Sustaining the future

Note to the reader from the UNU

This book is based on papers presented to a conference on "Sustainable Environmental and Resource Management Futures for Sub-Saharan Africa" held under the auspices of the United Nations University programme on "Sustainable Environmental Futures." The programme formed a part of the United Nations University Programme on Sustainable Environmental and Energy Futures, which is a response to the United Nations' *Agenda 21*. The programme focused on the complex interactions of physical and human activities in changing the environment, especially in the tropical regions of the world. The overall aim of the programme was to promote ecologically as well as socially and economically sustainable development through basic and applied research, training, and dissemination of research findings to policy makers. An earlier regional volume emanating from the research, entitled *South-East Asia's Environmental Future: The Search for Sustainability*, was published in 1993.

The authors were given the objectives of analysing the trends and processes of environmental change in Sub-Saharan Africa, and of identifying key issues for reaching sustainable environmental and resource management in the region within the medium-term future until around the year 2005. The aim was to provide policy-relevant conclusions for the benefit of decision makers in the countries concerned and in international agencies and other bodies concerned with African development. The work covered studies on how natural, socio-economic, cultural, and political causes affect the environmental future of Sub-Saharan Africa.

Sustaining the future: Economic, social, and environmental change in Sub-Saharan Africa

Edited by George Benneh, William B. Morgan, and Juha I. Uitto

United Nations University Press

TOKYO · NEW YORK · PARIS

© The United Nations University, 1996

The views expressed in this publication are those of the authors and do not necessarily reflect the views of the United Nations University.

United Nations University Press
The United Nations University, 53-70, Jingumae 5-chome, Shibuya-ku, Tokyo 150, Japan
Tel: (03) 3499-2811   Fax: (03) 3406-7345
Telex: J25442   Cable: UNATUNIV TOKYO

UNU Office in North America
2 United Nations Plaza, Room DC2-1462-70, New York, NY 10017
Tel: (212) 963-6387   Fax: (212) 371-9454
Telex: 422311 UN UI

United Nations University Press is the publishing division of the United Nations University.

Typeset by Asco Trade Typesetting Limited, Hong Kong
Printed by Princeton Academic Press, USA
Cover design by Jonathan Gullery/Abel Graphics, Thornwood, New York, USA

UNUP-918
ISBN 92-808-0918-0
03000 P

Contents

Contents

vi

Preface

Juha I. Uitto and William B. Morgan

Background

The quest for sustainable development has in recent years become a key concern for the developing regions of the world. Issues pertaining to the ecosystem's capacity to tolerate and respond to population growth and other human-induced stresses have become essential for the sustainable management of natural resources. Each year significant amounts of agricultural land are converted to urban land uses or lost owing to erosion, posing serious threats to local and global food security. At the same time, critical resources, such as water, become increasingly scarce and polluted. Physical and anthropogenic processes are intricately interlinked, but it can be argued that the present environment is largely a result of the interactions between man, natural resources, and technology in the socio-economic and cultural development process.

Finding and disseminating solutions to these problems is not only a matter of technology, but requires a multidisciplinary approach with inputs from both natural and social sciences, besides the cooperation of all sectors of the international community. Environmental considerations can no longer be separated from issues related to social and economic development, population, trade, food security, and the international system as a whole.

Regional environmental futures

The United Nations University (UNU) is concerned with promoting ecologically, as well as economically, socially, and culturally sustainable development through basic and applied research, policy reflection, capacity building, and dissemination of the research findings to policy makers. As part of the UNU's environmental programme, a series of regional conferences was organized focusing on issues affecting the sustainability of development and resource management in the medium-term future. The first of the conferences covered the South-East Asian region (Brookfield and Byron 1993).

This volume emanates from the second regional conference organized in Accra, Ghana, 22–26 March 1993. The theme of the conference was "Sustainable Environmental and Resource Management Futures for Sub-Saharan Africa" and it brought together leading experts on African environment and development issues from within the region, as well as from the outside. The objective was to analyse the trends and processes of environmental change in Sub-Saharan Africa and to identify key issues for reaching sustainable environmental and resource management within the medium-term future of some 20 years, given the current developments in the continent's social, economic, and political structures and demographic trends. The conference examined the driving forces of regional environmental change, including economic growth, development and poverty, population growth, migration and urbanization, energy consumption and production, and agricultural expansion and intensification. It further studied their relationship with environmental processes and the resource base, including climatic variability and change, the nature and incidence of drought, water supply, environmental transformation, and degradation in both rural and urban areas, and the threats to the more fragile ecosystems. It was recognized that some of the environmental problems arise partly from external factors, such as international trade, while others are of internal origin.

The main conclusions of the conference were rapidly published in a short summary report for quick dissemination to concerned individuals and organizations (Benneh et al. 1993). The present volume reproduces selected papers that were commissioned for and discussed at the conference. Based on the discussions, the papers contained here have undergone substantial rewriting, updating, and editing to form a complete book. This volume is in no sense a comprehensive treatise. It omits some aspects of interest, for example eco-tourism, although it does deal with a very wide range of issues and themes. It is the work of many scholars with different experiences and views. Although some integration of different aspects of environmental and resource problems and their management has been achieved, there are nevertheless differences of viewpoint and opinion.

References

Benneh, G., W. Manshard, W. B. Morgan, and J. I. Uitto. 1993. *Sustainable Environmental and Resource Management Futures for Sub-Saharan Africa: Summary and Recommendations*. Tokyo: The United Nations University.

Brookfield, H. and Y. Byron (eds.). 1993. *South-East Asia's Environmental Future: The Search for Sustainability*. Tokyo: United Nations University Press, and Kuala Lumpur: Oxford University Press.

Opening address by the Hon. Minister of Environment, Science and Technology

Christine Amoako-Nuama

It is indeed a great honour for me to be invited to participate in this United Nations University conference on a subject area that is professionally very close to my heart and also very much in line with my new assignment as Minister of Environment, Science and Technology. I am particularly pleased to add a word of welcome to you all. I am delighted that so many of you have come from afar to participate in this conference and also to catch a glimpse of the initial phase of the workings of the 4th Republic of Ghana. I trust that you will have a pleasant stay here and enjoy the traditional hospitality and warmth of the Ghanaian people.

Mr. Chairman, the subject of this conference is most significant and timely because, for developing countries, particularly those in Sub-Saharan Africa, sustainable environmental development and the management of our natural resources are fundamental to our livelihood security.

The Earth Summit in Rio de Janeiro in 1992 in many ways lifted the subject of sustainable development onto the international political agenda. The presence of so many Heads of State and Government in Rio and the general agreement reached on Agenda 21 and the Rio Declaration, which placed in perspective the balance between environment and development, are all clear testimonies of the importance of politics in environmental considerations. The Summit also acknowledged the concerns of the developing countries by bringing into sharp focus the link between poverty and environmental degradation.

Mr. Chairman, Ladies and Gentlemen, one of the messages that I would like to leave with you as you begin your deliberations is to emphasize that the attainment of sustainable development requires the concerted effort of government, the business community, the NGOs, scientific and technical organizations, and ordinary citizens in both rural and urban centres.

I am particularly concerned about the general attitude of some people who place all the responsibility for attaining sustainable environmental and resource management on the shoulders of governments. I am, however, confident that the many questions about how we are going to ensure the maintenance of our resource base and at the same time improve on our living standards through sustainable development will be answered with the total involvement and commitment of both the business community and government. It is on this premise that my new ministry, for example, will chart its course concerning the theme of this conference.

Mr. Chairman, please permit me to use this occasion to express the views of the Government of Ghana on the worldwide concerns about sustainable environmental and resource management.

Ghana, like so many other developing countries, has produced environmental strategy papers as well as various action plans within the context of our development programmes. In fact, since my own involvement in environmental protection at the technical level in Ghana, we have always felt the need to encourage the business and industrial communities to involve environmental considerations, from the very beginning, in their development plans. Unfortunately, the implementation of these strategies and national plans has been slow and limited because of other pressing financial commitments in our socio-economic development.

Although the Government has been most eager to develop the natural resources of the country, and is also fully aware and concerned about the environmental impact of rapid development in certain key sectors, it has not been easy to provide the right kinds of incentive packages to encourage the business and industrial communities to invest in environmentally sound technologies. Further, it is becoming increasingly evident that the right kinds of technology are not only environmentally friendly but also cost effective.

The Government therefore intends to work closely with industry to ensure that the most appropriate technologies are used in the conduct of their activities. In addition, my ministry will intensify its relations with each rural community by assisting to monitor constantly their local environment.

It is my hope that the donor countries and the multilateral funding agencies will work closely with us and assist us in funding a number of our environmental and technological programmes that have national, regional, and global significance.

In conclusion, Ladies and Gentlemen, it is my hope that the various papers that will be presented during the next few days will focus attention on the need for greater involvement of our people in all matters pertaining to sustainable development. Such action will hopefully result in an improved physical, social, and economic environment for the future of Sub-Saharan Africa.

Thank you.

1

Introduction

William B. Morgan

The 1980s and early 1990s witnessed serious economic decline or stagnation in most of Sub-Saharan Africa. The productivity of agriculture, Sub-Saharan Africa's most important industry, has failed to keep pace with the growth of population and has suffered particularly from falling productivity in the export sector and from declining markets and prices. Food imports are still essential in most Sub-Saharan countries to maintain an adequate total food supply and in certain cases to keep down food costs. Debt has mounted and pressures on resource use have increased, accompanied by evidence of environmental deterioration, so that attempts to arrest economic decline are now being questioned with regard to the immediate or potential environmental damage implied and the consequent inability to sustain either the economy or the resource base on which it depends. This double jeopardy has been compounded during the period by severe environmental difficulties relating to climatic change and associated in certain cases with drought and starvation, a deteriorating world market and world financial system, pressures on international loan capital from non-African sources such as the former USSR and the countries of Eastern Europe, declining international

investment interest, changes in African societies and political relationships, and a number of civil wars, which have imposed great
hardship on millions of people, besides the toll of death and injury.

Apart from South Africa, there have been very few signs of industrial progress, and the import-substitution policies dominant in most of
Sub-Saharan Africa's industrial economies have mostly failed to generate growth. The current economic difficulties have been described
as largely due to the agricultural crisis (see, for example, Pearce,
Barbier, and Markandya 1988, abstract 1 and 2), but Sub-Saharan
Africa's industrial failure has been more severe and the apparent
importance of agriculture in the African economies is largely the
result of the poor performance of industry. The depth of the economic recession in Sub-Saharan Africa has led some governments
and local authorities to encourage the development of national and
local self-sufficiency to compensate for the loss of overseas earnings,
while social services have been reduced, civil service labour forces
have been cut, and some state-controlled industries and parastatal
organizations have been privatized in order in certain cases to reduce
state budget costs.

In the past two decades in Sub-Saharan Africa much attention has
been focused on economic reform and the introduction of structural
adjustment and stabilization policies supported by advice and loans
from the World Bank and the International Monetary Fund. Growing
awareness of the importance of environmental relationships for effective economic management and the successful operation of economic
reform, mainly since 1983, has led to increased World Bank concern
with the role of environment in long-term development and has
encouraged the growth of new studies of environmental economics
and environmental accounting (Pearce, Barbier, and Markandya
1988; Ahmad, Serafy, and Lutz 1989). One may also cite the inclusion of "environmental indicators" in the United Nations Development Programme (UNDP) and World Bank publication *African Development Indicators* (1992), and the inclusion of data for "forests,
protected areas and water" in the World Bank's *World Development
Report* since 1991. However, it may be said that a great deal of the
more traditional economic analysis, which ignores the environmental
implications of economic policies, still persists (see, for example,
Chhibber and Fischer 1991).

There is also a heightened awareness of the problems of world
poverty and of Sub-Saharan Africa as one of the world's poorest
major regions, together with a growing concern that such poverty is

frequently accompanied by evidence of environmental degradation and of inefficient use of natural resources. These problems can have a "most immediate impact on rural poverty" amongst people whose survival is at stake as they are "forced to farm increasingly marginal soils, to reduce fallow periods which would permit the soil to renew its fertility, to cut vital forests in their search for arable land or fuel, to overstock fragile rangelands and to overfish rivers, lakes and coastal waters. These are the same people who have traditionally protected their resources by striking a balance between value extraction, resource conservation and regeneration" (Jazairy, Alamgir, and Panuccio 1992: 305). However, it is important not to exaggerate the role of poverty and of economic crisis in environmental and resource degradation. Wealthy communities can do as much, and more, damage in their pursuit of greater wealth, even though their wealth can provide a greater power to protect the environment, achieve more efficient resource use, or at least reduce loss and the damage rate. Much of the criticism of the environmental policies of third world countries comes from communities in wealthier industrial countries whose own environmental records are abysmal.

Economy and society: Development issues

According to World Bank estimates (World Bank 1990: 29 and 139), Sub-Saharan Africa has the second highest proportion of poor people of major world regions and is forecast to become proportionately the world's worst case by the year 2000, although its total of poor people will still be less than that of South Asia. The poor not only have problems in acquiring basic resources, but also have limited entitlements because of their status and low life expectancy owing to their vulnerability to disaster, exploitation, and social demands. In the Sub-Saharan countries for which data are available, rural poverty correlates most strongly with low levels of per capita energy consumption, of international trade, of imported food, and of value-added in agriculture, i.e. commercial agriculture, but has only a low positive correlation with the percentage of the labour force in agriculture, suggesting that many rural poor people are unemployed, underemployed, or employed in non-agricultural occupations. Large numbers of peasant farmers depend mainly on subsistence and are little affected by the market reforms and freeing of prices advocated by the World Bank, while many of the rural poor depend on the market to supply basic needs. Rural poverty is generally higher in

3

countries with poor economic development indicators and financial problems and there is evidence that it has been made worse in several countries, at least in the short term, by the financial policies and employment cuts associated with economic reform, following mounting international debt plus repeated drought and crop failure.

Marked economic and social inequity is evident in Sub-Saharan Africa, in some cases similar to the more extreme Latin American examples. Many resource use and environmental management problems are derived from inequitable management practices, which often claim superior scientific and technical knowledge, associated with alien systems of production and ideologies, and often support certain dominant economic, social, and bureaucratic vested interests. Formal orthodox environmental management offers technical efficiency, but is structured in a way that makes it the prerogative of a privileged group or class of nations or persons. It lacks the regard for social equity often built into indigenous popular environmental management. The answers to environmental questions and questions of sustainability are not necessarily scientifically determined, but may depend rather on the values, political positions, and vested interests of those called upon to provide them. The environmental end-users are the African people and it is with them that environmental management policy should begin, preferably in a much more participatory form than hitherto.

There is in Sub-Saharan Africa a vicious circle of population problems, producing mounting resource pressures and complicated by considerable migration, including strong rural–urban flows, urban–rural movement, migrant farmers and labourers, agricultural resettlement, pastoral nomads, and refugees from famine, warfare, and persecution. Despite high infant mortality rates, annual population growth rates of 3 per cent or more in most Sub-Saharan countries pose one of the greatest challenges to economic development and resource management, although the human resources are capable of improvement through better education and health facilities. Unfortunately these will become ever more difficult to provide with rapid population growth and the increasing social and economic liabilities of an urbanization that has failed to trigger industrialization or to produce higher levels of economic development. The future looks bleak for Sub-Saharan Africa because many countries have failed to improve standards of living or to provide for basic needs. The future demographic scenario both threatens natural resources and limits the effective development of human resources. The 1992 United Nations

4

Conference on Environment and Development at Rio de Janeiro indicated that the Sub-Saharan countries may have to shoulder a larger share of the burden of environmental problems than earlier envisaged, and in future will probably have to depend more on self-reliance and on their own funding for the required systematic multi-disciplinary policy research.

Africa has a long history of urbanization and, apart from East Asia and the Pacific, has currently the fastest rate of urban growth of the major global regions. However, it still has the lowest proportion of urban population and its urbanization has become increasingly a spatial concentration of poor people, who in many cases are forced to put today's needs ahead of tomorrow's environment. In large part the associated urban problems are the result of a failure to raise income levels by increasing industrial productivity. Sub-Saharan Africa is the least industrialized major region of the globe, yet industrialization is unlikely to expand and diversify significantly in the near future with poor prospects for foreign direct investment, which is mostly attracted elsewhere. Recession and state sector cutbacks under structural adjustment, whose severity was predicated partly on the assumption that foreign investment flows would increase, are exacerbating both unemployment and industrial pressures on the environment. Many people have been forced into dependence on informal economic activity, and the enforcement of conservation or pollution abatement legislation has become more and more difficult. The building material industry in particular is a prime case for improvement, while the informal and wider small business sectors need to play a more important role within integrated strategies. Poor management practice, particularly in urban development, has tended to encourage the exploitation of both people and environment and in consequence to create unstable situations. Extremely rapid urban growth accompanied by huge migratory inflows, pressure on peripheral land resources, poor or inadequate systems of supply, insecurity, and low-quality services are all factors encouraging social and political instability. They have resulted in a legacy of poor housing, depletion of vegetation for fuel, polluted drinking water, poor sanitation, and uncollected waste. Most municipalities lack sufficient resources to cope with their worsening social and environmental problems as the areas under squatter settlements and legalized areas of self-help housing expand. At root the basic problem is poverty, so it can be argued that employment and income-generating strategies should be given priority in urban planning.

Environmental issues and futures

If sustainable development or improvement in the quality of human life, whilst living within the capacity of supporting ecosystems, is to be effective in Sub-Saharan Africa it will require a more efficient economic performance capable of generating surpluses above the satisfaction of basic demands. It will also demand social systems able to resolve development tensions and create harmony between the production economy and the ecological basis for development, together with an evolved technology able to look for new solutions, sustainable international finance and trade, flexible administrative systems, and effective citizen participation in decision-making. Despite apparently low population densities in many regions of Sub-Saharan Africa, there are resource pressures owing to the increased scarcity of national capital and the decreased availability in most countries of international finance capital, which are worsened by the fact that economic indicators in many cases are giving the wrong signals about the sustainability of development in relation to environmental destruction, so that a new basis for the economy is required, informed by "environmental economics." In at least the short term, rather than attempt to raise the level of gross national product, it might be better to concentrate on environmental improvement, combined with income redistribution in order to minimize the poverty of the poorest. Modernization involves both losses and gains. Although it has brought education, science, technology, better health and sanitation, improved communication, water supply, and nutrition, and higher real incomes for many, it has also increased dependence on the West, introduced inappropriate technologies, weakened traditions, and created unsustainable lifestyles together with acculturation stress.

These problems are only part of a much larger set, including less abundant rains and recurrent droughts, especially in the semi-arid Sub-Saharan lands such as the Sahel region, where rainfall in the early 1970s was 15–35 per cent below normal. "Wet" or "dry" years seem to cluster in the Sahel, although not in southern Africa, so that Sahelian planning should focus on the driest years, not on the averages over given periods. Variations in time in the Sahel seem matched by variations in space, so that nearby villages can experience different rainfall regimes even when experiencing comparable rainfall totals. Desertification threatens the semi-arid lands as farming is taken beyond the limits of sustainable rain-fed agriculture and as strategies to combat it have met with only limited success, involving an apparent conflict of interest between foresters, farmers, and herders. Agro-forestry and small-scale "water-harvesting" techniques have the best potential to combat desertification and promote sustainable agricultural and fuelwood production.

Taking Sub-Saharan Africa as a whole, the chief source of environmental degradation considered in its entirety (including plant cover and species loss, destruction of fauna, climatic change, changes in water table levels and stream flow, and soil erosion) is deforestation, especially if followed by overcultivation and overgrazing. Although rates of deforestation seem to be highest in uplands and in dry deciduous forest, tropical rain forests provide particularly sensitive environments with generally highly weathered soils that are low in plant-available nutrient reserves and easily degraded by intensive land use. Yet more intensive use of existing land and the restoration of degraded lands are important strategies to reduce the need for additional deforestation as demand for food, industrial, and export crops increases with continued high rates of population growth and concentration, despite the generally low overall population densities by world standards. Science-based "best management practices" are available, but need to be fine-tuned to local conditions and adopted mainly on input-responsive prime agricultural land. It is estimated that over half the area of African climax tropical rain forest has been converted to other land uses (Richards 1990), but estimates are highly variable and erratic, and accurate inventories of land and its capability are needed for the rational utilization of forest resources.

The coastal zone and surrounding oceans of Sub-Saharan Africa have abundant resources of food, energy, and minerals, but consist of fragile ecosystems, subject to a variety of often conflicting uses, so that their potential for economic prosperity is threatened with environmental damage and resource loss. Most of the larger African cities are coastal, as are some of the larger population concentrations and much of the commercial and industrial development, together with a large part of the growing tourist industry. The considerable fish resources are threatened by the operations of large foreign fleets, while destructive fishing methods in the coastal zone include dynamite blasting and spear fishing on coral reefs and the unregulated use of unsuitable nets. Other damaging effects result from clearing mangroves, mining beach sand and gravel, metal pollution from coastal mining, constructing ports and harbours, disposing of urban sewage and wastes, pollution from the oil and gas industry, and some subsidence of sedimentary basins in the Niger delta from oil extraction. Oceans have no physical boundaries corresponding with national jurisdiction, so that remedies for current problems can be sought only within the framework of international agreements. However, on the whole the oceanic problems of the Sub-Saharan countries are less immediately damaging than those of the coastal zone, where adequate management requires legal controls.

Environment and resource management

The major issue in resource management is agriculture, which is still the leading productive sector by value and employment in most Sub-Saharan countries. It is also a source of concern, given the high rates of population increase and the evidence of widespread and recurring hunger, accompanied in several countries by dependence on food imports. Agricultural exports are also needed to repay debt, to pay debt service charges and import costs, and to pay in part the costs of investment. In the past two decades, increases in crop production and yields have been small, and modern intensive agricultural technologies have not been easily adopted by Africa's resource-poor farmers, many of whom are women, barely able to cope with highly variable rainfall, poor soils, and the damage inflicted by pests and diseases. Most success in developing sustainable agricultural production systems has been derived from the application of traditional methods that mimic natural ecosystems but that, for major yield increases, may need the support of biotechnology and investment in gene-related research.

The livestock industry has a smaller output volume and value than crop production, in part owing to the poverty of most African consumers, although, before the recession of the past decade and the financial restrictions of some economic reform programmes, demand had been rising in some areas faster than the increases in output. Increased production of meat and livestock products to satisfy future higher demand levels will require a more sedentary livestock-raising system and changes in land ownership, accompanied by lower stocking densities on open range land in order to create a more sustainable use of environment. There are, however, problems of social and cultural change in order that livestock owners can introduce the pasture plants developed by scientists and that are adapted to the agro-ecological zones of Sub-Saharan Africa. Other important changes required for sustainable, more sedentary systems include land tenure, infrastructures, and credit facilities. Genetic considerations are also just as important as the feed resource base. Whereas the objective of many governments is the sedentarization of herd owners in order to utilize the available technologies for increased intensity of production, the herd owners may have the different objective of developing their herds as capital and maximizing the numbers of their stock.

The rural population has to depend mainly on local resources, and the urban population, although consuming a high proportion of imported food, yet tends to depend on local wood fuels for its chief source of energy. The increasing demand for fuelwood is putting pressure on the producing rural areas and on the sustainability of farmed and forested environments. Policies aiming to reduce food imports and achieve food self-sufficiency, combined with policies to expand agricultural exports, are being achieved mainly at the expense of forest and woodland, producing fuelwood as a by-product, rather than by increased production intensity and higher yields. Rising urban fuelwood demand and rising prices have encouraged localized forest or woodland degradation. In the near future, with the poor prognosis for industrial expansion and the environmental pressures associated in many African countries with recession, greater demands on rural resources are likely, including increased dependence on agriculture to maintain employment, provide food and fuel, and achieve some economic growth.

One resource-based alternative to agriculture, pastoralism, and fuelwood production in order to provide an engine for development and economic growth is mining. In many Sub-Saharan countries, mining provides a vital export industry, although the hope of developing downstream industries for import substitution has failed in most cases. Environmental damage from mining activities has become an increasing problem, adding to operational costs at a time of competitive difficulty. Africa is endowed with enormous mineral potential, but in the past two decades has mostly missed the investment boom of international finance in mineral exploitation and development, apart from oil, and needs to attract the large mining companies back, encouraged by a more receptive attitude amongst African governments. However, the Republic of South Africa, with the most successful development of mining in Sub-Saharan Africa and a minerals industry sector that is the backbone of the rest of the economy, has a mining industry fully integrated into the domestic economy and largely without "enclave" or "offshore" transnational enterprises.

9

Institutional issues

International environmental institutions and organizations for international regional cooperation are at last facing up to threats to global
environments and the need to share and exchange scientific data and
knowledge concerning environmental issues. Particularly important
are the "global change" programmes and the role of certain United
Nations agencies, such as the UN Environment Programme and the
Man and the Biosphere Programme of the UN Educational, Scientific and Cultural Organization (UNESCO), in addition to such non-
governmental organizations (NGOs) as the International Council of
Scientific Unions with its International Geosphere–Biosphere Programme and the World Conservation Union (formerly known as the
International Union for the Conservation of Nature and Natural
Resources). An important joint initiative of the United Nations University (UNU), the International Social Science Council, the International Federation of Institutes for Advanced Studies, and UNESCO
has been the Human Dimensions of Global Environmental Change
Programme (HDP), set up to foster a global network of scientists,
select core projects such as global risk assessment, critical regions,
and potential sealevel rise, and develop appropriate information systems and methodologies. The programme on Critical Zones in Global
Environmental Change and an initiative on famine vulnerability are
carried out in collaboration with the International Geographical
Union. UNU's environmental research programmes, other than those
related to HDP, emphasize regional and local sustainability through
appropriate environmental and resource management. Major initiatives include the long-term project on Population, Land Management, and Environmental Change (PLEC) and the development of
an Institute for Natural Resources in Africa (UNU/INRA).

A very large number of non-governmental organizations is engaged
in problems of natural resource use and environmental management
in Sub-Saharan Africa. They are extremely diverse in scope, interest,
and size. Many, of particular importance for future environmental
democracy in Sub-Saharan Africa, are local or regional and operate
through communities or social groups at the "grass-roots" level.
Some of these are welfare oriented, while others are research based.
Generally they are driven by their feelings of unease about the economic order, the state of the resource base, and evidence of social
injustice. Often they have been able to spearhead strategies for wise

resource management and forge cross-border and inter-institutional links for cooperative research and policy formulation.

Environment and development in Ghana

The special problems of the host country, Ghana, provide detailed examples of the difficulties of policy implementation in resource and environmental management in relation to current social, political, and economic changes. In Ghana, legislation to protect the natural environment dates back to 1901 and the Wild Animals Preservation Ordinance, followed by the Rivers Ordinance of 1903 and the initiation of forest reservation in 1907. At present no fewer than 22 departments, commissions, research organizations, and corporations have responsibilities for land and other resources management. In 1974, only two years after the UN Conference on the Environment in Stockholm, the Ghana Environmental Protection Council (EPC) was created to organize research and educational programmes, to ensure observance of proper safeguards in all development projects, and to cooperate with national and international environmental organizations. The approach, however, was largely protectionist and cosmetic until the droughts and bush fires of the early 1980s and the realization that the natural resource base of Ghana was deteriorating rapidly.

In 1983 Ghana embarked on its Economic Reform Programme (ERP), which resulted in some environmental degradation and led the government to direct the EPC in 1988 to set up an environmental "think tank" to reconcile economic development and natural resource conservation. The ERP stopped economic decline and created some growth – especially in the rural areas, where commercial agriculture, mainly led by the cocoa industry, has played an important role in economic recovery. The terms of trade for food staples have tended to deteriorate, however. On average, poverty was reduced under the ERP, although admittedly the data are limited and there are some people below the poverty line whose condition has worsened.

The current development of palm oil provides an important special case. In the 1970s, peasant and state-owned plantation production of palm oil had failed to keep up with demand. After 1981 attempts were made to promote oil-palm plantations through private enterprise, foreign-aided government ventures, and joint government–private projects. These have expanded rapidly and have made a significant contribution to palm oil production, besides raising income and employment levels locally. The costs include local resistance to land expropriation and the creation of monocultural systems of plant production, which are vulnerable to insect pests and diseases. However, the development of nucleus estates by three major plantations in cooperation with smallholders and outgrowers under contract combines more traditional farming methods on small plantations with the technical advantages of modern agricultural production on core estates and may be able to offer a more sustainable future if production becomes more diversified on the basis of organic and other eco-farming and with low external input principles.

Recommendations

For several of the issues concerning the sustainability of environmental and resource management futures in Sub-Saharan Africa, the analyses and arguments produced at the conference provided the basis for a number of recommendations:

1. Only a marked acceleration of the pace with which cooperation is developed both between the countries of Sub-Saharan Africa and between the countries of the North and Sub-Saharan Africa in research programmes and in future policy-making and management of key resource problems will make it possible to cope with increasing environmental deterioration, but first the complex inter-relationships between population, environment, and sustainable development will require more study.

2. It is essential to halt the vicious spiral of worsening poverty and environmental degradation wherever it occurs, although most of the Sub-Saharan countries are poorly provided with the means to do so or even to undertake the necessary research. In fragile environments afflicted by poverty, with high levels of vulnerability to hazard and frequently dependent on external aid, the prospects for the long-term programmes required are bleak, more especially also where economies have been damaged or destroyed by warfare. In many cases the economic reforms meant to reverse current economic decline have incurred a heavy cost, worsening the condition of many poor people.

3. Promotion of social and political restructuring is required to make economic and environmental reforms effective, and should be combined with the development of more appropriate international relationships, particularly in the fields of world trade and interna-

tional finance, where Sub-Saharan Africa has a heavy burden of debt and declining levels of international investment.

4. In order to promote the rehabilitation of already degraded areas and prevent further degradation, wherever threatened, strategies are required to improve natural resource management. For this purpose the network of the UNU's Research and Training Centres, including UNU/INRA, should be developed further. The need to examine the political realities of financing such environmental activity, to improve the public accountability of the appropriate government departments, and to impose financial discipline was accepted, together with advice on how research organizations and government agencies should approach the Global Environmental Facility.

5. To minimize future environmental damage and degradation, research should be developed into modifying production systems in both agriculture and industry, including mining, and into developing new methods of production. Land use and labour efficiency need to be improved, including, for example, the minimization of drudgery in farm work, especially in the various operations performed by women, and this will have important implications for health, nutrition, and education.

6. Research and development in appropriate technology should also be expanded, particularly in the area of biotechnology, including, for example, the introduction of more productive seeds and livestock, the development of local capabilities in the use of biogas and more efficient woodstoves, the expansion of agro-forestry techniques, and the recycling of waste, in part to relieve resource pressure by widening the resource base and improving productive efficiency.

7. To improve the urban environment it is essential to promote the acceleration of key elements in the urbanization process. These include the training of urban management, the elimination of inequitable management practices, the improvement of the revenue and resource base, and the adoption of more realistic and practical development codes and standards, including strategies for upgrading squatter settlements and self-help housing and improving water supply and waste disposal.

8. The environmental institutions of Sub-Saharan Africa must be strengthened, particularly environmental education at all levels. A more holistic approach to a whole range of economic, social,

political, and environmental problems must be adopted and taught. Such an approach, based on both multi- and inter-disciplinary studies, is regarded as essential for policy formulation and should be based on sound monitoring, data recording, and analysis.

9. It is essential that research and development should be participatory. That is, the people of Sub-Saharan Africa should themselves be involved in and contribute to the design and implementation of programmes intended to change their lives and to create a sustainable environmental future that is technologically feasible, economically viable, and socially acceptable.

References

Ahmad, Y. J., S. El Serafy, and E. Lutz. 1989. *Environmental Accounting for Sustainable Development*. Washington D.C.: UNEP–World Bank Symposium, World Bank.

Chhibber, A. and S. Fischer. 1991. *Economic Reform in Sub-Saharan Africa*. Washington D.C.: World Bank Symposium, World Bank.

Jazairy, I., M. Alamgir, and T. Panuccio. 1992. *The State of World Rural Poverty: An Inquiry into Its Causes and Consequences*. London: Intermediate Technology Publications for International Fund for Agricultural Development.

Pearce, D. W., E. B. Barbier, and A. Markandya. 1988. *Environmental Economics and Decision-making in Sub-Saharan Africa*. London: International Institute for Environment and Development/University College London Environmental Economics Centre.

Richards, J. F. 1990. Land transformation. In: B. L. Turner et al. (eds.), *The Earth as Transformed by Human Action: Global and Regional Changes in the Biosphere over the Past 300 Years*. New York: Cambridge University Press, pp. 163–178.

UNDP (United Nations Development Programme) and the World Bank. 1992. *African Development Indicators*. Washington D.C.: World Bank.

World Bank. 1990. *World Development Report 1990: Poverty*. Oxford and New York: Oxford University Press.

———— 1991. *World Development Report 1991*. Oxford and New York: Oxford University Press.

Part 1
Economy and society:
Development issues

2

Poverty, vulnerability, and rural development

William B. Morgan

At the root of arguments about sustainable environments and the management of resource use lies a major preoccupation with poverty. For some social scientists it is the chief concern in the study of less developed countries, and its elimination or at least the raising of minimal living standards should be regarded as one of the main objectives of research and policy formulation. Economic reform combined with conservation of the environment should always be formulated with regard to what has now been seen in many countries and major regions as the crisis of the poor (for a comprehensive account of rural poverty in the third world, see Jazairy, Alamgir, and Panuccio 1992).

The nature of poverty

In Sub-Saharan Africa (SS Africa) we are concerned with both poor people and poor countries. Some poor countries are simply averagely low on some income scale, but some suffer in addition from being very small and therefore unable, for certain forms of production, to achieve economies of scale or to provide an adequate domestic market. The data for national wealth and productivity are more abundant than those for human groups, and the data for rural poverty (since this paper is concerned with rural development) are limited to just a few national attempts to measure such items as the percentage of poor people, income distribution, consumption levels, or access to services and resources. Poverty not only affects a particular human group such as an income or occupation group, but is a problem of gender, where, in many societies, women are likely to be more adversely affected than men, and of age, where old people and children are more likely to be adversely affected than people of working age.

Poverty may be seen as both relative and absolute, and in attempts to analyse it at world and national scales there is a major problem with a concept that has so many attributes varying in both time and space. Most attempts to measure poverty are forced into simplification and the use of poverty indicators or surrogates, which are rarely brought together in a way that reflects the real complexity of poverty. The problems are compounded by "us" and "them" attitudes, i.e. by social researchers who make up their minds what measures must truly reflect poverty without asking poor people themselves, often on the grounds that most poor people cannot adequately articulate their own problems, particularly in rural areas where educational standards in many countries are low.

In 1985 a World Bank report claimed that there were over 1 billion poor people in the less developed countries, of whom 180 million were in SS Africa (without South Africa) (World Bank 1990: 139). By the year 2000 it was thought that the world total would be reduced to 825 million while the SS African total would have increased to 265 million. The proportion of the SS African population in poverty in 1985 was estimated at nearly 47 per cent and was second in the world to that of South Asia. By the year 2000 it should be just over 43 per cent and proportionately the world's worst case because the South Asian figure should have reduced from 51 per cent to 26 per cent (World Bank 1990: 29 and 139). South Asia will, however, still have the largest total of poor people at 365 million. These somewhat heroic estimates were based on a global "poverty line" income for 1985 of US$370 per capita per annum (adjusted for purchasing power parity [PPP]). The World Bank also had an "extremely poor" upper income level of US$275 per capita per annum, which included 120 million or 31 per cent of the African total. All these estimates were derived from a range of country-specific poverty lines based on consumption estimates for a number of low-income countries, i.e. the expenditure necessary to buy a minimum standard of nutrition and other basic necessities plus the cost of participating in the everyday life of society (World Bank 1990: 26–30 and 139; Ravallion 1992: 25–33). They are probably the best global estimates that we have, providing one accepts a poverty line as at least some sort of indicator (criticized by Chambers and Conway 1992; see below p. 20). The United Nations Development Programme (UNDP) (1991: 15–18, 88–91, and 194–195) has provided estimates of numbers and percentages of people "below the poverty line" for a number of countries, totalling 1.2 billion for the less developed countries in 1990 (UNDP 1991: 125), and using "real GDP" in the calculation, i.e. gross domestic product per capita adjusted for PPP. The "poverty line" was defined as "that income level below which a minimum nutritionally adequate diet plus essential non-food requirements are not affordable" (UNDP 1991: 195).

Ravallion noted that real income poverty lines for different countries tended to rise with economic growth, but did so only slowly at the poorest levels, accelerating as growth increased. He argued that this suggested that the notion of "absolute poverty" (and therefore the World Bank's use of such a measure) appeared to be especially relevant to low-income countries, whereas "relative poverty" was of more relevance to high-income countries (Ravallion 1992: 31–33). Terms such as "minimum nutritionally adequate" and "essential non-food requirements", used with reference to poverty lines, are in a sense not absolute minima. Many poor people try to survive below these levels although their standards of living include poor diets, periodic hunger, and inadequate clothing.

For the purpose of global analysis, UN agencies such as UNDP and the World Bank generally prefer simple definitions of poverty and measurable practical attributes. Thus the World Bank defines poverty as "the inability to attain a minimal standard of living" and distinguishes it from inequality, which "refers to the relative living standards across the whole society" (World Bank 1990: 26). By contrast, some researchers offer more complex views of the nature of poverty in which they try to examine the interrelationships of a number of elements leading to deprivation. Thus Sen's (1984 and 1987) concept of "capability" referred to how far a person could avoid poverty by seeking to be adequately nourished and clothed and to avoid escapable morbidity and preventable mortality, but this was linked to the quality of life and the ability to choose valued activities (Sen 1987: 18). Capabilities also included the ability to cope with stress and shock and the ability to gain access to such things as services and information. In writing of hunger Sen argued that marked disparities in consumption might be concealed in data showing an adequate food supply for a given population and suggested that the problem was one of "acquirement." This is a central issue in problems of hunger and starvation and can be extended to most issues of deprivation and poverty. Sen added to this the concept of "entitlement," by which he meant *what can be acquired* or the set of alternative commodity bundles that a person of a given status and income can or should be able to obtain, together with bodily attributes such as labour power (Sen 1990: 34–41). The problem for poor people is not just a loss of or a fall in income resulting in an inability to buy essential goods, but a change in the minimum survival endowment, such as loss of land through alienation or sale to cover needs such as debt repayment, or loss of labour power owing to ill health.

Chambers has developed the notion of "integrated rural poverty" with its "clusters of disadvantage," including vulnerability (Chambers 1983: 1–27, 103–139; Chambers and Conway 1992). Chambers defined vulnerability as "a lack of buffers against contingencies," e.g. against the demands of social conventions, disasters, physical incapacity, unproductive expenditure, and exploitation. Vulnerability could also arise from a lack of power, demonstrated by the ease with which élites in some countries were able to intercept benefits intended for the poor. Rural people in the developing countries are in a deprivation trap in which powerlessness, vulnerability, physical weakness, poverty, and isolation combine. Poverty might also be affected by a process that could become irreversible – the so-called "poverty ratchet" – whereby assets (Sen's "endowment") were lost through the need to sell or mortgage them. Chambers and Conway (1992: 3) have developed these views in order to criticize production thinking (not producing enough food), employment thinking (the ideal of full employment), and poverty line thinking (the idea of a single deprivation continuum measured by incomes or consumption) as reductionist or having "an industrialized country imprint."

Poverty may also be seen as a many dimensional state in which a multidisciplinary approach to research into the processes that create or maintain it is essential. Survival within poverty includes many strategies, which are combined in a process aimed not just at income in the broadest sense but at assurance against the stresses and shocks to which poor people are particularly vulnerable. One such strategy is a mixture of jobs, some temporary, some full-time, some self-employed, some working for others. This strategy represents an evolution from a more traditional combination of occupations, which survives in many peasant households where farm work has a variety of tasks and is combined with household tasks, house-building, hunting, gathering, and trading. Such a strategy is a means of not just increasing income but broadening the income base, which provides a means of assurance against shock. This is not to suggest that many of the African poor would not prefer a well-paid, full-time, permanent, so-called "formal" occupation. The savings of many rural families may be used to pay for the secondary education of their more able children and this may be seen in one way as part of a multi-occupational strategy at the household or family level, but in another as an attempt to obtain the financial rewards available to those who choose to depend on a specialized, normally urban, occupation.

Rural poverty and development in Sub-Saharan Africa

Table 2.1 lists 43 countries of the conventional "Sub-Saharan Africa" (Africa south of the Sahara minus South Africa and some islands) by two wealth indicators, by one integrative "development" indicator, and by the data available for the percentage of rural population below the poverty line. The HDI (Human Development Index) is UNDP's merger of life expectancy and literacy rate with real GDP to give a composite index of "development." High levels of literacy and life expectancy suggest the probability of access to education, medical services, and nutrition by a wide spectrum of the population and possibly a more equitable distribution of wealth. There are problems about the way in which HDI is calculated, but these are less serious in the case of the poorer countries. The date of publication is 1991 and the data are derived from a mixture of years, best described as mid to late 1980s.

On the HDI basis, the six poorest countries are Sierra Leone, Gambia, Guinea, Mali, Niger, and Djibouti. Apart from Djibouti, it looks as though HDI poverty in 1991 was mainly a western West African and Sahelian phenomenon. The effect of major shocks such as war and drought can be obscured by the range of data years and one may suspect that some of the countries so affected must have poorer results in particular years. While the rankings under the different headings in Table 2.1 have serious differences for the poorest countries, there appears to be some partial agreement amongst them with regard to the six richest, which are mainly located in central

21

Table 2.1   **Sub-Saharan Africa: 43 countries ranked by per capita GNP in 1989 and listing UNDP's "real GDP" and Human Development Index together with the rural population below the poverty line**

Rank	Country	GNP (US$ per capita) 1989	Real GDP PPP[a] (US$ per capita) 1985–88	HDI[b] 1991	Rural population below poverty line	
					1990 million	1980–88 per cent
1	Mozambique	80	1,070	0.155	–	–
2	Ethiopia	120	350	0.166	26.5	65
3	Tanzania	130	570	0.266	–	–
4	Somalia	170	1,330	0.118	3.4	70
5	Guinea-Bissau	180	670	0.088	–	–
6	Malawi	180	620	0.179	6.3	85
7	Chad	190	510	0.087	2.2	56
8	Burundi	220	550	0.177	4.4	85
9	Sierra Leone	220	1,030	0.048	1.8	65
10	Madagascar	230	670	0.371	4.6	50
11	Gambia	240	650	0.064	0.3	40
12	Nigeria	250	1,030	0.242	–	–
13	Uganda	250	410	0.204	–	–
14	Zaire	260	430	0.299	17.4	80
15	Mali	270	500	0.072	3.6	48
16	Niger	290	610	0.079	2.0	35
17	Burkina Faso	320	650	0.081	–	–
18	Rwanda	320	730	0.213	6.0	90
19	Equatorial Guinea	330	700[c]	0.186	–	–
20	Sao Tomé and Principe	340	620[c]	0.399	–	–
21	Kenya	360	1,010	0.399	10.6	55
22	Benin	380	1,050	0.114	1.9	65
23	Central African Rep.	390	780	0.166	1.4	91
24	Ghana	390	970	0.311	3.7	37
25	Togo	390	700	0.225	–	–
26	Zambia	390	870	0.351	–	–
27	Guinea	430	910	0.066	–	–
28	Liberia	450[c]	890	0.220	0.3	23
29	Lesotho	470	1,390	0.432	0.8	55
30	Djibouti	480[c]	730[c]	0.083	0.0	51
31	Sudan	480[c]	970	0.164	16.7	85
32	Mauritania	500	960	0.140	–	–
33	Angola	610	840	0.150	–	–
34	Senegal	650	1,250	0.189	–	–
35	Zimbabwe	650	1,370	0.413	–	–
36	Cape Verde	780	1,410	0.428	–	–
37	Côte d'Ivoire	790	1,430	0.311	2.0	26
38	Swaziland	900	2,110	0.462	0.3	50

Table 2.1 **(cont.)**

Rank	Country	GNP (US$ per capita) 1989	Real GDP PPP*a* (US$ per capita) 1985–88	HDI*b* 1991	Rural population below poverty line 1990 million	Rural population below poverty line 1980–88 per cent
39	Congo, People's Rep.	940	2,120	0.374	–	–
40	Cameroon	1,000	1,670	0.328	2.6	40
41	Namibia	1,030	1,500*c*	0.440	–	–
42	Botswana	1,600	2,510	0.524	0.5	55
43	Gabon	2,960	3,960	0.510	–	–

Data sources: UNDP (1991); World Bank (1991a).
a. PPP = Purchasing Power Parity, i.e. based on a basket of goods.
b. HDI = Human Development Index (UNDP 1990: 9–16; 1991, 13–21).
c. Data from 1988 (GNP) or from UNDP estimates.

and southern Africa: Gabon, Botswana, Namibia, Cameroon, Congo, and Swaziland, although Lesotho, Cape Verde, and Zimbabwe have higher HDI values than Cameroon and Congo. Generally, the four variables in the table show some approximate relationship, although there are several striking exceptions.

Data for the rural population below the poverty line (UNDP 1991: 152–153) give some indication of the numbers of the rural poor. Perhaps we may regard them as an educated guess. Such data are available for only 24 countries and exclude some of the larger, including Nigeria. Probably the rural population of Sub-Saharan Africa in 1989 was 72 per cent of the total of 480 million, or 346 million. The rural population below the poverty line may be guessed at 60 per cent, or 208 million. Nigeria's rural poverty total must be the largest, possibly 44 million or more based on UNDP and World Bank data, and probably six countries have 60 per cent of the total of SS African rural poverty: (as percentages of SS African rural poverty; ? = personal estimate) Nigeria 21?, Ethiopia 13, Zaire 8, Sudan 8, Tanzania 5?, Kenya 5. (If the 1991 Nigerian census figure of 88.5 million is used instead of a guessed forecast of 120 million, then the Nigerian rural poor may total 38 million and the other figures be modified accordingly. In doing this Nigeria's population growth rate since the 1963 census is then reduced to the improbably low level of 1.67 per cent per annum!)

Table 2.2 offers some idea of relative poverty by household income

Table 2.2 **Household income distribution for nine Sub-Saharan African countries, 1967–1989 (percentage share of household income by percentile groups of households)**

Country	Period	Quintile					Highest 10%
		Lowest	2nd	3rd	4th	Highest	
Malawi	1967–68	10.4	11.1	13.1	14.8	50.6	40.1
Sudan	1967–68	4.0	8.9	16.6	20.7	49.8	34.6
Sierra Leone	1967–69	7.5	11.7	15.7	21.7	43.4	28.2
Tanzania	1969	5.8	10.2	13.9	19.7	50.4	35.6
Kenya	1974–76	2.6	6.3	11.5	19.2	60.4	45.8
Zambia	1976	3.4	7.4	11.2	16.9	61.1	46.4
Botswana	1985–86	2.5	6.5	11.8	20.2	59.0	42.8
Côte d'Ivoire	1985–86	2.4	6.2	10.9	19.1	61.4	43.7
	1986–87[a]	5.0	8.0	13.1	21.3	52.7	36.3
Ghana	1987–88	6.5	10.9	15.7	22.3	44.6	29.1
	1988–89[a]	7.1	11.5	15.9	21.8	43.7	28.5

Sources: World Bank, *World Development Report*, 1984: 272; 1987: 252; 1988: 272; 1990: 236; 1991: 262; 1992: 276.
a. Per capita expenditure.

distribution in 9 of the 36 larger countries (population of 1 million or more), but the data are spread over 20 years. In five of these countries the share of the lowest quintile is less than 5 per cent. In four – Kenya, Zambia, Côte d'Ivoire (1985–86), and Botswana – the difference in average household income level for the top and bottom quintiles is of the order of 20 times or more. The household income distribution in some at least of the SS African countries is more inequitable than in, for example, India (lowest quintile 8.1 per cent, highest 41.4 per cent) or in any Western country and is similar to the more extreme Latin American examples such as Brazil (lowest quintile 2.4 per cent, highest 62.6 per cent).

National data may be explored further by examining: (1) the relationships between a number of social and economic variables; (2) the ways in which some of these variables are grouped by components of economic and social behaviour.

Thirty-four variables were identified, mainly for 1989 (in a few cases 1988 or 1987 or averages over those years and including some growth variables over the previous decade), apart from illiteracy (1985) and the agricultural labour force (1985–1988). It might have been possible to take data averaged over three-year periods, but that would have involved further limitations on the data range and a considerable increase in labour in the time available. These variables, which were available for only 19 of the 43 countries of SS Africa, were derived from World Bank (1989b, 1990, and 1991a), UNDP (1991), and Food and Agriculture Organization of the United Nations (FAO 1991a,b,c, and 1992) (table 2.3). The examination of the results is confined to the elements relevant to the themes of this paper. Eight of the variables measure various aspects of agriculture, five measure wealth/poverty, six measure urban/industry/commerce, four measure rural economy, four measure food, three measure energy use, three

Table 2.3 **Key to names of 34 economic and social variables in Sub-Saharan Africa by 19 countries (mainly in the late 1980s)**

Variable names in programme:
1. Wealth/poverty

GNPC	Gross national product per capita in $US, 1989, calculated by the World Bank Atlas Method (problems of national accounting and official exchange rates – some adjustment by World Bank in extreme cases) (World Bank 1991a: 204, 273–274)
ODAC	Official development assistance (ODA): net disbursement from all sources in $ per capita, 1989 (World Bank 1991a: 242)
DEBG	Total external debt as % of GNP, 1989 (World Bank 1991a: 250)
GDPG	Growth rate per annum (%) of GDP, 1980–1989, at 1987 constant prices (World Bank 1991a: 206)
INFL	Average annual rate of inflation (%), 1980–1989 (growth rate of the GDP implicit deflator, based on calculating for each year of the period, using the annual price movements for all goods and services) (World Bank 1991a: 204, 274)

2. Agriculture

VAAG	Value-added in agriculture per capita of total population in current $, 1989 (calculated from World Bank 1991a: 210)
FERT	Fertilizer consumption in hundreds of grams of plant nutrient per hectare of arable land, 1987–1988 (crop year July to June) (World Bank 1991a: 210, 275)
EXOP	% share of merchandise exports in "other primary commodities" (food and live animals, beverages and tobacco, inedible crude materials, oils, fats and waxes), 1989 (World Bank 1991a: 234, 280)
AGRG	Growth rate per annum (%) of GDP in agriculture, 1980–1989, at 1987 constant prices (World Bank 1991a: 206)
ARLA	Arable land as a % of total land, 1987 (FAO 1991a: 205)
FOLA	Forest land as a % of total land, 1987 (FAO 1991a: 205)
HATR	Hectares of arable and permanent cropland per tractor, 1989 (FAO 1991b: 3–5, 263)

Table 2.3 **(cont.)**

HAPE   Imports of pesticides in $ per hectare of arable and permanent cropland, 1989 (FAO 1991b: 3–5; FAO 1991c: 311)

3. Food

IMFO   % share of merchandise imports in food, 1989 (World Bank 1991a: 232)

CALC   Daily kilocalorie supply per capita, 1988 (food supplies including net imports, stock changes, less animal feed, seeds, losses) (World Bank 1991a: 258, 285)

FIMD   Food import dependency ratio (ratio of food imports to food available for internal distribution) (UNDP 1991: 144–145, 194)

FPIN   Average index of food production per capita, 1987–1989 (1979–1981 = 100) (World Bank 1991a: 210)

4. Rural

RUPO   Percentage of the rural population below the "poverty line" in 1980–1988, defined as the income level below which a minimum nutritionally adequate diet plus essential non-food requirements are not affordable (UNDP 1991: 152–153, 195)

RURP   Rural population as % of total, 1990 (using national definitions of "rural") (UNDP 1991: 136–137)

LABA   % of labour force in agriculture, 1985–1988 (economically active population including armed forces and the unemployed, but excluding homemakers) (UNDP 1991: 150–151, 195)

POAR   Agricultural population per hectare of arable land, 1987 (FAO 1991a: 205)

5. Energy

ENCA   Energy consumption per capita in kilograms of oil equivalent, 1989 (World Bank 1991a: 212)

ENIM   Energy imports as a percentage of merchandise exports, 1989 ($ values) (World Bank 1991a: 212)

IMFU   % share of merchandise imports in fuels, 1989 (World Bank 1991a: 232)

6. Urban/industrial/commerce

VAMF   Value-added in manufacturing per capita of total population, 1988, in current $ 1988 (World Bank 1991a: 214)

EXPC   Value of merchandise exports in $ per capita, 1989 (calculated from World Bank 1991a: 230)

IMPC   Value of merchandise imports calculated as above

IMPM   % share of merchandise imports in machinery and transport equipment, 1989 (World Bank 1991a: 232)

EXFU   % share of merchandise exports in fuels, minerals, and metals, 1989 (World Bank 1991a: 234)

URBG   Urban population average annual growth rate (%), 1980–1989 (World Bank 1991a: 264)

Table 2.3 **(cont.)**

---

7. Population

POGR   Average annual growth of population (%), 1980–1989 (World Bank 1991a: 254)

FIVE   The annual number of deaths of children under 5 years of age per 1,000 live births, 1989 (UNDP 1991: 140–141, 196)

LIFE   Life expectancy at birth in years, 1989 (number of years a newborn infant would live if prevailing patterns of mortality at birth were to stay the same throughout its life – data do not yet reflect impact of HIV epidemic) (World Bank 1991a: 204)

8. Education

ILLI   Total adult illiteracy (%), 1985 (% of population >15 years who cannot, with understanding, read and write a short, simple statement on their everyday life) (World Bank 1991a: 204)

Names of countries in the programme

BENI	Benin
BURU	Burundi
CAFR	Central African Republic
CAME	Cameroon
CHAD	Chad
COTE	Côte d'Ivoire
ETHI	Ethiopia
GHAN	Ghana
KENY	Kenya
LIBE	Liberia
MADA	Madagascar
MALA	Malawi
MALI	Mali
NIGR	Niger
RWAN	Rwanda
SIER	Sierra Leone
SOMA	Somalia
SUDA	Sudan
ZAIR	Zaire

Sources: World Bank (1991a, 1990, 1989b); UNDP (1991); FAO (1991a,b,c, 1992).

Note: The "Africa" of this study is "Africa south of the Sahara." By convention it excludes South Africa. No doubt this practice will now change, but I have retained it in order to use standard data sets with that name. Africa south of the Sahara did include Botswana, Lesotho, Namibia, and Swaziland, but their trade figures are included with those of South Africa. So, lacking vital data, I excluded them, but they will be included in some of the total data analysis for SS Africa used, rather than spend time in calculating the sums for the countries available. Angola was also excluded from the list of countries because the data for 1989 or nearest years were simply inadequate.

measure population, and one measures illiteracy. The countries concerned were Benin, Burundi, Central African Republic, Cameroon, Chad, Côte d'Ivoire, Ethiopia, Ghana, Kenya, Liberia, Madagascar, Malawi, Mali, Niger, Rwanda, Sierra Leone, Somalia, Sudan, and Zaire.

The analysis included a correlation matrix (relationships) and tables of principal components (groups) (tables 2.4–2.6). Coefficients above .4000 have been identified as probably having some significance in indicating relationship possibilities, although some of the variables, particularly those with a financial base such as the value-added in agriculture, admittedly have somewhat skewed distributions.

The percentage of rural population below the poverty line (RUPO – table 2.4) correlated most strongly and negatively with energy consumption per capita (ENCA), international trade per capita (EXPC & IMPC), food supply per capita (CALC), value-added in agriculture (VAAG), food import dependency ratio (food imports to food available for internal distribution – FIMD), and GNP per capita (GNPC). There seem to be some positive relationship to arable land as a percentage of total land (ARLA) and weak negative relationships to the index of change in food production (FPIN) and population growth (POGR), but only a very weak or no correlation with the infant death rate per 1,000 live births (FIVE – sometimes regarded as an indicator of poverty), life expectancy at birth (LIFE), the percentage of adult illiteracy (ILLI), and the percentage share of exports in "other" primary commodities (EXOP – mainly agricultural). Obviously in some countries the rural poor will survive better than in others, possibly owing to better access to food. A high percentage of rural people below the poverty line in the late 1980s seems for this group of SS African countries to be mainly associated with a low general level of energy consumption and of international trade and a low value in agricultural production (although little association, whether negative or otherwise, seems indicated with the use of modern inputs such as fertilizers, pesticides and tractors). *The percentage of the labour force in agriculture* (LABA – table 2.4) has only a low positive correlation with the percentage of the rural population below the poverty line (RUPO), but like the latter has negative relationships to energy consumption (ENCA), trade (EXPC & IMPC), value-added in agriculture (VAAG), GNP (GNPC), and food import dependency (FIMD). It is positively related to the rural percentage of total population (RURP) and also to the rate of urban population growth (URBG – i.e. a high percentage of agricultural labour,

Table 2.4 **Twelve key variables from the correlation matrix**

						Key variables						
Variable	LABA	POGR	GNPC	INFL	LIFE	VAAG	POAR	HATR	HAPE	RUPO	FIVE	FPIN
GNPC	-.4022	.4276	—	-.1970	.5899	.9141	-.2641	-.2662	.3126	-.4361	-.4990	.1336
ODAC	.1908	-.0816	-.0087	-.1427	-.0451	.1467	.0463	.1705	-.0034	.1640	.2098	.2579
DEBG	-.2554	.1573	-.0301	.3018	-.1109	.1422	.1756	-.4371	-.1680	-.2445	.0556	.0616
GDPG	.1593	-.2254	-.0935	-.0436	.1363	-.1280	.0952	.0137	.2418	.2802	-.0759	.3647
INFL	-.5571	-.1806	-.1970	—	-.1052	-.1088	.0009	-.3881	-.2114	.2231	-.1299	.0445
VAAG	-.5097	.4017	.9141	-.1088	.4705	—	-.2575	-.2506	.1688	-.4532	-.4120	.2614
FERT	.0304	.5794	.0997	-.1913	.5327	-.0347	.5670	-.3581	.8495	-.1167	-.3083	.1413
EXOP	.2495	.0653	-.1331	-.3530	-.0071	-.0874	.2260	-.0846	.1162	.2489	.0569	.0180
AGRG	-.2485	-.0376	.0498	.2081	.1077	.0974	-.0968	-.0442	.0923	.0450	-.2138	.5007
ARLA	.3835	.0052	-.0782	-.1360	-.2073	-.0563	.0856	.1899	-.1643	.4201	.0910	-.2317
FOLA	-.3387	-.0127	.2306	.4165	.2736	.1402	-.3231	-.2423	-.2225	.2652	-.2370	-.0307
HATR	.4751	-.2303	-.2662	-.3881	-.4423	-.2506	-.2676	—	-.3023	.1570	.1895	-.0175
HAPE	-.0147	.4817	.3126	-.2114	.7087	.1688	.5668	-.3023	—	-.2650	-.5019	.2453
IMFO	-.3710	-.2599	-.0171	.3316	-.3778	.1240	-.3602	.0304	-.3557	.0457	.1096	.2427
CALC	-.1655	.4053	.4895	-.2534	.3356	.5349	-.1863	.0131	.0984	-.5612	-.2747	.3155
FIMD	-.5268	.1286	.3690	.2291	.0888	.5080	.1249	-.4772	.1133	-.4433	-.0400	.0770
FPIN	-.4092	.1126	.1336	.0445	.4137	.2614	-.0182	-.0175	.2453	-.3669	-.4397	—
RUPO	.3562	-.3654	-.4361	.2231	-.2970	-.4532	.0349	.1570	-.2650	—	.1763	-.3669
RURP	.5864	-.0598	-.4820	-.2322	-.3818	-.5434	.2357	.1824	-.0618	.3732	.3289	-.4188
LABA	—	-.2289	-.4022	-.5571	-.2882	-.5097	.3052	.4751	-.0147	.3562	.4344	-.4092
POAR	.3052	.3339	-.2641	.0009	.3230	-.2575	—	-.2676	.5668	.0349	-.1642	-.0182

Table 2.4 **(cont.)**

| | | | | | | Key variables | | | | | | |
Variable	LABA	POGR	GNPC	INFL	LIFE	VAAG	POAR	HATR	HAPE	RUPO	FIVE	FPIN
ENCA	-.6313	.5774	.7092	.1389	.6112	.7380	.1208	-.5383	.3900	-.6383	-.4997	.2426
ENIM	.0549	-.0018	-.4124	-.0655	-.2487	-.4695	-.0287	-.1012	-.2096	.2345	.2942	-.1671
IMFU	-.0799	.1805	-.3529	.1670	-.1507	-.3697	-.0815	-.2352	-.2740	.2312	.1330	-.1038
VAMF	-.2706	.4040	.9305	-.1871	.5167	.7822	-.2524	-.2300	.2691	-.3339	-.4772	-.0009
EXPC	-.4655	.5851	.6378	-.1196	.4190	.7033	-.0523	-.3250	.1895	-.6387	-.3649	.1495
IMPC	-.4216	.6016	.7421	-.2582	.4514	.7451	-.1318	-.1388	.3404	-.5608	-.4651	.3024
IMPM	.2433	-.0247	-.1533	-.1153	.1147	-.2247	.4444	-.1083	.1598	-.1615	.1692	-.3218
EXFU	-.2666	.0715	.1561	.3752	.0257	.0692	-.2099	.1458	-.1512	-.2862	-.2017	.0293
URBG	.5419	.3135	-.0977	-.3748	.0447	-.3024	.4381	.3685	.3829	-.0310	-.0771	-.3022
POGR	-.2289	–	-.4276	-.1806	.5913	.4017	.3339	-.2303	.4817	-.3654	-.6186	.1126
FIVE	.4344	-.6186	-.4990	-.1299	-.7930	-.4120	-.1642	.1895	-.5019	.1763	–	-.4397
LIFE	-.2882	.5913	.5899	-.1052	–	.4705	.3230	-.4423	.7087	-.2970	-.7930	.4137
ILLI	.1232	-.3526	-.1770	-.0728	-.5904	.0194	-.1492	.4063	-.3143	.0376	.5381	-.0064

Table 2.5 **Eigenvalues of the correlation matrix for the first 10 principal components**

	Cumulative	Eigenvalue	Difference	Proportion
PRINC1	0.2540	8.6369	3.7971	0.2540
PRINC2	0.3963	4.8398	1.2988	0.1423
PRINC3	0.5005	3.5410	0.4065	0.1042
PRINC4	0.5927	3.1344	0.3834	0.0922
PRINC5	0.6736	2.7510	0.4318	0.0809
PRINC6	0.7418	2.3192	0.6913	0.0682
PRINC7	0.7897	1.6279	0.3550	0.0479
PRINC8	0.8271	1.2729	0.0530	0.0374
PRINC9	0.8630	1.2199	0.1560	0.0359
PRINC10	0.8943	1.0639	0.3149	0.0313

but not necessarily of rural poor, seems likely to be linked with urbanward migration), the infant death rate per 1,000 live births (FIVE), and hectares per tractor (HATR), and negatively to the index of change in food production since 1979–1981 (FPIN). It also has a negative correlation with the average annual rate of inflation (are the governments of countries with a high percentage of agricultural labour less inclined to overspend?), but only a weak correlation with the agricultural population per hectare of arable land (POAR). *The agricultural population per hectare of arable land* (POAR – table 2.4) is itself related to very few of these variables – mainly to the use of fertilizers (FERT) and pesticides (HAPE – associated with the intensive development of agriculture), to urban growth (URBG), and to the share of merchandise imports in machinery and transport (IMPM).

In order to examine the way in which these variables group together, principal components have been identified. From a table of eigenvalues of the correlation matrix (table 2.5) it appears that 25 per cent of the values are in the first component and nearly 90 per cent in the first 10 (PRINC1–10), but even by the sixth component the level of so-called "explanation" has fallen to only 7 per cent. Three of the components identified seemed particularly relevant for this study: the first, the seventh, and the eighth (PRINC1, PRINC7, and PRINC8 in table 2.6).

The first principal component (PRINC1) has highest values on energy consumption, GNP, value-added in agriculture and manufacture, international trade, and life expectancy. Negative values

Table 2.6 Eigenvectors for the first 10 principal components

Variable	PRINC1	PRINC2	PRINC3	PRINC4	PRINC5	PRINC6	PRINC7	PRINC8	PRINC9	PRINC10
GNPC	.2838	.0145	.0302	−.1251	−.2047	.0963	−.1867	.0019	.1232	.0487
ODAC	−.0301	−.0933	.3879	−.0397	.0175	−.1095	−.0776	.0455	.1369	.4228
DEBG	.0866	−.1668	.1091	.1266	.3455	.1948	.0707	.2835	−.0822	.1409
GDPG	−.0687	.0970	.3001	.1765	−.2226	−.1014	−.1118	−.2006	−.1723	−.0876
INFL	.0115	−.2224	−.1624	.3124	.0818	−.1504	−.1402	.2914	−.0963	−.2023
VAAG	.2834	−.0710	.0961	−.1246	−.1400	.1552	−.1659	.0495	−.0166	.0396
FERT	.0874	.3065	.1446	.1920	.1352	−.0894	.1345	.0108	.1906	.1259
EXOP	−.0956	.1680	.3470	.1314	−.0877	.2833	−.0726	−.0138	−.0863	−.0886
AGRG	.0747	−.1761	.2526	.0997	.0858	−.2744	−.1583	.1718	−.0356	.2406
ARLA	−.1080	.1457	−.0434	−.0995	−.1867	.1811	−.1088	.4374	−.2393	−.0667
FOLA	.0720	−.1192	−.2737	.2091	−.2624	−.1364	−.1249	.0159	.1101	.4062
HATR	−.1466	−.0319	.0488	−.3680	−.1455	−.1706	.2196	.0029	.1676	−.0812
HAPE	.1473	.3065	.1384	.0737	.1044	−.2143	−.0746	−.0837	.1031	−.1203
IMFO	−.0081	−.3359	.2115	.1132	−.0160	.0542	.0290	.0903	.3276	−.2393
CALC	.1961	−.0081	.0202	−.2546	−.0421	−.0231	.3156	.1216	−.3790	.1836
FIMD	.1844	−.1433	.0340	.0338	.3501	.1808	−.2245	−.0173	.1136	−.1250
FPIN	.1324	−.0684	.2338	.1164	−.0673	−.2611	.2665	−.1877	−.2598	−.1767
RUPO	−.2221	−.0039	.0124	.1592	−.1774	−.0817	−.2593	.3165	.0352	.2333
RURP	−.2294	.2135	.0247	−.0289	−.0543	.1918	.1012	.2079	−.1356	−.2129
LABA	−.2178	.2052	.0588	−.2409	.0235	−.0400	−.0529	.0460	.0211	.2559
POAR	−.0106	.2815	.0601	.1196	.3488	−.1183	−.1189	.1839	−.0628	−.0375
ENCA	.3124	.0257	−.0840	.0345	.1281	.0823	−.0775	.0016	−.0197	−.0067
ENIM	−.1471	.0492	−.0724	.2950	−.0334	.2527	.2390	−.2551	.3118	.0578
IMFU	−.0925	.0442	−.1498	.3304	−.1017	.2453	.3743	.0157	−.0398	.1947

VAMF	.2355	.0646	.0139	−.0915	−.2807	.1496	−.2144	.0270	.1885	−.0206
EXPC	.2817	.0102	−.0494	−.0618	.0681	.2377	.1129	−.0249	−.0939	.1220
IMPC	.2713	.0489	.1065	−.0804	−.1030	.1774	.1525	−.0105	.0727	−.0203
IMPM	−.0070	.1803	−.2723	−.0953	.3099	−.0228	−.1616	−.2625	−.1805	.1660
EXFU	.0913	−.1395	−.3341	−.1154	−.0068	−.2615	.1990	.1202	.1295	−.1180
URBG	−.0521	.2904	−.0428	−.1912	.1243	−.1258	.0529	.1736	.4173	−.0622
POGR	.2041	.2260	−.0001	.0572	.0156	.1006	.2907	.2941	.1757	.0636
FIVE	−.2217	−.1254	−.0015	−.1361	.1706	.2292	−.0477	−.2219	−.0041	.2268
LIFE	.2423	.2164	.0220	.1383	−.0925	−.2006	−.0783	−.0782	−.0759	.1065
ILLI	−.0844	−.2214	.2491	−.2392	.1908	.0401	.0424	.0396	.0514	.0557

link to rural poverty, deaths of infants, and rural population percentage. This would appear to be a component of development, but with no particular link to general GDP growth or agricultural growth.

The seventh principal component (PRINC7) has a highest eigenvector value for fuel imports, followed by food consumption and population growth. It is also linked positively to the index of food production per capita and to a lesser extent to the export of minerals, metals, and fuels, but negatively to food import dependence and the percentage of rural population below the poverty line. This component would seem to be identified with a satisfactory level of local food production and self-sufficiency except for fuels paid for largely by minerals exports (the eigenvector for value-added in manufacture is negative).

The percentage of rural population below the poverty line has its strongest link (positive) to *the eighth principal component (PRINC8)*, of which it is the second largest eigenvector, the largest being the percentage of arable land. Component 8 is also linked to population growth, inflation, and debt percentage of GNP, and is low on imports of energy and of machinery and transport, and on value-added in agriculture. It would seem that this component represents rural poverty linked to arable production coupled with poor economic performance and financial problems.

However, the relationships described are only weakly developed in components 7 and 8, which have levels of "explanation" of only 7 per cent and 5 per cent respectively. The principal component analysis has had only a limited value, partly because of its complexity in grouping the variables and partly because the more relevant components had only low "explanatory" levels. The more significant components from this data set, apart from the first, reflected mainly urban growth, well-developed commercial agriculture, aid, and trade, and tended to suggest relationships of interest in a context outside the scope of this paper. However, the evidence does point to a link between rural poverty and a poor overall economic performance linked to dependence on agriculture, particularly non-commercial agriculture. Although this may suggest that improved productivity should reduce rural poverty, the marked income disparities shown in table 2.2 also suggest that attempts to increase wealth are likely to do more for the rich than for the poor unless linked to policies that are focused on improved income distribution.

Aspects of economy and society in SS Africa

In most developing economies, agricultural productivity both in total and per capita has been rising in the past decade despite world recession, whereas in the developing countries of Africa, on the basis that 1979–1981 = 100, the indices of agricultural production and food production per capita for 1989 were both 93 and were below 100 in 1985, 1987, and 1988 (FAO 1991a: 166, 169). For SS Africa, on the basis that 1971–1980 = 100, the index of food production per capita for 1987–1989 was 95, the lowest of all the major global regions, and compared with an index of 112 for "low- and middle-income" economies (World Bank 1991a: 211). One should add that revision of the SS African population figures to take account of the Nigerian 1991 census result does improve the SS African food and agricultural production per capita indices, although SS African figures without Nigeria only confirm the decline. This data problem and the agricultural "crisis" factor are discussed in Morgan and Solarz (1994).

The droughts that were widespread in the world in the 1980s were particularly severe in SS Africa, sometimes combined with warfare, creating huge refugee problems, and combined again with severe economic shocks such as the oil price hikes, rising international interest rates linked to the international debt crisis, and declining terms of trade. In the semi-arid marginal lands in particular there were marked crop production failures, leading to increased demands for imported staple grains and adding to SS Africa's growing dependence on imported food. However, in the 1980s many countries had little foreign exchange to spare to pay for these imports without further borrowing. Several came to depend on aid to cope with this and other economic problems. Aid as a percentage of GNP in SS Africa amounted to 7.9 in 1989 (compared with all "low- and middle-income" countries at 1.1 per cent, but a startling 59 per cent in Mozambique, nearly 39 per cent in Somalia, and 32 per cent in Tanzania) and rose from nearly US$6 billion in 1979 to US$13 billion in 1989. Direct food aid in cereals in most years in the 1980s varied between 2 million and nearly 5 million tons (World Bank 1991a: 242–243, 210–211, and earlier *World Development Reports* of the World Bank). Most SS African countries have been affected by macroeconomic disequilibrium, with inflation and unsustainable current account deficits. At the same time, in most countries the balance of investment has shifted to the towns while the productive sectors of their economies have continued to depend largely on the rural areas. Agriculture produces about one-third of GDP in SS Africa and is second only to services, while employing about two-thirds of the labour force. In several countries, mining rather than manufacture is the main alternative source of wealth, but was adversely affected in the 1980s by trends in the world markets.

In some ways the weakest feature of the SS African economies, apart from the low income and investment base, has been the failure to develop major industrial strength. Between 1965 and 1989 manufacture's contribution to GDP rose from 8 to 11 per cent compared with 15 to 17 in South Asia and 27 to 33 in East Asia. Zimbabwe seems to have produced the best performance with an increase from 20 to 25. Of all the developing global regions SS Africa has the worst overall economic performance, including the worst industrial performance. It is also worth noting that, in the few countries for which there are reliable figures, the urban–rural income disparity in SS Africa is of the order of 5–6 times (Lipton 1990a: xiii) and, despite several exceptions, clearly depends more on the contrast between employment in government and the service industries on the one hand and employment in agriculture on the other than on differences between manufacture and agriculture. There are also huge urban–rural disparities in access to health, water, sanitation, and child nutrition as listed in UNDP (1991: 136–137). Rates of growth of GDP and of the contributions to GDP of agriculture, industry, and services have been highly variable (fig. 2.1), but have tended to be mostly low or negative since 1976. The importance of agriculture compared with industry in sustaining GDP was especially noticeable in 1977, 1982, and 1985–1989.

Much of the rural poverty problem is connected with the existence of: increasing landlessness, a large class of farmers with very small holdings, a lack of investment resources for agricultural improvement, the urban effect, low levels of rural education and migration to the towns of those who do achieve some acceptable educational standard, overvalued exchange rates discouraging agricultural exports, and poverty amongst women.

Increasing landlessness

Increasing landlessness has emerged as a serious problem, especially in Kenya and Malawi (Addison and Demery 1989: 76; see also Morgan

Annual percentage growth

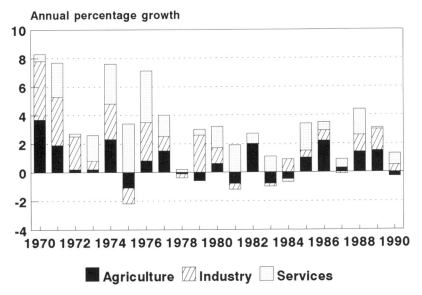

■ **Agriculture** ▨ **Industry** □ **Services**

Fig. 2.1 **Growth of GDP by sector in Sub-Saharan Africa, 1970–1990 (Source: World Bank, *World Tables 1992*, pp. 22–37)**

and Solarz 1994 for discussion of this and related agricultural problems). Land privatization in Kenya has become widespread, with evidence of a growing concentration of land ownership as some poorer farmers have been forced to sell (Wisner 1987: 24). The numbers of the landless have been swelled by those redundant urban workers who have chosen to return to the rural areas and who have lost their rural property rights. In much of SS Africa, traditional usufructuary systems of land tenure gave everyone at least some share in the land endowment. The growing commercialization of agriculture has increased the demand for private land in order to realize the benefits of long-term capital investment and even to use property as collateral. Privatization for some may be of benefit in transforming agriculture, but it is a loss for others, marginalized and made poor by the loss of their former rights.

A large class of farmers with very small holdings

The incomes from very small holdings are low and can be raised only by considerable investment in very intensive production and an increased labour input. For many of these farmers their living is precarious, partly dependent on market sales and partly on subsistence, which protects against market price fluctuations, but also dependent on inputs from their own production, with in consequence low yields and low output per man-day. Higher and more flexible prices for food and other agricultural raw materials, combined with less government interference and the introduction of higher-value crops, have been seen by the World Bank and by many monetarist economists as essential for transforming agriculture and as especially beneficial for smallholders (World Bank 1989a: 89–93). The World Bank's *Accelerated Development in Sub-Saharan Africa* (1981: 51) quoted in support of the case for smallholder agriculture the result of a survey in Kenya in 1974 that showed that holdings of less than half a hectare were 19 times more productive per hectare than holdings of over 8 hectares, but employment was 30 times greater, which may be excellent for reducing underemployment or unemployment but clearly is also a recipe for lower incomes.

The lack of investment resources for agricultural improvement

Investment has been discouraged in many countries by the poor prospects for profitability except in a few limited areas of export production and of specialized food production for urban markets, often in peri-urban zones. Peri-urban production in some cases has also been encouraged by the poor quality of rural roads and transport services. In the poorer African countries about 20 per cent of public investment in agriculture is provided by aid (World Bank 1982: 52; Lipton 1990b: 6–9).

The urban effect

Many of the evils of peasant poverty are primarily the result of decisions centred in, and made in the interests of, cities and urban groups (Lipton 1990a: xi). As Lipton points out (1990a: xii): "Where urban-based development depends on the flow of surpluses – marketed food; savings – from country to town, it is a natural urban reaction to put such resources as the rural sector does get at the disposal of larger farmers, who will use them to generate surpluses of that sort." The answer ought to be not large farms as such, but larger farms than the peasant average, able to use modern inputs and pay higher wages as farm incomes improve. But it also needs a successful urban sector, generating the wealth to pay higher prices and the ability to provide alternative employment for redundant farmworkers and dispossessed farmers.

Low levels of rural education, and migration to the towns of those who do achieve some acceptable educational standard

It is useless to improve rural education if there are no rewards at the end of the road (Lipton 1990a: xvii) and it is particularly important that the rewards to farmers are attractive to the educated if a more productive and more efficient agriculture is to be realized.

Thus in sum and substance, the man who is bound by traditional agriculture cannot produce much food no matter how rich the land ... Instead an approach that provides incentives and rewards to farmers is required. The knowledge that makes the transformation possible is a form of capital, which entails investment – investment not only in material inputs in which a part of this knowledge is embedded but importantly also investment in farm people. (Schultz 1964: 205–206)

This is not to deny that there is a case for promoting the use and development of traditional agricultural knowledge and methods of production. If more attention had been paid to such knowledge in the past, many mistakes could have been avoided, but systems of production that will offer substantially higher incomes will mostly require structural change and new inputs.

Overvalued exchange rates discouraging agricultural exports

Overvalued exchange rates have been true of some but not all SS African countries and keep the costs of food, fuel, machinery, and technical equipment imports low. They can also be part of an anti-inflation strategy. Attempts to promote industrial development can be protected by selective tariffs. Imported food can be cheap partly because Western countries, particularly those in the European Union (EU), subsidize their food exports, and may thus in certain cases help to undermine African agriculture and indirectly promote African rural poverty for the benefit of Western farmers, while keeping prices down to African urban consumers. More recently, however, food price inflation has occurred in certain cases of food import dependence. There is also the well-known example of the oil boom and "Dutch disease" in Nigeria, which was associated with the decline of non-oil tradables, i.e. export crop agriculture, and appeared to be an equivalent process in Nigeria to deindustrialization in the West (Collier 1987).

Poverty amongst women

The largest of the groups of particularly poor people is poor women, especially widows and the heads of single-parent households. Women participate in farming – in some communities they are the chief farmers, especially where men have migrated temporarily in search of work. In Lesotho the migratory labour system has left women to maintain households, look after children, search for cooking fuel, and look after the smallholdings. Most depend in part on remittances, but some, especially the growing number of divorcees and widows, are recognized as people at high risk (Wisner 1987: 25–28). Similar problems with women-headed households and difficulties in finding work for extra incomes or time in which to undertake the many duties imposed by women's precarious situation have been reported, for example, from Kenya (Wisner 1987: 24–25) and Nigeria (Morgan and Moss 1981: 32). In the latter case women, especially older single women, were often employed as fuelwood dealers, a job regarded as having low social status. In several SS African countries, e.g. Senegal and Tanzania, female labour force participation in work for wages or in trade is estimated at over 65 per cent of women of 15 years of age or more and women constitute 45 per cent of the labour force, but in others, e.g. Zambia, Kenya, Botswana, and Zimbabwe, women constitute only between one-quarter and one-third of the labour force and in some Islamic countries even less (Chant with Brydon 1989: 35).

Vulnerability

The vulnerability of the poor, as discussed in the introductory section on poverty, is a vulnerability to *stress*, including extremes of temperature and rainfall, general financial shortage, minor but especially persistent illness, family bereavements, which may be sudden but are often not unexpected, harvests below par but not severely deficient, damage to or deterioration of assets. It is also a vulnerability to *shock*, including war, civil war, riot, unexpected death, especially of a valued family mentor or earner, accidents involving severe or permanent injury, epidemic disease, not just amongst human beings but also amongst animals and plants, fire, drought with famine, flood, earthquake, landslides, volcanic eruption, bankruptcy, market collapse, sudden change in interest or exchange rates (poor people without savings or the need to travel across a border can still be affected by, for example, the consequent loss of a job), and changes in prices and wages (including hyperinflation).

Except in the poorest nations where welfare funding is totally inadequate, the worst effects of stress may be anticipated and at least some relief may be offered. In some cases international welfare may be available. Sudden shocks, however, often arrive without any or with very little national or household provision. A succession of climatically stressful years may, for example, be followed by the shock of severe drought, when the only recourse left is to migrate elsewhere more in the hope of relief than in the expectation of it. Even where national or international aid may be made available, it may be misdirected, opposed by those who see it as a threat to their interests, mismanaged, or arrive too late. Stress may also be offset by tradeoffs, particularly in the case where short-term adverse pressures are reduced by long-term payments: so future income expectations may be traded against immediate financial demands, or the environment may be subject to heavier, even damaging, demands in order to achieve a survival income (it may also be damaged to earn wealth, but the argument here is that part of the process of environmental damage and sustainability may be seen as a strategy for short-term survival). Unfortunately, environmental degradation may reduce the prospects for future livelihoods (Pearce, Barbier, and Markandya 1990: 13–14), especially where, as in the poorest countries, innovation in resource use and environmental management is limited. A sustainable development path occurs "only if the ecological boundary is shifted" by the application of appropriate technology (Pearce and Markandya 1989: 44). There can also be a trade-off with development, where investment has to be set aside and savings used for current expenditure. Finally, politically there can be a trade-off of the poor versus the rich, a trade-off in which the rich can be taxed or the poor can be further deprived in the interests of the other group.

Sustainability is not just about maintaining an economy or a given social condition, but about coping with stress and insuring against shock. To some extent the survival process of combining several activities and resources may offer some protection against stress and against the smaller shocks. However, it can rarely cope with the more severe shocks to which SS Africa is subject and which can overwhelm the more vulnerable communities whose range of strategies may be very limited. Some protection against future stress or shock may be achieved amongst the African poor by, for example, having large numbers of chidren, being part of an extended family, or using varied resources and storing whatever can be stored.

Shocks and disasters at the national instead of the family level need a different approach. In the richer capitalist nations people buy insurance. We have the World Bank, why not its parallel – a World Insurance Corporation that will operate at national and community levels? Of course there are nations that will not be able to afford a full subscription, but subscriptions to many of the international agencies are graded according to means and there is no reason why in this case it could not be similar and why insurance cover could not operate as of right. That still leaves the almost totally unexpected shocks, which may be regarded as unpredictable or "acts of God." But in these cases the richer nations and the relief agencies have normally attempted to provide aid and relief. It should not be beyond our global actuarial wit to widen the basis of cover and to provide funding and physical assistance on an organized instead of on an ad hoc basis as a kind of charity.

Poverty and economic reform

Economic reform provides a special case of the vulnerability of poor people in developing countries to rapid or sudden change in an economy. It is currently of particular interest in SS Africa in that most SS African countries have been affected by International Monetary Fund (IMF) and World Bank programmes of economic reform, with varying results for their economies and varying effects on the poorest people. All economic development as opposed to growth (i.e. structural change as opposed to increased production, savings, and consumption within an economy) involves investment that will require borrowing or the use of savings. For the most part development makes people poorer in the short to medium term, and also in the long term if it is unsuccessful, as much development in Africa has been. It is in effect a major contributor to poverty in the developing countries, whatever the long-term hopes. All change in the operation and structure of an economy has to be paid for. That payment is the investment that, even when profitable, may nevertheless reduce the standard of living of the poor where restructuring is loaded in favour of the richer members of a given community.

Structural adjustment and stabilization policies are normally the product of International Monetary Fund and World Bank advice, usually worked out in cooperation with a national financial team and linked sometimes to approval and loans from richer nations, sometimes from the G7 ("Group of Seven": Canada, France, Germany, Italy, Japan, the United Kingdom, and the United States). Differences in role between the IMF and the Bank have become blurred as the Bank's funding has become linked to structural adjustment programmes (SAPs) and to financial stabilization, which also appear to overlap (for discussion of the close relationship between the Bank and the IMF see *The Economist*, 12 October 1991). The roles of the two institutions in what has become in effect a world financial system are extremely powerful. There is a general consensus within the IMF and the Bank on the principles of economic reform, although there are differences amongst individual economists. This consensus may be described as either neoclassical or monetarist (for a useful summary see Hunt 1989: 305–307, 311–315, and 321–322, and in relation to agriculture see FAO 1991a: 81–107) and supports policies aimed mainly at monetary and fiscal stabilization and supply-side measures, usually including agricultural reform, input supply improvement, and market liberalization, mostly in sequenced operations in which the supply-side measures take longer to produce an effect than the monetary and fiscal measures. The latter have usually involved some or even all of the following: restraining demand, reducing current account deficits, devaluing exchange rates, eliminating hyperinflation and controlling inflation, reducing government expenditure, restraining wages, raising interest rates, encouraging savings, and liberalizing international and national trade by removing subsidies and protective tariffs. Some of these measures have been described as "getting the prices right" (Green 1989a: 39) and are based on a belief in the removal of factor distortions in economies and in the attempt to seek equilibrium through the operation of a free market.

What makes the changes of policy associated with the monetarist approach to economic reform of special importance for this paper is the effects on the poor of the introduction of these formidable reform packages, including the short-term nature of many of the measures introduced, involving economic shock and often including the removal or reduction of many of the welfare services and other forms of protection for the poor, thus greatly increasing the stresses put upon them. Of course, one should allow against this the effects on the poor of either not introducing the programmes or taking other courses of

action, both of which, unfortunately, are hypothetical or even spec-
ulative. Here one can only examine what has happened.

Structural adjustment programmes have been adopted by more
than 30 SS African countries, more especially in the 1980s, although
African countries were affected by World Bank and IMF policies
even in the 1960s, e.g. Zaire, which was one of the first countries to
accept such policies. Despite all these programmes, real GDP growth
in SS Africa in 1980–1988 averaged only 0.8 per cent per annum,
compared with 4.8 per cent in 1965–1980, international debt grew at
12 per cent per annum, and social conditions deteriorated. Obviously
world recession problems had to be overcome and African governments cooperated with the Bank and the IMF in various ways and to
varying degrees. Nevertheless the results have given cause for debate,
criticism, and the expression of doubt (Stein and Nafziger 1991).

The World Bank contrasts its "shock treatment" or reforms implemented in less than two years, usually to resolve a crisis, with what it
calls "gradualism" or reforms spread over rather more than two
years, but essentially even these are what many social scientists would
regard as short to medium term (World Bank 1991a: 117). The model
the Bank has in mind was shown in *World Development Report 1990*
(1990: 105) where a diagram indicated the supposed effects of adjustment in Ecuador, including an increase in the percentage of total
population in poverty above the percentage level predicted for "no
adjustment" for three years in the rural areas and four years in the
urban, while real GDP fell below that expected under "no adjustment" before it eventually rose. The same model included a "no
external shock" case, but such a scenario does not appear to have
occurred in SS Africa. The World Bank claimed that the real beneficiaries of the SAPs were the rural poor (World Bank 1991a: 106)
because even in the "short run" they were protected in relation to the
urban poor by depreciation of the real exchange rate, which stimu-
lated exports and increased farm incomes, offsetting in part the
effects of a general decline in wages. But how many of the rural poor
are engaged in export crop production, which has declined severely
in SS Africa, and what is the time-lag on the expected growth of
export production? Several years in the case of tree crops. In some
countries there is increasing privatization of land and the introduction of herbicides, pesticides, and machinery to reduce labour use,
tending to encourage the growth of larger private farms and adding
to the numbers of rural landless and urbanward migrants. In some
cases the rural areas have been forced to accept people returning to

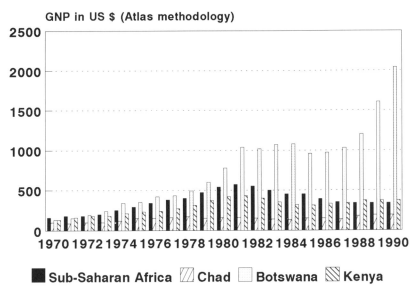

Fig. 2.2 **GNP per capita in Sub-Saharan Africa, 1970–1990 (US$ at current purchaser values) (Source: World Bank, *World Tables 1992*, pp. 2–3)**

the family farm after being made redundant in the town. It is in any case unsafe to argue on the basis of a rural–urban dichotomy. What, for example, is happening to rural incomes partly dependent on remittances from urban workers?

SS Africa in the 1980s experienced far worse levels of shock from deteriorating terms of trade and interest rates than did East or South Asia or Latin America, and these were on top of macroeconomic imbalances and severe structural weaknesses (World Bank 1990: 107). Figure 2.2 shows the decline in GNP for SS Africa as a whole since 1980 (for comparison, examples of high [Botswana], medium [Kenya], and low [Chad] GNP trends have been provided). SAPs aimed to reduce imports and raise export earnings, but also generally raised the prices of tradable goods relative to the non-tradables. Pinstrup-Andersen (1989: 94) argued that many of the poor were more occupied with non-tradables than with tradables and were in consequence made worse off. Higher retail prices, where passed on to full-time farmers, have benefited that particular rural group, but those part-time farmers who depend more on the market for their basic goods have gained little. Only the mainly subsistence farmers who could maintain a low level of dependence on markets have managed to escape the effects of sudden changes in market prices and

45

of changes in the demand for agricultural goods, more especially of any rise in the prices of inputs needed for export production or for commercial food production.

Three examples will illustrate these points.

First, in Uganda the implementation of IMF–World Bank policy packages since 1980 has been claimed to have been followed by reduced food remittances from rural to urban areas, reduced cash remittances from urban to rural, a decline in food production, and a decline in the social services. From 1980 to 1984 overall real wages fell, but agricultural producer prices rose 12–15 times, only to be partly offset by a rise in the consumer price index by 10 times, adversely affecting those peasant families depending on the market for a major part of their domestic consumption (Banugire 1989). Uganda began an economic recovery programme in 1987, but this was followed by inflation, which reached 240 per cent per annum at the end of 1988. More devaluation plus higher interest rates and other measures followed, but inflation still persisted. Conditions were made worse by the collapse of the International Coffee Agreement in 1989 (World Bank 1991b: 550–555).

Secondly, Zambia received an IMF programme in 1985, abandoned it in 1987, and returned to the IMF conditions in mid-1989, when consumer prices were decontrolled and the kwacha was devalued. Inflation rose to more than 120 per cent per annum by early 1990 and there was a considerable foreign cash shortage. The agricultural marketing boards were abolished and attempts were made to increase maize production, mainly through subsidies, which contributed significantly to the budget deficit, and unfortunately involving increased marketing costs and serious transport and storage problems. In 1989 maize had to be rationed and maize meal prices rose, followed by riots in Lusaka (FAO 1991a: 50–53). Some progress has been made since in financial reform and in reducing the power of the parastatals, although the toll on living standards has been heavy, including deterioration of all the key indicators of social development (World Bank 1991b: 599–605). Although Zambia has a higher GNP per capita than most SS African countries and a measure of industrial development, it is overdependent on the world metals markets and has shown a marked disparity of income levels (table 2.2).

Thirdly, in the Sudan in the 1970s economic reform measures included a wage freeze, limits on government employment levels, and limits on government expenditure, but seven years later the Sudan had failed to achieve its economic targets and by 1985, after some help from the US government, the Sudan was deep into economic crisis and the government was swept from office. The debt service ratio climbed to 150 per cent of GDP and the country was forced in part to engage in counter-trade. There is evidence that the economic austerity required in the Sudan imposed severe burdens on the poor, and Cheru (1989) asked whether the IMF was "the enemy of the poor." By the late 1980s the disposable income of the Sudanese peasant was only 30 per cent of what it had been in 1970, and GDP per capita had been markedly reduced. Social services had been cut, wages and salaries frozen, and the purchasing power of the poor had been reduced by devaluation and the removal of price controls. Severe shortages of essential inputs and consumer goods became commonplace. Investment as a proportion of GDP fell together with national and public savings. Budget deficits led to high levels of inflation, jumping by 1989–1990 to 120 per cent. More economic reforms were introduced in 1991, but unfortunately on an ad hoc and inconsistent basis, which has undermined their effectiveness (World Bank 1991b: 507–512). The Sudan has a harsh environment combined with considerable irrigation potential. It has been severely affected also by civil war and pressure from time to time from Ethiopian refugees. In the complex process of combining several strategies against poverty the Sudan suffers from its limitations, and the Sudanese poor are in consequence amongst the more vulnerable.

Despite the limitations discussed, current SAPs and World Bank programmes have claimed an intention to benefit the poor, at least in the longer term, by enhancing the rates of return on the few assets they hold, by increasing their access to the factors of production, by creating employment opportunities, by maintaining their human capital, and by increasing income and consumption transfers (Addison and Demery 1989: 71–89; FAO 1991a: 111–113). The FAO report on *The State of Food and Agriculture 1990* (1991a), much of which was focused on structural adjustment and agriculture (pp. 81–152), claimed that SAPs had a negative effect on the chronically poor, while creating a new poor sector with extra burdens on women, very small farmers, and low-income groups (pp. 113–114). Attempts have been and are still being made to reduce the social costs of adjustment, such as the PAMSCAD programme in Ghana (Programme of Actions to Mitigate the Social Costs of Adjustment), but, although "it is true that no social group has lost out massively in Ghana,... it is equally true that those who have lost, even if not massively, are those with relatively poor ability to withstand such losses" – particularly the

47

poor northern farmers, the women food farmers in the south, and the petty retail traders (Toye 1991: 169).

Conclusion

"Poverty, vulnerability, inequality and threats to the social fabric in Africa are not a product of the 1970s or 1980s, much less of Fund and Bank prescriptions for stabilization and adjustment. Nor are they purely imported colonial phenomena" (Green 1989b: 32). SS Africa, in common with the rest of the world, has a history of poverty, war, and famine extending over millennia. However, it is evident that the SS African economic and financial problems were made very much worse in the 1970s and the 1980s by a combination of:

1. an investment in growth and development that failed to earn the expected rewards;
2. the international debt crisis, oil price hikes, and rising interest rates, plus the inadequacy of the aid programmes that were meant to provide relief;
3. repeated drought, crop failure, and widespread famine;
4. the failure of agricultural production to contribute significantly to growth and the increased dependence on imported food;
5. widespread warfare and civil unrest;
6. the fact that SAPs have been only partially successful and that that success has been in terms of system rather than people, who somehow have to survive in the hope that decisions linked to short- or medium-term deterioration based on theories that are unknown or unappreciated could solve their problems in the future.

Price incentives have been held up as one of the most important means of promoting agricultural production and reducing rural poverty, but they will not solve the problems of extremely poor people dependent wholly or at least in part on the market. They and the urban poor need cheaper food, which only a more efficient use of inputs in agriculture can provide, and they need employment.

The evidence of the general review of the nature of poverty, the statistical examination, and the study of vulnerability has shown the existence in SS Africa of a mass of rural people who are on or below margins regarded as the minimum for the avoidance of malnutrition and whose condition has been severely worsened by the combination of economic crises and droughts and then further impoverished by some aspects of the economic reforms attempted. The evidence suggests that their condition can be relieved only in the long term, not just by economic reform but by appropriate investment and trade in a world in which the major powers are concerned to promote growth rather than restrict it and to encourage open access to world markets. Perhaps "don't do as I do, do as I say" may be said to express a great deal about some of the major development problems of today's poor countries and poor rural people, which are as much a problem of double standards in the world trading system and in the politics of international finance as they are the product of their own development problems.

References

Addison, T. and L. Demery. 1989. The economics of rural poverty alleviation. In: S. Commander (ed.), *Structural Adjustment and Agriculture: Theory and Practice in Africa and Latin America*. London: ODI with Currey and Heinemann, pp. 71–89.

Banugire, F. R. 1989. Employment, incomes, basic needs and structural adjustment policy in Uganda, 1980–87. In: B. Onimode (ed.), *The IMF, the World Bank and the African Debt. Vol. 2, The Social and Political Impact*. London and New Jersey: Zed Books, pp. 95–110.

Chambers, R. 1983. *Rural Development: Putting the Last First*. London and New York: Longman.

Chambers, R. and G. R. Conway. 1992. Sustainable rural livelihoods: Practical concepts for the 21st century. Institute of Development Studies Discussion Paper 296.

Chant, S. with L. Brydon. 1989. Introduction to L. Brydon and S. Chant (eds.), *Women in the Third World: Gender Issues in Rural and Urban Areas*. Aldershot, UK: Edward Elgar.

Cheru, F. 1989. The role of the IMF and World Bank in the agrarian crisis of Sudan and Tanzania: Sovereignty versus control. In: B. Onimode (ed.), *The IMF, the World Bank and the African Debt. Vol. 2, The Social and Political Impact*. London and New Jersey: Zed Books, pp. 77–94.

Collier, P. 1987. Macroeconomic effects of oil on poverty in Nigeria. *Institute of Development Studies Bulletin* 18(1): 55–60.

Economist, The. 1991. *Sisters in the Wood: A Survey of the IMF and the World Bank*, 12 October.

FAO (Food and Agriculture Organization of the UN). 1991a. *The State of Food and Agriculture 1990*. Rome: FAO.

———— 1991b. *Production Yearbook 1990, Vol. 44*. Rome: FAO.

———— 1991c. *Trade Yearbook 1990, Vol. 44*. Rome: FAO.

———— 1992. *The State of Food and Agriculture 1991*. Rome: FAO.

Green, R. H. 1989a. Articulating stabilisation programmes and structural adjustment: Sub-Saharan Africa. In: S. Commander (ed.), *Structural Adjustment and Agriculture: Theory and Practice in Africa and Latin America*. London: ODI with Currey and Heinemann, pp. 35–54.

———— 1989b. The broken pot: The social fabric, economic disaster and adjustment in Africa. In: B. Onimode (ed.), *The IMF, the World Bank and the African Debt*.

Vol. 2, The Social and Political Impact. London and New Jersey: Zed Books, pp. 31–55.

Hunt, D. 1989. *Economic Theories of Development: An Analysis of Competing Paradigms*. New York and London: Harvester Wheatsheaf.

Jazairy, I., M. Alamgir, and T. Panuccio. 1992. *The State of World Rural Poverty: An Inquiry into Its Causes and Consequences*. London: Intermediate Technology Publications for International Fund for Agricultural Development.

Lipton, M. 1990a. Foreword to K. Puttaswamaiah (ed.), *Poverty and Rural Development: Planners, Peasants and Poverty*. London: Intermediate Technology Development Publications, pp. xi–xxiii.

——— 1990b. Aid to agriculture and rural development. In: K. Puttaswamaiah (ed.), *Poverty and Rural Development: Planners, Peasants and Poverty*. London: Intermediate Technology Development Publications, pp. 1–20.

Morgan, W. B. and R. P. Moss. 1981. *Fuelwood and Rural Energy: Production and Supply in the Humid Tropics*. Dublin: Tycooly International for the UN University.

Morgan, W. B. and J. A. Solarz. 1994. Agricultural crisis in Sub-Saharan Africa: Development constraints and policy problems. *Geographical Journal* 160(1): 57–73.

Pearce, D. and A. Markandya. 1989. Marginal opportunity cost as a planning concept in natural resource management. In: G. Schramm and J. J. Warford (eds.), *Environmental Management and Economic Development*. Baltimore, Md.: Johns Hopkins University Press for the World Bank, pp. 39–55.

Pearce, D., E. Barbier, and A. Markandya. 1990. *Sustainable Development: Economics and Environment in the Third World*. London: Earthscan.

Pinstrup-Andersen, P. 1989. The impact of macro-economic adjustment: Food security and nutrition. In: S. Commander (ed.), *Structural Adjustment and Agriculture: Theory and Practice in Africa and Latin America*. London: ODI with Currey and Heinemann, pp. 90–104.

Ravallion, M. 1992. *Poverty Comparisons: A Living Standards Measurement Study*. Working paper no. 88. Washington D.C.: World Bank.

Schultz, T. W. 1964. *Transforming Traditional Agriculture*. New Haven and London: Yale University Press.

Sen, A. K. 1984. *Resources, Values and Development*. Oxford: Blackwell.

——— 1987. *The Standard of Living*. Cambridge: Cambridge University Press.

——— 1990. Food, economics and entitlements. In: J. Drèze and A. K. Sen (eds.), *The Political Economy of Hunger. Vol. 1*. Oxford: Clarendon Press, pp. 34–52.

Stein, H. and E. W. Nafziger. 1991. Structural adjustment, human needs and the World Bank agenda. *Journal of Modern African Studies* 29(1): 173–189 (review article of World Bank, *Sub-Saharan Africa: From Crisis to Sustainable Growth*, 1989).

Toye, J. 1991. Ghana. In: P. Mosley, J. Harrigan, and J. Toye (eds.), *Aid and Power: The World Bank and Policy-based Lending. Vol. 2, Case Studies*. London and New York: Routledge, pp. 150–200.

UNDP (United Nations Development Programme). 1990. *Human Development Report 1990*. Oxford and New York: Oxford University Press for UNDP.

——— 1991. *Human Development Report 1991*. Oxford and New York: Oxford University Press for UNDP.

Wisner, B. 1987. Rural energy and poverty in Kenya and Lesotho: All roads lead to ruin. *Institute of Development Studies Bulletin* 18(1): 23–29.

World Bank. 1981. *Accelerated Development in Sub-Saharan Africa: An Agenda for Action*. Washington D.C.: World Bank.

———— 1982. *World Development Report 1982*. Oxford and New York: Oxford University Press for the World Bank.

———— 1989a. *Sub-Saharan Africa: From Crisis to Sustainable Growth*. Washington D.C.: World Bank.

———— 1989b. *World Development Report 1989*. Oxford and New York: Oxford University Press for the World Bank.

———— 1990. *World Development Report 1990: Poverty*. Oxford and New York: Oxford University Press for the World Bank.

———— 1991a. *World Development Report 1991: The Challenge of Development*. Oxford and New York: Oxford University Press for the World Bank.

———— 1991b. *Trends in Developing Economies 1991*. Washington D.C.: World Bank.

3

Environmental management and social equity

Tade Akin Aina

Introduction

Recent times have seen a rise of what can be called the sustainable development movement in terms of a heightened concern with the state and future of the environment and the extensive politicization and institutionalization of environmental questions on a global scale. The result of this has been innumerable initiatives and efforts at many levels, which include the internationalization of knowledge, practices, strategies, and institutions to understand and predict environmental trends better and to arrest environmental decline and degradation. As part of these, a series of strategies, approaches, and techniques is being developed to plan, organize, and manage the environment. Increasingly a body of knowledge and expertise is growing around these efforts and is beginning to constitute what is formally defined as orthodox environmental management.

However, formal or orthodox environmental management, like all "managerialist" perspectives, is structured in such a way that it is defined as the prerogative of a privileged group or class of nations and persons. Because of this definition, it poses several problems in terms of relevance, appropriateness, long-term effectiveness, and, more fundamentally, social justice and equity. These problems, however, contain far-reaching implications for the expression and acceptance of the key elements of the sustainable development approach, of which orthodox environmental management claims an important executing component. One of the major questions here relates to the specific current to which one adheres within the broad and eclectic sustainable development movement and approach. Another, proceeding from this, is whether the attainment of sustainable development objectives is either a scientific/technocratic or humanistic issue, or rather an embodiment of these various elements of human civilization. It is these questions that form the concern of this paper.

To explore the most important dimensions of these issues effectively, this paper is structured as follows: (a) clarification of key notions such as sustainable development, environmental management, and social equity, (b) a brief examination of the political-economic context of contemporary environmental management, (c) a discussion of social equity and environmental management, in terms of exploring some of the practices in Sub-Saharan Africa, and (d) finally an exploration of the options for sustainable futures.

The key notions

Sustainable development

According to the authoritative document *Nigeria's Threatened Environment: A National Profile* (Nigerian Environmental Study/Action Team (NEST) 1991: 282):

Sustainable development is a notion, a movement and an approach which has developed into a global wave of concerns, study, political mobilization, and organization around the twin issues of environmental protection and economic development ... The approach embodies the notion and ideal of a development process that is equitable and socially responsive, recognizing the extensive nature of poverty, deprivation, and inequality between and within nations, classes and communities. It also seriously advocates that the world be seen as one ecosystem and that the economic development process should include ecological and environmental issues as an essential component.

However, the conventional usage of the notion has a wide range of concerns embodied in it that has made it broadly eclectic. It has therefore not been expressed within a theoretical framework of any great rigour, though it is more identifiable in a general common-sensical and programmatic nature (Redclift 1987; Aina 1990: 194). This openness of concerns has given rise to a wide variety of currents across different ideologies and a proliferation of definitions and interpretations.

An attempt that has perhaps popularized the notion most is the report of the World Commission on Environment and Development (WCED) entitled *Our Common Future* (1987) and known as the "Brundtland Report" after Mrs. Gro Harlem Brundtland, the former prime minister of Norway who chaired the Commission. That report and the range of activities that it generated, including the United Nations Conference on Environment and Development (UNCED) held in Rio de Janeiro, Brazil, in June 1992, have all elevated the notion of sustainable development to the level of an operational concept. Within this are principles, ideals, and values that see it as desirable and necessary if humankind is to tackle the problem of the crisis of environment and development effectively.

What needs to be pointed out however, and the WCED document and later positions have emphasized this, is the centrality of social equity to a sustainable development approach. Repeatedly, the document emphasized the importance of intergenerational and intragenerational equity, the meeting of the basic needs of all, the conquest of poverty, and the extension of the opportunity to fulfil the aspiration of all for a better life (WCED 1987: 8).

The centrality of the question of social equity in coming to a meaningful analysis, or practical action, becomes evident from the above issues.[1]

Environmental management

Environmental management as it is conventionally understood today refers to a formal body of techniques, rules, and practices for the planning, organization, and social and technical control of the human utilization of, and interaction with, nature and natural resources.

However, an important position that we need to consider, particularly in the African case, is to see environmental management rather as a wider range of human practices and actions involved in our interaction with natural resources and the environment. These include the use of a whole range of institutions, values, customs, and strategies through which ordinary peoples have interacted with nature and organized their needs and use of natural resources. From this definition, it can be seen that even the poorest peoples and the most rudimentary societies possess specific strategies and an armoury of cultural equipment with which they manage natural resources and cope with their ecology, economy, and society. In this light, it might be necessary to make a distinction between *popular environmental management*, which is what ordinary peoples and indigenous communities do, and *orthodox environmental management*, which is the formal body of professional and technical approaches and system that is currently dominant. For the purpose of attaining social equity and effectiveness both approaches have to be integrated. The direction for this is taken up later in this paper.

Social equity

To those familiar with the Anglo-American common law traditions, the notion of equity denotes the legal concept of "technical equity." This is the application of principles of natural justice and the collective conscience to temper the rigidity of the common law, whose concern with technicalities and precedents might deny a litigant the chance of receiving justice in the courts. In other words, principles of fair play and justice based on the defined collective conscience and the guiding values of natural justice are brought into play. Social equity takes its departure from here. It means in its simplest terms that which is fair and just (Adigun 1987: 10–11).

Of course, the problem of arriving at a consensus on what these imply, particularly across cultures, is tremendous. But this is really why it becomes an issue particularly in orthodox environmental management in cases where value systems differ and perceptions of rights, obligations, and duties also differ. This has been the case with several indigenous peoples and communities when they confront the definitions of laws, proprietorial rights, tenure, and duties as defined by the modern state and related Western institutions. The result has been and is still devastating for them. Social equity therefore, particularly in a situation of clash of cultures and in environmental management, requires that we recognize the values and norms of other peoples and that our decisions and actions are guided by notions of justice and fairness that accept the integrity and validity of other cultures and lifestyles.

55

The political-economic context of contemporary environmental management

To understand effectively why questions of social equity become central to contemporary forms of environmental management it is necessary to look at the overall political-economic context. In the case of Sub-Saharan Africa, given its specific history and the nature of its environmental problems, this is an important point of departure.

The political-economic context of most countries, particularly those of Sub-Saharan Africa, can be identified as possessing four broad levels with implications for the management of the environment. These are the global, the regional, the national, and the local or grassroots level. As has been pointed out in an earlier work (Aina 1990: 196), these levels are sites and sources not only from which actions are expressed but also within which effects are felt. At these different levels, a wide array of vested interests and social forces interplay and interact. In a lot of cases these interactions cut across the levels, while in some cases actions and effects are localized.

Also expressed at these levels are three cross-cutting issues that affect the nature of the political-economic context of most Sub-Saharan African countries. These are: (a) inequality and poverty, (b) domination and conflicts, and (c) unsustainable economic and social development processes. The three are closely interrelated, often feeding on each other, and to a great extent co-determining the vicious cycles of poverty, misery, and environmental degradation characteristic of many parts of Sub-Saharan Africa.

The global/regional contexts

The global/regional levels include what goes on within the global political-economic system, particularly within its influential multilateral institutions such as the International Monetary Fund, the International Bank for Reconstruction and Development, the United Nations System, and similar institutions. At this level, the problems related to inequality and poverty, domination and conflicts, and unsustainable economic and social development processes continuously play themselves out but on a more macro and systematic scale. The history of most Sub-Saharan African countries as ex-colonies, their dependent and weak economies, their narrow technological base, and their recent high indebtedness make them extremely vulnerable. This vulnerability is not only in economic terms but also in ecological, social, and cultural terms.

Such countries, particularly in the context of the debt crisis and the application of the economic recovery programmes initiated from the centres of the global system, are often forced through deregulation mechanisms to open all aspects of their economy and society. In this context, social and economic priorities tied to either debt repayment or rescheduling are imposed on them and these often reinforce or expand unsustainable social and economic development processes, particularly with regard to the exploitation of natural resources that are exported for hard currency. In a lot of cases, the imperatives of debt servicing and adjustment management have pushed equity and sustainable development questions into the background. In fact economic reforms have by their nature favoured the well-off and reinforced unsustainable strategies.

These have implications for the environment in terms of an accelerated process of natural resources degradation and in a lot of cases often repressive and inequitable environmental management responses.

National/local contexts

At national or local levels all three issues – inequity and poverty, domination and conflicts, and unsustainable economic and social development processes – find expression. There is scarcely any country in Sub-Saharan Africa that is free from one or all of these problems.

Quite often the problems have their origins in the colonial history of the specific countries. It is at this point that the transformation and internationalization of the national/local environments begin through specific forms of insertion into the global economy based on some form or combination of forms of exploitation of natural resources through cash-crop production, mining, timber, forestry, etc. This process often involves a redefinition of the relationships of the people to nature and natural resources through production, consumption, laws, the growth of bureaucracies and institutions of enforcement, and, in several cases, through direct physical and spatial segregation of the colonized and the colonizer.

Because colonial interests were often about the exploitation of natural resources, the central concern of environmental management was often with environmental sanitation in the urban areas and with agricultural productivity and the securing of the reserves of other natural resources in the rural areas. Commitment to these objectives led to the growth of management techniques that confronted erosion, land degradation, and pest control only in relation to the obstacles they created to producing economic goods or to the leisure of the colonial and the indigenous élites.

Of course there was the creation of forest reserves to conserve the sources of forest products and the institution of national parks projects to promote tourism and conserve wildlife.[2] But in essence the dominant techniques utilized were reactive, Western in origin and style, and concerned more with the definition and protection of interests either identified or possessed by the colonial élites. Environmental management in this context was specialized, alienated, and élitist in form, and in some cases motivated by romantic and adventurist conceptions of the "native" and his natural habitat. All of this was inherited and applied in the post-colonial era and, with the deteriorating conditions imposed by the economic and political crises that plagued the continent from the mid-1970s, some of the institutions decayed while others were seriously perverted. It is in this context that the current situation of multifaceted crises of the economy, polity, society, and ecology have come together to plague the African continent.

Social equity and environmental management: Some examples

Examples of inequitable environmental management practices abound both in the field and in the literature (see Enghoff 1990; Hallward 1992). The majority of these examples relate to major differences in environmental management approaches between the ordinary peoples and the élites, whether foreign or local, who determine policies and politics.

Environmental management of the orthodox type covers a wide range of inequitable practices that can be found in both urban and rural areas. In this paper, I consider the manifestation of inequitable management practices or prescriptions mainly with regard to three environmental issues: pastoralism and wildlife conservation, the population question, and urban poverty. For each of these the significant property of the inequitable management is that it alienates and often represses and oppresses the people it is meant for. It is also distant from their own approaches and forms. As Paul Richards (1985) has pointed out, orthodox environmental management strategies are often not more effective and successful than those that come from indigenous technical knowledge, although they often tend to be contemptuous of them. More often than not, the orthodox practices are sectoralist in design and implementation as well as repressive and enforcement oriented. There is also a deep-seated mistrust and suspicion of the motives and activities of the people being managed. Perhaps of greater significance is that these practices are built and controlled by specific vested interests, such as those of tourism, plantation and other large-scale agriculture, commercial forestry, or ranching, or those of orthodox environmental managers such as urban planners, sanitation engineers, agronomists, and wildlife conservationists.

Of course, the claim to superior scientific and technical knowledge, a great deal of which is ethnocentric, is often used as legitimation for the imposition of the practices and techniques. Yet there is very little integration of the ecological, cultural, and sociological reality of the contexts of concern. But this is how reality is defined for most indigenous and ordinary peoples, ranging from the Peul of the Futa Djalon highlands to the urban poor of the Mathare Valley slum in Nairobi, Kenya.

Inequitable management practices often include the following:
- violations of fundamental rights such as: the right to life, the right to livelihoods, the right to shelter, the right to freedom of movement and association;
- violations of access to the basic human needs identified by Abraham Maslow, such as: safety, other physiological needs, self-esteem, and actualization needs.[3]

The strategies and tactics often utilized include:
- evictions without compensation and adequate resettlement in both rural and urban areas;
- restrictions on mobility, such as entry and exit into traditional zones of operations such as game reserves and forests;
- restrictions on traditional or popular environmental management activities and livelihood strategies such as range burning, grazing patterns, cultivation, hunting, fishing, gathering, and street trading.
- the imposition of culturally alien practices, an example being extraordinary family planning strategies such as involuntary sterilization;
- deliberate and systematic neglect in the provision of services as they affect the poor, such as those of public health or those of effective crime control.

Such measures ensure the continuity of high mortality risks for the poor.

Various aspects of these broad strategies express themselves in the three areas of environmental management identified above.

Pastoralism and wildlife conservation

NEST (1991) described the Fulani pastoralists of Nigeria as a culture threatened by modernization. This seems to be the case for most pastoralists of the African continent. The economic development process, the forces and institutions of the modern state, and the introduction or enforcement of wildlife conservation practices and reserves threaten both the cultures and the livelihoods of these people. Evidence abounds for this in the experience of countries such as Nigeria, Niger, Chad, Somalia, the Sudan, Ethiopia, Kenya, and Tanzania.[4]

In fact the experience of the Masai pastoralists in Kenya and Tanzania exemplifies clearly the inequitable environmental management approach that focuses on wildlife conservation while threatening the very livelihood and essence of the Masai pastoralist culture.

Martin Enghoff (1990), in a study of parks and peoples in East Africa, clearly shows the origin of this form of inequitable environmental management and its current patterns. The colonial imperatives of wildlife conservation negatively affected the Masai and other pastoralists, first and foremost involving the alienation of their land and the imposition of various limitations and prohibitions on their activities.

As Enghoff points out, the pastoralists lost important grazing lands to the creation of national parks, which greatly restricted their mobility over their traditional range lands. Their systems of bush burning, grazing patterns, and cultivation activities were also equally restricted. An important element of their loss of control was the creation of a negative image for them. They were accused of being responsible for the wide incidence of environmental degradation, which was said to be related to their overstocking and overgrazing of pasture lands. However, the accusations and analyses were one-sided because pastoralists also suffer greatly from contacts with wildlife. For example, their stock have been infected with wildlife diseases. Moreover, some of the practices carried out by the pastoralists such as bush burning contain positive implications for the regeneration of grazing lands and the control of both tick-borne diseases and the spread of non-edible grass species.

The sad fact, however, is that pastoralists are not offered either the chance or the opportunity to defend themselves, while the inequitable management strategies imposed on them continue to attack the very basis of their existence. The intention here is neither to romanticize nor to idealize the culture of the pastoralists but to point out that the pattern of external interaction with it, particularly with regard to wildlife conservation, contains strong elements of inequitable environmental management practices.

The population question

Discussion of the population question can be very sensitive, in particular because the issues touch on fundamental values related to sexuality and the physical and social reproduction of peoples. Also present is the possibility of racist interpretations of other peoples and cultures. But perhaps the strongest cause of distrust is the question of religion and the religious definition of the purpose and basis of procreation. All of these issues extend the population question beyond mere science to the realm of values, ethics, and politics. But science indeed has a role to play, not in defining what is to be done but in pointing out the increasingly delicate balance between population, ecology, and natural resources. The extension of the conception of "carrying capacity" beyond its formal usage to making it the basis of prescribing public health policies demonstrates this delicate balance. As a result, the population question becomes an environment and development question that has to be addressed. However, this must be done with serious consideration of ethics and issues of social equity.

Several specialized agencies, particularly in North America, have developed to address these issues.[5] These have used every opportunity to bring the "population question" to the fore. The intensity and urgency of the problem in fact raise serious ethical questions about whether or not inequitable or socially unjust management strategies and practices should be used. In this particular context, does the end justify the means, however unjust and inequitable these are? These are questions that most of science by its very positivist nature does not and cannot answer. But they are questions that environmental managers and some scientists try to answer.

An interesting position with far-reaching implications for environmental management is that of Maurice King (1990), who introduces the idea of the "demographic trap" and "ecosustainability." Concerned with the implications of current population trends for future generations, King advocates a new global strategy that will impose "extra-ordinary family planning" strategies: the "one-child family" option and the need no longer to promote reduced child mortality as an element of public health strategy for countries described as caught in the demographic trap. King criticizes what he considers the unsustainable orientation of the World Health Organization and the United Nations Children's Fund (UNICEF), which both provide what are perceived as desustaining measures, such as oral rehydration therapy on a public health scale. To the discerning reader, what King is advocating is a particular form of environmental management strategy. The problem here is that on closer examination it denies the "right to life" and advocates a deliberate and systematic neglect of the provision of collective services, particularly in the area of public health.

This is the problem with some of the orthodox environmental management strategies advocated for family planning and as responses to the population question. They often breach the right to life and contain the tacit acceptance of involuntary mechanisms that are defined as unacceptable to "civilized" Western culture.

Urban poverty

Contemporary urbanization in many parts of Africa contains many unsavoury features that threaten the urban environment. As discussed in another work (Aina et al. 1994), the urban condition often includes large-scale poverty, overcrowding in the low-income settlements, inadequate provision of basic services such as water, roads, drainage, schools, and health centres, blighted dwelling places, insecurity of tenure of both land and shelter, and a generally poor quality of life. The urban environment in most low-income settlements often suffers from deliberate systematic neglect of the most basic services and infrastructure, resulting in extensive pollution from poor waste management and industrial and other economic activities, perennial flooding, and the exposure of the populace to a wide variety of environmental and health hazards.

In this context, the life of the ordinary low-income urban dweller is difficult, oppressed, and miserable. It is not made easier by the wide range of policies, institutions, and legislation utilized in the course of urban management, which contribute to blaming the victims and penalizing them for the very condition in which they find themselves. In a study of the environmental problems of Metropolitan Lagos, it was found that most of the indicators utilized by governments and planning authorities to determine the extent of blight in low-income settlements can be traced to government neglect and/or inaction, such as the failure to provide basic services or to plan the settlements (Aina et al. 1994).

However, the image of the "underdog" remains consistent in orthodox environmental management, whether in the urban settlements or in rural areas. Although the urban poor contribute extensively to the building and maintenance of their settlements and have over the years generated a wide range of strategies and practices for organizing and managing these settlements, orthodox urban environmental managers continue to ignore or/and despise these efforts and knowledge. These are often not integrated in any meaningful way into city development and planning strategies. Rather, a specifically urban variant of the inequitable management practices such as denial of the fundamental human rights identified above and the violation of access to the fulfilment of basic human needs continues to constitute the essence of urban environmental management. Thus the lives of the urban poor in Africa are characterized by large-scale evictions and demolitions such as that of the Maroko slum on the outskirts of Lagos, Nigeria, in 1990 and those of Nairobi, Kenya, in the same year.

As pointed out elsewhere (Aina et al. 1994), the policies and laws that govern urban environmental management seem to be oblivious to the notion of sustainable development. The emphasis is on enforcement and policing of breaches of environmental sanitation laws and the provisions of public order and the criminal code. Even then, the state and the level of the institutional capacity of the agencies of urban environmental management – the shortage of skilled manpower, funds, and capacity, coupled with corruption and the manipulation of these institutions – have rendered the enforcement of laws generally problematic. What currently happens is that city authorities and their agents focus on the lines of least resistance, which are the urban poor and their settlements.

The way forward

This paper has painted a picture of the extent to which environmental management as we know it contains extensive elements of social inequity. It has also shown that efforts at managing the environment can be classified broadly into two approaches: *formal orthodox environmental management* and *indigenous popular environmental man-*

agement. Both approaches contain strengths and weaknesses in terms of efficiency and effectiveness. Although the orthodox approach might contain a greater element of built-in technical efficiency, it lacks strong elements of social equity. It often tends to be inappropriate, can be irrelevant, and of course at times is less effective. The popular strategies are themselves limited when they confront large-scale problems, although they cope more effectively with community-based micro-scale issues, and they have been found to work quite well in many contexts in Africa. This has been well stated by Paul Richards (1985).

The question here is, how do we integrate both and build on their strengths? The answer is readily available in trends and practices in development thinking and work and can be found in the participatory approach to development. The point is that environmental management must become *participatory environmental management.*

This of course means that it must begin with the people; it must be based on their needs in terms of both their perceptions and their definition of their needs. Managers and researchers must therefore change their strategies and orientation and learn to work with and for ordinary people in fulfilling their needs in the order of priority that they place on them. Every element of environmental management must incorporate the knowledge, values, and energies of the end-users – the communities. More significantly, groups that are at the moment considered irrelevant and are marginalized, such as pastoralists, peasants, women, children, and youth, must become the central subjects of policies and actions whenever these affect their lives and locations.

There is of course the need for a review and reform of institutional operations, their structure, functions, and responsibility. Policies and legislation require quick, effective, and self-sustaining review mechanisms. An important element is effective decentralization to local authorities or those closest to the points where action will be felt. The institutions responsible for producing formal environmental managers also require a reorientation of their training programmes and their professional ideologies. This means new approaches, methods, and curricula. It also means retraining and training of practitioners in the field.

Above all, environmental managers need to adopt and internalize the values, principles, and practice of effective *participatory management.* This, if genuinely done, would help to guarantee the protection of popular economic and social rights and would lead to a more human-centred strategy of environmental management. That way the most important and universal features of social equity are guaranteed.

Notes

1. For an elaboration of this position, see Aina and Salau (1992).
2. On this, see Enghoff (1990); also Toure (1986).
3. Abraham Maslow, the humanist psychologist, was one of the earliest scholars to give scientific expression to the fact of basic human needs, their hierarchy, and their importance for human motivation. See Maslow (1943).
4. A special issue of *Nomadic Peoples*, no. 25–27 (1990) on "Pastoralism and the State," is devoted to a treatment of this question.
5. There is indeed a lot of concern. In some cases the concerns are genuine but again they can be misguided. Several international non-governmental organizations are working in this field.

References

Adigun, O. 1987. *Cases and Texts on Equity, Trusts and Administration of Estates.* Abeokuta: Ayo Sodimu Publishers.

Aina, T. A. 1990. The politics of sustainable third world urban development. In: D. Cadman and G. Payne (eds.), *The Living City: Towards a Sustainable Future.* London: Routledge.

Aina, T. A. and A. T. Salau. 1992. "The challenge of sustainable development in Nigeria: The way forward." In: Tade Akin Aina and A. T. Saulau (eds.), *The Challenge of Sustainable Development in Nigeria.* Ibadan: Nigerian Environmental Study/Action Team.

Aina, T. A., F. E. Etta, and C. I. Obi. 1994. The search for sustainable urban development in Metropolitan Lagos, Nigeria: Prospects and problems. *Third World Planning Review*, special issue on "Sustainable Cities," pp. 201–219.

Enghoff, M. 1990. Wildlife conservation, ecological strategies and pastoral communities: A contribution to the understanding of parks and peoples in East Africa. *Nomadic Peoples*, no. 25–27: 93–107.

Hallward, P. 1992. The urgent need for a campaign against forced resettlement. *The Ecologist* 22(2): 43–44.

King, M. 1990. Health is a sustainable state. *The Lancet*, 15 Sept., vol. 336: 664–667.

Maslow, A. H. 1943. A theory of human motivation. *Psychological Review* 50: 370–396.

NEST (Nigerian Environmental Study/Action Team). 1991. *Nigeria's Threatened Environment: A National Profile.* Ibadan: Nigerian Environmental Study/Action Team.

Redclift, M. 1987. *Sustainable Development: Exploring the Contradictions.* London: Methuen.

Richards, P. 1985. *Indigenous Agricultural Revolution.* London: Hutchinson.

Toure, O. 1986. The pastoralists of northern Senegal. *Review of African Political Economy*, no. 42: 19–31.

WCED (World Commission on Environment and Development). 1987. *Our Common Future.* Oxford: Oxford University Press.

65

4

Introduction to population, resources, and sustainable development in Sub-Saharan Africa

John O. Oucho

Introduction

The demographic structure of Sub-Saharan Africa in all its complexity is a considerable subject. This paper will therefore focus mainly on the major subcontinental and regional features of Sub-Saharan Africa's demography and will provide a brief introduction to the subject to serve as a foundation on which other more detailed discussions of poverty, development, sustainability, and resource management may rest. Many of the topics relevant to demography, such as urbanization, urbanward migration, natural resources, and environmental sustainability, have specialized treatment elsewhere in this collection of conference papers, and will receive only preliminary or partial treatment here.

Amongst the major regions of the third world, Sub-Saharan Africa has one of the smaller populations in total, at an estimated 543 million in mid-1992 (World Bank 1994: 163), more than Latin America and the Caribbean but much less than either South Asia or East Asia and the Pacific. It shares with Latin America and the Caribbean a very low population density of only 22 per km², compared with 229 in South Asia and 103 in East Asia and the Pacific. However, in contrast with Latin America and the Caribbean, there are few great urban concentrations and virtually no major industrial regions outside South Africa. A much higher proportion of its population is rural (71 against 27 per cent) and widely dispersed, a feature of considerable significance in its economic development. Sub-Saharan Africa's population is one of the poorest and depends in many of its subregions on fragile tropical environments, for whose sustainable management its peoples often lack the skills required to cope with current economic and technological changes. There is also the problem of increasing pressure on resources generated by the highest rate of population increase in the world apart from that of the Middle East and North Africa – 3.0 per cent per annum in 1980–1992 against 3.1 per cent (World Bank 1994: 211).

Population structure and characteristics and their relation to the resources for sustainable development will be examined largely at the subregional and national level. Table 4.1 shows some of the basic demographic data for Sub-Saharan Africa estimated in 1990 (Population Reference Bureau 1990). The largest population of the subregions was in western Africa, with 206 million or 39.8 per cent of the estimated total of 518 million. Eastern, central, and southern Africa had 38.4, 13.1, and 8.7 per cent respectively. Doubling time for most of the subregions was estimated to be 23 years. Projected populations for Sub-Saharan Africa were nearly 702 million with approximately the same subregional balance by the year 2000, and 1.2 billion by 2020. Some differential size changes will occur, mainly by countries, reflecting different rates of population growth – three of the four subregions recorded the same rate of natural increase and doubling time (table 4.1, columns 2–5). In western Africa, half the countries listed had annual natural increase rates of 3 per cent or more, as did more than two-thirds of eastern African countries (at 3.8, Kenya and Zambia had the highest rates in Sub-Saharan Africa), while in central and southern Africa rates tended to be lower. As might be expected, very high total fertility rates (TFR) are widespread, with 13 countries listed as having 7.0 or more births per woman. Rwanda has the remarkable figure of 8.3, one of the highest in the world. It should be noted that, although there is some variation in the country-level data between published sources, all agree that Sub-Saharan Africa currently has the highest rates. Although Sub-Saharan Africa succeeded in reducing its infant mortality rate (IMR) from 142 per 1,000 live births in 1970 to 99 in 1992, compared with a reduction from 97 to 60 in the world IMR (World Bank 1994: 215), most of the countries in

Table 4.1 **Demographic indicators: Estimates and projections for Sub-Saharan Africa by subregion and country, 1990**

Subregion/country	Population estimate, mid-1990 (million)	Birth rate (per '000 pop.)	Death rate (per '000 pop.)	Natural increase (annual, %)	Population "doubling time" in years (at current rate)	Population projected to 2000 (million)	Population projected to 2020 (million)
	(1)	(2)	(3)	(4)	(5)	(6)	(7)
Eastern Africa	199.0	47	17	3.0	23	272.8	474.5
Burundi	5.6	48	15	3.2	22	7.7	13.7
Comoros	0.5	47	13	3.4	20	0.7	1.3
Djibouti	0.4	47	18	3.0	23	0.6	1.0
Ethiopia	51.7	44	24	2.0	34	70.8	126.0
Kenya	24.6	46	7	3.8	18	35.1	60.5
Madagascar	12.0	46	14	3.2	22	16.6	29.6
Malawi	9.2	52	18	3.4	20	11.8	22.0
Mauritius	1.1	19	7	1.3	54	1.2	1.3
Mozambique	15.7	45	19	2.7	26	20.4	31.9
Réunion	0.6	24	6	1.8	39	0.7	0.8
Rwanda	7.3	51	17	3.4	20	10.4	19.7
Seychelles	0.1	25	8	1.7	41	0.1	0.1
Somalia	8.4	51	20	3.1	23	10.4	18.7
Tanzania	26.0	51	14	3.7	19	36.5	62.8
Uganda	18.0	52	17	3.6	20	25.1	42.2
Zambia	8.1	51	14	3.8	18	11.6	22.0
Zimbabwe	9.7	42	10	3.2	22	13.1	20.9
Central Africa	68.0	45	16	3.0	23	91.1	156.0
Angola	8.5	47	20	2.7	26	11.1	18.5
Cameroon	11.1	42	16	2.8	26	14.5	23.5
CAR	2.9	44	19	2.5	27	3.7	5.9
Chad	5.0	44	20	2.5	28	6.2	9.4
Congo	2.2	44	14	3.0	23	3.0	5.0
Eq. Guinea	0.4	43	17	2.6	27	0.5	0.8
Gabon	1.2	39	16	2.2	31	1.6	2.6
São Tomé/Principé	0.1	36	9	2.7	25	0.2	0.3
Zaire	36.6	47	14	3.3	21	50.3	90.0
Western Africa	205.7	47	17	3.0	23	279.3	480.9
Benin	4.7	51	19	3.2	22	6.6	11.7
Burkina Faso	9.1	50	18	3.2	21	12.5	23.0
Cape Verde	0.4	38	10	2.8	25	0.5	0.8
Côte d'Ivoire	12.6	51	14	3.7	19	18.5	35.4
Gambia	0.9	47	21	2.6	27	1.1	1.7
Ghana	15.0	44	13	3.1	22	20.4	33.9
Guinea	7.3	47	22	2.5	28	9.2	14.4
Guinea-Bissau	1.0	41	20	2.1	33	1.2	2.0
Liberia	2.6	45	13	3.2	22	3.7	6.5
Mali	8.1	52	22	3.0	23	10.7	19.2
Mauritania	2.0	46	19	2.7	25	2.7	4.5

Infant mortality rate (per '000 live births)	Total fertility rate	% population under 15/ over 65	Life expectancy at birth (years)	Urban population (%)	% married women using contraception (total)	Government view of fertility level[a]	Population density (persons/km² arable land)
(8)	(9)	(10)	(11)	(12)	(13)	(14)	(15)
116	6.7	47/3	50	18	–		
114	7.0	45/3	51	5	9	H	422
94	7.1	48/3	55	23	–	H	555
122	6.6	46/3	47	78	–	S	n.a.
154	6.2	46/4	41	11	–	H	320
62	6.7	50/2	63	20	27	H	1,083
120	6.6	45/3	54	22	–	S	404
130	7.7	48/3	49	14	7	H	304
25.2	2.0	30/5	68	41	75	S	1,036
141	6.4	44/3	47	19	–	S	430
14	2.4	32/5	71	98	–	–	–
122	8.3	49/2	49	6	10	H	348
17	2.7	36/6	70	52	–	H	n.a.
132	6.6	47/3	45	33	–	S	304
106	7.1	49/2	53	19	–	H	551
107	7.4	49/2	49	9	5	H	316
80	7.2	49/2	53	45	–	H	313
72	5.8	45/3	58	25	43	H	135
118	6.1	45/3	50	37	–		
137	6.4	45/3	45	25	–	H	297
125	5.8	44/3	50	42	2	H	1,167
143	5.6	42/3	46	35	–	H	6
132	5.9	43/4	46	27	–	S	159
113	6.0	45/3	53	40	–	L	264
120	5.5	43/4	50	60	–	L	302
103	5.0	33/6	52	41	–	L	340
61.7	5.4	42/5	65	38	–	S	n.a.
108	6.2	46/3	53	40	–	S	512
119	6.6	46/2	48	30	6		
110	7.0	48/4	47	39	9	S	291
126	7.2	43/4	51	8	–	H	301
66	5.2	42/5	61	27	–	H	325
96	7.4	49/2	53	43	3	S	355
143	6.4	44/3	43	21	–	–	438
86	6.3	45/3	55	32	13	H	1,140
147	6.2	43/3	42	22	–	H	405
132	5.4	41/4	45	27	–	H	307
83	6.4	46/3	56	43	6	H	1,675
117	7.2	47/3	45	18	5	S	390
127	6.5	44/3	46	35	1	S	929

Table 4.1 **(cont.)**

Subregion/country	Population estimate, mid-1990 (million)	Birth rate (per '000 pop.)	Death rate (per '000 pop.)	Natural increase (annual, %)	Population "doubling time" in years (at current rate)	Population projected to 2000 (million)	Population projected to 2020 (million)
	(1)	(2)	(3)	(4)	(5)	(6)	(7)
Niger	7.9	51	21	3.0	23	11.1	20.6
Nigeria	118.8	46	17	2.9	24	160.8	273.2
Senegal	7.4	46	19	2.7	26	9.7	15.2
Sierra Leone	4.2	48	23	2.5	28	5.4	8.9
Togo	3.7	50	14	3.6	19	5.2	9.9
Southern Africa	44.9	36	9	2.7	26	58.7	95.3
Botswana	1.2	40	11	2.9	24	1.6	2.2
Lesotho	1.8	41	12	2.8	24	2.4	3.9
Namibia	1.5	44	12	3.2	22	2.1	3.9
South Africa	39.6	35	8	2.7	26	51.5	83.5
Swaziland	0.8	46	15	3.1	22	1.1	1.8

Sources: Population Reference Bureau (1990); UN Economic Commission for Africa (1988) for col. 15.

a. H – too high; S – satisfactory; L – too low.

table 4.1 had IMRs above 100 (column 8), putting some brake on population growth. Very high IMRs were recorded in Sierra Leone, Ethiopia, Guinea, the Gambia, the Central African Republic, and Mozambique.

Rapid population growth rather than population size *per se* poses one of the greatest challenges for Sub-Saharan Africa because it has tended not only to press on the management of the resource base, but also to act as a drag on economic development, which must achieve a gross domestic product growth above 3 per cent per annum in order to produce a per capita gain. The limited birth control data available indicate that in Sub-Saharan Africa less use is made of contraception than in any other major global region. Over the period 1988–1993 the percentage of married women of childbearing age using contraception was lowest in Uganda, Nigeria, Senegal, and the Sudan at 5, 5, 11, and 9, respectively, and highest in Mauritius, Zimbabwe, Botswana, Togo, and Kenya at 75, 43, 33, 34, and 27 respectively (World Bank 1994: 212–213). For several African countries no data were available. Rapid population growth, largely attributed to high and sustained fertility, has induced many Sub-Saharan governments to

Infant mortality rate (per '000 live births)	Total fertility rate	% population under 15/ over 65	Life expectancy at birth (years)	Urban population (%)	% married women using contraception (total)	Government view of fertility level[a]	Population density (persons/km² arable land)
(8)	(9)	(10)	(11)	(12)	(13)	(14)	(15)
135	7.1	47/3	45	16	–	H	164
121	6.5	45/2	48	31	5	H	334
128	6.4	44/3	46	36	11	H	123
154	6.5	44/3	41	28	–	H	223
114	7.2	49/2	55	22	34	S	218
61	4.7	40/4	62	53	45		
64	5.3	46/3	59	22	33	L	79
100	5.8	43/4	56	17	5	H	513
106	6.1	45/3	56	51	–	–	n.a.
55	4.5	40/4	63	56	43	H	–
130	6.2	47/2	50	26	20	H	369

adopt population limitation policies (e.g. family planning) and population-responsive development programmes in order to reduce fertility rates and improve the quality of population. In 27 of the 44 Sub-Saharan countries for which information is available, fertility rates were considered too high, in 13 satisfactory and in only 4 – the Congo, Equatorial Guinea, Gabon, and Botswana – too low (Population Reference Bureau 1990).

Rapid population growth tends to produce a youthful population structure, shown by the percentages of children under 15 years of age in column 10. Apart from Gabon and the three Indian Ocean island countries, all the countries listed have 40 per cent or more of their population in this age group. The age group over 65 years is low, being in the range of 2–3 per cent of population in most cases. Nevertheless, with the high proportion of children, most of Sub-Saharan Africa has high dependency ratios by world standards. A consuming rather than producing population can cripple national development and sectoral planning efforts, where overall productivity tends to be very low and where unemployment and underemployment are rife.

Despite the evidence of rapid population increase, there is low life expectancy at birth in Sub-Saharan Africa (column 11). Generally life expectancy is between 40 and 55 years; the few exceptions above this range include Kenya, Zimbabwe, Botswana, South Africa, and the islands. Southern Africa has much higher life expectancy than any of the other regions, owing mainly to better health infrastructure, well-trained health personnel, and a favourable ratio of population per physician (Sub-Saharan Africa has the worst ratio of the world's major regions). There are fears that the addition of Acquired Immune Deficiency Syndrome (AIDS) to the catalogue of Africa's diseases will seriously reduce life expectancy and will reshape Africa's demographic profile.

Internal and international migration

All types of internal migration (rural–rural, rural–urban, urban–urban, and urban–rural) and international migration (permanent, labour, refugee, and undocumented/illegal) are represented in Sub-Saharan Africa, but only the broad outline of population movement can be discussed here.

Internal migration

The two dominant forms of internal migration are: the less studied but more diverse rural–rural migration and the more studied and pervasive rural–urban. Rural–rural migration consists of:
1. nomadism, especially in the Sahel, the Horn of Africa, northern Kenya, northern Tanzania, north-eastern Uganda, Botswana, and Namibia (Oucho and Gould 1992);
2. spontaneous migration for purposes of land colonization by farmers (e.g. in Kenya, Zimbabwe, and revolutionary Ethiopia, and in Tanzania during "ujamaa");
3. resettlement of peasants from densely occupied areas to marginal lands, and migration from areas of traditional agriculture to areas of modern agriculture or to mining areas.

Approximately 29 per cent of Sub-Saharan Africa's population was estimated to be urban in 1992 (World Bank 1994: 223), but the definition of "urban" varies between countries. African cities generally lack strong economic bases, often attract rural–urban migration in the face of widespread unemployment (Todaro 1969, 1976), lack decent housing (Ohadike and Teklu 1990), and have overburdened educational and health facilities (Gould 1990; for discussion of rural–urban links see Oucho 1985, 1988, 1990). Attempts by many Sub-Saharan governments to limit or control rural–urban migration have mostly failed. The nature and magnitude of internal migration and the problems of spatial distribution of population are demonstrated by the fact that in 1987, out of 45 countries, 28 perceived both to be inappropriate and 26 adopted policies to decelerate the processes involved (UN Department of International Economic and Social Affairs 1988).

International migration

International migration in Sub-Saharan Africa has two dominant forms: labour migration and refugee movements. In western Africa, labour migration mostly has a north to south alignment, particularly to Côte d'Ivoire, and a south to north flow outside the continent to Europe (Adepoju 1991) and the Gulf states. In Sub-Saharan Africa, migration has involved flows mainly from weaker to stronger economies, such as, in western Africa, to Côte d'Ivoire (where by 1975 some 22 per cent of the population were foreign born), Nigeria, Liberia (21 per cent foreign born in 1974), Equatorial Guinea, and Gabon, and, in central and southern Africa, mainly to Zambia and South Africa (Bohning 1981; UN Economic Commission for Africa 1988). In western Africa, labour migration has sometimes precipitated sour relations between some countries, e.g. between Ghana and Nigeria (Afolayan 1988), ending in the repatriation of between 0.5 and 1 million Ghanaians in 1983. Many of these were from Nigerian towns and were forced back into rural areas in Ghana.

Apart from economic refugees, as in Ghana, most Sub-Saharan refugees have been and are still being forced to move by civil war or by drought. Many millions in the Sudan, Ethiopia, Uganda, Rwanda, Liberia, Mozambique, Angola, and Namibia are still displaced. However, the refugee flows also include movements back home, as in Uganda, where rehabilitation programmes have been undertaken, in recently independent Namibia, and in Mozambique and Angola.

Natural resources

There are many different ways to classify natural resources. The classification used here is a simple ad hoc method related to the link between natural resources and population, beginning with land as the basic resource for agricultural production, which is the most important element in many Sub-Saharan economies.

Land

Table 4.2 provides broad land-use categories, from which it can be seen that Sub-Saharan Africa is nearly 34 per cent pastoral, 30 per cent forest and woodland, and just under 7 per cent cropland (which also supports large numbers of trees) (World Resources Institute 1994: 284). Another 30 per cent is "other land" – a small part urban and roads, and the rest chiefly sand, rock, and poorly vegetated terrain. Because Africa as a whole has 16 per cent of its soil area without "serious limitations" (FAO 1980: 4) it would seem probable that the cropland area could be considerably expanded (of these soil limitations, the most serious in Africa was drought, affecting 44 per cent, followed by nutritional deficiency or chemical toxicity, affecting 18 per cent). However, the demand for cropland is highly variable and some countries have little room for expansion. The highest proportions of cropland and permanent pasture are in western and eastern Africa, and the highest percentages of cropland by country are in Burundi (52.3), Mauritius (52.2), Rwanda (46.9), Nigeria (35.4), and Uganda (33.7). These three countries, particularly Rwanda, have little scope for the expansion of agricultural production other than by intensification. It is worth noting that some of the countries with advanced commercial agriculture, e.g. Kenya and Zimbabwe, have only low to average proportions of cropland, although Kenya does have a considerable area with serious environmental limitations.

In many African countries, small family farms are the basis of agricultural production and the amount of cropland per capita tends to be low. In 1991, Africa as a whole had an average of 0.27 hectares per capita – nearly twice the Asian figure and less than half that for North and Central America, but the same as for Europe. Botswana had most cropland per capita, with 1.10 ha, but very low figures were recorded in Kenya (0.10), Guinea and Somalia (0.12), Tanzania (0.13), and Liberia (0.14) (World Resources Institute 1994: 294–295). Pressure on land resources has led to increasing individual ownership of land in place of traditional use right systems and associated with the growing commercialization of agriculture (Migot-Adholla et al. 1991).

Atmospheric resources

Apart from the southern subtropical extreme and the more temperate conditions of the high plateaux and mountain environments, especially in Ethiopia and elsewhere in eastern Africa, temperatures

Table 4.2 **Agricultural and forest/woodland land use in Sub-Saharan Africa, 1989–1991**

Regions/countries[a]	Land area ('000 ha.)	Cropland (%)	Permanent pasture (%)	Forest/ woodland (%)
SUB-SAHARAN AFRICA	2,124,784	6.7	33.7	29.5
East Africa	604,892	7.6	46.1	27.6
Burundi	2,565	52.3	35.6	2.6
Djibouti	2,318	0.0	8.6	0.0
Ethiopia	110,100	12.7	40.8	24.6
Kenya	56,969	4.3	66.9	4.1
Madagascar	58,154	5.3	58.5	26.7
Malawi	9,408	17.8	19.6	38.6
Mauritius	203	52.2	3.4	28.1
Mozambique	78,409	4.0	56.1	18.2
Rwanda	2,467	46.9	18.8	22.5
Somalia	62,734	1.7	68.5	14.4
Tanzania	88,604	3.8	39.5	46.2
Uganda	19,955	33.7	9.0	27.9
Zambia	74,339	7.1	40.4	38.8
Zimbabwe	38,667	7.3	12.6	49.5
Central Africa	648,910	3.8	17.7	52.7
Angola	124,670	2.7	23.3	42.0
Cameroon	46,540	15.1	17.8	52.7
Central African Rep.	62,298	3.2	4.8	57.5
Chad	125,920	2.5	35.7	10.1
Congo	34,150	0.5	29.3	62.0
Eq. Guinea	2,805	8.2	3.7	46.2
Gabon	25,767	1.8	18.2	77.1
Zaire	226,760	3.5	6.6	76.9
Western Africa	605,211	9.1	27.5	13.9
Benin	11,062	16.8	4.0	31.4
Burkina Faso	27,380	13.0	36.5	24.1
Côte d'Ivoire	31,800	11.6	40.9	23.1
Gambia	1,000	17.9	9.0	15.6
Ghana	22,754	12.0	22.0	35.5
Guinea	24,586	3.0	25.0	59.3
Guinea-Bissau	2,812	12.0	38.4	38.1
Liberia	9,675	3.9	58.9	18.0
Mali	122,019	1.7	24.6	5.7
Mauritania	102,522	0.2	38.3	4.3
Niger	126,670	2.8	7.0	1.6
Nigeria	91,077	35.4	43.9	13.1
Senegal	19,253	12.2	16.1	54.8
Sierra Leone	7,162	8.9	30.8	28.8
Togo	5,439	12.3	32.9	29.4

75

Table 4.2 **(cont.)**

Regions/countries[a]	Land area ('000 ha.)	Cropland (%)	Permanent pasture (%)	Forest/ woodland (%)
Southern Africa	265,771	5.9	5.9	12.7
Botswana	56,673	2.4	58.2	19.3
Lesotho	3,035	11.1	16.0	0.0
Namibia	82,239	0.8	46.2	22.0
South Africa	122,104	10.8	66.6	3.7
Swaziland	1,720	12.0	68.8	6.0

Sources: Calculations of percentages based on data from World Resources Institute (1994: 284–285); FAO (1993).

a. Some island countries included in table 4.1 have been omitted.

are high throughout Sub-Saharan Africa and winter as such is non-existent. Climatic types range from hot–wet to hot–dry; i.e. the main seasonal variations concern rainfall and humidity. The regularly arranged climatic regions each side of the equator have been a factor in north–south population movements and constitute a major resource on which most productivity depends. Sub-Saharan Africa has abundant sunshine throughout the year and therefore has substantial solar energy, utilized so far mainly by indirect means, chiefly in agriculture and in biomass energy sources such as fuelwood or crop plant waste. Solar energy is the greatest potential source of renewable energy in the region, providing the technology for its use can be developed.

Although the more humid regions provide Sub-Saharan Africa's agricultural base and support most of its population, even they have been affected periodically by droughts that have brought severe livestock and crop losses, especially to the climatically marginal areas. Since the mid-1960s, Sub-Saharan Africa has been the major global region worst affected by drought, mainly in 1968–1971 in the Sahel, Ethiopia, the Sudan, and Somalia, in 1982–1985 in both the Sahel and southern Africa, and again in 1990.

Water resources

Sub-Saharan Africa has about 10 per cent of the world's annual internal renewable water resources for 18 per cent of the world land area and about 10 per cent of the world population. Estimates for Africa as a whole suggest that 6,140 m^3 per capita was available in 1992, of which 245 (4 per cent) was withdrawn, mainly for agriculture

(World Resources Institute 1994: 346). However, data are provided by only 17 Sub-Saharan countries and the rest have to be estimated from other related information. Some countries are mainly riparian users of water from external sources over which they have little or no control and for which they compete. Only 45 per cent of Sub-Saharan Africa's population has access to safe water (UNDP 1994: 133) – the worst figures are for the Central African Republic (12 per cent), Uganda (15 per cent), and Congo (21 per cent). The prospects of increased water scarcity are considerable, given the evidence of poorer precipitation in the past three decades and the reduction in volume of several water bodies, associated with some evidence of worsening vegetation conditions or "desertification."

Energy resources

Sub-Saharan Africa has substantial mineral fuel resources, including oil, coal, and uranium. Nigeria is the biggest oil producer and exporter, with about 27 per cent of production in 1991. South Africa has over 90 per cent of the coal production and reserves and two-thirds of the recoverable uranium. There are also extensive renewable resources, including fuelwood and hydroelectric power. Locally, fuelwood is often the cheapest form of heat for cooking and readily available for the dispersed rural population. Where market and supply systems are well developed, kerosene can now be cheaper, apart from the capital cost of buying an oil stove. Hydropower is the greatest most readily available renewable energy resource, but, apart from very small schemes, can involve considerable capital costs, force the resettlement of rural communities, and cause the loss of agricultural land. It is not very economic for the supply of power to a largely dispersed rural population. Greatest hydro-power potential is in Zaire and Zambia, which also have the greatest installed capacity.

The biggest producer and consumer of energy in Sub-Saharan Africa is South Africa, which is the richest in developed commercial energy resources. Gabon, Zimbabwe, and Botswana come next. Some countries, such as Zambia and Kenya, saw a steep decline in energy use in the 1980s owing to rising fuel costs and falling demand.

Natural vegetation and deforestation

The extent of forest and woodland in tropical Africa is difficult to estimate owing to differences in classification and measurement techniques. The estimates for 1990 published by the Food and Agriculture Organization (FAO 1993) and the World Resources Institute (1994: 308) suggest that of the forested area of tropical Africa, including the tropical islands, 47.6 per cent is moist deciduous forest (mainly moist savanna woodland with 1,000–2,000 mm annual rainfall), 16.4 per cent is rain forest, with over 2,000 mm, and 17.5 per cent is dry deciduous, with 500–1,000 mm. The rest (18.5 per cent) is very dry deciduous and desert, with less than 500 mm, and hill and montane forest (500 mm with about a three-month rainy season is marginal for tropical agriculture dependent on rainfall). More or less 80 per cent of the forest and woodland area, occupying rather less than a quarter of the area of Sub-Saharan Africa, is moist enough and with large enough trees to be threatened by agricultural clearance (subject to soil limitations), logging, and fuelwood cutting, apart from protected areas occupying less than 5 per cent of the Sub-Saharan land area.

Tropical rain forest, savanna woodlands, and subtropical forests are being depleted in Sub-Saharan Africa at a rate that many observers find alarming. The highest subregional rate of deforestation (percentage annual reduction) estimated for 1981–1990 was for western Africa at 1.0 and the lowest was for central Africa at 0.5 (World Resources Institute 1994: 308, using the WRI regional classification).

Other primary resources

In minerals, Sub-Saharan Africa provides one of the world's greatest resources in both production and potential. Southern Africa is a particularly rich metalliferous zone, with gold, diamonds, iron, nickel, lead, chromium, vanadium, and manganese, but central Africa is one of the world's greatest sources of copper and cobalt and western Africa of bauxite and iron. Mining has played a major role in developing African economies and, including the production of mineral fuels, has provided the chief basic financial resource for the richest African economies. It has attracted large numbers of migrant labourers and has produced the largest concentrations of urban and industrial population in Sub-Saharan Africa.

Wildlife resources are more important in Africa than in any other comparable global region. Apart from experiments in farming wildlife, aimed at a higher production of meat per unit area than from conventional livestock, wild animals are a valuable genetic resource and one of the most important elements in African tourism, especially in eastern Africa.

Human resources

There is widespread agreement that a country's most important resource is its people. Simon (1981) called people the ultimate resource, requiring improved education, health care, and nutrition. Population growth can thus be regarded as an asset to development, depending nevertheless on its rate in relation to the rate of production growth.

Sub-Saharan Africa had the lowest percentages amongst the major global regions of the appropriate age group enrolled in primary, secondary, and tertiary education in 1990 and 1991 (UNDP 1994: 156–159; World Bank 1994: 216–219). Primary enrolments are particularly low in Ethiopia, the Niger, Burkina Faso, Mali, and Guinea. Senegal, Mauritania, the Sudan, and Sierra Leone are also below the Sub-Saharan average, i.e. there is a marked concentration of low levels of primary education enrolment in the part-Sahelian countries for a variety of reasons, including problems of accessibility and warfare (Chad is an exception, with only just below-average enrolment). Most Sub-Saharan countries show a sex differential in favour of males, but the difference has in most cases been considerably reduced over the past two decades.

In health care, too, Sub-Saharan Africa had the worst ratios of population per doctor or per physician in 1990 ("doctor," the term used by the United Nations Development Programme, is evidently much broader than "physician," as used by the World Bank: UNDP 1994: 150–153; World Bank 1994: 214–215). Infant mortality and under-5 mortality rates were also the worst, and several African countries had high rates of malnutrition amongst children under 5 for 1987–1992, although the worst figures recorded were in India and Bangladesh. The data suggest that health-care problems are particularly severe in Burkina Faso, Malawi, Rwanda, the Niger, and Ethiopia.

Women are arguably the most wasted human resource in Sub-Saharan Africa. Their access to credit, technology, and production resources in agriculture – especially land – is constrained by social and legal barriers. With certain exceptions, notably the trading women of southern Nigeria and Ghana, their earning capacity is much poorer than that of men, and most women spend their lives

79

chiefly in rearing children, household maintenance, headloading water and fuelwood, pounding grain, and cultivating certain crops, usually of lower value – the "women's crops." They are mostly less educated than men and less well nourished, although the proportion of educated women has improved in the past two decades.

Population, agricultural land, and food supply

Tables 4.1 and 4.2 suggest that population growth may well be a threat to land-carrying capacity in several of the Sub-Saharan countries. As the population totals have increased (and even rural populations have increased, despite urbanward migration and expansion of the agricultural area), so landholdings have tended to decrease in size and the fallow area, still important for restoring fertility, has been reduced.

Dependence on agriculture will involve greater pressures and a more precarious food situation in future, possibly entailing greater dependence on food imports and food aid, combined with more intensive production using improved agricultural technology and innovations. Much of the agricultural base is widely dispersed, with long distances to market and high transport costs plus poor market information. Imported food is more centrally marketed, often cheaper than locally produced food for the urban consumer, and easier to subsidize in order to support the poor or keep down urban wages. In some cases food imports are not the effect of low agricultural productivity but, at least in part, the cause.

Population, economy, and sustainable development

In Sub-Saharan Africa one can contrast the poorest countries such as Ethiopia, where high population growth and poor productivity mean that people have to struggle even to provide basic needs, with more productive countries such as Kenya, where high population growth constrains the development effort. Population growth is not the cause, even the main cause, of poverty and decline in Sub-Saharan Africa, but it does mean that high rates of growth in productivity must be achieved in order for the economy to do more than stand still. The World Bank argues that economies need to grow by at least 4–5 per cent a year. The target for agricultural production should be 4 per cent to meet food requirements and generate the foreign exchange needed for development, and for industrial production 5–8 per cent, with a rapid expansion of jobs to reduce unemployment (World Bank 1989: 4).

Unfortunately, the World Bank devoted all too little space in its 1989 study of Sub-Saharan Africa to the implications for, and the costs of sustaining, the natural environmental base, although in looking at the case for increasing agricultural production it did point out that agricultural expansion cannot be adequate to meet needs without adverse environmental consequences and that there was a need to reverse "the degradation of natural resources that threatens long-term production" (World Bank 1989: 8–9, 89–91, 100–103). However, more recently the Bank has shown increasing environmental concern by proposing to assist in national environmental assessments (see below). In 1991 the Bank set up the Global Environmental Facility to invest in green projects of global importance by paying for research and for the incremental cost of protecting the environment above that which is in the interests of the developing countries themselves (Reed 1993; World Resources Institute 1994: 229–231). Although clearly an advance in Bank policy, nevertheless the Facility has met with criticism for its financial limitations.

It is becoming increasingly difficult in Sub-Saharan Africa to provide adequate educational and health facilities as productivity falls or remains stagnant and the need to repair or improve deteriorating and inadequate infrastructures grows. In almost all the Sub-Saharan countries, structural adjustment and stabilization programmes, mostly advised or managed by the World Bank and the International Monetary Fund, have become necessary in attempts to cope with enormous international debt and debt service payments, to deal with external trade deficiencies, and to resolve internal debt problems, overspending, fiscal imbalances, inflation, and productive decline. In many cases these programmes have led to a worsening of the more adverse social effects, including reduced availability of health services and education as rising costs have forced up charges.

On the basis of gross national product, the World Bank classifies 27 Sub-Saharan countries as low-income economies, 5 as middle-income, and 4 as upper-middle-income. Low income per capita leaves little room for savings and investment or for the finance required to support an adequate infrastructure and services. The United Nations Development Programme employs a "Human Development Index" (HDI), from which Sub-Saharan Africa's situation emerges just as bleakly (UNDP 1994: 130–131). In 1992 only six Sub-Saharan countries had HDIs over 0.5 and two of these were island groups; the mainland countries, in descending order of HDI, were Botswana, South Africa, Gabon, and Swaziland. Outside southern Africa only small, mineral-rich Gabon showed any promise.

Sub-Saharan Africa also has low and declining levels of foreign investment, partly because of doubts about future political stability, despite the spread of greater democracy, and some evidence of capital flight. External factors, such as the demise of communism in Central and Eastern Europe and the former USSR and the economic boom in East and South-East Asia, have encouraged major investment flows to poorer countries to go elsewhere. However, more aid flows into Sub-Saharan Africa than into any other major global region – more than one-third of the official development assistance to the less developed countries in 1991. In nine Sub-Saharan countries it provided more than one-fifth of the gross national product (World Bank 1994: 198–199). It has been argued that the Sub-Saharan countries will need a greater measure of self-reliance in the face of falling terms of trade, mounting debt, and low levels of investment (Ikoku 1980). Greater self-reliance, with the implication of more independent policies and greater self-sufficiency, may well be necessary in some of the Sub-Saharan countries, but such a policy should not neglect comparative advantage in production and trade or the need to build a more productive export industry to fund the new inputs needed for development.

Clearly the sustained use of natural resources is likely to be increasingly difficult in the face of the economic and social pressures listed and the natural inclination of poor people and poor countries to seek short-term solutions to their problems, which at least offer immediate survival, combined where possible with rapid growth, even at the cost of some environmental damage. For the poor, growth has been claimed to be not an option but an imperative (Husain 1994: 163). In part some of the "short termism" implicit in structural adjustment policies may have encouraged environmental degradation by quick "solutions," coupled with considerable pressure to raise export performance and increase local food production, although some environmental degradation has a long history, often linked to institutional distortions (Husain 1994: 163). Currently it is not so much increasing productivity that is the problem but the speed with which it has to be undertaken to offset rapid decline and rapidly increasing population. Incentives are needed for improved resource use, but these are affected by both price-related and institutional factors.

One of the most hopeful signs has been the introduction of National Environmental Action Plans (NEAPs) incorporating a holistic approach. These were in effect suggested in 1987 in an offer by the president of the World Bank of the Bank's assistance in nationwide environmental assessments. They were pioneered in Madagascar, Lesotho, and Mauritius. Other countries engaged in similar national environmental planning include Ghana, Burkina Faso, Rwanda, and the Seychelles (Falloux and Talbot 1993). There are some external resources to support NEAPs, but they are limited. Many of the developed countries were reluctant to sign the Biodiversity Treaty at the Earth Summit in Rio de Janeiro and some never signed it. Undoubtedly this was discouraging to the developing countries, most of which have been left to provide a large part of the funding required by their environmental management programmes. Yet without such funding and management, limited as it is at present, growth can hardly be sustained without undermining the environmental basis. Probably more commercial considerations will have to be taken into account in future conservation initiatives, or the costs of conservation will be seen as an immediate drain on very limited and even decreasing resources, despite the essential long-term advantages (Moyo, O'Keefe, and Sill 1993: 4).

References

Adepoju, A. 1991. South–North migration: The African experience. *International Migration Review* 29(2): 205–222.

Afolayan, A. 1988. Immigration and expulsion of ECOWAS aliens in Nigeria. *International Migration Review* 22(1): 4–27.

Bohning, W. R. 1981. *Black Migration to South Africa*. Geneva: International Labour Office.

Falloux, F. and L. M. Talbot. 1993. *Crisis and Opportunity: Environment and Development in Africa*. London: Earthscan (originally published in French by Masonneuve and Larose, Paris, 1992).

FAO (Food and Agriculture Organization of the United Nations). 1980. *Natural Resources and the Human Environment for Food and Agriculture*. Rome: FAO.

——— 1993. *Agrostat-PC* (on disk). Rome: FAO.

Gould, W. T. S. 1990. Migration and basic needs in Africa. In: Union for Africa Population Studies, *Conference on the Role of Migration in Development: Issues and Policies for the '90s*, Nairobi, 19–24 February 1990. Dakar: Union for Africa Population Studies, pp. 142–155.

Husain, I. 1994. Structural adjustment and the long-term development of Sub-Saharan Africa. In: R. van der Hoeven and F. van der Kraaij (eds.), *Structural Adjustment and beyond in Sub-Saharan Africa*. London and Portsmouth: Currey and Heinemann, pp. 150–171.

Ikoku, E. U. 1980. *Self-reliance: African Survival*. Enugu, Nigeria: Fourth Dimension Publishers.

Migot-Adholla, S. E., P. Hazell, B. Blarel, and F. Place. 1991. Indigenous land right systems in Sub-Saharan Africa: A constant on productivity? *World Bank Economic Review* 5(1): 155–175.

Moyo, S., P. O'Keefe, and M. Sill. 1993. Profiles of the SADC countries 1993. *The Southern African Environment*. London: Earthscan.

Ohadike, P. O. and T. Teklu. 1990. Migration and shelter in a suburban African setting. In: Union for Africa Population Studies, *Conference on the Role of Migration in Development: Issues and Policies for the '90s*, Nairobi, 19–24 February 1990. Dakar: Union for Africa Population Studies, pp. 156–180.

Oucho, J. O. 1985. Co-existence of rural–urban migration and urban–rural links in Sub-Saharan Africa. *Development Policy and Administration Review* 11(2): 33–60.

——— 1988. The rural bias of first generation rural–urban migration: Evidence from Kenya migration studies. *African Population Studies*, October: 61–78.

——— 1990. Migration linkages in Africa: Retrospect project. In: Union for Africa Population Studies, *Conference on the Role of Migration in Development: Issues and Policies for the '90s*, 19–24 February 1990. Dakar: Union for Africa Population Studies, pp. 109–141.

Oucho, J. O. and W. T. S. Gould. 1992. *Internal Migration, Urbanization and Population Distribution*. Paper commissioned by Panel on Population Dynamics in Sub-Saharan Africa, Commission on Behavioral and Social Sciences and Education, National Research Council, Washington D.C.

Population Reference Bureau. 1990. *World Population Data Chart 1990*. Washington D.C.: Population Reference Bureau.

Reed, D. (ed.) 1993. *The Global Environment Facility: Sharing Responsibility for the Biosphere*, 2 vols. Washington D.C.: World Wide Fund for Nature.

Simon, J. L. 1981. *The Ultimate Resource*. Princeton, N.J.: Princeton University Press.

Todaro, M. P. 1969. A model of labor migration and urban unemployment in less developed countries. *American Economic Review* 59(1): 138–148.

——— 1976. *Internal Migration in the Developing Countries*. Geneva: International Labour Office.

UN Department of International Economic and Social Affairs. 1988. *World Population Trends and Policies: 1987 Report*. New York.

UNDP (United Nations Development Programme). 1994. *Human Development Report 1994*. Oxford and New York: Oxford University Press.

UN Economic Commission for Africa. 1988. *Demographic Handbook for Africa*. Addis Ababa: UNECA.

World Bank. 1989. *Sub-Saharan Africa: From Crisis to Sustainable Growth*. Washington D.C.: World Bank.

——— 1994. *World Development Report 1994*. Oxford and New York: Oxford University Press.

World Resources Institute (in collaboration with the UN Environment Programme and the UN Development Programme). 1994. *World Resources 1994–95*. Oxford and New York: Oxford University Press.

5

Urbanization and industrialization: What future for Sub-Saharan Africa?

David Simon

Introduction

It is inevitably impossible within the scope of a short paper to do justice to the diversity of urban conditions in the 46 countries[1] comprising Sub-Saharan Africa. For this the reader is referred to the several comprehensive accounts that are available (e.g. O'Connor 1983, 1991; Gilbert and Gugler 1992; Simon 1992). Only a brief summary of the five most salient recent trends and issues is given here. Many recent urban and economic studies have focused upon tropical Africa rather than Sub-Saharan Africa as a whole. South Africa, Namibia, and the BLS countries (i.e. Botswana, Lesotho, and Swaziland) have thus unfortunately been excluded, as if they formed a distinct and discrete subregion. This is difficult to defend. South Africa, in particular, is vital, given its historically pivotal role in southern and central Africa, its status as Sub-Saharan Africa's most highly urbanized and industrialized country, and the current implications of this as its economic and political relations with the rest of the Sub-Saharan countries mushroom even before the formal demise of white minority rule.

The continuing rapid rate and scale of urbanization

Although Sub-Saharan Africa is the world's poorest and least urbanized and industrialized continental region, it does now have several metropolises with over 3 million inhabitants and problems comparable in intensity to those in megacities elsewhere in the third world. However, the Pretoria–Witwatersrand–Vereeniging (PWV) complex, centred on Johannesburg, Lagos, Kinshasa, Durban, Cape Town, Kano, and Ibadan are still the exceptions. Most capital cities and major industrial centres in Sub-Saharan Africa have populations below 2 million; in the smallest states they house no more than 100,000–150,000. In international terms, these would rank as merely modest intermediate or secondary cities. Yet the majority of urban Africans still live in cities, towns, and villages of this size or smaller.

Nevertheless, it is misleading to focus exclusively on absolute urban size. Far more critical in terms of the ability to absorb, house, and employ people is the rate of urban growth. In this respect, Sub-Saharan Africa has for some time now led the world, with rates of 5–6 per cent per annum. Many primate centres and some secondary cities have experienced persistent growth of 9–11 per cent per annum, which means that their populations double in less than a decade. These rates are two to three times higher than the respective national population growth rates, which average 3–4 per cent per annum and are themselves among the highest in the world.

Although obviously increasing, the levels of urbanization in the Sub-Saharan countries remain among the lowest in the world. International comparisons are impeded by the widely differing definitions of urban areas adopted by national statistical offices, as well as great variation in the coverage, accuracy, and base years of national censuses. Nevertheless, World Bank compilations are useful as an indicator of orders of magnitude (fig. 5.1). South Africa and Zambia were the only two countries in Sub-Saharan Africa with over half their populations classified as urban in 1990. Congo, Gabon, Cameroon, the Central African Republic, Côte d'Ivoire, Liberia, Mauritania, and Zaire fell in the 40–49 per cent range, but the majority of countries had levels of between 20 and 39 per cent. The average in Sub-Saharan Africa is just over 30 per cent.

It follows from the above that, in contrast to Latin America and much of Asia, rural–urban migration remains the principal source of urban growth, although the contribution of natural increase is rising in the more highly urbanized countries such as Zambia and South

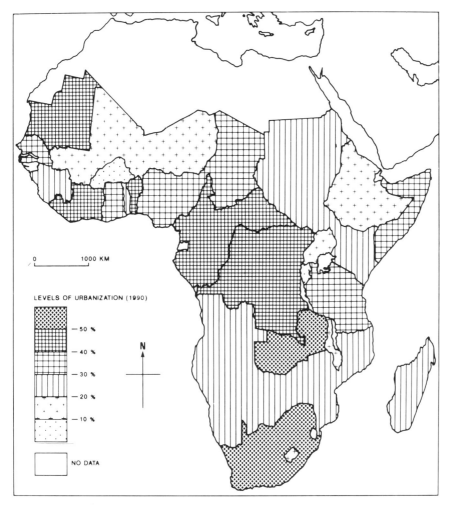

Fig. 5.1 Levels of urbanization in Sub-Saharan Africa, 1990 (Source: World Bank 1992)

Africa. One of the principal reasons for such rapid urbanization has been poverty and the persistence of longstanding urban–rural disparities in the diversity of income-earning opportunities, average incomes, infrastructure, and service provision. Conditions obviously vary across the continent but, on the whole, agricultural mechanization has been rather less of a contributory factor to migration than in more intensively farmed regions of the world. On the other hand, over the past 20 years or so, drought, famine, and armed conflict have forced millions of Africans off the land.

87

The urban environment

Although urban areas are generally better served with infrastructure and public utilities than are peri-urban and rural areas, major disparities in access to these forms of collective consumption exist within towns and cities. Whereas the urban élites and most of the middle classes enjoy adequate facilities, in some cases on a par with first world standards, the urban poor endure varying degrees of deprivation. Two components of inaccessibility can be distinguished:

1. Inadequate service or infrastructure provision, in that the resources and political will to expand piped water and reticulated sewerage networks, refuse and other solid waste collection services, and health care and education systems in accordance with urban growth have proved lacking. Even the reduction of standards, e.g. pit latrines and communal standpipes, as commonly incorporated in site and service or shanty upgrading schemes, for example, has not enabled such services to reach anything like all urban residents. Many peripheral and poor neighbourhoods are thus unserved, while infrastructural maintenance in older low-income areas, even of formal dwellings, has often been deficient or neglected (Hardoy and Satterthwaite 1984; Hardoy, Mitlin, and Satterthwaite 1992; Simon 1992).

2. The unaffordability to the poor of services that do exist. This problem is particularly acute in the absence of state health care, for example, or when residents are unable to afford the cost of water and electricity installations and payments. As discussed below, the situation in this regard has deteriorated markedly since the early 1980s as a result of public expenditure cutbacks and widespread retrenchments under the impact of structural adjustment and economic recovery programmes. Class, ethnicity, gender, and access to employment are becoming, more than ever, the critical determinants of urban quality of life in urban Sub-Saharan Africa.

The urban environment of large cities is also suffering increasingly as a result of industrial pollution. Although there have fortunately been no disasters on the scale of Bhopal or Mexico City in Sub-Saharan Africa, industry is a major polluter in metropolitan areas such as the PWV and Lagos. On calm days, the smog enveloping Cape Town is on a par with that choking Los Angeles. Here and elsewhere, high motor vehicle concentrations play a role. In addition to atmospheric pollution, groundwater and soil contamination by toxic chemical discharges, leaks, and unscrupulous dumping is wide-spread across the continent. Notorious cases of imported toxic dumping in several African countries have hit the headlines in recent years (O'Keefe 1988). Factory workers are often at great risk from hazardous substances and processes, for which they commonly receive inadequate training and/or protective clothing.

In many countries, the basic problem is the absence or inadequacy of environmental legislation and emission controls. However, even in countries such as Nigeria and to some extent South Africa, which now have relevant laws on the statute book, the problems persist. This reflects inadequate enforcement of the regulations on account of staff and equipment shortages, lack of muscle, political corruption and nepotism/clientelism, or executive decisions to play down environmental considerations in the pursuit of employment and industrial output. A recent United Nations Environment Programme/World Health Organization (UNEP/WHO) study found that, overall, mega-cities in countries of the South now suffer more severe air pollution than their counterparts in the North (UNEP/WHO 1992). Although no African city was included, the implications for large cities such as Cairo, the PWV complex, and Lagos are ominous.

Finally, in this context, it is necessary to record that poverty is also a source of urban air pollution. The great majority of urban Africans still rely on fuelwood, charcoal, or coal as their primary energy source for cooking and heating. At night, especially in winter, large low-income areas are often submerged under thick blankets of smoke.

The limitations of industrialization

It is no coincidence that Sub-Saharan Africa is not only the world's least urbanized continental region but also (apart from the Carib-bean) the least industrialized. There are no newly industrializing countries (NICs) and no industrial cities on the scale of Shanghai, Hong Kong, São Paulo, or Mexico City. Even where industry forms a significant activity and has diversified since the 1960s, as in the major metropolitan centres and cities such as Bulawayo, it is geared essentially to import substitution for the domestic market rather than for export (Simon 1992). Many inappropriate prestige industrial projects have failed to operate efficiently, and such investments, especially when funded by the state, have drained resources from other sectors of the economy.

The emphasis has remained on primary import substitution, i.e.

production of consumer non-durables, whereas Latin America and South-East Asia have made considerable progress in the spheres of consumer durables and light capital goods and in adopting successful export-substitution strategies. Moreover, the benefits to Sub-Saharan Africa of import-substituting industrialization have been reduced by its continued heavy import dependence on inputs and intermediate goods. Currency devaluations, especially as an element of structural adjustment of the economy over the 1980s, have aggravated the problems, leading to poor utilization even of existing industrial capacity. Even in South Africa, the most sophisticated Sub-Saharan economy, manufacturing (as distinct from all industry) provides only about a quarter of gross domestic product.

The impact of structural adjustment

The role of structural adjustment and associated policies deserves specific attention. Their impact across the continent has been profound, often exacerbating macroeconomic conditions, at least in the short to medium term, and having the most severe consequences for the poorest countries, the most powerless groups (notably the poor and female-headed households), and the environment, which is now subject to even more intense exploitation pressures. Many infrastructural, social, and related programmes that were vital to the urban (and rural) poor have been savagely cut or abolished, while the loss of subsidies and rapid decline in purchasing power of low- and most middle-income earners have hit people hard (see Save the Children Fund/Overseas Development Institute 1988; Onimode 1988, 1989; South Commission 1990; O'Connor 1991; Cornia et al. 1992; Stewart et al. 1992; Woodward 1992). Let me add at once that I do not deny the need for radical economic restructuring and political change; nor is it realistic to blame Sub-Saharan Africa's predicament exclusively on external forces. Africa undoubtedly bears significant responsibility too. My problem is far more with the treatment and its wider consequences than with the diagnosis.

Sub-Saharan Africa as the global periphery

Furthermore, it is important to underscore the seriousness of the African situation in comparison with other third world regions. Africa has become the outer periphery of the world economy, the poorest continental region of the world (Simon 1992, 1993) and commensurately marginal politically (Harbeson and Rothchild 1992). A glance at some World Bank and OECD data underscores the point.

Sub-Saharan Africa's dismal economic performance, relative both to all low-income countries and to other continental regions of the South, is starkly illustrated in table 5.1. Whereas the region experienced the fastest growth of value-added in industry until 1973, it has been the slowest growing since then and even declined during 1980s. In fact, during the 1980s, Sub-Saharan Africa's results for all three sectors were the poorest. This situation is clearly unsustainable, given population growth rates and rising expectations.

The rate of return in industry has been so low that transnational corporations (TNCs) disinvested during the 1980s (Bennell 1990; Simon 1992, 1993). Even in South Africa, sanctions proved little more than an expedient political flag under which TNCs withdrew. The Sub-Saharan countries now account for an insignificant percentage of the industrial foreign direct investment (FDI) portfolios of most TNCs, given the strong performance of the Pacific Rim economies, for example. Thus, in respect of global industrial FDI by United Kingdom firms, Sub-Saharan Africa's share fell from around 4 per cent in the mid-1970s to 0.5 per cent in 1986 (Bennell 1990). I see little prospect of major new net FDI flows into Sub-Saharan Africa as a whole in the foreseeable future, despite the severity of structural adjustment having been predicated largely on the assumption by the IMF and the World Bank, in particular, that creating the "right" economic conditions would prove attractive to large-scale FDI. Yet, although still the world's least urbanized continental region (30–35 per cent), Africa (and Sub-Saharan Africa) – the poorest continent – is actually experiencing the most rapid rate of urbanization (O'Connor 1991; Gilbert and Gugler 1992; Simon 1992).

From table 5.2 it is evident that, although the net indebtedness of the Sub-Saharan countries is comparatively small in US dollar terms, it is extremely serious and unsustainable relative to the size and structure of the continent's economies – as measured by debt service ratios. Moreover, Sub-Saharan Africa's position deteriorated dramatically during the 1980s and is now worse than that of Latin America, the continent that precipitated the debt crisis and that has shown modest improvement over the 1980s on some indicators. Table 5.2 includes three slightly different forms of debt service ratio in order to highlight both the consistency of the region's deterioration across these variables and the sensitivity of the magnitude of such change to the particular variable(s) used. Table 5.3 shows the extent of Sub-

Table 5.1 **Sectoral growth rates, 1965–1989 (average annual percentage change of value-added)**

Country group	Agriculture			Industry			Services		
	1965–73	1973–80	1980–89[a]	1965–73	1973–80	1980–89[a]	1965–73	1973–80	1980–89[a]
Low-income economies	2.9	1.8	*4.3*	10.7	7.0	*8.7*	6.3	5.3	*6.1*
Middle-income economies	3.2	3.0	*2.7*	8.0	4.0	*3.2*	7.6	6.3	*3.1*
Severely indebted middle-income economies	3.1	3.6	*2.7*	6.8	5.4	*1.0*	7.2	5.4	*1.7*
Sub-Saharan Africa	2.2	–0.3	*1.8*	13.9	4.2	*–0.2*	4.1	3.1	*1.5*
East Asia	3.2	2.5	*5.3*	12.7	9.2	*10.3*	10.5	7.3	*7.9*
South Asia	3.1	2.2	*2.7*	3.9	5.6	*7.2*	4.0	5.3	*6.1*
Latin America and the Caribbean	3.0	3.7	*2.5*	6.8	5.1	*1.1*	7.3	5.4	*1.7*

Source: World Bank (1990: 162).

a. Figures in italic in the 1980–89 columns are not for the full decade.

Table 5.2 **The external debt burden, 1990 and 1980**

Region/income category[a]	Total external debt as % of exports of goods and services		Total debt service as % of exports		Interest payments as % of exports	
	1990	1980	1990	1980	1990	1980
Sub-Saharan Africa	324.3	96.8	19.3	10.9	8.9	5.7
Low-income						
countries, *of which*	218.5	105.1	20.1	10.3	9.3	5.1
1 Mozambique	1,573.3	–	14.4	–	7.7	–
2 Tanzania	1,070.7	317.8	25.8	19.6	10.9	10.0
3 Ethiopia	480.3	136.2	33.0	7.6	8.1	4.7
4 Somalia	2,576.2	252.0	11.7	4.9	5.8	0.9
9 Malawi	328.5	260.8	22.5	27.7	9.1	16.7
17 Nigeria	242.7	32.2	20.3	4.2	12.1	3.3
18 Niger	464.2	132.8	24.1	21.7	8.9	12.9
25 Kenya	306.3	165.1	33.8	21.4	14.8	11.3
27 Ghana	353.4	116.0	34.9	13.1	9.9	4.4
34 Lesotho	41.2	19.5	2.4	1.5	0.8	0.6
Lower-middle-income						
countries, *of which*	179.0	115.2	20.3	18.8	8.4	9.1
45 Zimbabwe	155.0	45.4	22.6	3.8	9.6	1.5
46 Senegal	236.8	162.7	20.4	28.7	8.1	10.5
48 Côte d'Ivoire	487.4	160.7	38.6	28.3	13.3	13.0
56 Congo	352.5	146.7	20.7	10.8	10.5	6.7
71 Botswana	22.9	17.8	4.4	1.9	1.6	1.1
Upper-middle-income						
countries, *of which*	132.1	159.6	17.9	31.0	8.2	16.6
93 Gabon	138.4	62.2	7.6	17.7	5.0	6.3
East Asia and Pacific	91.1	88.8	14.6	13.5	5.8	7.7
South Asia	281.5	162.9	25.9	12.2	13.1	5.2
Bangladesh	448.2	345.6	25.4	23.2	7.7	6.4
India	282.4	136.0	28.8	9.3	15.9	4.2
Europe	125.7	90.6	16.9	15.9	6.8	7.1
Middle East and North Africa	180.3	114.9	24.4	16.4	8.1	7.4
Latin America and Caribbean	257.4	196.8	25.0	37.3	13.3	19.7
Mexico	222.0	259.2	27.8	49.5	16.7	27.4
Brazil	326.8	304.9	20.8	63.1	8.2	33.8

Source: World Bank (1992).

a. Regional and income category averages are weighted by size of flows.

Table 5.3 Official development assistance (ODA) by region and origin, 1984–1990 (current US$m)

	1984	%	1988	%	1989	%	1990	%
Europe:								
Net disbursements (all sources), *of which*	414.7	1	522.6	1	356.7	1	1,496.5[a]	3
from DAC countries	302.0	73	477.1	91	358.7	101	783.5	52
by multilateral agencies	74.3	18	86.0	16	39.7	11	41.5	3
Africa:								
Net disbursements (all sources)	11,375.2	37	17,694.0	38	18,286.2	39	25,512.0	43
from DAC countries	7,515.9	66	12,532.1	71	12,654.0	69	16,561.9	65
by multilateral agencies	2,823.3	25	4,924.6	28	5,528.8	30	6,104.2	24
Africa north of Sahara:								
Net disbursements (all sources)	2,424.3	8	2,527.2	5	2,445.9	5	7,146.4[b]	12
from DAC countries	2,156.0	89	2,205.9	87	2,090.8	85	4,142.3	58
by multilateral agencies	211.0	9	286.1	11	355.0	15	265.4	4
Africa south of Sahara:								
Net disbursements (all sources)	8,211.1	27	14,801.6	32	15,304.3	32	17,879.4	30
from DAC countries	5,216.1	64	10,123.5	68	10,220.7	67	12,146.3	68
by multilateral agencies	2,506.7	31	4,482.4	30	4,983.5	33	5,626.1	31
North & Central America:								
Net disbursements (all sources)	2,248.4	7	3,213.6	7	3,380.4	7	3,991.1	7
from DAC countries	1,775.3	79	2,697.3	84	2,865.0	85	3,471.8	87
by multilateral agencies	473.2	21	515.9	16	514.5	15	519.6	13
South America:								
Net disbursements (all sources)	1,101.6	4	1,639.4	4	1,885.6	4	2,078.0	3
from DAC countries	774.5	70	1,271.6	78	1,518.0	81	1,631.9	79
by multilateral agencies	329.6	30	368.1	22	368.3	20	446.2	27

Middle East:							
Net disbursements (all sources)	3,456.2	11	2,441.5	5	2,305.4	5	4,118.2^c	7
from DAC countries	1,537.1	44	1,913.9	78	1,806.9	78	2,200.5	53
by multilateral agencies	233.7	7	232.8	10	364.0	16	560.2	14
South Asia:							
Net disbursements (all sources)	4,544.7	15	6,718.9	14	6,309.8	13	6,334.6	11
from DAC countries	2,184.2	48	3,991.2	59	3,658.7	58	3,343.3	53
by multilateral agencies	2,310.3	51	2,767.5	41	2,693.7	43	3,004.4	47
Far East:							
Net disbursements (all sources)	2,852.4	9	5,520.9	12	6,292.2	13	6,997.9	12
from DAC countries	2,205.2	77	4,326.4	78	5,086.1	81	5,595.4	80
by multilateral agencies	547.8	19	1,200.0	22	1,208.1	19	1,364.2	19
Oceania:							
Net disbursements (all sources)	971.7	3	1,436.4	3	1,361.6	3	1,348.5	2
from DAC countries	912.4	94	1,291.3	90	1,273.6	94	1,214.7	90
by multilateral agencies	59.3	6	144.9	10	87.8	6	133.5	10
TOTAL							
Net disbursements (all sources)	30,984.9	100	46,370.1	100	47,281.1	100	59,828.2	100
from DAC countries	19,693.8	64	33,155.9	72	34,228.1	72	40,225.7	67
by multilateral agencies	7,637.0	25	11,326.9	24	11,736.3	25	13,447.1	22

Source: OECD, *Geographical Distribution of Financial Flows to Developing Countries: Disbursements, Commitments, Economic Indicators, 1987/1990*, Paris, 1992.

Note: Neither the annual totals nor percentages for all regions add up exactly to the global totals because of various unspecified and unallocated disbursements.

a. Turkey received a dramatically increased allocation in 1990.

b. Egypt received a dramatically increased allocation in 1990.

c. Syria received a dramatically increased allocation in 1990 (back to levels of 1987 and earlier).

Saharan Africa's current high aid reliance relative to other regions, a picture unlikely to change much in the near future.

Implications for urbanization and industrialization

The preceding analysis leads me to the following set of linked contentions with respect to the future prospects for urbanization and industrialization in Sub-Saharan Africa.

1. Urbanization in Sub-Saharan Africa is increasingly urbanization of and by the poor; urban environments are increasingly environments of poverty, with all the attendant pressures and problems – not least for the poor themselves.

2. In the struggle to survive, poor people inevitably put today's food and income ahead of tomorrow's environment, be it urban or rural. Generally, the environment suffers, although refuse-pickers and associated scrap-recycling activities may reduce urban solid waste disposal and litter problems significantly – albeit under unhealthy and even hazardous conditions (see Furedy 1990; Bouverie 1991).

3. Industrialization in Sub-Saharan Africa is highly unlikely to expand and diversify dramatically or to provide a great many more jobs in the near future, even after restructuring, more selective investment, and greater domestic sourcing of inputs where possible. The most significant industrial growth is likely to occur in the relatively small-scale sector (see 5 below).

4. Moreover, recession and state sector cut-backs under structural adjustment are exacerbating industrial pressures on the environment and often make the enforcement of conservation or pollution abatement legislation – even where such does now exist, as in Nigeria – more rather than less difficult.

5. Existing urban conditions and current trends are clearly unsustainable, and rather more radical changes will be required to promote sustainability than is implied in more official pronouncements by local, regional, or national state bodies and private companies around the world on the subject. Equally, the view that the environment is of secondary importance to the imperative of employment generation and economic growth must be challenged as untenable in the face of the wealth of available evidence. The basic prerequisite is action on poverty in the broadest sense. Different forms and types of industrialization, technology, and energy policies must be explored, promoting local suitability,

greater local and sustainable resource use, and, where appropriate, more labour-intensive techniques (*Environment and Urbanization* 1992). The building materials industry is a prime case for treatment (Simon 1992), with major potential environmental and economic benefits. Generally, the "informal" and wider small business sectors can play a significant role within integrated strategies but do not represent a panacea in themselves. There is now a well-established case for addressing the problems and needs of small enterprises (both formal and "informal") in an integrated manner (Bromley 1993).

6. Urban management and government (or "governance," in contemporary international agency parlance) will also need to undergo major reorganization in line with these objectives, the need to democratize structures, and fuller public participation and control (Stren and White 1989; *Environment and Urbanization* 1991; Devas and Rakodi 1993; chap. 6 in this volume). Although the new rhetoric is now being widely adopted, substantive change is still rarely evident. Addressing the continued alienation of a sizeable proportion of the urban population represents a formidable challenge.

7. Given Sub-Saharan Africa's global position, greater collective self-reliance and innovativeness will be necessary. The shift in emphasis underlying the reconstitution of the Southern African Development Co-ordination Conference (SADCC) as the Southern African Development Community (SADC) in August 1992 is indicative of such thinking. Counter-trade and other unconventional forms of exchange may need to be expanded. Current democratization across Sub-Saharan Africa could also be instrumental, if it proves genuine and substantive rather than purely symbolic. Overall, the problems remain formidable but I do sense renewed hope and energy amid the poverty, despair, and violence in many parts of the continent. Although the much-vaunted dawning of a post–Cold War "new world order" has clearly proved premature – in Africa as elsewhere – some significant gains have been made in many states, even as Angola and Somalia sink ever deeper into chaos. It is also worth reminding ourselves that the critical instability currently gripping Sub-Saharan Africa's most populous and well-endowed countries (Kenya, Nigeria, South Africa, and Zaire) symbolizes the difficulties and resistance to be overcome in moving to a more open, democratic, participatory – and therefore potentially sustainable – order.

Note

1. Eritrea, Africa's newest state, became independent only in May 1993.

References

Bennell, P. 1990. British industrial investment in Sub-Saharan Africa: Corporate responses to economic crisis in the 1980s. *Development Policy Review* 8(2): 155–177.

Bouverie, J. 1991. Recycling in Cairo: A tale of rags to riches. *New Scientist*, 29 June, no. 1775: 52–55.

Bromley, R. 1993. Small-enterprise promotion and an urban development strategy. In: J. Kasarda and A. D. Parnell (eds.), *Third World Cities: Problems, Policies and Prospects*. Newbury Park, Calif.: Sage.

Cornia, G. A., R. van der Hoeven, and T. Mkandawire (eds.) 1992. *Africa's Recovery in the 1990s: From Stagnation and Adjustment to Human Development*. London: Macmillan.

Devas, N. and C. Rakodi (eds.) 1993. *Managing Fast Growing Cities: New Approaches to Urban Planning and Management in the Developing World*. Harlow, England: Longman.

Environment and Urbanization. 1991. Rethinking local government – Views from the third world. *Environment and Urbanization* 3(1).

———— 1992. Sustainable cities: Meeting needs, reducing resource use and recycling, re-use and reclamation. *Environment and Urbanization* 4(2).

Furedy, C. 1990. *Social Aspects of Solid Waste Recovery in Asian Cities*. Environmental Sanitation Reviews 30. Bangkok: Environmental Sanitation Information Centre, Asian Institute of Technology.

Gilbert, A. and J. Gugler. 1992. *Cities, Poverty and Development: Urbanization in the Third World*, 2nd edn. Oxford: Oxford University Press.

Harbeson, J. and D. Rothchild (eds.) 1992. *Africa in World Politics*. Boulder, Colo.: Westview Press.

Hardoy, J. E. and D. Satterthwaite. 1984. Third world cities and the environment of poverty. *Geoforum* 15(3): 307–334.

Hardoy, J. E., D. Mitlin, and D. Satterthwaite. 1992. *Environmental Problems in Third World Cities*. London: Earthscan.

O'Connor, A. 1983. *The African City*. London: Hutchinson.

———— 1991. *Poverty in Africa: A Geographical Perspective*. London: Belhaven.

O'Keefe, P. 1988. Toxic terrorism. *Review of African Political Economy*, no. 42: 84–90.

Onimode, B. 1988. *A Political Economy of the African Crisis*. London: Zed Books.

———— (ed.) 1989. *The IMF, the World Bank and the African Debt*, 2 vols. London: Zed Books.

Save the Children Fund/Overseas Development Institute. 1988. *Prospects for Africa*. London: Hodder & Stoughton.

Simon, D. 1992. *Cities, Capital and Development: African Cities in the World Economy*. London: Belhaven.

———— 1993. Debt, democracy and development: Sub-Saharan Africa in the 1990s. Paper presented to the Trilateral Conference on Structural Adjustment and

Access to Economic, Political, Social and Environmental Resources, University of Amsterdam, 29–31 March.

South Commission. 1990. *The Challenge to the South: Report of the South Commission*. New York: Oxford University Press.

Stewart, F., S. Lall, and S. Wangwe (eds.) 1992. *Alternative Development Strategies in Sub-Saharan Africa*. London: Macmillan.

Stren, R. E. and R. R. White (eds.) 1989. *African Cities in Crisis: Managing Rapid Urban Growth*. Boulder, Colo.: Westview Press.

UNEP/WHO. 1992. *Urban Air Pollution in Megacities of the World*. Oxford: Blackwell.

Woodward, D. (ed.) 1992. *Debt, Adjustment and Poverty in Developing Countries*, 2 vols. London: Belhaven.

World Bank. 1990. *World Development Report 1990*. New York: Oxford University Press.

―――― 1992. *World Development Report 1992*. New York: Oxford University Press.

6

Urban environmental management and issues in Africa south of the Sahara

R. M. K. Silitshena

Introduction

Africa is the least urbanized continent but one where the rate of urbanization is among the highest. The rapid rate of urban growth is causing social and economic strains, some of which manifest themselves in environmental problems. An environmental problem has been defined as "either an inadequate supply of a resource essential to human health or urban production (e.g. sufficient fresh water) or the presence of pathogens or toxic substances in the human environment which can damage human health or physical resources such as forests, fisheries or agricultural land" (Habitat 1989: 6).

A number of environmental problems that occur at varying spatial scales from the home through the neighbourhood, the city to the region are reviewed. The problems include the crowded and cramped living conditions and the presence of pathogens in the human environment because of lack of basic infrastructure; the dangerous and unhealthy sites of some neighbourhoods and the irregular or non-collection of garbage in some neighbourhoods; the city-wide problems of the disposal of toxic/hazardous wastes, and water, air, and noise pollution; and the problem of energy and vegetation, which encompasses a much wider region.

There are many causes or factors contributing to these problems. They include massive rural–urban migration, poor planning and ineffective development control, weak urban institutions, and inadequate financial resources.

A number of suggestions are made for the improvement of the situation. They include institutional reform, improvement of financial viability, and a review of standards.

The paper starts with the background to the process of urbanization in Africa. I then deal with the nature of environmental problems and give explanations for the present situation. Finally, I look at what can be done to improve the situation.

The process of urbanization in Sub-Saharan Africa

Africa is the least urbanized continent but one currently experiencing the fastest rate of urbanization (O'Connor 1983). Africa, however, has a long history of urbanization (Hance 1970), although the most formative period started with colonialism. There are therefore many traditions of urbanism in Africa, and O'Connor has identified six, namely: indigenous, Islamic, colonial, European, dual, and hybrid city (O'Connor 1983: 28–41). Even this is not a neat categorization because "many individual cities will occupy only marginal positions between these categories" (ibid.). But it serves to underline the need to recognize the diversity of urban centres between and within African countries. The complexions of urban problems, as indeed policy prescriptions, will vary from one type of town to another.

The colonial influence has, however, been widespread and pervasive. In much of eastern and southern Africa most towns are creations of colonial exploitation and domination. The cities were created to facilitate the exploitation and export of natural resources to metropolitan countries of Europe. They started as commercial, administrative, and mining towns and as ports. The pre-existing indigenous towns, most widespread in western Africa, have been affected by colonial and post-colonial policies. All types of African city have experienced growth, although this has been much slower with indigenous cities (O'Connor 1983). Other common elements of African urbanization include the existence of a primate city (or cities) superimposed on a large number of small settlements; the rapid physical expansion of the towns, resulting in the loss of agricultural land or absorption of nearby villages; ever-increasing demand for water, fuel, services, transport, and housing, all of which are beyond the cities' budget to satisfy; and the thorny issue of waste disposal. These problems are partly manifestations of poor management.

The main engine of urban growth is rural–urban migration (Todaro 1976; Gugler 1982; O'Connor 1983; Van Western and Klute 1986). The urban population in the selected African countries has at least doubled since 1960, with changes in proportions and growth rates as shown in table 6.1. The main motivation for migration is economic – the search for better-paying jobs, especially by young men. The trend, however, is for women migrants as well as the older married men to increase. Some studies have found that women migrants were in fact in the majority (Gwebu 1982; Van Western and Klute 1986). Many women are wives, daughters, and fiancées arriving to join their male relatives in town, but they also come to seek employment.

The increase in the numbers of females partly explains one trend of rural–urban migration – the tendency for migration to be long term or even permanent and to reflect a shift from individual to family migration. Long-term migration has been explained by the increasing difficulty of finding jobs in the formal sector (Van Western and Klute 1986). This has implications for urban planning: increasingly, policy makers and planners are having to plan not for circulating but for permanent and stable urban populations.

There are other reasons for migrating to towns. They include personal security in countries where there is political strife and warfare and the desire for better services, which are located in urban areas. As a result of urban-biased development, the quantity and quality of health and education services are higher in urban than in rural areas (Sparks 1990). Although there is evidence of stepped migration in some countries, most migration is directed to the large cities. More than 42 per cent of all urban populations live in cities of more than 500,000, compared with only 8 per cent in 1960 (Sparks 1990). There were only two cities in the region with a population exceeding 500,000 in 1960; if present trends persist, there will be 60 cities with more than 1 million by the year 2000.

The phenomenon of rural–urban migration cannot be fully comprehended outside some of the problems in the structure of African economies. There has been a general economic decline since independence, so that some poor countries are poorer now than they

Table 6.1 **Urban growth of selected African countries, 1960–2000**

Country	Urban population (as % of total)			Urban population annual growth rate (%)		Population in largest city (%)
	1960	1990	2000	1960–90	1990–2000	1980
Botswana	2	28	42	13.5	7.9	–
Gabon	18	46	54	6.3	4.9	–
Swaziland	4	33	45	10.5	6.7	–
Namibia	15	28	34	4.8	5.4	–
Lesotho	3	20	28	8.6	6.3	–
Zimbabwe	13	28	35	5.9	5.4	–
Zambia	17	50	59	7.1	5.5	35
Cameroon	14	41	51	6.5	5.7	21
Ghana	23	33	38	3.9	4.6	35
Côte d'Ivoire	19	40	47	6.5	5.5	34
Zaire	22	40	46	4.8	5.0	28
Nigeria	9	29	37	5.8	6.2	17
Rwanda	2	8	11	7.4	7.6	–
Uganda	5	10	14	6.1	6.6	52
Senegal	32	38	45	3.5	4.4	65
Equatorial Guinea	25	29	33	1.5	4.0	–
Malawi	4	12	16	6.5	6.5	19
Ethiopia	6	13	17	4.8	5.8	37
Sudan	10	22	27	5.4	4.8	31
Mozambique	4	27	41	9.5	7.2	83
Angola	10	28	36	5.9	5.4	64
Benin	9	38	45	7.4	5.0	63
Chad	7	30	39	7.1	5.4	39
Burkina Faso	5	9	12	4.6	6.3	41
Niger	6	20	27	7.4	6.7	31
Mali	11	19	23	4.4	5.2	24
Guinea	10	26	33	5.3	5.8	80
Gambia	13	23	30	5.2	5.3	–
Sierra Leone	13	32	40	5.2	5.1	47

Source: UNDP (1991).

were at independence. In the process of impoverishment, Africa has lost the ability to feed itself and both food imports and food aid have continued to rise (Sparks 1990). The major explanation for this malaise lies in the neglect of agriculture, Africa's most important activity:

Many governments have pursued economic policies that were designed to keep urban wages (and living conditions) high and farm prices low; have maintained the value of currencies at unrealistic rates of exchange ... This is understandable and obvious. Political power in Africa rests in the city, not in the village. (Sparks 1990: 35)

In Mali, for example, the government policy in the 1960s was to curb rural–urban migration by forcibly repatriating unemployed migrants as a means of reducing the build-up of political opposition (Van Western and Klute 1986). Subsequent policy relaxed migration regulations but alleviated the effects of low wages by keeping prices of food products low. This policy resulted in lower producer prices and further depressed conditions in the rural areas (ibid.).

A recent study in Kenya found that "often the husband brings home maize and other commodities bought in town where competition deflates prices" (Andreasen 1990: 165). The study found a strong dependency of rural families on urban wages. The men, who live and work in town separated from their families, experience very harsh conditions: "There is no doubt that the image of life in rural areas which urban residents maintain, often is an illusion referring to a situation as it was many years ago, and perhaps sustained under the influence of hardships of urban life" (ibid.: 166).

On top of these unfavourable terms of trade against agricultural products must be added the ecological stresses of the African environment. Hjort af Ornäs (1990) argues that the people in the Horn of Africa live in such a marginal environment that they have little room to manoeuvre. Thus the 1984 drought disaster left "as many as two thirds of the population as temporary refugees in towns and cities" (Hjort af Ornäs 1990: 152).

The loss of soil productivity is a result of a number of factors that were set in motion by the colonial regimes: the introduction of export cash crops, which increased demand for land and reduced self-sufficiency in food crops; the expansion of cultivated land into grazing land as a result of rapid population growth; and the creation of state boundaries, which have put a brake on transhumant migrations and thus contributed to overgrazing, etc. (Vis 1989). All these factors manifest themselves in the shortage of land.

In some areas, holdings are no longer economic even under more intensive forms of agriculture (White 1989: 15; Andreasen 1990). These areas are characterized by landlessness. The alternative for people in these situations is rural–urban migration.

The role of rural–urban migration in contributing to urban population growth has been stressed because of the key role it plays in many countries. However, it must be realized that natural growth is assuming greater importance in long-established cities and some countries with a relatively long history of urbanization. Indeed, the rural population of the region has continued to grow and these trends are expected to persist (United Nations 1991). The rate of urbanization is projected to decline by 1995–2000 (ibid.).

To conclude this section, Sub-Saharan Africa is the world's poorest region with an estimated two-thirds of the rural population living in absolute poverty (Sparks 1990). The gap between rural and urban incomes is at least fourfold (White 1989). A number of countries have had to accept various structural adjustment programmes since the mid-1980s. Continuing drought in much of the region and lack of protection from excessive competition in years of overproduction (e.g. 1985–1986) have further undermined the rural economy. In the meantime, the rational thing to do for any African on the land has been to migrate to urban areas.

The nature of environmental problems

We can discuss the environmental problems at different but inter-connected scales that range from those that affect the home to those that operate at a regional level (Habitat 1989).

Environmental problems of the home

The majority of the urban population – e.g. 65 per cent in Dar-es-Salaam (Mosha 1990), 67 per cent in Blantyre (Mwafongo 1991), and 80 per cent in Luanda (Hill 1992) – live in squatter settlements. Squatter settlements refer to shanty towns, most of which start as illegal settlements. These settlements are characterized, among other things, by poorly constructed houses, poor sanitary conditions, lack of all services (power, running water, and garbage collection), and lack of legal status as residential dwellings. Izeogu (1989) has described such a settlement in Port Harcourt as follows:

There is a total lack of public services and infrastructure such as piped water and residential access roads. There is no provision for sanitation and drainage facilities, separate kitchens or children's play areas. The population density is also very high ... Most houses are below acceptable standard; their condition may also be deteriorating; the level of household facilities such as kitchen, flush toilets, and piped water to the house is very low; most residents depend upon a bucket toilet. (Izeogu 1989: 62)

105

Houses suffer from the prevalence of pathogens because of the lack of basic infrastructure and services such as sewers, drains, or services to collect solid and liquid wastes and safely dispose of them (Habitat 1989). These pathogens are a cause of many debilitating and endemic diseases that afflict poor households. The diseases include diarrhoea, dysentery, typhoid, food poisoning, and intestinal parasites.

One of the basic problems is lack of running water. The majority of residents living in squatter settlements have no access to potable (clean) water. In Nigeria, for example, only a limited number of houses have running water (Nwaka 1990). The majority of households depend upon various, and often unsafe, sources of water such as streams, wells, itinerant vendors, stagnant pools, and springs (Mosha 1990; Nwaka 1990; Mwafongo 1991). Such water is often contaminated by untreated effluents from industry and by sewage and is a source of many children's diseases. Where standpipes are provided, they are so few as to make a very limited impact.

With a few exceptions (e.g. Mutizwa-Mangiza 1990; Musandu-Nyamayaro 1991), sanitation is poor. Large parts of towns are not sewered. Most urban residents use pit toilets; others use a variety of unhealthy systems such as the bucket system. Nigerian towns are characterized by open drains, which are never cleaned and often clogged with all types of debris and garbage (Nwaka 1990). Even where sewers are provided, they are often blocked and overflow into the streets and attract harmful insects and bacteria (Mosha 1990).

The health problems are exacerbated by often crowded and cramped housing conditions. The numbers of persons per room are high (Izeogu 1989), which contributes to the spread of diseases such as tuberculosis, influenza, and meningitis. The spread of diseases is facilitated by limited resistance because people also suffer from malnutrition. Among children, diseases such as mumps and measles take a heavy toll. Accidents, particularly among children, are also common from fires, stoves, and kerosene heaters (Habitat 1989).

The unhealthy home environment is paralleled by an equally unhealthy environment in the workplace arising from dangerous concentrations of toxic chemicals and dust, inadequate lighting, ventilation, and space, and inadequate protection of workers from machinery and noise (Habitat 1989). These problems arise because of inadequate legislation and lack of enforcement.

Many factors have brought about the development of squatter settlements. The basic causes include the high demand for housing in the wake of rapid rural–urban migration, the slow growth of the housing stock, and the low incomes of the majority of migrants. It has been observed that, where the minimum standard of accommodation is costly, environmental quality may be sacrificed in favour of other goals: "Each low-income individual or household will choose the sacrifice to be made in terms of size of accommodation, the terms under which it is occupied, the suitability of the site, housing quality, the location and access to infrastructure and basic service" (Habitat 1989: 15). For many African urban residents the choice of where to live is almost predetermined; they cannot afford the cheapest low-cost housing. In most instances such housing is not even available, so that even those who might afford it are forced to join the squatters. The waiting lists for low-income housing are typically long. In Mozambique, for example, the construction of new houses ceased in 1976 (Gumende 1990), while in Malawi "new construction and servicing of new plots has drastically declined" (Mwafongo 1991: 21).

In Zimbabwe, the government has always been hostile to squatting and has not allowed the process to take root. Recently, however, with government inability to cope, there are signs of softening on the policy as squatting is grudgingly being accepted (*Africa South* 1992). Harare suffers from a scarcity of serviced land, insufficient funds, rapid population growth, and a shortage of building materials (*Southern African Economist* 1990).

Problems of the neighbourhood

The problems of the home merge into or are part of the wider problems afflicting the neighbourhood. Two problems, the siting of settlements and the poor collection of household garbage, will be discussed.

Squatters often select land that is likely not to be demanded for any other use in order to minimize the possibility of eviction. Such sites are likely to be dangerous or unhealthy. They include hillsides, flood plains, and polluted land sites (e.g. near solid waste dumps or industrial areas or areas with high levels of noise pollution such as in proximity to airports). Such land may have the additional advantage of being cheap or close to jobs (Habitat 1989). Squatter settlements in the Cameroon towns of Douala and Yaounde occupy quarry sites and marshy sites in valley bottoms.

The second major problem is waste disposal. A variety of wastes is generated. Izeogu (1989) found six factors that affect solid waste generation in Nigeria, including population growth, urbanization, social development, income class composition, and diffusion of technical competence. He found that, with improvements in incomes of the urban employed, consumption patterns changed so that the emphasis shifted to packaged products, which tend to produce large amounts of litter such as plastics, tins, and bottles.

Most cities do not have sufficient capacity to deal with the garbage that is generated. Dar es Salaam, for example, generates an estimated 2,000 tonnes of refuse a day but the city's removal capacity is only 100 tonnes a day (Mosha 1990). In Nigeria, Nwaka has estimated that only 30 per cent of waste is satisfactorily disposed of; the rest is dumped by the roadside or into nearby rivers and streams (Nwaka 1990). In many cases, refuse collection is restricted to high-income areas (Leduka 1991; Mwafongo 1991). There are no regular collections, if any, in the squatter areas, and the uncollected refuse soon attracts rodents, flies, and other vermin.

Where refuse is collected, it is often dumped at the edge of the city. The waste is untreated and is often a mixture of both domestic and industrial waste (Segosebe and Van der Post 1990). This causes pollution of the soil and the ground water. Meanwhile the built area gradually extends towards the dumps and in time surrounds the waste dump (White 1989; Musandu-Nyamayaro 1991).

The situation with respect to waste disposal is very serious because its direct effect on the quality of the environment is tremendous. Izeogu has observed: "By 1983 the large volumes of solid waste generated in Port Harcourt had changed the aesthetics of the urban environment. Garbage completely blocked some streets in Diobu and various parts of the city were dirty, unhealthy and visually unpleasant" (Izeogu 1989: 64).

It is unfortunate that, in cities such as Harare that have been coping, "residents are now resorting to emptying uncontrolled refuse in open spaces" (Musandu-Nyamayaro 1991: 8).

Problems of the city environment

Just as the home merges into the neighbourhood, so the neighbourhood merges into the city region. The main environmental problems at the city level are related to various aspects of pollution. Although pollution problems such as air pollution may be considered unimportant because of the low scale of industrialization, they may be as serious as in developed countries in certain localized areas. These are the major centres, particularly capital cities, where industries are concentrated.

The first problem concerns the disposal of toxic or hazardous wastes. The main sources of hazardous wastes include heavy metals, oxides of nitrogen and sulphur, and petroleum hydrocarbons (Habitat 1989; Christiansson 1993). Most of these come from the chemical industries, although other industries such as primary and fabricated metal and petroleum industries and leather tanning industries also produce significant quantities of hazardous substances (Habitat 1989; Izeogu 1989; Christiansson 1993). Effluents are discharged into the rivers, lakes, or estuaries, some of which are sources of drinking water (Izeogu 1989; Christianson 1993). Alternatively they may be dumped with ordinary domestic garbage and thus cause soil and groundwater contamination (Segosebe and Van der Post 1990). There are no effective regulations and institutions regarding the handling and disposal of such materials (Segosebe and Van der Post 1990; Habitat 1989).

It has been observed that: "The major cause of industrial pollution is the lack of consideration given to pollution and human health aspects when formulating and assessing industrial projects. Most of these projects are planned and assessed according to technical, economic and, in some cases, political criteria" (Christiansson 1993: 3).

As already indicated, water pollution from industrial effluents is a serious problem. Other sources of water pollution are sewage, garbage, and human excreta. In Port Harcourt, the piped water supply in some parts of the city was found to contain unacceptable levels of coliform (Izeogu 1989). As already noted above, most residents of squatter settlements depend upon contaminated sources for their water supply.

Air pollution is becoming a serious problem in some big centres. The sources of air pollution are industry, fuels for heating and electricity generation, the burning of garbage, some mining operations such as quarrying, and motor vehicles (Habitat 1989; Izeogu 1989; Mosha 1990). Motor cars, which are often poorly maintained and congested in narrow streets, contribute substantially to air pollution through emissions of carbon monoxide, oxides of nitrogen, and hydrocarbons. In addition, there is lead pollution as a result of less stringent regulations on the lead content of petrol.

Noise pollution is one of the problems in large cities. The sources of noise pollution include highway traffic, industrial operations, and aircraft (Habitat 1989). In some cases, desirable maximum levels of outside noise (65 decibels) are exceeded. In Port Harcourt, measurements in excess of 80 decibels were recorded (Izeogu 1989). The major cause of the problem is the lack of regulations and institutions to check noise pollution (Habitat 1989).

We can conclude this section by noting that, although various types of pollution are generally not yet a major problem, they constitute serious hazards in some large cities.

Environmental problems affecting the region beyond the city

The effects of some of the problems discussed above go beyond the city boundaries. A good example is water pollution. The effluents dumped in streams pollute the water used by rural communities (Izeogu 1989).

The other way in which the city affects its neighbouring communities is through the exhaustion of natural resources. Thus, as cities grow, the demand for water increases and sources further afield must be tapped. In these cases cities may compete with local communities for water and contribute to the fall in the levels of aquifers (Claassen 1990).

The other area of natural resource stress is energy. The main source of energy in urban areas is charcoal, followed by fuelwood (White 1989). The advantage of charcoal is that it is lighter and therefore easier to transport, but it is 40 per cent less efficient than fuelwood (ibid.). Consequently, urban dwellers cause greater deforestation per capita than do rural dwellers. In Malawi, it is feared that the shift from commercial fuels to wood may increase deforestation (Mwafongo 1991).

Causes of the current problems

The preceding section has described the various environmental problems found in African towns. Why is the situation this bad? How can we explain it? There are many answers to these questions and I shall explore some of them in this section.

The role of rural–urban migration

The first explanation for the terrible conditions found in some African towns is that rural–urban migration is so massive as to make it impossible for cities to cope with demands for the various services (e.g. El Sammani et al. 1989; Osman 1990). Rural–urban migration is accelerated by war and by urban-biased development. Studies do not see any changes in these trends. The suggestion is that cities could cope with much slower growth. But could they? Other fundamental issues are discussed below.

The problems of urban institutions

One of the key issues is institutional. In many countries there are many institutions that are involved in the provision of urban services and some of their activities overlap (Leduka 1991; Mwafongo 1991). Invariably, most of them are controlled by the central government and there is limited devolution of authority to local government; there is no clear division of functions between the various levels of government and there is lack of coordination of their various activities. In Lesotho, the Maseru city council was torn between the central government, the councillors, and the council administration, resulting in dissipated efforts (Leduka 1991). In Malawi, a study showed that there was a multiplicity of agencies delivering urban services and there was no coordination between them (Mwafongo 1991). On the other hand, in Abidjan, the council was weak because power was concentrated in the hands of the mayor, whose style of management was management by crisis (Attchi 1989). In discussing the situation in Kinshasa, Mbuyi (1989) showed that lack of effective management had led to conditions that were deleterious to the environment.

Even where devolution appears to have taken place and participatory institutions exist, the centre tries to exert some control. Musandu-Nyamayaro (1991: 5) has noted with respect to Harare that: "Despite the municipality possessing power and authority to act without referring to the Minister for approval, the centre maintains control and influence through a number of traditional avenues."

The effect of inadequate financial resources

Financial resources are crucial in urban management. Many cities have various sources of income but collection is neither comprehensive nor efficient and more sources could be identified. In Khartoum, for example, El Sammani et al. (1989: 268) have observed: "On the income side, the tax base is both outdated and structurally inadequate to meet current demands. This deficiency is further exacerbated by incompetence and corruption in the collection of the revenue due to the local government."

Even more serious is the lack of data on the cost of urban services, which prevents city councils from instituting cost-recovery measures (Mbuyi 1989). Zimbabwe, however, is an example of local authorities with financial independence (Mutizwa-Mangiza 1990; Musandu-Nya-mayaro 1991), and it shows the variety of sources that can be tapped.

The major problem with increasing the tax base is the widespread unemployment that is characteristic of African urban areas. Unemployment is increasing in a number of countries, including South Africa (e.g. Mwafongo 1991; Bond 1992), and the only alternative is the informal sector.

Unemployment and other conditions are likely to be worsened by the various International Monetary Fund and World Bank structural reform programmes, whose aims include the elimination or reduction of food subsidies, price controls, the reduction of the urban wage structure to market levels, and the reallocation of government capital investment away from subsidies for urban industrial production and public service provision. What monetary reform and a free market can do, following IMF loans and advice, is shown by the recent South African experience: "Even in industrial South Africa it becomes almost impossible to provide low-income housing and jobs because of exorbitant interest rates, bank strangle holds on development, land speculation, and the cartel of building materials producers" (Bond 1992: 7). According to Mabogunje (1991), whether the structural adjustment programmes fail or succeed, they will result in increased rural–urban migration.

Finance is central to effective and efficient urban management. First, it determines the level or quality of services that can be provided. For example, Dar es Salaam would have required a minimum of 240 trucks in 1990 to remove refuse and yet it had only 30, some of which were out of service (Mosha 1990). Shortage of finance has also affected, *inter alia*, housing delivery for low-income groups in Harare and refuse removal (Musandu-Nyamayaro 1991). Secondly, finance affects the level of salaries. Many city councils are not able to pay competitive salaries, with the consequence that they lose skilled manpower not only locally to the private sector but also to foreign countries (see El Sammani et al. 1989).

According to Wekwete (1990), the problems of African cities go even deeper and derive from their economic and social setting. Following Harvey's (1985) analysis, he identifies in African cities three circuits of capital accumulation and circulation. The primary circuit comprises the primary industries – mining, agriculture, industry, etc. –

and is generally characterized by the surplus production of capital. This excess capital is absorbed into the secondary circuit, which is concerned with the built environment in the city. The tertiary circuit "comprises of investment in science and technology and a wide range of social expenditures that relate to the process of production of labour power" (Wekwete 1990: 11).

In African cities, the primary circuit is dominated by foreign and international capital and therefore the surpluses generated are expropriated elsewhere. As a result, the secondary and tertiary sectors are undeveloped, a situation that is exacerbated by the absence of financial institutions "for pooling whatever little surplus might exist after multinational expropriation". Consequently,

Urban expansion was based largely on service provision and expanding government bureaucracies. It was urbanisation propelled by the service and administrative sectors, and in any cases sponsored by public sector investment.... Hence as economies have receded and or declined in their performances and the states have retreated as providers, the cities have collapsed or are in the state of collapse. (Wekwete 1990: 13)

The Wekwete model applies generally to southern Africa and to parts of eastern Africa. In many countries, large-scale mining and commercial agriculture are absent. The primary circuit, dominated by subsistence producers, does not produce much surplus. Even if surpluses were available, it would need more viable institutions and a less corrupt bureaucracy to ensure that they channelled the funds in the proper direction.

For much of black Africa, however, the role of government in the urban sector, through various subsidies, has been extensive. When this role is curtailed, as is the case under various restructuring programmes, this has far-reaching consequences for the urban economy and environment.

The role of planning

According to *The Economist*, most African cities "were designed with the grandeur and selfishness of empire, spread-out, tree-lined suburbs separated by open land from barracks for Africa labourers" (*The Economist* 1990: 21). And certainly, in many Commonwealth African countries, town planning was initiated by the colonial government, which also created embryonic planning departments (Ling 1988). In some cases, such as Kampala in Uganda, the colonial master plan provided a blueprint that was followed for many years after independence (Kajugira 1988).

Virtually every country has physical planning and development control legislation on its statute books. Yet a number of development problems have come to the fore and have intensified over the years. They include the following:

• a great deal of development of a commercial and educational nature has taken place outside planned centres;
• land use inside the towns is usually at variance with the approved plans;
• within or on the fringes of several large cities, unplanned and unserved squatter settlements have grown; and
• there has been a clearly visible spiralling deterioration of the environment (Kajugira 1988; Ling 1988; Mosha 1989).

There are several reasons why planning and development control have not worked effectively in Africa. First, physical planning is not given priority in Africa. It is generally treated as a sectoral activity concerned with works, housing, communications, and local government (Ling 1988). Yet it should be regarded as part and parcel of economic and social planning because it is the spatial expression of economic and social policies.

Secondly, planning and development control have been applied only to small areas. In some countries, development control was first introduced to cope with the development of large formal projects such as offices, banks, and hotels, "whilst the remaining building activity remains uncontrolled in people's hands" (Ling 1988: 17). In Port Harcourt, planning is restricted to low- and medium-density residential areas catering for only 15 per cent of the city's residents. Here live the top civil servants and business executives. The rest of the population lives in unplanned squatter settlements (Izeogu 1989).

A major factor in the lack of effective control is the shortage of professional and technical staff (e.g. Matope 1988; Ohas 1988; Kajugira 1988). Working conditions and salaries are not attractive, which makes it difficult for local authorities to retain trained and experienced manpower (El Sammani et al. 1989; *The Economist* 1990).

This situation is also symptomatic of the organizational weakness that has already been discussed. The overriding factors are lack of political and administrative action. This often reflects lack of political will resulting from a lack of real power or from corruption (Ohas 1988; Mosha 1989). Thus some old master plans have never been revised or the new ones have never been implemented.

Mosha (1989) has identified six factors that lead to weak enforcement of development control in Tanzania. They include:
(a) corruption on the part of enforcing officials;
(b) the long period taken to complete the construction of structures, which makes the monitoring of projects difficult;
(c) the lack of vehicles for officials, which precludes adequate development control;
(d) a scarcity of serviced land; and
(e) "a lack of follow-up and unwillingness in many cases to effect prosecution or revocation of leases for breach of covenant."

In summary, there is generally a lack of proper planning. Even where planning is done, there is no enforcement of development control. Thus much of urban development is not directed to ensure that the environment and the health of the people are protected.

The way forward

There are many views on the solutions to the problems identified above. A few of them are discussed below and it is important to realize that they are not mutually exclusive.

One recurring theme is institutional reform. The weaknesses of urban institutions have been noted. In addition these institutions are highly centralized and lack accountability (*The Economist* 1990). The principles of sound administration have been given as (Habitat 1987: 115):
(a) Organisational structure in tune with their defined functions.
(b) Power and authority commensurate with responsibility.
(c) Managers accountable for specific programmes.
(d) Service delivery constantly monitored, and systems of rewards and punishments institutionalized.
(e) Continuity and stability of personnel, and ongoing training.
(f) Availability of qualified staff and appropriate arrangements to encourage secondment and exchange of staff.

The system needs to be decentralized right down to the neighbourhood level (ibid.). Mabogunje (1991) has argued for investing neighbourhoods with "greater visibility and authority" in urban management. He has concluded:

In general, more attention to the neighbourhood structure can serve many other vital management purposes. It can enhance revenue collection for urban services, provide useful data, and improve delivery of urban services. It can also increase residents' participation in city administration and encourage a high standard of environmental quality. To assist neighbourhoods in this crucial role, some real decentralization of power is essential and can be expected to contribute to greater transparency and accountability in government. (Mabogunje 1991: 204–205)

It is necessary to have proper grass-roots participation if the environmental problems are to be solved. People must feel part of the process and they must accept the problems and the proposed solutions. Thus:

The best way for any administration to prove that it represents the interests of those that it administers is to establish the necessary mechanisms to allow and encourage participation, and to adopt a well-designed system of communication and information so as to make the development process easily understandable. Public participation should be instituted as a permanent feature of the management process, supported by the necessary legal framework, and integrated in the management structure. (Habitat 1987: 104)

Participation must be encouraged in all levels of decision-making – planning, programming and budgeting, implementation, and operational activities (ibid.: 104–105).

The second issue concerns financial reform. As already indicated, many cities are experiencing shrinking revenues because of, among other things, cuts in grants as a result of economic austerity (*The Economist* 1990). Secondly, cities have been forbidden to raise some charges for fear of riots. Thus cities are owed huge sums of money in the form of rents and water and electricity bills. The shrinking revenues are not matched by increased responsibilities.

Local government must be given more power to raise revenues (*The Economist* 1990; Habitat 1987). The tax base must be widened and the central government must not siphon off revenues collected by local government. Possibilities of cost recovery should be investigated but care must be taken that it does not become "hidden subsidies to high-income" residents (Habitat 1987). Further, in the present economic climate of many African countries there are limits to cost recovery. What should be done is to target subsidies in such a way as to exclude groups or sectors that do not deserve them.

The third area relates to the need to reappraise existing standards and therefore the need to introduce appropriate and affordable standards. It has been observed that African governments insist that high standards must be maintained (*The Economist* 1990). These standards, inherited from the colonial era, are often so high and demanding that it is impossible to upgrade most of the houses in the squatter areas. For example, they prohibit the use of local materials and may require that every dwelling be accessible by car (ibid.).

It is important to relax building standards and to allow people to put up "tolerable but cheap housing." In this way squatter settlements can be improved or avoided.

Indeed, there is now considerable experience with squatter upgrading. The most important objectives have generally been as follows (Habitat 1987: 175):

(a) projects should be "affordable" for the urban poor;
(b) projects should be self-financing and have high levels of cost recovery;
(c) projects should lead to the gradual improvement of housing on the basis of realistic standards as well as overall costs;
(d) projects should provide for income generation and employment creation;
(e) projects should be "integrated," providing for the systematic and coordinated delivery of physical and social infrastructure;
(f) programme and project impacts should be extensive in terms of coverage and reach.

The three areas of concern discussed above are the key to the solution of a number of urban environmental problems.

Concluding remarks

It is clear from this survey that the majority of urban residents in Africa live under unacceptable environmental conditions. However, these conditions do not act as a deterrent to further cityward migration. Instead, large numbers of migrants continue to flock to urban areas in an effort to improve their lot and thus make it even more difficult to cope with the present problems.

The problems include deforestation of surrounding regions to supply fuelwood or charcoal; the reduction or depletion of water supplies in surrounding regions; polluted water supplied to low-income areas; water, air, and noise pollution; inadequate collection and inappropriate disposal of wastes; and poor housing conditions.

The many causes of these problems include rapid rural–urban migration, a lack of finance, and inadequate institutions. However, some authorities contend that the problem is mainly structural – that what is listed above is a manifestation of something that is more serious and deep-seated.

A number of remedies have been suggested. A thorough institutional reform is essential and lies at the heart of any changes that might be proposed. In addition there is need for reform of the financial system and a review of standards in the building industry.

References

Africa South. 1992. Harare: Signs of a thaw. June.

Andreasen, J. 1990. Urban–rural linkages and their impact on urban housing in Kenya. In: J. Baker (ed.), *Small Town Africa.* Uppsala: Scandinavian Institute of African Studies.

Attchi, K. 1989. Cote d'Ivoire: An evaluation of urban management reform. In R. E. Stren and R. R. White (eds.), *African Cities in Crisis.* Boulder, Colo.: Westview Press.

Bond, P. 1992. The region's citizens have to live with cycle of continuous eruption. *Africa South,* June.

Christiansson, C. 1993. Environmental degradation in Tanzania. Paper presented at the Conference on Environment and Development in a North/South Perspective, Oslo University, 30 September – 3 October.

Claassen, P. E. 1990. Environmental concerns in third world cities: A case study of Khayelitsha, South Africa. In: International Society of City and Regional Planners (ed.), *The Environment and the City – Case Studies.* Amsterdam: ISCRP.

Economist, The. 1990. Africa's cities. 15 September.

El Sammani et al. 1989. Management problems in Greater Khartoum. In: R. E. Stren and R. R. White (eds.), *African Cities in Crisis.* Boulder, Colo.: Westview Press.

Gugler, J. 1982. The rural–urban interface and migration. In: A. Gilbert and J. Gugler, *Cities, Poverty, and Development.* Oxford: Oxford University Press.

Gumende, A. 1990. Halting decay in a siege city. *Southern African Economist* 3(2).

Gwebu, T. 1982. Rural–urban migration. In: Central Statistics Office (ed.), *Migration in Botswana: Causes, Patterns and Consequences.* Gaborone: CSO.

Habitat. 1987. *Global Report on Human Settlements.* Oxford: Oxford University Press.

———— 1989. *Urbanization and Sustainable Development in the Third World: An Unrecognized Global Issue.* Nairobi.

Hance, W. 1970. *Population, Migration, and Urbanization in Africa.* New York: Columbia University Press.

Harvey, D. 1985. *The Urbanization of Capital.* Oxford: Blackwell.

Hill, H. 1992. Concrete and clay: Angola's parallel city. *Africa South,* June.

Hjort af Ornäs, A. 1990. Town-based pastoralism in Eastern Africa. In: J. Baker (ed.), *Small Town Africa.* Uppsala: Scandinavian Institute of African Studies.

Izeogu, C. V. 1989. Urban development and the environment in Port Harcourt. *Environment and Urbanization* 1(1): 59–68.

Kajugira, D. K. 1988. Uganda. In: A. Ling (ed.), *Urban and Regional Planning and Development in the Commonwealth.* Howell: Howell Publications.

Leduka, R. C. 1991. Aspects of urban management in Lesotho. Paper presented at the RUPSEA Conference on Urban Management in Southern and Eastern Africa, Lilongwe, Malawi, 7–10 October.

Ling, A. 1988. Gambia. In: A. Ling (ed.), *Urban and Regional Planning and Development in the Commonwealth*. Howell: Howell Publications.

Mabogunje, A. L. 1991. A new paradigm for urban development. In: *Proceedings of the World Bank Annual Conference on Development Economics*. Washington, D.C.: World Bank.

Matope, J. J. 1988. Malawi. In: A. Ling (ed.), *Urban and Regional Planning and Development in the Commonwealth*. Howell: Howell Publications.

Mbuyi, K. 1989. Kinshasa: Problems of land management, infrastructure, and food supply. In R. E. Stren and R. R. White (eds.), *African Cities in Crisis*. Boulder, Colo.: Westview Press.

Mosha, A. C. 1989. Urban planning in Tanzania at the cross roads. *Review of Rural and Urban Planning in Southern and Eastern Africa*, no. 1: 79–91.

―――― 1990. Urbanisation and environment – Case study: Dar es Salaam. In: International Society of City and Regional Planners (ed.), *The Environment and the City – Case Studies*. Amsterdam: ISCRP.

Musandu-Nyamayaro, O. 1991. Urban management in Zimbabwe: The case of Harare. Paper presented at the RUPSEA Conference on Urban Management in Southern and Eastern Africa, Lilongwe, Malawi, 7–10 October.

Mutizwa-Mangiza, N. D. 1990. Urban local government in Zimbabwe: A case study of Bulawayo city with special reference to finance and delivery of service. Paper presented at the RUPSEA Workshop on Planning the Urban Economies in Southern and Eastern Africa, University of Zimbabwe, Harare, 12–16 November.

Mwafongo, W. M. K. 1991. Rapid urban growth: Implications for urban management in Malawi. Paper presented at the RUPSEA Conference on Urban Management in Southern and Eastern Africa, Lilongwe, Malawi, 7–10 October.

Nwaka, G. I. 1990. Urban planning and environmental protection in Nigeria. In: International Society of City and Regional Planners (ed.), *The Environment and the City – Case Studies*. Amsterdam: ISCRP.

O'Connor, A. 1983. *The African City*. London: Hutchinson University Library for Africa.

Ohas, J. M. 1988. Kenya. In: A. Ling (ed.), *Urban and Regional Planning and Development in the Commonwealth*. Howell: Howell Publications.

Osman, A. 1990. A toll of many cities. *Southern African Economist* 3(2).

Segosebe, E. and C. Van der Post. 1990. Urban industrial solid waste pollution in Botswana: Practice, attitudes and policy recommendations. Gaborone, University of Botswana, mimeo.

Southern African Economist. 1990. Harare's housing headache, 3(2).

Sparks, D. L. 1990. Economic trends in Africa south of the Sahara, 1990. In: *Africa South of the Sahara 1991*. London: Europa Publications.

Todaro, M. P. 1976. *Internal Migration in Developing Countries*. Geneva: International Labour Organization.

United Nations. 1991. *World Urbanization Prospects 1990*. New York: UN.

UNDP (United Nations Development Programme). 1991. *Human Development Report 1991*. New York: Oxford University Press for UNDP.

Van Western, A. C. M. and M. C. Klute. 1986. From Bamako, with love: A case study of migrants and their remittances. *Tijdschrift voor Econ. en Soc. Geografie* 77(1).

Vis, H. L. 1989. Nutrition in sub-Saharan Africa. *The Courier*, no. 118, Nov.–Dec.

119

Wekwete, K. H. 1990. Planning the urban economies in southern and eastern Africa. Paper presented at the RUPSEA Workshop on Planning the Urban Economies in Southern and Eastern Africa, Harare, University of Zimbabwe, Harare, 12–16 November.

White, R. R. 1989. The influence of environmental and economic factors on the urban crisis. In: R. E. Stren and R. R. White (eds.), *African Cities in Crisis*. Boulder, Colo.: Westview Press.

Part 2
Environmental issues and futures

7

Towards sustainable environmental and resource management futures in Sub-Saharan Africa

Bede N. Okigbo

Introduction

To the layperson, the environment consists simply of anything animal, plant, and mineral, in addition to other things around us such as the atmosphere, sun and, moon. To the ecologist, the environment is a more complex, multifaceted, interlocking, and overlapping phenomenon that is physical, biological, anthropic, and resource generating in nature (Pomeroy and Service 1986). The physical environment consists of: a *terrestrial component*, made up of land, water, wind, and climatic elements such as solar radiation and temperature; the *aquatic component*, made up of bodies of water, dissolved and suspended matter, currents, light, and other elements; the *resources*, made up of food of plant and animal origin, air (including oxygen, nitrogen, and carbon dioxide), water, shelter, etc.; the *biological environment* or component, consisting of living things made up of a diversity of species and their wide range of characteristics; and last, but not least in importance, the anthropic component consisting of *humans and human multisectoral activities* in agriculture, building, construction, fishing, hunting, industry, tourism, etc. It is of interest to note that humans and human activities are grouped into a separate category despite the fact that humans are also animals. This is because of the overwhelming influence or effects that humans have on the environment, shaping and conditioning things in the present and in the future. The implication of humans and human activities as a special component of the environment is that they give rise to other environments that are economic, political, and cultural in nature.

Again, to the layperson the above environmental resources (plant, animal, and mineral) are synonymous with natural resources. But, to the resource economist, in the human ecosystem humans assign utility to various elements of the environment, thus conferring on them the role of resources (Chapman 1969). A *resource* is the result of human interaction with elements of the environment. When humans make use of any element of the environment, thus changing its status to that of a resource that fulfils one or more human needs, this involves a different kind of interaction or interrelationships in which humans play a central role.

A component of the environment that humans use as a resource acquires an economic or rarity value, whose magnitude depends on its nature and the size of the requirements humans place on it, which depend on the size of population using it, humans' needs and desires, and humans' values and skills (Chapman 1969). The implications of this are that the economic value of a resource depends a lot on the magnitude of its reserve(s), its characteristics, including ease of extraction and processing, and the technologies available for rendering it into forms that satisfy human needs. Consequently, according to Chapman (1969):

- Resource availability is the result of interactions among the nature and size of humans' requirements, the physical occurrences of the resource, and the means of producing it.
- The future availability of resources can be determined on the basis of assessment of:
  - the particular combination of economic and technological conditions that determine present production,
  - the level of production that would take place under different economic conditions,
  - the level of production that could take place under different technological conditions (i.e. types, mixes, sequences, and timing),
  - the nature and quantity of the total physical stock of both renewable and non-renewable resources.
- The total stock or *resource base* is the sum of all components of

the environment that would be resources if they could be extracted from it.

- The resource constitutes the proportion of the total stock that humans can extract and make available under prevailing technological and economic conditions.

- The *reserve* is that proportion of the resource that is known with reasonable certainty to be available under prevailing technological, economic, and social conditions.

- The requirements and availability of resources very much depend on their interrelationships with time, space, and technology. The relative importance of time lies in the fact that, whereas certain biological processes take a very long time, some ecological processes may require a relatively short time, and human activities may take only a very short time to change the result of thousands of years of evolution. Furthermore, technological changes occur with time, and the economics of the availability of resources may depend on the distribution in space or distance between sources and where they are used, and the technology available at a given time or stage for facilitating access to the resources.

The importance of science and technology then lies in the fact that, through their applications, we can (a) identify the presence and determine the amount (quantity) and the characteristics (quality) of reserves, (b) conserve/manage them, and (c) process them with increasing cost-effectiveness in order to ensure rational utilization of resources. Management and economics are of importance in that resources are often scarce and/or exhibit inequalities in availability and distribution. Management also is very important in the processing and utilization of scarce resources as cheaply as possible. It is not surprising then that, in sustainable development, there is increasing realization of the interrelationship between economics and ecology. In fact it is for this reason that, in an age of sustainable development, Goodland (1991) maintains that conventional economics and conventional ecology should be integrated into ecological economics (fig. 7.1 and table 7.1).

The complex interrelationships that exist among resources and humans in various sectoral development activities are shown in figure 7.2. It is necessary to emphasize that, in the development process, both general and specialized education are important in our understanding and managing of natural resources. Education provides a solid foundation for the research needed to develop new technologies

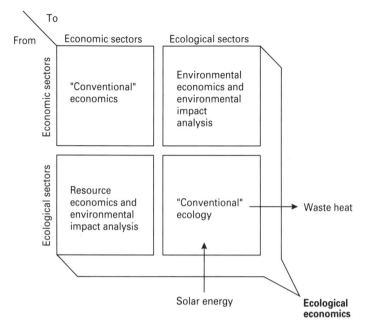

Fig. 7.1 **The domains of conventional economics, conventional ecology, environmental and resource economics, and ecological economics (Source: Constanza 1991)**

and expand the frontiers of knowledge, while training is necessary for imparting the skills needed for conservation, management, and rational utilization of resources.

The problem of renewable and non-renewable resources

In the development process, strategies and technologies used in the conservation, management, and utilization of renewable resources should be different from those used for non-renewable resources, such as minerals. *Non-renewable* resources should be conserved and wisely utilized so as substantially to extend the time of their availability and existence. Such a long period of time is necessary for seeking and finding alternatives. Although *renewable* resources can be regenerated, they have to be conserved and carefully utilized in order to realize their renewability. For example, although the soil is renewable, if it is managed in such a way that rates of loss and degradation exceed the rate of soil formation, the result is lack of renewability and sustainability. Similarly, although plants or animals are renewable, the extermination of certain species that are necessary

126

Table 7.1 **Comparison of "conventional" economics and ecology with ecological economics**

	"Conventional" economics	"Conventional" ecology	Ecological economics
Basic world-view	Mechanistic, static, atomistic	Evolutionary, atomistic	Dynamic, systems, evolutionary
	Individual tastes and preferences taken as given and as the dominant force. The resource base viewed as essentially limitless owing to technical progress and infinite substitutability	Evolution acting at the genetic level viewed as the dominant force. The resource base is limited. Humans are just another species but are rarely studied	Human preferences, understanding, technology, and organization co-evolve to reflect broad ecological opportunities and constraints. Humans are responsible for understanding their role in the larger system and managing it for sustainability
Time frame	Short	Multi-scale	Multi-scale
	50 years maximum, 1–4 years usual	Days to eons, but time-scales often define non-communicating sub-disciplines	Days to eons, multi-scale synthesis
Space frame	Local to international	Local to regional	Local to global
	Framework invariant at increasing spatial scale; basic units change from individuals to firms to countries	Most research has focused on relatively small research sites in single ecosystems. but larger scales becoming more important recently	Hierarchy of scales
Species frame	Humans only	Non-humans only	Whole ecosystem including humans
	Plants and animals included only rarely for contributory value	Attempts to find "pristine" ecosystems untouched by humans	Acknowledges interconnections between humans and rest of nature

127

Table 7.1 (**cont.**)

	"Conventional" economics	"Conventional" ecology	Ecological economics
Primary micro goal	Max. profits (firms) Max. utility (individuals)	Maximum reproductive success	Must be adjusted to reflect system goals
	All agents following micro goals leads to macro goal being fulfilled. External costs and benefits given lip-service but usually ignored	All agents following micro goals leads to macro goal being fulfilled	Social organization and cultural institutions at higher levels of the space/time hierarchy ameliorate conflicts produced by myopic pursuit of micro goals at lower levels, and vice versa
Assumptions about technical progress	Very optimistic	Pessimistic or no opinion	Prudently sceptical
Academic stance	Disciplinary	Disciplinary	Transdisciplinary
	Monistic; focus on mathematical tools	More pluralistic than economics, but still focused on tools and techniques. Few rewards for comprehensive, integrative work	Pluralistic; focus on problems

Source: Constanza (1991).

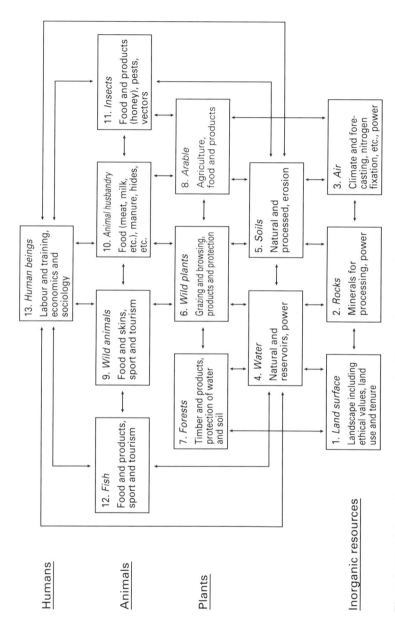

Humans

Animals

Plants

Inorganic resources

Fig. 7.2 **The interactions among components of natural resources in sectoral development activities (Source: B. Brouillette, N. J. Graves, and G. Last, *African Geography for Schools*, London: Longman; Paris: UNESCO, 1974)**

129

for their breeding and continuous regeneration may ultimately lead to their extinction. Thus the loss of species or even individuals with unique characteristics results in the loss of their irreplaceable unique genetic information and make-up.

Futures in normal commercial everyday usage are used to designate goods and stocks sold for future delivery. Here the term is used in a prognostic manner to forecast what the future portends in terms of the status of resources and the condition of the environment for future generations as a result of the impacts of multifarious human activities. It requires an assessment of past and present development policies, strategies, technologies, and programmes with regard to the extent to which they have resulted in unsustainability, lack of it, or enhancement of the resource base. A sustainable future will be possible only where appropriate and effective measures are taken now to replace the past and present non-environmentally friendly development policies, strategies, technologies, and programmes, and in addition to introduce the requisite changes in attitudes, morals, and behaviours in different cultures.

The concept of sustainable development and its implications

Definition

Sustainable development as a concept and development paradigm for lasting progress was originally defined by the World Commission on Environment and Development (WCED) to mean "development that meets the needs of the present generation without compromising the ability of future generations to meet their own needs" (WCED 1987). The Commission further added that "this concept does not imply limits – not absolute limits but limitations imposed by the present state of technology and social organization on environmental resources and by the ability of the biosphere to absorb the effects of human activities." This definition implies that sustainable development involves policies, strategies, and programmes that do not make it more difficult for the development process to be continued by future generations than it is for present generations. It would appear that this definition emphasizes the objectives to be achieved rather than explicitly defining sustainable development.

One of the earlier concepts of sustainable development was advanced by Sachs (1973), who used the term *eco-development*. Eco-development was defined to consist of strategies designed for particular eco-zones with a view to:

(a) making fuller use of specific resources in each eco-zone in order to meet the basic needs of its inhabitants while safeguarding the long-term prospects by rational management of these resources instead of their destructive exploitation;
(b) reducing to a minimum the negative environmental effects and even as far as possible using waste products for productive purposes;
(c) designing adequate technologies for achieving these goals. (Ominde 1977)

There does not appear to be any substantial difference between eco-development and sustainable development, both of which embody environmental concerns in development activities and programmes. The real difference lies in the fact that, whereas the former was a development paradigm born at the beginning of the period of environmental and "limits of growth" concerns, the latter came at a time when environmental activism and pressures from green parties all over the world necessitated not only a new development paradigm but a slogan and buzzword christened *sustainable development*.

The United Nations Environment Programme (UNEP 1992) argues that the WCED (1987) definitions of sustainable development have been criticized as ambiguous and confusing because "sustainable development," "sustainable growth," and "sustainable use" have been used interchangeably even though they do not have the same meaning. "Sustainable growth" is regarded as contradictory in that nothing physical can grow indefinitely, while "sustainable use" is applicable only to renewable resources in terms of "using them at rates within the capacity for renewability." Based on these arguments, UNEP (1992) put forward the following relevant definitions:

- *Sustainable development* means improving the quality of human life while living within the carrying capacity of supporting ecosystems.
- *Sustainable economy* is the product of sustainable development; it maintains its natural resource base and it can continue to develop by adapting to changing circumstances and through improvements in knowledge organization, technical efficiency, and wisdom.
- *Sustainable living* indicates the lifestyle of an individual who feels the obligation to care for nature and for every human individual, and who acts accordingly.

According to MECCA (1992), sustainable development is said to exist if each generation per capita inherits a more valuable stock of capital (human-made and natural) than the earlier generations. This definition raises the question of what are valuable resources and the problem of how far one can be more specific about sustainability without bringing in value judgements on what is important for ensuring a given quality of life.

Recently, Benneh (1993) presented an African concept of sustainability that constitutes an extension of the WCED (1987) definition of sustainable development by emphasizing that sustainable development is not simply a question of managing resources in a manner that meets current needs while not making it more difficult for future generations to meet theirs. Rather, it is a strategy of resource management that regards the capital stock as a baton in a relay race handed down to us by our ancestors, and it is our duty to ensure that it is successfully transferred to future generations more or less intact and without much decline in value.

Although this concept, like the WCED (1987) definition, does not specifically indicate what sustainable development entails, it raises an issue that the WCED (1987) discussed but did not include or allude to in its definitions. This is the problem of *transition*, which takes into account the past, the present, and the future. It is perhaps the most difficult challenge and implication of sustainable development: it recognizes that maintenance of environmental quality, productivity potentialities, biological diversity, and resilience of ecosystems should go hand in hand with development activities, but it does not stipulate how the necessary changes from a past of exploitative squandering of the earth's natural resources and degradation of the environment to a sustainable future can be effected through the present period of transition when the necessary changes in attitudes, ethics, morality, culture, and lifestyles against the driving forces of polarization and momentum of the modernization process and other change factors discussed later will be made.

In this paper, sustainable development is defined as consisting of policies, strategies, plans, production systems, and technologies used in executing projects and programmes aimed at satisfying real human needs in perpetuity while maintaining environmental quality, biodiversity, the resilience of ecosystems, and the welfare of all organisms by integrating conservation, management, and rational utilization of resources at individual, institutional, community, national, regional, and global levels. Conservation here, according to Jacobs (1988), is an indispensable part of a wide field known as "the wise utilization of natural resources" aiming at utilization *ad infinitum*. It aims at (a) maintaining essential ecological processes and life-support systems, (b) preserving genetic diversity, and (c) ensuring the sustainable utilization of species and ecosystems.

What sustainable development entails

Requirements for sustainable development, according to WCED (1987), include: a *political system* that secures effective citizen participation; an *economic system* that is able to generate surpluses and technical knowledge on a self-reliant basis; a *social system* that provides for solutions for tensions arising from disharmonious development; a *production system* that respects the obligation to preserve the ecological base for development; a *technological system* that can search continuously for new solutions; an *international system* that fosters sustainable patterns of trade and finance; and an *administrative system* that is flexible and has the capacity for self-correction.

Caring for the Earth: A Strategy for Sustainable Living (IUCN/ UNEP/WWF 1991) enunciated nine principles for sustainable development:
• Respect and care for the community of life.
• Improve the quality of human life.
• Conserve the earth's vitality and diversity.
• Minimize the depletion of non-renewable resources.
• Keep within the earth's carrying capacity.
• Change personal attitudes and practices.
• Enable communities to care for their own environments.
• Provide a national framework for integration, development, and conservation.
• Create a global alliance.

It is obvious from the above that sustainable development not only entails the embodiment of environmental concerns in development activities and technology use but also necessitates changes in attitudes, behaviour, philosophy, moral and ethical values, religious practices, and relationships among human beings and between humans on the one hand and organisms or things on the other at the local, national, regional, and global levels.

Implications and challenges in sustainable development

In addition to the above requirements for sustainable development, there are several implications of the sustainable development paradigm that pose serious challenges for mankind now and in the future.

Some of these implications and challenges are discussed in Pearce et al. (1990), Goodland et al. (1991), and Sachs (1992). Only salient aspects of these are considered here.

According to Pearce et al. (1990), a key prerequisite for sustainability is maintaining the constancy of the stock of natural resources and environmental quality. But because this condition has already been breached, in that the environment in many situations has become degraded by human activities, the problem of maintaining the constancy of the capital stock is not just one of stopping further environmental degradation but undoubtedly one of enhancing the environment. The implications of this are addressed from different viewpoints by the Brundtland Report (WCED 1987), which stipulates that sustainable development requires non-depletion of the natural capital stock as indicated in the World Conservation Strategy (IUCN/UNEP/WWF 1980), although WCED (1987) insists that, if needs are to be met on a sustainable basis, the earth's natural resources have to be both conserved and enhanced. Reasons for conserving the natural capital include moral obligation and the supposed mutual interdependence of development and natural capital conservation.

Goodland (1991) presents very convincing arguments and undeniable evidence to conclude that the limits of growth, in which the earth functions as a source of inputs and sink for waste products, have been reached and that options for ensuring sustainability in future are running out. Evidence for this conclusion includes: (a) over 80 per cent of the earth's net primary productivity is already being consumed to meet humans' food and other needs while population is still increasing, (b) global warming owing to increasing levels of carbon dioxide is already producing adverse climatic effects that threaten humans and various ecosystems, (c) ozone depletion is taking place owing to increasing levels of greenhouse gases (methane, CFCs, and nitrous oxide), which are eating up the protective ozone layer with adverse consequences for humans and other living things, (d) land degradation and loss of soil fertility and productivity make it difficult to produce enough food, feed, and fibre for rising populations of humans and animals, and (e) biodiversity has been lost with increasing deforestation, especially in species-rich tropical ecosystems, with loss of species estimated at 500 per annum.

Daly (1991) notes that the human economy has passed from an era in which human-made capital was the limiting factor to an economic development era in which increasingly scarce natural capital has become the limiting factor. He recommends that priority should be given to "qualitative development" based on more efficient use of energy and natural resources, an increase in end-use efficiency of the product through recycling, and the reduction of waste and pollutants.

Tinbergen and Hueting (1991) as well as Serafy (1991) consider equity issues, sustainability constraints under low rates of economic growth, uneven/varying population growth rates, and the effects of North–South trade on the environment and development in the South. Doubts are raised about the soundness of some WCED (1987) equity considerations in economic growth and the strategies aimed at increasing economic growth and development in developing countries going *pari passu* with lower non-increasing growth rates in developed countries in order to ensure that developing countries achieve higher per capita income and alleviation of poverty in order to narrow the gap between the rich and the poor countries. The fallacy in this is that, because growth in developed countries has naturally acquired momentum, it is very likely that its rate will continue to rise rather than decrease. Moreover, the intended objective can be achieved only if the developed countries transfer the resources needed to redress the negative effects of richer countries' arrested growth to the developing countries, thereby reducing poverty.

It is observed that the time-horizon of development should be taken into account, for some obvious reasons. First, sustainable development usually aims at a long-term time-frame of several generations, but politicians and policy makers plan on short-term time-frames of four to five years. Secondly, sustainable development that involves many generations or centuries cannot go on indefinitely where both population and per capita use of the earth's finite resources grow significantly. Even where population and economic activities remain static, the accumulation of pollutants and waste will continue to increase with the growth of entropy beyond nature's capacity for self-repair.

The principle of the free market mechanism as a way of creating certain optimal conditions has not often yielded the expected results in sustainable development because the blessings of free trade have associated with them (a) production pollution arising from the production process, (b) consumption pollution, which is the indirect effect of pollution produced by consumers in enjoying goods and services, and (c) negative impacts on the environment of the production process. Sustainable development cannot be achieved in a world where developed countries with higher technical skills for producing a wide range of technology selfishly focus on consumer goods and services instead of focusing on more basic improvements in using the world's resources to the benefit of the poor. Furthermore, sustainability cannot be achieved and inequalities eliminated through the trickle-down process from the developed countries unless the increasing ability to use resources more efficiently and to reduce waste and pollution is used to assist less fortunate people who cannot provide the minimum level of basic needs.

Liberalization and an increase in North–South trade and aid cooperation have not significantly contributed to equity and sustainable development, especially where the poor developing countries are tempted to exhaust their valuable natural reserves at lower prices in order to feed the trend-setting and unsustainable consumption patterns of the North in return for consumer goods and machinery. Such trade involves the depletion of natural resources by the sale of non-renewable minerals and harvests from soils, forests, and oceans, and the soils being increasingly used as the dumping sites of undesirable waste. Related to this is the fact that aid to developing countries to develop the same technologies that degrade the environment and cause the same pattern of polluting consumption as in the West cannot contribute to sustainable development.

Droste and Dogsé (1991) observe that investments in education, science, and technology that contribute to human welfare and the decisions surrounding them are also often contributors to environmental problems. Examples include:
- investments in short-term income-generating activities such as deforestation, intensive agriculture, and plantations, without concomitant investments in soil conservation and protection measures;
- spending more money on combating pollution or on remedial measures than would be needed for preventive measures;
- the use of subsidies, trade barriers, and various production technologies (including biotechnology) in the developed countries to produce surpluses that undermine the production of farmers in developing countries, making it difficult for the latter to compete or even ensure access to the inputs needed.

Constanza (1991) maintains that, to achieve global sustainability, it is necessary to switch from the concept of ecological and economic goals being in conflict, to one of economic systems being dependent on ecological life-support systems, and also to incorporate it into our thinking and actions at a very basic level. In other words, human beings must realize that:
(a) humans are only part of the subsystem in both local and global ecosystems;

(b) sustainability is a relationship between dynamic human economic systems and larger but normally slower-changing ecological systems in which human life can continue indefinitely, human cultures can develop, but the effects of human activities must remain within bounds, so as not to destroy the diversity, complexity, and function of the ecological life-support system.

It is necessary that the idea of economics being in conflict with ecology be replaced by one of the integration of conventional economics and conventional ecology into ecological economics, as shown in figure 7.1 and table 7.1. There is also a need to ensure continued adequate investment in natural capital and in finding ways of limiting physical growth so as to encourage development with an emphasis on qualitative improvement.

The above survey of the implications of sustainable development is necessary because it emphasizes that the problem is not mainly one of having a better definition of what sustainable development is. The main issue or critical factor is how to rehabilitate the natural resource base and repair the damage already done while not contributing to making things worse by continuing unsustainable living – locally, nationally, regionally, or globally. In this regard, it is also obvious that the greatest challenge is how to engender a transition that is steady, continuous, and on an even keel in all sectors at individual, community, national, regional, and global levels.

Driving forces

The problem of environmental degradation as a result of various development and other activities that constitute driving forces has to be understood as a basis for determining measures for ensuring sustainability. The driving forces considered here include:
- modernization
- agriculture, including livestock production and fishing
- population explosion
- fuelwood and energy management and associated deforestation
- industrialization
- poverty and affluence
- urbanization
- other miscellaneous activities and phenomena.

Holdgren, Daily, and Ehrlich (1995) recently included among driving forces: excessive population growth; maldistribution of consumption and investment; misuse of technology; corruption and mis-management; and powerlessness of the victims. The authors also refer to underlying human frailties such as: greed, selfishness, intolerance, and shortsightedness; and ignorance, stupidity, apathy, and denial. These are among the miscellaneous activities and phenomena listed above but only modernization is considered in detail here, although they are implied when it is stressed that, for sustainable development, changes are needed in attitudes, lifestyles, morals, ethics, behaviour, and philosophy.

Modernization

Modernization may be defined as a process of transformation of the way of life (culture, social and economic structures, and attitudes) from the characteristics of traditional societies to those dictated by changes brought about by industrialization, urbanization, trade, and communications. Of major importance in the modernization process is the West European influence, which was most pronounced during various periods of colonialism. This was followed by a period of political/ideological, technical, cultural, and other influences related to American/West European and East European aspects of modernization associated with the Cold War. With the end of communism, Westernization influences have become dominantly more American. However, it must be admitted that, just as with sustainable development, modernization has many interpretations. Its meanings and indicators range from its being equivalent to industrialization to a more complex process affecting all aspects of human life, with the indicators ranging from GNP, income, or number of cars per 100 people to combinations of major economic indicators ranging from life expectancy to numbers of scientists per 1,000 of population and quality of life indices. A few definitions of modernization are considered below to clarify the situation.

Todaro (1986) defines modernization as the transformations in attitudes, institutions, and ideologies that are associated with processes such as urbanization and industrialization, whose characteristic ideals include: rationality, which is the substitution of modern methods of thinking, acting, producing, distributing, and consuming for age-old traditional practices; planning or the search for a rational coordinated system of policy measures that can bring about and accelerate economic growth and development, with the plan period usually in units of five years; social and economic equalization aimed at promoting more equality or equity in status; improved institutions and attitudes, including changes that are deemed necessary to increase labour efficiency and diligence; the promotion of effective competition, social and economic mobility, and individual enterprise, raising living standards, changing outmoded land tenure systems, and changing educational and religious structures.

Hoogvelt (1982) defines modernization as a process by which developing countries were to be made either efficient producers and exporters of agricultural products and raw materials, or consumers of industrial products from the West, or both, thereby participating in world economic relations. Modernization started at the end of World War II in underdeveloped countries as a process in development activities regarded in liberal progressive circles as a necessary complement to the economic reconstruction in war-ravaged industrial countries and of a prosperous world capitalist economy based on free trade. In order to accomplish this goal rapidly, it was felt that fast changes from "stone age" to the twentieth century through the modernization process were necessary. According to the neo-evolutionary theory of development, modernization involved structural compatibility between certain primary consequences of modernization, consisting of advanced economic institutions (money markets, occupational specialization, profit maximization, etc.), and certain second-order consequences, consisting of Western "modern" political, social, and cultural institutions, with second-order institutions such as social mobility of individuals, nuclear family patterns, nationalism, formal education, a free press, voluntary associations, urbanization, and consumerism regarded as prerequisites for economic development. There was also some collusion of interests between Western international capitalism and the ruling élites of the new ex-colonial territories, who in many cases dictated the goal of development to be economic, involving the wholesale adoption of Western social, economic, and political structures. Traditional elements or counterparts of these consequences and characteristics of modernization, such as kinship and the extended family, were condemned as obstacles to development.

Until the second United Nations Development Decade, the above primary and secondary characteristics of modernization of the neo-evolutionary modernization theories led to the use of indicators for comparing developing countries that included such economic, political, and social factors as degree of urbanization, industrialization, political democracy, secularization, social mobility, occupational differentiation, free enterprise, and independent judiciary. The World Bank and other international organizations used these factors to outline the socio-economic programmes that contain these elements as a basis for qualifying for aid. Western technology, Western methods of production, and Western economic enterprises were also welcomed as vital agents of development.

Dube (1988) observes that, following World War II and the escalation of the number of independent countries, modernization was born as a new development paradigm. At that time, as new independent states launched massive economic development and technical change programmes aimed at getting them in a few years to where their erstwhile colonial rulers had taken centuries to reach, the developed countries were forced by conscience and humanitarian interest, in addition to strategic power interests and promise of long-term economic gain, to extend their cooperation in a limited way. Modernization emerged as one of the formulations of social scientists aimed at evolving stable patterns of relationship that were mutually beneficial, with prospects of short-term and long-term national interest weighing heavily on both developed and developing countries. In putting forward the theories of modernization, social scientists were determined not to offend the sensitivities of the new nations. "Modernization" was invented as a more acceptable term to replace "Westernization." Because of its academic respectability, funds flowed easily to research on this new paradigm, and aid was extended to programmes aimed at achieving it.

Dube (1988) also notes that modernity was understood to be a common behavioural system associated with the industrial, literate, and participant societies of Western Europe and North America. Developing countries were impressed by the varying degrees of success of the countries that early in the twentieth century joined the race for industrialization, such as Japan (the first Asian country to do so) and Russia. The basic underlying assumptions were that:

1. inanimate sources of power could be tapped with a view to solving human problems and ensuring minimum acceptable standards of living, the ceiling of which will rise progressively;
2. both industrial and collective efforts should be channelled to achieve this;
3. to create and run complex organizations, radical personality changes and attendant social structures and values were necessary.

As to the nature of modernization, it is regarded as a process very similar to development (see table 7.2). However, although many of

the attributes of the two processes – such as their being revolutionary, complex, systematic, lengthy, and phased – are acceptable, others
are open to question, including the following:

- some of the benefits have been widely diffused but large sections of
  human society often remain unaffected;
- the extent of their being global is debatable;
- although the world is increasingly being described as a global village on account of homogenization, the rise of ethnicities and plu-
  ralities of culture is tearing it apart;
- whether the process is irreversible remains to be seen – the rise of
  fundamentalism and what is happening in the Soviet Union indicate
  that it is not;
- whether the processes are progressive remains a matter of opinion,
  with individual alienation and social anomalies occurring and collective violence increasing;
- although the benefits are substantial, the social cost and cultural
  erosion (coupled with environmental degradation) are escalating.

There are several dilemmas associated with modernization and
development:

- there are inequalities in wealth and affluence, with many countries
  not attaining high growth rates of GNP;
- many countries (developed or developing) face cycles of recession,
  severe inflation, and growing unemployment;
- the rationality of the system is in question, with current gaps in
  access to resources among countries and between men and women;
- there is increasing violence and crime;
- corruption is a way of life in many places;
- the lifestyles of the affluent in developed countries are taking hold
  in developing countries;
- there is misdirection of science and technology and even funds for
  development to military and disharmonious pursuits;
- although developed countries spend billions of dollars on tools
  of destruction, they cannot devote 1–2 per cent of their GNP to
  development in the developing countries;
- developing countries spend millions on military hardware while
  millions of their people die of hunger;
- the world's finite energy resources of coal, tar, petroleum, oil,
  natural gas, and uranium not only are unevenly distributed but
  are becoming exhausted, while the capabilities for generating alternatives and their sustainable use vary from one country to
  another;

Table 7.2 **The similarities between modernization and development**

Modernization	Development
1. Revolutionary process with significant technological and cultural consequences, e.g. rural agrarian cultures being transformed into urban industrial cultures	1. Same
2. Complex and multidimensional process with series of cognitive, behavioural, and institutional modifications and restructuring	2. Same
3. Systematic process with variations in one dimension producing important co-variations in other dimensions	3. Same
4. Global process, with ideas spreading from one centre of origin to other parts of the world	4. Same
5. Lengthy process with no known way of producing it instantly	5. Same
6. Phased process that, according to experience, involves known phases and sub-phases, namely: (i) traditional (ii) transitional (iii) modernized	6. Same, namely: (i) underdeveloped (ii) developing (iii) developed
7. Homogenizing process, with advanced stages significantly narrowing differences between national societies and ultimately reaching a stage when the universal imperative of modern ideas and institutions prevails, and various societies are so homogenized as to be capable of forming a world state	7. Same
8. Irreversible process, although there may be occasional upsets and temporary breakdowns	8. Same
9. Progressive process regarded as inevitable and desirable, ultimately contributing to human well-being culturally and materially	9. Same
10. Painful process and in some instances in the past built on painful and ruthless exploitation of segments of society, dividing or integrating peoples, and resulting in privileged or underprivileged people	10. Same for areas that have been under colonial rule
11. Multilinear and multi-path process, with societies not necessarily all taking the same route but sometimes alternative paths	11. Same
12. Cannot be visualized as continuous or unending path since they are conditioned by outer and inner limits and human perceptions can change and have changed course	12. Same

Source: Adapted from Dube (1988).

- non-fuel mineral resources are also running out, as well as being unequally distributed;
- world forest resources are disappearing fast and rapid loss of bio-diversity is also taking place;
- billions of tonnes of soil are being lost to erosion and vast areas of agriculture are being degraded;
- increasing emissions of carbon dioxide and greenhouse gases are causing ozone depletion and climatic change.

Dube (1988) identifies several factors that obstruct moderniza-tion and observes that many nations are torn between their allegiance to tradition and a commitment to modernization. Several barriers to modernization of an ideological, motivational, institutional, and orga-nizational nature are encountered, as well as problems of a decline of the paradigm, ambiguities and inadequacies, environmental con-straints, and global problems.

Modernization and sustainable development in Africa
Modernization has associated with it several benefits, including: edu-cation and educational infrastructure; applications of science and technology in banishing ignorance and superstition; improved health and sanitation; improved communications; improved water supplies; improved nutrition; and employment and high incomes. Most of these consequences, except that of high incomes, are very likely to enhance sustainability in development.

There are also many changes associated with modernization that have adverse effects on sustainability in development. These include: increased dependence on the West for what Africans wear or how they think; the importation of inappropriate technologies; a change in standards associated with lack of appreciation of traditional things; unsustainable lifestyles; and acculturation stress owing to massive exposure to Western media and communication channels to an extent that Africans are unable to fight back. It is a paradox, for example, that improved health and medical services, better sanitation, a decline in infant mortality, and longer life expectancy, which are associated with modernization, are causes of rapid population growth and its obvious adverse environmental and socio-economic consequences.

Modernization has made deep inroads into African culture and has also caused changes in attitudes and overall changes in lifestyles that are not as sustainable as some traditional African ones. Increased dependence on Western or imported clothes, food, and drink results in loss of income and foreign exchange needed for development. The importation and use of excessive amounts of certain pesticides, chemicals, and inappropriate technologies result in damage to the environment. Some technologies, such as agricultural and forest logging machinery, can do serious damage to the soil and vegetation. The emergence of a global culture has adverse effects on the attitude of the youth towards traditional African culture and sense of standards. In African culture, work is appreciated and a farmer has status depending on his productivity. With modernization, farmers have lower status irrespective of their productivity. As a result of modernization, indigenous knowledge is not appreciated or utilized, yet, without a good understanding, knowledge, and appreciation of indigenous knowledge, traditional resource management strategies, and technologies, African research and development activities cannot develop production systems for the location-specific conditions in Africa. Exposure to the media has significant effects on Africans and not only causes the development of unsustainable attitudes and habits but also causes acculturation stresses.

Agriculture, livestock production, and other driving forces

Modernization has been given detailed treatment here because it has an all-pervading influence on all human sectoral development activities, attitudes, value systems, and way of life. The other driving forces are only briefly addressed because they are covered in greater detail elsewhere in this volume. A summary of the environmental impacts of these driving forces is presented in table 7.3. Reference to this indicates that population is a major driving force because its rapid growth exerts considerable pressure on resources, renders sustainable traditional farming systems outmoded and unsustainable, and contributes to the adverse effects of urbanization, scarcity-triggered deforestation, fuelwood management, etc.

At the same time, such forces as commercialization of agricultural production, related market forces, and, more recently, measures necessitated by structural adjustment (SAP) often also cause exploitative damage to the environment and the resource base.

Levels of environmental effects of human activities and sustainability concerns

The environmental impacts of development activities occur at the local, national, regional, and global levels. Concern about them also

Table 7.3 **Major driving forces and some of their main environmental impacts**

Driving forces	Some of the main environmental impacts
1. Agriculture, livestock production, fishing and hunting	• Under high population pressure and intensification of farming, traditional farming systems become outmoded, causing land degradation including erosion. • Increasing livestock numbers beyond carrying capacity also cause land degradation. • Cash cropping can result in excessive deforestation, loss of biodiversity, and environmental pollution. • Mechanical clearing and excessive tillage cause land degradation and erosion. • Land degradation causes expansion of farming and grazing often into more marginal areas, resulting in more deforestation and land degradation. • Deforestation and damage to vegetation cover in farming and grazing, in addition to unregulated fishing and hunting, result in rapid loss of biodiversity. • Burning of vegetation in farming and pasture management produces greenhouse gases, which pollute the air, smoke, and suspended particulate matter. • Ruminants produce methane, which pollutes the atmosphere. • Intensification of farming without adequate fertilizer/manure application causes land degradation, while excessive use of fertilizers and pesticides also causes environmental pollution. • Soil erosion and excessive runoff cause siltation of streams and rivers, with adverse effects on aquatic resources.
2. Population growth	• Rapid growth intensifies pressures on resources, resulting in excessive deforestation and environmental degradation because sustainable traditional farming systems cannot cope. • Population growth drastically reduces available land per capita, resulting in removal of all natural vegetation and loss of biodiversity of plants, animals, and micro-organisms. This either eliminates national parks and reserves or causes sharp declines in areas available. • High population pressure on forestry and fishery resources also causes serious loss of biodiversity. • Population concentration generates enormous amounts of waste, which pollutes the environment, while concentrations of livestock also degrade the environment.

Table 7.3 **(cont.)**

Driving forces	Some of the main environmental impacts
3. Industrialization	• Some industrial technologies and processes cause atmospheric pollution, with greenhouse gases, acid rain, and loading of the air with suspended particulate matter. • Undegraded plastic products produced by industry constitute a major environmental hazard. • Industry produces enormous quantities of solid and liquid waste in addition to toxic chemicals, which pollute the environment. Some of these hazardous wastes in developed countries are transported to Africa. • Industrial accidents (such as the one that occurred in Bhopal in India) endanger life and property in addition to destroying the environment.
4. Urbanization	• Urbanization causes climatic, hydrological, geomorphological, vegetational, and environmental quality changes. • The production of large amounts of liquid and solid waste, in addition to contaminants, causes pollution of land, water bodies, and atmosphere. • Urban transport produces greenhouse gases and smog. • Urbanization increases flooding and lowers water quality and hydrological amenities. • Urbanization increases crime rates and drug trafficking and breeds slums.
5. Fuelwood and energy management	• Over 80% of the energy in Sub-Saharan Africa comes from fuelwood and biomass. • The collection of fuelwood and charcoal to satisfy this demand results in rapid rates of deforestation, which exacerbate the environmental degradation caused by forest clearing for agriculture, pastures, ranges, and other land uses. • The making of charcoal and burning of fuelwood produce greenhouse gases and particulates that pollute the atmosphere and contribute to climate change and ozone depletion. • The building of large dams for hydroelectric power results in eutrophication. Sedimentation behind dams for irrigation increases the incidence of parasitic waterborne diseases such as bilharzia, aquatic weed problems, etc.

Table 7.3 **(cont.)**

Driving forces	Some of the main environmental impacts
6. Poverty and affluence	• The poor have limited access to resources and wreak havoc by exploiting the environment to the extent that there is rapid irreversible degradation. • The poor, who cannot purchase inputs for farming, mine the soil, thereby causing land degradation. • The poor cannot afford to provide sanitation services, with the result that land, water, and atmosphere are polluted. • Affluence causes people to destroy the environment through the excessive use of chemicals and pesticides and the maintenance of unsustainable livelihoods.
7. Other miscellaneous activities and phenomena	• Examples of miscellaneous factors that also have adverse impacts on the environment include greed, excessive consumption patterns, war and social conflicts, etc., which result in environmental degradation and damage to life and property.

occurs at all levels but the magnitude of the adverse effects of certain activities may be more seriously felt at one level than at the others. Similarly, measures to be taken in dealing with the problems caused by adverse environmental impacts may be more effective if taken at one level than at another.

Local impacts

Certain effects of human or development activities may be highly localized. For example, if a whole tree falls in a tropical forest it knocks down or carries with it broken branches of surrounding vegetation or lianas and may smash and kill several small seedlings, herbs, and shrubs that are in its way. Within the damaged area, called the *chablise*, some light is allowed into the canopy. Within a short time most of the non-woody and succulent material decomposes and releases nutrients to the soil, from where they are recycled in a more or less closed cycle. Within a few years the *chablise* is covered by vegetation and there is no movement of materials outside the ecosystem. Similarly, a small clearing in the forest for shifting cultivation may have only a limited localized effect and even the gases produced in the slash and burn clearing do not travel very far away since the volume of the gases produced may be very small.

National and regional impacts

Most environmental effects that might attract attention or have impacts at the national level start in a small way locally and then gather momentum to become important at both national and international levels. For example, many river basins cut across several countries. According to UNEP (1992), the proportion of river basins in Africa that are international, out of a total of 56 river basins, is 26 per cent, compared with 22 per cent in Europe, 19 per cent in Asia, 17 per cent in South America, and 16 per cent in North and Central America. It is obvious that in such river basins as in the Niger and the Nile, development activities and natural disasters such as floods upstream may have trans-boundary effects along the river basin. Although small isolated forest fires have only local effects in Africa, during the dry season north or south of the equator fires in hundreds of small clearings produce smoke and gases that combine to contribute a considerable amount of greenhouse gases, which in turn gather momentum to have regional impacts. When they join jet streams in the upper atmosphere they may have global effects. It is obvious from this example that some of the environmental impacts, whether local or regional, are related to time. For example, whereas Africa's contribution to the global load of carbon dioxide and greenhouse gases constituted less than 100 million tonnes in 1900, by 1980 the CO_2 released by burning fuelwood and by deforestation, which minimizes the sink capacity for CO_2, amounted to about 700 million tonnes per year (see fig. 7.3).

The activities and impacts of tropical deforestation also occur at different levels. In fact, Wood (1990) observes that "at the local level deforestation primarily affects shifting cultivators and a growing population of rural peasants" but "the same problem multiplied over thousands of locations and combined with extensive logging can exacerbate the global issue of accelerated build-up of carbon dioxide." Wood (1990) likens the environmental politics of deforestation, consisting of four expanding layers of eco-political interaction at local, national, multilateral, and global levels, to the four sides of an upside-down pyramid (fig. 7.4). Each of the sides of this "upside-down pyramid" – number of actors; number of political jurisdictions; complexity of ecological cause and effect relationships; and institutional obstacles to enforcement – represents an attribute of the deforestation problem that is compounded as it moves up the hierarchy. Thus deforestation not only becomes more complex ecologi-

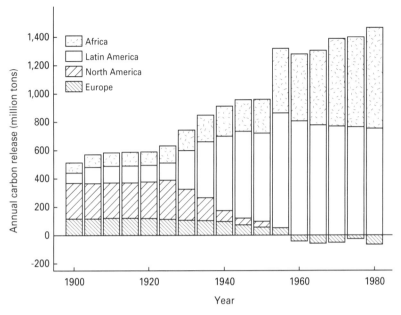

Fig. 7.3 **Annual carbon release for the biomass system of the world's four major regions, 1900–1980 (Note: Whereas Africa's CO$_2$ emissions from petroleum fuels in the 1980s were low – 0.25 tons/capita, equivalent to 8% of the figure for the United Kingdom – its CO$_2$ emissions due to deforestation were about 700 million tons, or 1.5 tons/capita, at a time when such emissions were negligible or negative for European countries. Source: G. Leach, Agroforestry and the way out for Africa, in M. Suliman, ed.,** *The Greenhouse Effect and Its Impact on Africa,* **London: Institute for African Alternatives, 1990)**

cally as it moves from the local level to the global but also becomes more intransigent politically.

A peculiar kind of trans-boundary environmental impact involves locally generated toxic waste in developed countries, which is transported across the seas to be deposited at minimum cost in some developing countries. This made it a global problem and the United Nations had to step in and formulate a convention to deal with such wastes.

Problem of transmission of cultural behaviour and standards at the international or global level

An aspect of modernization that could have very adverse effects on sustainability is the globalization of culture and economy that has

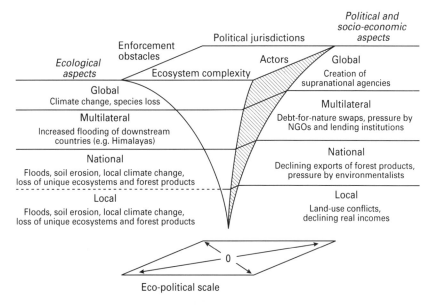

Fig. 7.4 **Hierarchy of eco-political interactions in tropical deforestation (Source: Wood 1990)**

exposed Africans and some indigenous peoples to advertisements via global television, video, radio, newspapers, and other media. Not only is it possible to advertise by television and radio, but fashion shows and behaviour patterns of people in Europe and America are projected to Africans in their own bedrooms, thereby making them interested in the material luxury consumption propensities of the North.

Not only fashion but also criminal acts and lifestyles that are by no means sustainable are being "marketed" through the media. There is no doubt that the lack of strong cultural discipline in Africa as compared with Asia is one of the reasons that the level of savings in Africa is much lower than that in Asia. Although we have considered environmental impacts that start locally and gather momentum at the regional level to become global and affect millions of people physically, there is also a situation where people's attitudes and cultures are altered at the global level, and whereas certain global conventions have been passed to combat the former situation, it is not so easy to inculcate sustainable lifestyles or attitudes in the face of market forces and the globalization of culture that have become or are fast becoming deeply entrenched.

Constraints on sustainable development in Sub-Saharan Africa

Constraints on sustainable development in Sub-Saharan Africa are legion. Some are general and others are sectoral or specific. Some are local while others are national or regional. It must also be admitted that, prior to the adoption of the current sustainable development paradigm, Sub-Saharan Africa lagged behind other regions in food security, standard of living, and various aspects of development. Consequently, the adoption of a new development paradigm that places more emphasis on environmental resource conservation does not eliminate the existing constraints on development. Rather it requires more interdisciplinary or systems approaches, greater sensitivity to environment in policies, strategies, planning, and execution of development programmes, and stringency in defining the characteristics and nature of technologies that can be used to ensure the maintenance of environmental quality and the conservation of natural capital stock, which is imperative for sustainable development.

General constraints

The general constraints on sustainable development are political, socio-economic, and technological in nature.

Political constraints

THE COLONIAL LEGACY. At the time when explorers established contact with Africa and pushed further inland and developed a lucrative trade in spices, ivory, and forest products in exchange for alcohol and various manufactured goods, the prevailing development ideology in Europe was based on the Old Testament idea expressed in Genesis that God gave man "dominion over the fish of the sea, over the fowl of the air, and over every living thing that moveth upon the earth." Consequently, it was generally believed that humans had the right to exploit the natural resources of Africa and other parts of the world as desired. No serious effort was made to conserve natural resources until late in the eighteenth century when it was observed that with the extinction of the dodo in Mauritius it became necessary for measures to be taken to ensure the survival of diverse species of organisms through the establishment of reserves. The establishment of colonial spheres of influence and the arrival of Christianity, which in some areas preceded colonial administrations, dealt a death blow to the appreciation of even ecologically sound sustainable traditional or indigenous resource management strategies, practices, systems, attitudes, and behaviour patterns in African culture. This was most pronounced where these practices were applied as taboos associated with traditional African religion. It is not surprising, therefore, that taboos dealing with hunting and fishing were abolished outright and in agriculture such practices as intercropping were regarded as primitive. With colonialism came changes in the African perspective of looking at things, Westernization, and the propensity for consumption patterns of a more materialistic kind that are satisfied only with imports of food and manufactured goods, leading to increasing dependence on the developed countries.

POLITICAL INSTABILITY. No sustainable development can be achieved in Sub-Saharan Africa with the kind of endemic political instability that has been the order of the day since independence in the 1960s. The instability is not unrelated to the artificial boundaries cutting across ethnic groups or groupings of incompatible people in the same country. Although inter-tribal wars were in existence before colonial administrations were established, there are indications that Europeans actually encouraged inter-tribal conflicts that supplied captives or prisoners to be sold in the slave trade. Moreover, the divide-and-rule policies prior to independence often led to incompatibilities and unequal development among different areas or peoples lumped together in the same country. Coups and frequent changes in government have resulted in inconsistencies in policies and development programmes and a lack of continuity in development activities, all of which are incompatible with sustainable development. Figure 7.5 shows the extent of political instability in African countries, as indicated by the numbers of military regimes, by civil strife, and by stages in the democratization process.

CORRUPTION AND DEFICIENCIES IN GOVERNANCE. It has been indicated earlier that one aspect of modernization is the collusion between the élite or politicians in power in African countries with businessmen or agents of the former colonial powers and, in fact, other countries to ensure that certain development activities are executed in ways that are of mutual benefit to the individuals or businesses involved, often to the detriment of the common people in the African countries concerned. It is also well known that, while some African countries are unable to allocate funds to vital development projects, some of

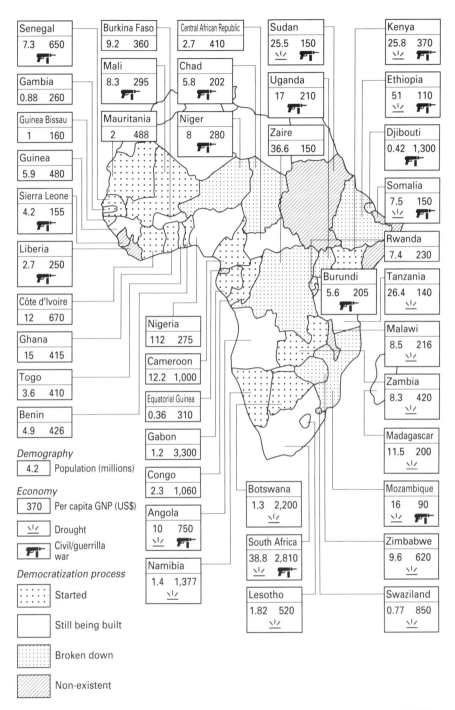

Senegal	Burkina Faso	Central African Republic	Sudan	Kenya

Fig. 7.5 **Stage of democratization, civil stability, and economic status of African countries, October 1992 (Source: *L'Express*, Paris, 8 October 1992)**

the politicians are busy stashing millions of dollars of ill-gotten money in Swiss banks or in investments in property in foreign countries. Related problems are a lack of accountability, waste, and a lack of grass-roots democratic institutions and participation in decision-making. In the past, more emphasis was given to top–down approaches to extension work and development programme execution. It is only recently that emphasis is being given to bottom–up participatory approaches.

DEFICIENCIES IN PLANNING. Sustainable development necessitates the adoption of holistic or systems approaches, which call for multidisciplinary interaction involving all relevant disciplines and ministries simultaneously working together in the planning process in an integrated manner. In sustainable development, environmental concerns are best integrated into the programme at the planning stage, when measures are taken to ensure the compatibility of all sectoral plans and the integration of environmental and developmental concerns at all stages. This necessitates special training and orientation of all concerned.

INAPPROPRIATE POLICIES AND STRATEGIES. Concern about the environment must be embodied in development policies and strategies. In other words, policies must be formulated in relation to the objectives to be achieved, and the strategies to be adopted must aim at a range of alternative strategy options that ensure conservation of resources and as far as possible enhancement of the quality of the resource base.

DEFICIENCIES IN LEGAL AND LEGISLATIVE SUPPORT OF DEVELOPMENT PROGRAMMES. There is need for economic incentives and legal and legislative instruments as a back-up for development projects in which maintenance of environmental quality and the conservation of resources are given high priority. Without such instruments, it would be difficult to ensure the achievement of resource conservation and environmental quality and to take the necessary measures to enforce compliance. In developing such legal and legislative instruments, it would be necessary to develop appropriate guidelines based on ecological and economic principles.

LACK OF EFFECTIVE REGIONAL INTEGRATION AND COLLABORATION IN DEVELOPMENT. Since the 1960s when many African countries became

154

independent, all regional R&D organizations such as the CCTA (Commission for Technical Cooperation in Africa), EAFFRO (East African Freshwater Fisheries Research Organization), and related inter-territorial research organizations have broken down. Yet, with the small size of many countries, the limited resources available, the potentialities for sharing information, and experience and participation in R&D activities of mutual interest, there is no reason why African countries should be more strongly linked to their former colonial masters than to their African neighbours. This is the case not only in trade but sometimes also in the sharing and exchange of information on natural resources management and utilization. Even political and economic organizations such as OAU (Organization of African Unity), ECA (Economic Commission for Africa), and ECOWAS (Economic Community of West African States) rarely function as well as intended.

Socio-economic constraints
Socio-economic constraints on sustainable development include deficiencies in education and training, the lack of an effective campaign of public enlightenment and orientation, poverty, unfavourable economic conditions, and limitations in financial support.

Doubts continue to be expressed about the relevance of African education at all levels to the requirements of human resource and institutional capacity-building for innovative R&D in African countries. Sustainable development calls for environmental education at all levels and the development of appropriate curricula in science and technology embodying various aspects of natural resources conservation and management. The recommended ratio of 60:40 of students in science and technology to arts and humanities, respectively, in African schools and universities is rarely achieved at all levels in any African country. There are also deficiencies in the education of women, with the number of women at all levels far below the number of men, especially in the sciences.

With the change in development paradigm, there is a need for a public enlightenment campaign aimed at creating better awareness about sustainable development, what it is, what it entails, and the role of the masses in ushering it in sooner rather than later in Africa. Special training courses need to be developed in environmental monitoring, resources inventorying, and environmental impact assessment.

The prevailing poverty and adverse economic conditions in African

155

countries owing to heavy debt burdens, unfavourable economic effects of structural adjustment, and two decades of continuing decline in commodity prices have left African countries with limited funds to maintain adequate levels of relevant R&D activities, to purchase, repair, and replace scientific equipment, as well as to acquire journals and literature in relevant scientific disciplines.

Technological constraints
Development involves the application of science and appropriate technologies to the conservation, management, processing, and rational utilization of natural resources. Since most African countries have neither the critical mass of trained personnel in many fields and at different levels, nor the institutional capacity for the generation and adaptation of technologies in order to make them appropriate for executing development programmes, self-reliance and success in development have eluded them. In the past, many development projects have been either disappointing or total failures owing to attempts at horizontal transfer of technologies and use of inappropriate technologies in location-specific situations. Moreover, because sustainability was not an explicit objective of development projects, no serious effort was made to choose and develop technologies that ensure economic viability, ecological soundness, and cultural acceptability.

Specific or sectoral constraints

In addition to the above general constraints on sustainable development, there are sectoral constraints on agriculture, including forestry and fisheries, industrial development, and mining.

Constraints on agriculture
The major constraints on sustainable agricultural production in tropical Africa are physico-chemical, biological, and socio-economic in nature. They are listed in table 7.4.

Constraints on industrial development
Constraints here are of three types, namely: environmental and natural resource constraints, technical and technological constraints, and socio-economic constraints.

The environmental and natural resource constraints include: high levels of environmental pollution and an inability or lack of means

Table 7.4 **Constraints on agricultural production in tropical Africa**

Physical constraints
Unfavourable *climatic* conditions include:
- rainfall that is unreliable in onset, duration, and intensity
- unpredictable periods of drought, floods, and environmental stresses
- reduced effective rainfall on sandy soils and steep slopes
- high soil temperature for some crops and biological processes (N-fixation)
- high rates of decomposition and low level of organic matter
- cloudiness and reduced photosynthetic efficiency

Most *soils* of the humid and subhumid tropics
- are intensely weathered, sandy, and low in clay
- have very low cation exchange capacity (CEC) and thus also less active colloidal complex
- have very low inherent fertility (except on hydromorphic and young volcanic soils)
- have very high acidity and sometimes high surface temperatures
- are extremely subject to multiple nutrient deficiencies and toxicities under continuous cultivation
- have very high P-fixation
- are extremely leached, and thus at high risk of erosion under prevailing rainstorms
- have serious salinity problems under poor irrigation management

Biological constraints
- unimproved crops and livestock
- low yields and low potential
- susceptibility to disease and pests
- high incidence of disease, pests, and weeds owing to environment that favours these phenomena
- drastic environmental changes, brought about by human activities that have adverse effects on ecological equilibrium

Socio-economic constraints
- small farm size, more drastically reduced by population pressure
- unfavourable land tenure systems, often resulting in fragmentation of holdings
- shortage of labour
- lack of credit and low income
- poor marketing facilities and pricing structure
- high cost and extreme scarcity of inputs
- poor extension services
- illiteracy and superstition, which sometimes hamper adoption process
- poor transportation
- inappropriateness of inputs
- lack of package approach to technology, development, and use

Source: Okigbo (1982).

for enforcing safety standards; dependence on imports for a substantial proportion of raw materials and equipment needed in industries; and limited allocation of resources for the conservation of natural capital stock and environmental protection.

Technological and technical constraints include: dependence on imported equipment, which often does not meet safety standards in the originating countries; lack of adequate capabilities for the maintenance and repair of equipment; deficiencies in human resources development, experience, and training; and limited research in promoting energy efficiency and the use of alternative energy resources.

Socio-economic constraints consist of: a lack of clear-cut industrial policies and strategies for sustainable development; high priority given to heavy industries at the expense of agricultural and light industries based on available renewable natural resources; high priority given to the achievement of rapid economic growth at the expense of environmental quality; limitations in industrial managerial experience; inability to monitor, control, and enforce environmental safety standards, and deficiencies in legal and economic instruments to support these; use of subsidies to promote practices that are environmentally degrading; the existence of poverty among large segments of the population, with markedly unequal distributions of wealth; and deficiencies in legal provisions for the protection of workers and for ensuring a safe and healthy work environment.

Constraints on mineral industry development

Constraints on sustainable development in the mining industry, as in industry, consist of environmental and resource constraints, technological and technical constraints, and socio-economic constraints.

Environmental and natural resource constraints consist of: a lack of adequate environmental safeguards to minimize environmental damage and degradation, especially in several sectoral development activities including road construction and open-cast mining; the fact that mining activities and practices sometimes cause gullies and considerable damage to the landscape and surrounding useful land; deficiencies in laws and regulations concerning the safety and protection of workers; considerable amounts of sediments and waste released into rivers and streams where they pollute the environment; limited provision for environmental rehabilitation of mined sites.

Technical and technological constraints may arise because mining, except for semi-precious stones, is often under the monopolistic control of multinational companies that conduct very little research and training in the host countries. The main constraints include: a lack of improved technologies for small-scale mining; limited endogenous capabilities for exploration and mining R&D activities; the monopolization by multinationals of information on reserves and characteristics of mineral resources; limited research on the rehabilitation and afforestation of mined sites; limited capabilities for attaining a reasonable level of minerals-based manufacturing to ensure the realization of the benefits of the value-added.

Socio-economic constraints include: deficiencies in policies that give multinationals control of relevant information on mineral resources; limited capabilities in mineral resource economics and the ecological economics of mineral resources; deficiencies in legal instruments; deficiencies in policy research; a lack of provision for the effective monitoring of environmental impact and the enforcement of regulations; frequent fluctuations in commodity market prices; and the social problems of female-headed households resulting from the migration of men to mines in southern Africa.

Recommendations

Sustainable development in Africa can be achieved only where appropriate policies, strategies, and priorities in research and development are carefully chosen and adhered to with the continuous commitment and allocation of resources and the creation of an enabling environment by governments. The elements of necessary ingredients for such sustainable development are briefly summarized below.

The adoption of a holistic or systems approach in planning, policies, and R&D

Sustainable development applies to the conservation, management, and rational utilization of natural resources in such a way as to maintain the integrity of each ecosystem, support all life, ensure no loss in biodiversity, and prevent environmental degradation. This calls for compatibility in sectoral development programmes in such a way that activities in any one sector do not have adverse environmental impacts, which would make it difficult to achieve the desired sustainable management of resources in any other sector now and in the future. For this to be successful it must involve the interaction of relevant disciplines in the planning and policy formulation stages, and in all stages of research and development (R&D) activities at local, national, regional, and global levels.

Conservation and development

There is need in all countries to adopt an environmental perspective in the management of natural resources in development programmes so as to ensure that conservation goes hand in hand with development in order to enhance sustainability. Conservation is defined as "the rational use of the earth's resources to achieve the highest quality of living for mankind" (UNESCO/FAO 1968), with the additional qualification that the quality of life also should apply to humans and to other organisms since this is the way to ensure conservation of biodiversity. When environmental quality is good for the survival of humans and other organisms then it is obvious that the environment is being given the due consideration it deserves in development if the earth is to function largely as a self-regulating planet.

Integration

Sustainable development calls for the adoption of a holistic and integrated approach in natural resource management. Opportunities for this exist in the following situations:

Land use
The adoption of an integrated land-use plan in which integrated watersheds as units for planning and development are a component entails the development of a master plan that provides for all the competing multiple land-use options, ranging from land for wildlife reserves and forest plantations to land for mining and human settlement, at least at national and regional levels.

Traditional and modern systems and technology
The integration of traditional, modern, and emerging resource management systems and technologies is one way of ensuring the relevance of technologies to the farmer's needs and circumstances, thereby facilitating rapid and widespread adoption. It involves the integration of desirable compatible elements of the different technologies in order to achieve sustainability. This approach also ensures

160

that systems of production and their component technologies are ecologically sound, economically viable, and culturally acceptable.

Cropping systems and animal production systems
The integration of production systems involving, for example, the integration of arable (field) crop production with agro-forestry species in hedgerows and sometimes also with livestock into agrisilvo-pastoral systems can achieve a wider spectrum of objectives than can any of the systems alone.

Pest and disease management systems
Reliance on environment-polluting pesticides and chemical control in pest management can be minimized by mixing different strategies that interact synergistically to produce the desired effects. The combination of compatible chemical, biological, physical, and/or cultural methods in the control of pests and diseases aims to reduce reliance on any one method that, when used alone, may have adverse environmental effects – e.g. using a resistant variety and a few sprays of dilute chemical pesticide, instead of high concentrations and several sprays of more pesticides, which causes environmental pollution.

Species of crops and/or animals
Growing different species of crops or using different species of animals can ensure higher and more stable yields over time than growing only one commodity.

Alternative energy systems

It is necessary to develop alternative energy systems because reliance on fuelwood as the main energy source will not only lead to depletion of fuelwood resources and deforestation but also cause erosion and desertification.

Monitoring of resources and environment

For sustainable development to succeed, there must be monitoring of the status of various natural resources and analyses of the data in order to predict the likely consequences of environmental change in the future. Related to this is the inventorying of natural resources so as to determine changes in biodiversity causes and remedial measures.

Regulatory and guidance measures

Monitoring provides the basis for legislation and enforcement measures for protecting the environment. The results can also be used to guide actions to be taken or to enforce related laws and regulations.

Education, training, and orientation priorities

The existing educational curriculum needs to be modified so as to facilitate the provision of environmental education at different levels and the provision of training in environmental monitoring and assessment, in addition to orientation of the public so as to enhance popular participation in sustainable development projects. Any effort aimed at combating the development of inappropriate attitudes or standards as a result of the influence of the media can best be achieved through the educational system, formally or informally.

Other strategies

The above strategies are by no means exhaustive. It would be necessary to take appropriate measures to see that there are in place policies, strategies, technologies, systems, and other actions that are needed for combating or eliminating any of the constraints identified above.

References

Benneh, G. 1993. Population, environment and sustainable development in Africa. Paper presented at the General Conference and 25th Anniversary Celebration of the AAU, University of Ghana, Legon, 13–18 January.

Chapman, J. D. 1969. Interactions between man and his resources. In: Committee on Resources and Man, NAS-NRC, *Resources and Man: A Study and Recommendations*. San Francisco: W. H. Freeman, pp. 31–42.

Constanza, R. 1991. The ecological economics of sustainability: Investing in natural capital. In: R. Goodland, H. Daly, S. el Serafy, and B. von Droste (eds.), *Environmentally Sustainable Economic Development: Building on Brundtland*. Paris: UNESCO, pp. 83–92.

Daly, H. E. 1991. From empty world to full world economics: Recognising an historical turning point in economic development. In: R. Goodland, H. Daly, S. el Serafy, and B. von Droste (eds.), *Environmentally Sustainable Economic Development: Building on Brundtland*. Paris: UNESCO, pp. 29–40.

Droste, B. von and P. Dogsé. 1991. Sustainable development: The role of investment.

In: R. Goodland, H. Daly, S. el Serafy, and B. von Droste (eds.), *Environmentally Sustainable Economic Development: Building on Brundtland*. Paris: UNESCO, pp. 71–82.

Dube, S. C. 1988. *Modernization and Development – The Search for Alternative Paradigms.* Tokyo: UNU, and London: Zed Books.

Goodland, R. 1991. The case that the world has reached limits: More precisely that current throughput growth in global economy cannot be sustained. In: R. Goodland, H. Daly, S. el Serafy, and B. von Droste (eds.), *Environmentally Sustainable Economic Development: Building on Brundtland*. Paris: UNESCO, pp. 15–28.

Goodland, R., H. Daly, S. el Serafy, and B. von Droste (eds.) 1991. *Environmentally Sustainable Economic Development: Building on Brundtland*. Paris: UNESCO.

Holdgren, J. P., G. C. Daily, and P. R. Ehrlich. 1995. The meaning of sustainability: Bio-geophysical aspects. In: M. Munasinghe and W. Shearer (eds.), *Defining and Measuring Sustainability: The Biophysical Foundations.* Tokyo: United Nations University Press, and Washington D.C.: World Bank.

Hoogvelt, A. M. M. 1982. *The Third World in Global Development.* London: Macmillan Education.

IUCN/UNEP/WWF. 1991. *Caring for the Earth: A Strategy for Sustainable Living.* Gland, Switzerland: IUCN/UNEP/WWF.

Jacobs, M. 1988. *The Tropical Rain Forest: A First Encounter*, edited by R. Kruk et al. Berlin: Springer-Verlag.

MECCA (Morogoro Environmental Charter Consulting Agency). 1992. *Environment and Development.* Vienna: MECCA.

Okigbo, B. N. 1982. Agriculture and food production in tropical Africa. In: *The Development Effectiveness of Food Aid in Africa.* New York: Agricultural Development Council, pp. 11–68.

Ominde, S. H. 1977. The integration of environmental and development planning for ecological crisis areas in Africa. In: K. W. Deutsch (ed.), *Eco-social Systems and Eco-politics.* Paris: UNESCO, pp. 115–130.

Pearce, E. et al. 1990. *Sustainable Development: Economics and Environment in the Third World.* London: Earthscan Publications.

Pomeroy, D. and M. W. Service. 1986. *Tropical Ecology.* Harlow, England: Longman.

Sachs, I. 1973. Eco-development: A contribution to the definition of development styles for Latin America. United Nations Symposium on Population Resources and Environment, Stockholm, 26 September – 5 October (E/CO NF 60/SYM – 111/26, 18 September 1973).

——— 1992. Transition strategies for the 21st century. *Nature and Resources* 28(1): 4–17.

Serafy, S. el. 1991. Sustainability, income measurement and growth. In: R. Goodland, H. Daly, S. el Serafy, and B. von Droste (eds.), *Environmentally Sustainable Economic Development: Building on Brundtland*. Paris: UNESCO, pp. 59–70.

Tinbergen, J. and R. Hueting. 1991. GNP and market prices: Wrong signals for sustainable economic success that mask environmental destruction. In: R. Goodland, H. Daly, S. el Serafy, and B. von Droste (eds.), *Environmentally Sustainable Economic Development: Building on Brundtland*. Paris: UNESCO, pp. 51–58.

Todaro, M. P. 1986. *Economic Development in the Third World.* New York: Longman.

UNEP (United Nations Environment Programme). 1992. *Saving Our Planet: Challenges and Hopes. The State of the Environment (1972–1992).* Nairobi: UNEP.

UNESCO/FAO. 1968. *Conservation and Rational Use of the Environment.* Report to the Economic and Social Council of the United Nations (ECOSOC), 44th Session, Doc. E/4458.

WCED (World Commission on Environment and Development). 1987. *Our Common Future.* Oxford: Oxford University Press.

Wood, W. B. 1990. Tropical forest – deforestation. *Global Environmental Change,* December: 23–41.

8

Drought, desertification, and water management in Sub-Saharan Africa

Edouard G. Bonkoungou

Introduction

For Sub-Saharan Africa as a whole, consisting of 45 countries, gross national product per person in constant dollars fell by 20 per cent between 1977 and 1986. May (1988) reports that the average person in many of these countries is now poorer than at the time of independence about 30 years ago. Whereas Latin America and Asia have become almost self-sufficient in cereals, Africa has grown more dependent on imports and food aid. Total food production has, in fact, increased but not enough to keep pace with population growth. During the past 30 years agricultural production in Sub-Saharan Africa has risen by 2 per cent a year, while population is growing at the rate of about 3.2 per cent a year, faster than any other region has ever experienced (World Bank 1989).

The constraints on development in Sub-Saharan Africa are many and varied, including the following: a difficult climate with frequent episodes of severe drought in the semi-arid lands; fragile soils prone to erosion and nutrient depletion; a very fast rate of population growth; a heavy external debt burden. The world economy has not favoured Africa. Declines in Africa's commodity export prices and increases in the import prices of manufactured goods and oil have deteriorated the terms of trade and worsened Africa's external debt burden. Although this is true of all third world economies, the impasse in Sub-Saharan Africa is most striking.

Yet, as Harrison (1987) points out, the economic crisis is dwarfed by the continent's deepening environmental crisis. In the semi-arid regions, for example, recurrent droughts and population pressure have led to destruction of vegetation resulting in desertification, erosion, and depletion of soil fertility. Although the outlook is rather gloomy, there are individual projects that have succeeded against a background of general failure. If we could read the lessons of their successes, we might be able to piece together the formula, as Harrison (1987) puts it, and find some way of breaking through the development impasse.

This paper highlights some of the major environmental constraints in Sub-Saharan Africa and points to their implications for sustainable development strategies in the region, with a focus on semi-arid lands.

Droughts in Sub-Saharan Africa and their implications for planning and development

Recurrent droughts are a salient feature of the semi-arid lands of Sub-Saharan Africa, especially the Sahel. Rainfall fluctuates widely in time and space in a way that has not yet been understood and therefore cannot be easily forecast. The implication of this extreme variability for planning and development is that the concept of "mean" or "average" rainfall has little value.

Some of the main characteristics of the drought-prone climate of the region are presented below.

Rainfall fluctuation in time

The recent drought in the Sahel is not unique in the history of the region. Droughts of this magnitude and extent have occurred in the past. Nicholson (1982), using records of harvest quality, lake levels and river flow, rainfall data, and climatic description, reconstructed past episodes of droughts and good rainfall (see figs. 8.1 and 8.2).

For example, a wet episode lasted from about 1870 to 1895. Harvests were consistently good in the semi-arid regions of Namibia, southern Angola, and South Africa. North of the equator, the Niger Bend region near Timbuktoo, Mali, in the Sahel yielded abundant

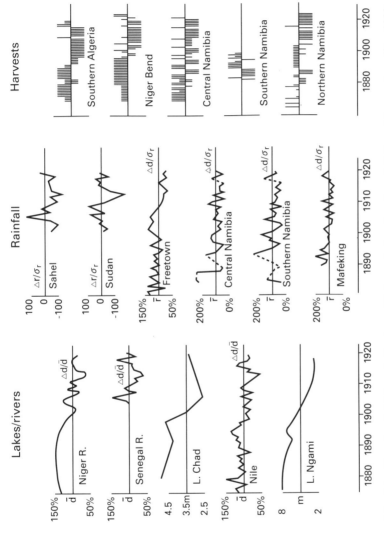

Fig. 8.1 Trends of African indicators of lake and river levels, rainfall, and harvest quality, 1880–1920 (Source: Nicholson 1982)

167

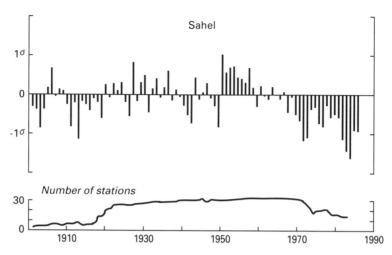

Fig. 8.2 **Annual rainfall fluctuations in the Sahel, 1900–1982 (Source: Sircoulon 1992)**

crops and the region became the "bread basket" of West Africa. Today, annual rainfall in the area is only about 200 mm, below the rain-fed agriculture boundary.

About 1895, a major change towards more arid conditions occurred and the "desiccation" culminated in severe drought around 1913–1914.

In more recent decades, rainfall was more abundant in the 1950s, with records as high as 30 to 60 per cent above "normal." But this episode ended abruptly towards the end of the 1960s, giving way to the extreme drought of the early 1970s when rainfall went down 15 to 35 per cent below normal in the Sahel. In some areas, rainfall during the 1968–1973 period was 50 per cent lower than during the 1950s.

Fluctuations are often abrupt and extreme, with droughts recurring at irregular intervals. The change from wetter conditions to persistent drought cannot as yet be forecast. Thus the implication for planning and development is that the carrying capacity of the land should be that of the driest years, not the "average" year.

Clustering and persistence of abnormal years

An unusual feature of rainfall fluctuations in the region is their extreme persistence for one to two decades or more.

168

In most humid areas, dry and wet years are generally randomly interspersed. In some arid regions, however, abnormal years tend to cluster together. In the Sahel, this characteristic is extreme: wet or dry conditions may persist for one or two decades. As an example, the period 1960–1980 was rather consistently dry. Droughts lasting one or two decades are also evident in the historical records mentioned earlier.

A study by the International Crops Research Institute for the Semi-Arid Tropics (ICRISAT 1988) illustrates this feature. Change in rainfall variability in semi-arid lands in India and the Sahel was compared by analysing long-term climatic records for Niamey in Niger and Hyderabad in India. The variability in annual rainfall at the two locations is shown in figure 8.3. In 87 years (1901–1987) at Hyderabad, the time-series showed no significant trend, and the rainfall in a given year is not correlated with that of the preceding or the following years. At Niamey in the Sahel, variability of annual rainfall from 1905 to 1987 revealed a different pattern. Compared with Hyderabad, Niamey has longer sequences of consecutive "dry" years with below-average rainfall, and much fewer "wet" years. Droughts are longer in the Sahelian zone.

The clustering of abnormal ("wet" or "dry") years seems to be unique to the Sahel. Other semi-arid lands in Africa do not exhibit this characteristic. Comparison of climatic data between the Kalahari region in southern Africa and the Sahel showed that, although drier (and wetter) periods tend to occur synchronously in both areas, the decadal persistence observed in the Sahel is not a distinct feature of rainfall fluctuation in the semi-arid lands of southern Africa; dry episodes coincide in the two regions but the years of most intense drought do not (Nicholson 1982). Although the recurrence of drought has been shown to be cyclic in some semi-arid regions, this has not been clearly established for the West African Sahel.

Spatial variability

High spatial variability is a well-known characteristic of Sahelian rainfall (figs. 8.4 and 8.5). The reason for this spotty distribution is the convective nature of the rains, i.e. the showery type, as shown in figure 8.6; the falling of rain from a cloud generally signals the onset of dissipation of the cloud, which may grow again and produce intense rainfall further away.

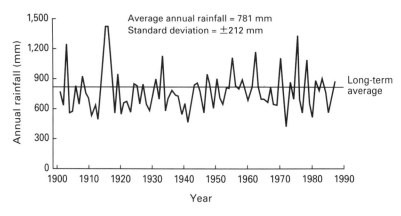

Annual rainfall at Hyderabad, India, 1901–1987

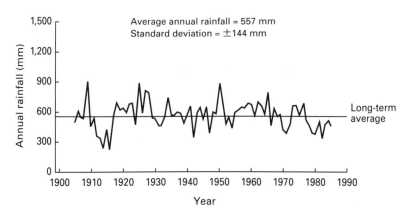

Annual rainfall at Niamey, Niger, 1905–1987

Fig. 8.3 Variability in annual rainfall in Niamey, Niger, and Hyderabad, India (Source: ICRISAT 1988)

Implications for planning and development

The implication of this extreme spottiness for regional planning is frightening. Two villages only 1 km apart can experience entirely different rainfall regimes at one time or another during the season, even during a year when total rainfall is comparable in both locations. For a given rainstorm, one village may be drenched while its neighbour remains dry. If this happens at a crucial time for crop

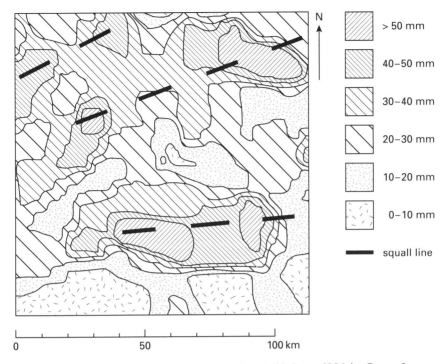

Fig. 8.4 **Spatial variability of rainfall on 12 and 13 June 1986 in Ouagadougou, Burkina Faso (Source: Rochette 1989)**

development – e.g. when seedlings are establishing themselves or grain is maturing – this can mean a good harvest for one village and total crop failure for its neighbour.

Other features of the Sahelian climate described earlier pose equally serious constraints for planning. Persistent years of above-average rainfall can create a false sense of the true climatic conditions and mislead farmers and pastoralists to extend their activities into the marginal desert fringe beyond the true agronomic dry boundary. They may then become trapped in this fragile environment during a drier period; the environmental damage that then occurs is intensified. This may have contributed to the disaster accompanying the droughts of the 1970s, which succeeded a very "wet" period in the 1950s.

As Nicholson (1982) summed it up, the characteristics of the Sahelian climate that should be kept in mind include the low and highly variable rainfall, the prevalence of dry years, the extreme magnitude of the variability, the rapidity with which new persistent conditions can be established, and the spottiness of rainfall even in

171

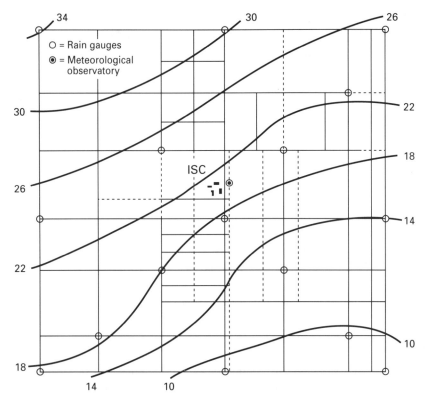

Fig. 8.5 **Spatial variability of rainfall shown as isoheyets measured on a 400 m grid over 500 ha at the research station of the ICRISAT Sahelian Centre, Niger, 22 July 1986 (Source: ICRISAT 1988)**

"normal" years. The "persistence" feature of the Sahelian climate is a clear message to planners that technologies and strategies that have produced good results in other semi-arid regions of the world may not be expected necessarily to work in the Sahel.

The task ahead is immense. A complete understanding of the climatic peculiarities of the semi-arid lands of Sub-Saharan Africa and the tuning of development planning to these characteristics deserve sustained efforts. On-going programmes/projects and recent initiatives in this direction include those by the Regional Agrometeorological-Hydrological Centre, the Sahelian Centre of ICRISAT, the African Centre of Meteorological Applications for Development, the Sahara and Sahel Observatory, and the International Geosphere-Biosphere Programme in the region. This development is encouraging, but a breakthrough is still awaited.

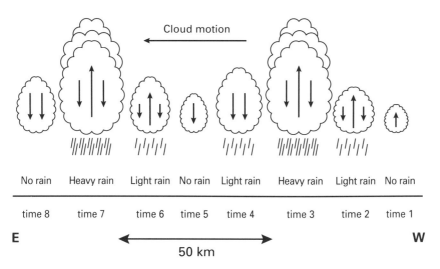

Fig. 8.6 **Continual growth and decay of a typical convective cloud as it moves downstream with the wind (Source: Nicholson 1982)**

Desertification

The problem

Pressures from human and livestock populations coupled with the effect of recurrent drought have led to serious degradation of vegetation cover, erosion, and depletion of soil fertility on a large scale in many parts of Sub-Saharan Africa. Desertification, as this tragic land degradation is referred to, threatens the drylands of Sub-Saharan Africa in a larger proportion than any other region in the world. Once the vegetation cover is removed, the fragile soils are exposed to winds and battering rains. Erosion is inevitable. Early storms are often accompanied by strong winds. Wind speeds exceeding 100 km/hour have been recorded at ICRISAT Sahelian Centre in Niger. Blowing sand subjects seedlings to abrasion and often results in their being completely covered by sand, causing serious problems in crop establishment (Kalij and Hoogmoed 1993). In many areas this takes dramatic forms: shifting sand dunes that swamp villages and fields, formation of deep gullies, crusts that seal the soil surface and markedly increase runoff.

Desertification has been described as self-propagating (Harrison 1987): as expanding areas become useless for crops or livestock, the pressure on the islands of remaining fertility increases. Farming is

173

taken beyond the limits of sustainable rain-fed agriculture. Whole families, sometimes whole villages, migrate to better-watered areas. There they begin the process of deforestation, overcultivation, and overgrazing anew.

Implications for development

The traditional solution

Over the centuries African pastoralists and farmers had developed efficient systems of land use compatible with their environment. For example, nomadic pastoralists traditionally moved with herds of animals to different areas of good grazing and water supply. With low stocking levels they were able to move to new areas before the reserves of any single area were depleted and the soil laid bare.

The parkland system of cropping under tree cover, a widely practised farming system in the Sahel, is probably the most elaborate traditional agro-forestry practice known today in any of the semi-arid zones of the world. In most instances, however, farmers have relied on natural processes for the regeneration of the woody component.

The current level of population pressure, however, precludes true nomadic grazing or passive reliance on natural regeneration to maintain adequate tree densities in the farmlands. Many of the traditional solutions are no longer viable. The severity of land degradation alerted the governments and the international community and led to the creation in 1973 of CILSS (Comité Permanent Inter-Etats de Lutte contre la Sécheresse dans le Sahel). Major efforts by the international community to combat desertification include the 1977 UN Conference on Desertification in Nairobi, Kenya, the creation of the United Nations Sudano-Sahelian Office, and the agreement at the Rio Summit in 1992 to negotiate a convention on desertification. The agreement commits governments, relevant non-governmental organizations, and the scientific community to prepare and adopt an international convention to combat desertification in all affected areas of the world, particularly in Africa.

Technical interventions introduced so far to combat desertification have met with very limited success. Some of the reasons for this débâcle include the misunderstanding of the nature of the problem, which was initially conceived solely as the responsibility of the government departments in charge of forestry; hence, the overemphasis on planting fast-growing species in woodlots and green belts. The failure properly to diagnose people's perception of the problem and to identify the felt needs of local populations fuelled antagonistic relationships between foresters and peasants. This was because modern forestry, contrary to traditional wisdom in the region, has been considered to be separate from agriculture and livestock. Harrison (1987) noted that "foresters viewed farmers and herders as vandals, destroyers of forests to be kept out at all costs. Peasants saw foresters as policemen who excluded them from land that was traditionally theirs to control and use. Under such conditions the forests did not flourish." I have expressed similar views elsewhere (Bonkoungou 1985, 1987, and 1990) and pointed out the risk of some foresters failing to see the people for the forest.

The situation described above explains many of the failures in the fight against desertification. Yet trees and shrubs have a crucial role to play in the future of farming and pastoralism in Africa, as is becoming convincingly clear from research results of the International Centre for Research in Agroforestry (ICRAF).

The potential of agro-forestry to combat desertification and sustain agricultural production

Baumer (1987) extensively discusses the potential of agro-forestry to combat desertification. As mentioned above, research results from ICRAF indicate that agro-forestry has great potential for mitigating tropical deforestation, land depletion, and rural poverty. Trees integrated with crops or livestock meet wider needs than do woodlots. If properly spaced and managed, they serve as windbreaks and shelterbelts. They mark boundaries and strengthen terraces. They supply not only fuel, timber, stakes, and poles but also cash crops, fodder, fruits, nuts, leaves, and pods for human and livestock feed, gums, and medicines. In addition to the above products and many others, trees and shrubs also render various services in environmental protection: shade, improvement of soil fertility, etc.

As Harrison (1987) so ably advocates, agro-forestry offers by far the speediest road to reforesting Africa. Many African farmers already practise one form or another of agro-forestry but have relied mostly on natural regeneration of woody species, which is no longer reliable because of the much-shortened fallow periods. The task ahead then, as Harrison (1987) puts it, is "to convert African farmers and herders from *passive* to *active* agroforesters; from users of self-planted trees, to tree farmers."

ICRAF does just that. Established in 1978, with headquarters in Nairobi, Kenya, ICRAF implements research jointly with national institutions through networks associated with the major eco-regions. One such network, the agro-forestry research network for the Semi-Arid Lowlands of West Africa was launched in 1989 with the objective of generating appropriate agro-forestry technologies for the eco-region and strengthening national agro-forestry research capabilities in the subregion.

Land degradation and management of soil and water

The problem

From the discussion presented above on drought and desertification, it is apparent that the fragile soils of semi-arids lands of Sub-Saharan Africa are exposed to increasing threats of wind and runoff erosion. It is also evident that water is a scarce, high-value economic resource in the region. In addition to high rates of evaporation, because the rains usually come during the hot period of the year, other major routes of water loss include soil evaporation and runoff owing to poor infiltration in the soil. Rains in the semi-arid lands of Sub-Saharan Africa do not fall gently and evenly; they come predominantly in convective storms as described earlier. Rain that falls this way in torrents is more destructive than the gentler rain of temperate zones. More is lost in runoff and less filters into the ground.

Yet water management is less advanced in Sub-Saharan Africa than in any other developing region, including Africa north of the Sahara where water management is more developed. In Sub-Saharan Africa, almost half of the irrigated area is concentrated in two countries only: the Sudan and Madagascar. In the rest of the region, irrigated land is only about 2 per cent of the cultivated area. This compares with 8.5 per cent in Latin America and 29 per cent in Asia (Harrison 1987).

Most of the large-scale irrigation schemes and soil conservation work tried out in Sub-Saharan Africa in the past have met with little success. As Critchley (1991) points out, concern about soil conservation is nothing new in Africa. Several colonial administrations recognized from the early part of the twentieth century that there was an erosion problem. Programmes of one sort or another continued in most countries until independence. But the majority of these schemes were resented by the local people, who were forced to supply labour.

However, the cycles of drought that have affected Sub-Saharan Africa in recent decades have drawn renewed attention to the role of soil and water management in ensuring crop production in semi-arid lands. The need for conservation programmes is much greater now, because of population increase, than when the first unpopular programmes were started. However, new approaches need to be developed to avoid the many mistakes of the past.

The way ahead: How to make every drop count

At least two major lessons can be learnt from past failures (Critchley 1991): first, for subsistence farmers, the idea of preventing future loss of soil is irrelevant to present pressing needs; and, secondly, the farmers themselves have, in the past, simply not been consulted about their knowledge and understanding of the processes of erosion. Both traditional technologies and social organizations have usually been ignored.

The way ahead calls for alternative strategies to large-scale conventional irrigation schemes or soil and water conservation projects. One such alternative being implemented with success in the Sahel is a low-cost water-harvesting technique adapted by incorporating a traditional practice, in Burkina Faso, of placing lines of stones to slow down runoff. But slopes in the Yatenga region where the project was developed are too gentle (between 0.5 and 2 per cent) and levels are impossible to get right by eye, although runoff erosion is quite severe. In response to this constraint, the Oxfam project devised an inexpensive (and rather ingenious) tool: the water-tube level, which accurately identifies the contour lines. Originally developed in the arid Negev desert 3,000–4,000 years ago, the water-harvesting technique is now being tried out with various adaptations in many parts of the Sahel, and is now widely adopted by farmers in the Yatenga region in Burkina Faso (Wright and Bonkoungou 1985; Younger and Bonkoungou 1989; Critchley 1991). The success of the technique has exceeded expectations.

In the course of four to five years, the Oxfam project perfected a traditional technique into a now highly valued water-harvesting technology that successfully collects water and holds it on the field, preventing soil erosion and increasing water infiltration and crop yields. Thousands of farmers now use the technique, and the number is growing rapidly as others observe its success. Scientists are now studying the possibility of using agro-forestry technologies to improve the technique even further by planting suitable trees and shrubs along the contour lines.

Supplementary irrigation and rain harvesting are a useful way to increase the water available to crops. However, Cooper and Gregory (1987) indicate that this is only one of many ways to make every drop count. They point out that in rain-fed farming systems, where lack of moisture limits crop production, agronomists frequently assess innovative management practices in terms of water use efficiency, which is the ratio of dry matter produced to water used for the production of that dry matter. This is expressed in units of kg/ha/mm and can be increased either by increasing total water supply, as in the case of the water-harvesting technique described above, but also by increasing transpiration efficiency or by reducing evaporation from the soil surface, e.g. through mulching. In terms of water conservation, the principal effect of mulching is to reduce soil evaporation. This is often complemented by many other beneficial effects. In the acid sandy soils (Psammentic Paleustalfs) of the Sahelian zone in West Africa, Kretzschmar et al. (1991) report that crop residues play a key role in increasing pearl millet (*Pennisetum glaucum* L.) yield, a beneficial effect likely due to improvement of P nutrition through both an increase in P mobility in the soil and enhancement of root growth. Although alternative uses of crop residues for fuel and animal feed limit their availability as mulch, the development of agroforestry techniques could make leaves and small branches of multipurpose trees available for mulching, a traditional practice known to small farmers in the rain-fed agriculture region of the West African Sahel.

The success of the water-harvesting technique demonstrates that a project that proceeds with a low budget and pursues a low-technology method can yield significant returns. Of course, this does not imply that all agricultural research should follow such a strategy – many high-technology projects have also yielded high rates of return – but it does suggest that a place exists for simpler technological changes, and that planners should not forget them. Small-scale measures on a large scale could be a viable alternative to the large-scale projects that so conspicuously failed in the past.

Conclusion

"Sustainability" and "sustainable development" have become the key terms in addressing the world's general concern over environment and development issues. In Sub-Saharan Africa, the development process seems to have reached an impasse. Food production per person has declined steadily during the past three decades. People in many countries of the region are poorer now than they were 30 years ago around the period of independence. The environmental crisis is equally tragic and plagued by desertification and recurrent droughts in the semi-arid lands and high rates of deforestation in the humid eco-zones.

Scattered in the gloomy picture, however, some success stories offer useful lessons and point to the direction that could lead to sustainable development in Sub-Saharan Africa. This paper has underlined the potential of agro-forestry and a small-scale water-harvesting technique to combat desertification and promote sustainable agricultural production. These alone would not be enough to reverse the current negative economic growth of Sub-Saharan Africa. Without them, however, it appears that sustainable agricultural development in the region could remain an insurmountable challenge for the near future.

Acknowledgements

I gratefully acknowledge the help received from Dr. Peter Cooper and Chin Ong at ICRAF, Dr. Joseph Menyonga at OAU/STRC-SAFGRAD in Ouagadougou, and Professor Bakhit, University of Khartoum.

References

Baumer, M. 1987. *Agroforesterie et Désertification*. ICRAF/CTA.
Bonkoungou, E. G. 1985. Forestry research in the Sahel: Process and priorities. *Rural Africana* 23/24.
———— 1987. Management of natural forest versus afforestation in the Sahel region of Africa. Future prospects. In: San José and R. Montes (eds.), *La Capacidad Bioproductiva de Sabanas*. Caracas, Venezuela: Centro Internacional de Ecologia Tropical, pp. 489–512.
———— 1990. Problématique des forêts et de la foresterie en zones sèches tropicales. Bilan et perspectives. In: *IUFRO XIX World Congress Report B*. Montreal, Canada, pp. 54–73.
Cooper, P. and P. J. Gregory. 1987. Soil water management in the rain-fed farming systems of the Mediterranean region. *Soil Use and Management* 3(2): 57–62.
Critchley, W. 1991. *Looking after Our Land. New Approaches to Soil and Water Conservation in Dryland Africa*. Oxford: Oxfam Publications.
Harrison, P. 1987. *The Greening of Africa – Breaking Through in the Battle for Land and Food*. London: Paladin Grafton Books.
ICRISAT (International Crops Research Institute for the Semi-Arid Tropics). 1988. *ICRISAT Annual Report 1987*. Patancheru, India.
Kalij, M. C. and W. B. Hoogmoed. 1993. Soil management for crop production in

the West African Sahel. II. Emergence, establishment, and yield of pearl millet. *Soil and Tillage Research* 25: 301–315.

Kretzschmar, R. M., H. Hafner, A. Bationo, and H. Marschner. 1991. Long- and short-term effects of crop residues on aluminum toxicity, phosphorus availability and growth of pearl millet in an acid sandy soil. *Plant and Soil* 136(2): 215–233.

May, D. H. 1988. *Africa Heading for Tomorrow. A Bretton Woods Committee Special Report on Economic Reform in Sub-Saharan Africa*. Washington D.C.: Bretton Woods Committee.

Nicholson, S. E. 1982. *The Sahel: A Climatic Perspective*. CILSS/OECD.

Rochette, R. M. (ed.) 1989. *Le Sahel en Lutte Contre la Désertification. Leçons d'Expériences*. Berlin: CILSS/PAC.

Sircoulon, J. 1992. Le réseau pluviométrique en Afrique de l'Ouest. In: S. Janicot and B. Fontaine (eds.), *La Variabilité Climatique en Afrique de l'Quest*. Paris: Ministère de la Recherche et de la Technologie.

World Bank. 1989. *Sub-Saharan Africa from Crisis to Sustainable Growth. A Long-Term Perspective Study*. Washington D.C.: The World Bank.

Wright, P. and E. G. Bonkoungou. 1985. Soil and water conservation as a starting point for rural forestry: The Oxfam project in Ouahigouya, Burkina Faso. *Rural Africana* 23/24.

Younger, S. D. and E. G. Bonkoungou. 1989. Burkina Faso: The *Projet Agro-Forestier*. A case study of agricultural research and extension. In: *Successful Development in Africa. Case Studies of Projects, Programs and Policies*. Washington D.C.: World Bank, pp. 11–26.

9

Tropical deforestation and its impact on soil, environment, and agricultural productivity

Rattan Lal

Introduction

The humid tropics comprise about 31 per cent of all tropical biomes, cover 11 per cent of the earth's total surface, occupy about 1.5 billion ha of land area, and are home to about 2 billion people (WRI 1990–91). Of the 1.5 billion ha of the humid tropics, 45 per cent lie in the Americas, 30 per cent in Africa, and 25 per cent in Asia and Oceania. Within the generic term "tropical rain forest" (TRF), there are three principal types of forest vegetation including: lowland rain forest (80 per cent of the humid tropical vegetation), premontane forest (10 per cent), and lower montane and montane forests (10 per cent). The TRF ecosystems are characterized by constantly high temperatures and relative humidity, high annual precipitation, highly weathered and leached soils of low chemical fertility, and high total biomass. High total biomass production, despite low soil fertility, is due to the effect of high temperatures and relative humidity, abundant rainfall, and low moisture deficit. The natural vegetation of the TRF is characterized by a high degree of biodiversity. The TRF ecosystem has global importance in terms of soil and climatic interactions and its impact on several processes. For example, local and global climatic

181

patterns are influenced by the interaction of the TRF with the atmosphere (Salati et al. 1983; Myers 1989; Houghton 1990). An important aspect with global influences involves the impact of the TRF on biogeophysical cycles, e.g. C, N, S, and H_2O. Conversion of the TRF to other land use disrupts these cycles, which are critical in regulating several global processes; e.g. emission of radiatively active gases into the atmosphere, change in the total water vapour present in the atmosphere. It is because of these local, regional, and global interactions that the TRF and its conversion are a major concern.

TRF and its conversion

In prehistoric times, the geographical area of undisturbed TRF was about 1.5 billion ha. It is estimated that 45 per cent of the original TRF has been converted to other land uses, with a regional loss of about 52 per cent in Africa, 42 per cent in Asia, and 37 per cent in Latin America (Richards 1991). Because of the wide diversity in vegetation type and in the mode and degree of conversion, however, there is a large variation in the estimates of the extent of the remaining TRF and rates of its conversion. The areal extent of TRF from 1700 to 1990 for three regions is depicted in table 9.1. Over the 290 years, the TRF decreased by 36 per cent in tropical Africa, 26 per cent in Latin America, and 30 per cent in Asia. The most drastic conversion happened between 1920 and 1950. The data in table 9.2 are an estimate of the total deforestation that occurred in different regions over a 328-year period. Low and high estimates of total forest conversion range from 484 million ha (32 per cent of the total) to 538 million ha (36 per cent of the total).

Present estimates of the remaining area of tropical rain forest and annual rates of deforestation are also highly variable and erratic (Myers 1991). Estimates of the total area of TRF for the year 1990

Table 9.1 **Global change in tropical rain forest and woodland, 1700–1990 (million ha)**

Region	1700	1850	1920	1950	1980	1990	Total change
Tropical Africa	1,358	1,336	1,275	1,188	1,074	869	−489
Latin America	1,445	1,420	1,369	1,273	1,151	1,067	−378
South & South-East Asia	558	569	536	493	415	410	−178

Sources: Richards (1991); WRI (1990).

182

Table 9.2 **Estimated area of deforestation, 1650–1978 ('000 km^2)**

Region	Level[a]	Pre-1650	1650–1749	1750–1849	1850–1978	Total deforestation 1650–1978 High	Low
Central America	H	18	30	40	200	288	
	L	12					282
Latin America	H	18	100	170	637	925	
	L	12					919
Oceania	H	6	6	6	362	380	
	L	2	4	–			368
Asia	H	974	216	606	1,220	3,016	
	L	640	176	596			2,632
Africa	H	226	80	–16	469	759	
	L	96	24	42			631
Total	H	1,242	432	806	2,888	5,368	
	L	762	334	848			4,832

Source: Williams (1991).
a. H = high estimate; L = low estimate.

Table 9.3 **Present estimates of TRF and the annual rate of deforestation**

	WRI (1992–93)		FAO (1991)	
Region	Total area (ha m.)	Annual rate (%)	Total area (ha m.)	Annual rate (%)
Africa	600.1[a]	5.0	241.8	4.8
Latin America	839.9	8.3	753.0	7.3
Asia	274.9	3.6	287.5	4.7
Total	1,714.9	16.9	1,282.3	16.8

a. Includes wooded land area and closed forest.

range from 1,282 million ha (FAO) to 1,715 million ha (WRI) (table 9.3). The principal discrepancy in the data in table 9.3 lies in the estimate of TRF for Africa. The WRI estimate of 600 million ha includes both closed forest and wooded areas. There are several categories of vegetation called TRF. These include closed forest, forest land, woodland, shrub land, forest land under shifting cultivation, and miscellaneous land (FAO 1981). The closed forest is the

Table 9.4 **Different categories of TRF and their conversion rate**

Region	Total area (ha m.)		Conversion rate (ha m./yr)	
	Closed forest	Wooded land	Closed forest	Wooded land
Africa	217	652	1.33	2.34
Latin America	679	388	4.12	1.27
Asia	306	104	1.82	0.19
Total	1,202	1,144	7.27	3.81

Source: WRI (1988–89).

true TRF. The distinction between these categories is difficult to make, and estimates vary widely. Estimates of the area of closed forest and wooded land and the rate of conversion are shown in table 9.4.

There are several problems with the available data. Original data based on recent and direct surveys are not available. Most estimates are 10–20 years old and obsolete. Furthermore, there are differences in the criteria used, and the accuracy of most estimates is questionable. As with the area, the rate of deforestation is also hard to estimate. However, reliable estimates of the areas of TRF and rate of conversion are needed for: (i) land-use planning, and (ii) predicting the impact of forest conversion on soil and environment.

Soils of the TRF ecosystem

The predominant soils of the humid tropics are oxisols, ultisols, and alfisols (table 9.5). Oxisols and ultisols comprise 63 per cent of soils of the TRF (table 9.6). These soils are highly weathered, leached, devoid of basic cations, and relatively infertile. Young soils of moderate to high fertility (mollisols, inceptisols, and entisols) occupy about 15 per cent of the total land area. There are several soil-related constraints on intensive food crop production in the humid tropics. The principal constraints are listed in table 9.7. Oxisols and ultisols have low nutrient reserves and are prone to toxicity owing to high concentrations of Al and Mn. In general, these soils have high P-fixation capacity. Alfisols are relatively more fertile than oxisols and ultisols. However, alfisols have weakly developed structure and are highly prone to accelerated soil erosion. The effective rooting depth for food crops and annuals is generally 20–30 cm owing to either physical (compacted, concretionary, or gravelly subsoil) or chemical (Al

Table 9.5 **Geographical extent and distribution of major soils of the humid tropics (ha million)**

Soil type	Region			
	America	Africa	Asia	Total
Oxisols	332	179	14	525
Ultisols	213	69	131	413
Inceptisols[a]	61	75	90	226
Entisols[b]	31	91	90	212
Alfisols	18	20	15	53
Histosols	–	4	23	27
Spodosols	10	3	6	19
Mollisols	–	–	7	7
Vertisols	1	2	2	5
Aridisols	–	1	1	2
Total	666	444	379	1,489

Source: NRC (1993).
a. Inceptisols include Aquepts, Tropepts, Andepts, and Entisols.
b. Entisols include Fluvents, Psamments, and Lithic Entisols.

Table 9.6 **Soils of the humid tropics (% of the total area)**

Principal feature	Soil type	Region			
		America	Africa	Asia	Total
• Acid, infertile	Oxisols and ultisols	82	56	38	63
• Moderately fertile, & well-drained	Alfisols, vertisols, mollisols, inceptisols, andisols, fluvents	7	12	33	15
• Poorly drained	Aquepts	6	12	6	8
• Very infertile, sandy	Psamments, spodosols	2	16	6	7
• Shallow	Lithic entisols	3	3	10	5
• Organic	Histosols	–	1	6	2
		100	100	100	100

Source: NRC (1982).

or Mn toxicity, low P) limitations. Coupled with low plant-available water reserves, water deficiency can be a problem for shallow-rooted annuals. In contrast, upland crops can be subjected to periodic inundation and anaerobiosis. With proper management, however, the agricultural productivity of these soils can be greatly improved while minimizing risks of soil and environmental degradation. An impor-

185

Table 9.7 **Soil-related constraints on intensive land use for food crop production in the TRF ecosystem**

Constraint	Oxisols	Ultisols	Alfisols	Inceptisols	Mollisols	Andisols
Physical						
Accelerated erosion	2	2	3	2	1	1
Soil compaction & crusting	2	2	3	2	1	1
Root impedance	3	3	3	1	1	1
Moisture imbalance	2	2	3	1	1	1
Shallow depth	2	2	3	1	1	1
Nutritional						
N deficiency	3	3	2	2	1	1
P deficiency	3	3	2	1	1	1
Al & Mn toxicity	3	3	1	1	1	1
Micro-nutrient deficiency	3	3	2	1	1	1
Biological						
Soil fauna	2	2	2	1	1	1
Biomass carbon	2	2	2	1	1	1

3 = severe; 2 = moderate; 1 = slight.

tant strategy in enhancing the productive potential of these soils is to reduce the adverse effects of forest conversion.

Forest conversion and soil productivity

Deforestation and conversion to arable land use have drastic impacts on soil properties, water and energy balance, and soil erosion hazard (Lal 1987). The worst-case-scenario local effects are outlined in table 9.8. The principal soil degradation effects include adverse effects on soil structure leading to crusting, compaction, and hardsetting. Reduction in infiltration, increase in surface runoff, and soil exposure to raindrop impact and to the shearing effect of overland flow accentuate soil erosion risks. Alterations in pore size distribution and reduction in the colloid content of the surface soil, owing to eluviation, and preferential removal of clay and organic carbon by erosion drastically reduce plant-available water reserves. High soil temperatures, often reaching 40–45°C at 0–5 cm depth for 4 to 6 hours a day, further aggravate the frequency and intensity of drought stress experienced by shallow-rooted crops.

The principal impact of deforestation on chemical and nutritional

Table 9.8 **Worst-case scenario regarding the adverse effects of deforestation on soil productivity**

Physical effects	Chemical and nutritional effects
• Compaction, crusting, increased strength • Accelerated erosion • Loss of clay and soil colloids • Drought stress • High soil temperatures	• Loss of soil organic matter, nitrogen, and sulphur • Leaching of bases • Acidification • Reduction in soil biological activity • Disruption of nutrient recycling

Table 9.9 **Technological options to minimize the adverse effects of deforestation**

Activity	Recommended practice
Time of land clearing	• During dry season when soil moisture is low
Method of land-clearing	• Manual felling with chainsaw
Mechanized clearing	• Preferably with shearblade
Management of fell biomass	• *In situ* burning, no windrows
Stumping and root removal	• Remove manually from the top 30 cm, or leave intact
Protective cover	• Plant an aggressive cover crop, e.g. *Mucuna*, *Desmodium* spp. *Puereria*, etc.
Seedbed preparation	• No-till or conservation tillage
Erosion management	• Vegetative hedges, e.g. *Vetiver*, *Leucaena*, etc.

properties is related to a decrease in the organic matter content of the soil and to disruption in nutrient-recycling mechanisms owing to the removal of deep-rooted trees. The decrease in soil organic matter content is mostly due to the high rate of mineralization caused by high temperatures. The absence of actively growing roots in the sub-soil horizon leads to leaching of bases (e.g. Ca, Mg, K, Na) and increase in soil acidity. In addition to leaching, loss of N and S also occurs owing to volatilization.

The magnitude of these adverse effects depends on the method of deforestation and on the soil and crop management practices. In addition, there exists a strong interaction with soil type, rainfall regime, nature of the existing vegetation, ambient soil moisture content, and microclimate. Technological options for minimizing the adverse effects of deforestation are outlined in table 9.9. It is well known that the adverse effects of deforestation are more severe for mechanical than for manual land-clearing. The adverse effects of mechanical clearing (soil compaction and accelerated erosion) are generally less severe for shearblade than for treepusher or bulldozer blade methods of tree felling. Compaction and structural degradation are more severe when soil wetness is high at the time of land-clearing (Ghuman and Lal 1992). Stumping and removal of roots, which is necessary only to facilitate mechanized farm operations, should preferably be done manually. Root ploughing is disruptive and causes considerable soil disturbance. Windrowing also scrapes topsoil and concentrates nutrient-rich ash in narrow strips. Management of the soil structure and erosion control can be achieved by sowing a quick-growing cover crop. The cover crop should preferably be a legume, e.g. *Mucuna utilis, Pueraria phaseoloides, Centrosema* spp., or *Desmodium* spp. Erosion control on sloping lands can be achieved by establishing vegetative hedges (e.g. *Vetiver, Leucaena, Gliricidia*) and other multi-purpose trees and woody shrubs. Adoption of agro-forestry practices also enhances nutrient recycling and minimizes leaching losses of bases.

Enhancing the nutrient capital of the soil is critical to increasing the agricultural productivity of these soils of low inherent fertility. Soil fertility is further depleted by deforestation and biomass removal and/or burning. Therefore, judicious application of fertilizer needs careful consideration. To some extent, nitrogen can be supplied through biological fixation. However, other nutrients, including Ca, Mg, and P, must be made available from off-farm sources. Admittedly, resource-poor farmers cannot afford capital-intensive inputs. None the less, essential nutrients must be supplied, through application of either organic manure or mineral fertilizer, if high yields are expected on a sustained basis.

Deforestation and the emission of radiatively active gases

Deforestation strongly affects the dynamics of soil organic matter. Experiments conducted in Africa (Greenland and Nye 1959; Nye and Greenland 1960; Lal 1976; Juo and Lal 1977; Aina 1979; Lal et al. 1980; Ghuman and Lal 1991, 1992) show rapid decline in soil organic matter content following deforestation and cultivation. The magnitude of carbon decline in the top 5 cm depth can be as much as 50 per cent in 12 months and 60 per cent in 18 months. The organic carbon (C) content of the top 30 cm depth declines by about 50 per cent within 10 years of deforestation and intensive cultivation. Examples of the carbon loss from soils of the humid tropics within 10 years of

Table 9.10 **Loss of organic carbon with continuous and intensive cultivation with no-till and agro-forestry in 10 years following deforestation**

Depth (cm)	Organic C (%)		Bulk density (mg/m^3)		Total soil carbon (mg/ha)		Carbon emission in 10 years (mg/ha)
	Initial	Final	Initial	Final	Initial	Final	
0–10	2.50	1.50	1.10	1.40	27.5	21.0	6.5
10–25	1.40	1.00	1.25	1.45	26.3	21.8	4.5
25–50	0.90	0.80	1.30	1.45	29.3	29.0	0.3
Total					83.1	71.8	11.3

Source: Lal (1991).

Table 9.11 **Loss of organic carbon with continuous and intensive cultivation using plough-based mechanized systems in 10 years following deforestation**

Depth (cm)	Organic C (%)		Bulk density (mg/m^3)		Total soil carbon (mg/ha)		Carbon emission in 10 years (mg/ha)
	Initial	Final	Initial	Final	Initial	Final	
0–10	2.5	0.5	1.10	1.5	27.5	7.5	20.0
10–25	1.40	0.4	1.25	1.45	26.3	8.7	17.6
25–50	0.9	0.3	1.30	1.45	29.3	10.9	18.4
Total					83.1	27.1	56.0

Source: Lal (1991).

deforestation and intensive cultivation are shown in tables 9.10–9.12. The rate of C loss may be as much as 1.13 mg/ha/yr from soil managed by conservation tillage and agro-forestry to 5.60 mg/ha/yr for soils managed with a plough-based conventional tillage system. That being the case, newly cleared land in the humid tropics may release between 98.7 billion kg C/yr and to 218.8 billion kg C/yr, with a mean emission rate of about 154.3 billion kg C/yr.

The loss of organic C from soils under shifting cultivation is less than that from soils under intensive cultivation. Nye and Greenland (1960) observed that the loss of organic carbon in 100 years may be 20 per cent for a soil with 12-year fallow cycle to 45 per cent for a soil with 4-year fallow cycle. The annual loss of C due to shifting cultivation may be as much as 0.27 mg/ha. If shifting cultivation is prac-

Table 9.12 **Changes in soil organic carbon (SOC) content of the surface 0–5 cm layer of two soils in southern Nigeria**

	Alfisol at Ibadan[a]				Ultisol at Okomu[b]		
			ΔC				ΔC
Year	Organic carbon (%)	%/yr	Average (%/yr)[c]	Year	Organic carbon (%)	%/yr	Average (%/yr)[c]
1978	2.17	–	–	1984	1.8	–	–
1979	1.61	−25.8	−25.8	1985	1.4	−22.2	−22.2
1982	1.54	−1.5	−7.3	1986	1.45	+3.6	−9.7
1984	1.14	−13.0	−7.9	1987	1.05	−27.6	−13.9
1985	1.24	+8.8	−6.1	1988	1.15	+9.5	−9.0
1986	1.30	+4.8	−5.0				
1987	1.09	−16.2	−5.5				

a. The data from Ibadan are from Watershed 1.
b. The data from Okomu are from the manually cleared plots; data recalculated from Ghuman and Lal (1991).
c. The average (%/yr) is calculated for each year on the basis of the original SOC content.

tised on about 25 million ha, the total loss of C due to shifting cultivation is estimated at 6.25 billion kg C/yr. In addition to C, biomass burning also causes release of several other greenhouse gases, e.g. CO_2, CO, CH_4, and NO_x.

Deforestation and hydrological balance

Deforestation of TRF can drastically alter the components of the hydrological cycle:

$$P = I + R + \Delta S + D + \int Ed_t,$$

where P is precipitation, I is infiltration, R is surface runoff, ΔS is soil-water storage, D is deep drainage, E is evapotranspiration, and t is time. Deforestation decreases I and ΔS and increases R and D components. In general, deforestation may also increase E. The change in E, however, may also depend on the land use.

Several experiments have demonstrated the effects of clear-cutting on the increase in total water yield. The impact of deforestation on the hydrological balance of a 44 ha watershed was studied at the International Institute of Tropical Agriculture (IITA), Ibadan, Nigeria. Prior to partial deforestation in 1978 and complete defor-

Table 9.13 **Effects of partial clearing in 1978 on total water discharge from Watershed 1**

Parameters	
Rainfall (mm)	785.8
Surface flow (mm)	42.7
Surface flow (% of rain)	5.4
Subsurface flow (mm)	9.4
Subsurface flow (% of rain)	1.2
Total yield (mm)	52.1
Total yield (% of rain)	6.6

Note: The partial clearing was of 3.1 ha out of 44.3 ha.

Table 9.14 **Hydrological components on an annual basis for Watershed 1, 1979–1986**

Year	Annual rainfall (mm)	Subsurface flow[b] (mm)	Surface flow (mm)	Total water yield		Apparent evapotranspiration[a]	
				mm	% of rainfall	mm	% of rainfall
1979	1,435.5	28.0	73.4	101.4	7.1	1,334.1	92.9
1980	1,449.7	73.1	90.0	163.1	11.3	1,286.6	88.8
1981	1,074.5	58.9	28.9	87.8	8.2	986.7	91.8
1982	851.5	50.9	25.9	76.8	9.0	774.7	91.0
1983	897.6	45.8	21.3	67.1	7.5	830.5	92.5
1984	1,162.2	58.9	27.1	86.0	7.4	1,076.2	92.6
1985	1,675.7	18.5	93.2	111.7	6.7	1,563.9	93.3
1986	1,164.1	1.9	51.7	53.8	4.6	1,110.3	95.3

a. Evapotranspiration includes soil water storage and groundwater recharge.
b. Subsurface flow is underestimated during wet years because it is computed as a part of surface flow during the storm runoff.

estation in 1979, measurements of surface and subsurface flow were made under the forest cover from 1974 to 1977. Under the forest cover, the interflow was 0.4 per cent to 1.4 per cent and total flow 0.8 per cent to 2.7 per cent of the total rainfall. Partial clearing in 1978 increased interflow to 1.2 per cent and increased total flow to 6.6 per cent of the total rainfall (table 9.13).

The entire watershed was cleared in 1979 and cultivated to food crops. The data in table 9.14 show that the total water yield ranged from 4.6% to 11.3% of the rainfall received. Because of the bimodal

Table 9.15 **Hydrological components for the first growing season (March–July), 1979–1987**

Year	Seasonal rainfall (mm)	Subsurface flow[b] (mm)	Surface flow (mm)	Total water yield mm	Total water yield % of rainfall	Apparent evapo-transpiration[a] mm	Apparent evapo-transpiration[a] % of rainfall
1979	846.1	7.0	89.8	96.8	11.4	749.3	88.6
1980	604.3	1.2	7.0	8.2	1.4	596.1	98.6
1981	636.8	20.2	17.3	37.5	5.9	599.3	94.1
1982	615.2	28.4	17.6	46.0	7.5	569.2	92.5
1983	580.9	22.3	15.2	37.5	6.5	543.4	93.5
1984	681.6	23.6	13.9	37.5	5.5	644.1	94.5
1985	935.7	10.8	52.1	62.9	6.7	872.8	93.3
1986	714.2	1.8	36.9	38.7	5.4	677.3	94.8
1987	723.5	36.4	49.2	85.6	11.8	637.9	88.2

a. See notes to table 9.14.
b. See notes to table 9.14.

Table 9.16 **Hydrological components for the second growing season (August–November), 1979–1986**

Year	Seasonal rainfall (mm)	Subsurface flow[b] (mm)	Surface flow (mm)	Total water yield mm	Total water yield % of rainfall	Apparent evapo-transpiration[a] mm	Apparent evapo-transpiration[a] % of rainfall
1979	585.8	0.03	4.6	4.6	0.8	581.2	99.2
1980	845.4	71.90	81.1	153.0	18.1	692.4	81.9
1981	432.4	33.50	11.6	45.1	10.4	387.3	89.6
1982	223.6	19.20	8.1	27.3	12.2	196.3	87.8
1983	230.6	19.20	6.1	25.3	11.0	205.3	89.0
1984	480.6	30.50	13.2	43.7	9.1	436.9	90.9
1985	735.5	6.90	41.1	48.0	6.5	687.5	93.5
1986	379.2	0.10	13.9	14.0	3.7	365.2	96.3

a. See notes to table 9.14.
b. See notes to table 9.14.

distribution of the rainfall, the hydrologic balance was computed separately for each growing season. The hydrologic balance showed that total water yield ranged from 1.4% to 11.8% for the first season (table 9.15) and from 0.8% to 18.1% for the second season (table 9.16). The intermittent stream, with a trace of flow after heavy rain

Table 9.17 **Hydrological components for the dry season (December–February) for Watershed 1, 1979–1987**

Year	Seasonal rainfall (mm)	Subsurface flow (mm)	Surface flow (mm)	Total water yield (mm)
1979	3.6	0.0	0.0	0.0
1980	23.6	0.0	0.0	0.0
1981	5.3	2.0	0.08	2.1
1982	12.7	5.0	0.10	5.1
1983	0.0	3.6	0.03	3.6
1984	86.1	4.1	1.1	5.2
1985	0.0	3.6	0.0	3.6
1986	7.6	0.0	0.0	0.0
1987	18.8	3.9	0.0	3.9

Note: The data for December are taken from the previous year.

and no flow during the dry season, became a perennial stream that recorded a measurable flow throughout the dry season (table 9.17).

An increase in the magnitude of interflow and its continuous discharge throughout the dry season may be attributed to the replacement of deep-rooted perennials with high water requirements with shallow-rooted annuals with relatively fewer water requirements. Further, annuals were not grown during the dry season.

Sustainable use of the TRF ecosystem

Criteria for sustainable land use

The tropical rain-forest ecosystem must be used, improved, and restored. Continuous depletion of these resources has economic and ecologic ramifications at local, regional, and global scales. Sustainable use of soil and water resources in the TRF ecosystem should take the following into consideration:
• the nutrient capital of the soil resources should be enhanced by applications of chemical and organic fertilizers;
• the management systems adopted must optimize energy flux as well as energy use efficiency – energy efficiency alone is not adequate in view of increasing population pressure;
• losses of nutrients and water out of the ecosystem should be minimized;
• nutrient recycling mechanisms from subsoil to surface horizons must be an integral aspect of the land-use system;

193

• land degraded by past mismanagement must be restored by afforestation with ecologically adapted and quick-growing species.

Land capability assessment

Land capability assessment is necessary for the rational utilization of forest resources. Sustainable use of TRF resources necessitates a detailed and accurate inventory of the soil, water, vegetation, and climatic characteristics of the region. These inventories/surveys should be conducted at reconnaissance scales (1:50,000 to 1:1,000,000) and detailed scales (1:10,000 to 1:50,000). The land resources should then be classified according to their potential capability as follows (FAO 1982):

Forest land

There are several types of forest land:

(a) *Natural forested land* should be preserved as natural forest and left alone. It has limitations of topography, shallow/stony soils, poor water regime, etc. Some examples are marginal steep lands, forests in the vicinity of regions with short supplies of firewood, inaccessible areas, small islands, and regions with other sociopolitical connotations.

(b) *Production forests* are suitable for managed logging of timber and other forest products.

(c) *Planted or man-made forests* are fertile, prime lands and are suitable for tree plantations, e.g. *Gmelina*, teak, Cassia.

(d) *Protected forests* are forest reserves protected in order to preserve the natural biodiversity.

Arable land

Arable land is prime agricultural land and is suitable for supporting continuous and intensive agriculture for food-crop and livestock production. Such land should be developed and managed according to ecologically compatible methods of deforestation and land development. When deforestation for arable land use is inevitable, land development should be carefully planned and implemented according to scientific guidelines.

Guidelines for land use in the TRF ecosystem

The development of TRF for alternative land uses has become a global issue. For some countries, the question is no longer whether to remove tropical forest for alternative land uses; the important consideration is how much to remove and by what method so that ecological concerns are adequately addressed. It is the ill-planned and improper management of TRF that has created severe ecological, economic, and socio-political problems. The sequence of steps needed to achieve a rational use of the TRF ecosystem is outlined below:

1. land capability assessment;
2. choice of proper land use (e.g. arable land, protected forest, man-made forest);
3. use of proper methods and time of deforestation (e.g. manual, chainsaw, shearblade);
4. adoption of soil conservation measures (e.g. cover crop, mulch farming, vegetative hedges);
5. use of science-based agronomic techniques of soil and crop management (e.g. balanced fertilizer use, proper crop rotation and cropping sequences, appropriate tillage methods, and integrated pest management).

Best management practices for sustainable agriculture

Some soils supporting the TRF ecosystem can be converted to intensive arable land use with sustained production provided that:

(a) expectations of agronomic yields are not too high,
(b) the soil and crop management systems adopted ensure the replenishment of plant nutrients harvested in crops and the maintenance of biophysical resources,
(c) the soils are taken out of production and put to restorative land use long before the degradative processes are set in motion.

Some research-proven agronomic practices based on these guidelines are listed in table 9.18. Just as use of prime agricultural land is essential not only for food-crop production but also for establishing pasture and forest plantations, so is the use of chemical and organic fertilizers for enhancing soil fertility. Most soils of the TRF ecosystem are of low inherent fertility. Enhancing soil fertility, therefore, is crucial to sustained agricultural productivity.

Imperata control

Land misuse and severe soil degradation encourage encroachment by *Imperata cylindrica* and other noxious weeds. It is important to

Table 9.18 **Best management practices for sustainable land use in TRF ecosystems**

Arable land use	Pasture development	Agro-forestry	Forest plantations
• Use prime land, and avoid marginal, steep, or shallow soils	• Use prime land, and avoid steep and shallow soils	• Use prime land of high inherent fertility	• Use prime land with no serious limitations
• Remove forest by manual methods, or by shearblade	• Use proper clearing methods, e.g. manual, slash and burn, etc. Tree defoliants can also be used in regions with low tree density. Dead trees can be left standing	• Clear land by manual methods or shearblade techniques	• Clear existing vegetation by manual methods of slash and burn or by shearblade. Some roots and stumps can be left intact
• Use cover crop and mulch farming techniques for soil and water conservation		• Choose native tree species that do not aggressively compete with annuals	• Seed a leguminous cover crop immediately
• Make frequent use of planted fallows	• Seed with suitable and ecologically adapted mixture of grass and legumes	• Proper tree management is crucial.	• Establish tree seedlings through the leguminous cover by suppressing it through chemical or mechanical means. Cover crop management is crucial to tree establishment
• Wherever feasible, integrate woody perennials and livestock with food-crop annuals		• Choose appropriate crops and cropping sequences	
• Use chemical and organic fertilizers judiciously	• Maintain soil fertility as per soil test values. Balanced fertilization is important	• Manage soil fertility in relation to cropping intensity and soil test values	• Use balanced fertilizer based on soil test values and tree requirements
• Choose appropriate crops and cropping sequences			• Use effective soil and water conservation techniques

maintain soil fertility at a high level to curtail encroachment by *Imperata* and to reclaim already infested lands. Reclamation of *Imperata*-infested land requires a combination of mechanical, chemical, and biological measures. Soil inversion, to uproot rhizomes and expose them to high temperatures during the dry season, followed by the use of systemic herbicides and sowing an aggressively growing cover crop, is essential to eradicate the noxious weed. Biological methods of *Imperata* control, slow as they may be, are often effective on a long-term basis. Preventing encroachment by adoption of the best management practices (BMPs) outlined in table 9.18 should be the best overall strategy.

Restoring degraded forest lands

Restoration of degraded lands in TRF ecosystems is a high priority if the rate of new deforestation is to be reduced. The choice of land restorative measures to be adopted depends on the type of degradation, the processes involved, and antecedent soil properties and vegetation. Knowing the critical/threshold levels of soil properties, beyond which the soil's life support processes are severely jeopardized, is crucial in this endeavour. Land restorative techniques for soils degraded by different processes are outlined in table 9.19.

Research needs

In view of the ever-increasing demand on limited and fragile resources, the question most often asked is whether soil productivity in TRF ecosystems can be sustained with intensive and continuous farming. The available research data indicate that most tropical soils can be intensively cultivated and produce high and sustained yields by adopting BMPs based on an ecological approach to agriculture. In this connection, land-clearing techniques play an important role. The effects of improper land-clearing methods are observed even 8–10 years after the land has been cleared, and especially when the overall soil fertility has drastically declined. Adopting a land-use system that may produce, say, 60–80 per cent of maximum returns and that avoids causing environmental degradation is a better choice than land-use systems that bring high short-term returns but severely degrade the resource base.

An optimum resource utilization should be based on scientific data obtained through well-designed and adequately equipped long-term

Table 9.19 **Land restorative techniques**

Soil degradative process	Strategies	Land restorative techniques
Soil compaction	Enhance soil structure	Grow planted fallows and deep-rooted perennials
	Improve aggregation	Use mulch farming techniques
	Enhance activity of soil fauna, e.g. earthworms	Avoid excessive vehicular traffic
		Use subsoiling discriminatingly and judiciously
Soil erosion	Divert run-on	Isolate the area
	Prevent runoff	Construct diversion channels
	Minimize raindrop impact	Establish permanent ground cover
	Enhance soil structure	Use fertilizers and manures
		Establish vegetative hedges on the contour
		Establish micro-catchments and water-spreading devices to enhance water infiltration
Nutrient depletion	Stop fertility mining practices	Take land out of production and establish planted fallows
	Use balanced fertilizer	Augment nutrient capital by the addition of chemical and organic fertilizers
	Develop nutrient re-cycling mechanisms	Establish native trees and deep-rooted shrubs to facilitate nutrient recycling

experiments. To start meeting this objective, additional research information is needed on evaluating the following:

- land capability and the development of criteria for the choice of rational land use and for appropriate methods of removing vegetation,
- the economic and environmental consequences of different land-use systems,
- methods of restoring forest vegetation and soil quality degraded by land misuse,
- ecologically compatible methods of *Imperata* control,
- adaptability of those methods of soil and crop management that enhance production from existing land, thereby reducing the need to clear new land.

Considering the limited resources available and the urgent need to use forest resources efficiently, it is important that priorities are defined and research goals are sharply focused. A coordinated effort is needed to achieve these objectives.

References

Aina, P. O. 1979. Soil changes resulting from longterm management practices. *Soil Science Society of America Journal* 43: 173–177.

FAO (Food and Agriculture Organization of the United Nations). 1981. *Forest Resources of Tropical Africa, Asia and Americas.* Rome: FAO.

———— 1982. *Tropical Forest Resources.* FAO Forestry Paper no. 30. Rome: FAO.

———— 1991. *Production Year Book.* Rome: FAO.

Ghuman, B. S. and R. Lal. 1991. Land clearing and use in the humid Nigerian tropics. II. Soil chemical properties. *Soil Science Society of America Journal* 55: 184–188.

———— 1992. Effects of soil wetness at the time of land clearing on physical properties and crop response on an Ultisol in southern Nigeria. *Soil & Tillage Research* 22: 1–11.

Greenland, D. J. and P. H. Nye. 1959. Increase in the carbon and nitrogen contents of tropical soils under natural fallows. *Journal of Soil Science* 9: 284–299.

Houghton, R. A. 1990. The global effects of tropical deforestation. *Environment Science Technology* 24: 414–422.

Juo, A. S. R. and R. Lal. 1977. The effect of fallow and continuous cultivation on the chemical and physical properties of an Alfisol in the tropics. *Plant Soil* 47: 567–584.

Lal, R. 1976. No-tillage effects on soil properties under different crops in western Nigeria. *Proceedings Soil Science Society of America* 40: 762–768.

———— 1987. *Tropical Ecology and Physical Edaphology.* Chichester: Wiley.

———— 1991. Agricultural activities and carbon emission from soils of the tropics. Washington D.C.: US Environmental Protection Agency, mimeo.

Lal, R., D. DeVleeschauwer, and R. M. Nganje. 1980. Changes in properties of newly cleared Alfisol as affected by mulching. *Soil Science Society of America Journal* 44: 827–833.

Myers, N. 1989. *Deforestation Rates in Tropical Forests and Their Climatic Implications.* London: Friends of the Earth.

———— 1991. Tropical forests: Present status and future outlook. In: N. Myers (ed.), *Tropical Forests and Climate.* Boston: Kluwer Academic Publishers, pp. 3–32.

NRC (National Research Council). 1982. *Ecological Aspects of Development in the Humid Tropics.* Washington D.C.: National Academy of Sciences.

———— 1993. *Sustainable Agriculture and the Environment in the Humid Tropics.* Washington D.C.: National Research Council.

Nye, P. H. and D. J. Greenland. 1960. *The Soil Under Shifting Cultivation.* Technical Comm. 51. Harpenden, England: Commonwealth Bureau of Soils.

Richards, J. F. 1991. Land transformation. In: B. L. Turner, W. C. Clark, R. W. Kates, J. F. Richards, J. T. Mathews, and W. B. Meyer (eds.), *The Earth as Transformed by Human Action: Global and Regional Changes in Biosphere over the Past 300 Years.* New York: Cambridge University Press, pp. 163–178.

Salati, E., T. E. Lovejoy, and P. B. Vose. 1983. Precipitation and water recycling in tropical forests. *Environmentalists* 3: 67–72.

Williams, M. 1991. Forests. In: B. L. Turner, W. C. Clark, R. W. Kates, J. F. Richards, J. T. Mathews, and W. B. Meyer (eds.), *The Earth as Transformed by Human Action: Global and Regional Changes in Biosphere over the Past 300 Years.* New York: Cambridge University Press, pp. 179–201.

WRI (World Resources Institute). 1988–89. Forests and rangelands. In: *An Assessment of the Resource Base That Supports Global Economy.* Washington D.C.: WRI, pp. 285–295.

――― 1990–91. Forests and rangelands. In: *A Guide to the Global Environment.* Washington D.C.: WRI, pp. 101–120.

――― 1992–93. *Towards Sustainable Development.* Washington D.C.: WRI.

10

The coastal zone and oceanic problems of Sub-Saharan Africa

A. Chidi Ibe

Introduction

The coastal zone and oceans surrounding Sub-Saharan Africa, with their vast resources of food, energy, and minerals, not only are composed of various fragile ecosystems, but are scenes of a variety of often conflicting uses. At present, the uncontrolled development of the coastal zone and ocean and the almost haphazard exploitation of their natural resources threaten to turn the promise of economic prosperity into an environmental nightmare that portends great dangers for present and future generations. There is the urgent need to put in place national management policies that address the environmental controls and procedures to be applied in pursuit of economic development. However, the oceans have no physical boundaries corresponding to national jurisdiction and problems originating from one country easily become those of another. Consequently, although it is recognized that remedies should be effected at the national level, such remedies should be undertaken in the framework of and as part of wider regional and global agreements and policies aimed at the sustainable development of the entire coastal and ocean environment.

The value of the coastal zone and oceans

The coastal zone and oceans of Sub-Saharan Africa constitute a huge storehouse of food, energy, and mineral resources that, if exploited rationally, could be the basis for sustainable development. The coastal zone is in addition a site of human habitation and of concomitant infrastructures for agriculture, industrial development, recreation, and communication (including harbours and ports).

The northern and southern sectors of the western African coastline are the scene of periodic profound upwelling, and upwelling, although weaker, has also been reported in the equatorial sections (Longhurst 1962; Ibe and Ajayi 1985). On the eastern African coast, the picture is much the same, and the Ras Hafun upwelling off the northern coast of Somalia has been extensively described (Newell 1957, 1959; Winters 1976). These areas of upwelling are particularly rich in fish production. Various species of crustacea, including lobsters, deep water shrimps, and prawns, are common. In the coastal lagoons, fish, prawns, and molluscs are also abundant and help to sustain the needs of local populations.

In addition to species of economic importance, there are vulnerable and endangered species such as sea turtles, dugongs, and manatees whose preservation contributes to marine biological diversity (Howell 1988a). Waterbirds are also important; over 100 species from over 25 families are associated with the eastern African coast but are threatened (Howell 1988b).

Some of the coastal countries in Sub-Saharan African are, to varying degrees, oil producers and a few, such as Nigeria and Gabon, are important exporters; others have important refineries and the potential for the development of further production and refining appears substantial. Besides oil and gas, commercial energy production is dominated by hydropower and coal. A survey of the potential of ocean energy in the West and Central African region noted that attractive resources exist for ocean thermal energy conversion, oceanic bioconversion, tides and salinity exchange, but the prospects for wave and current energy are rather poor, except along the southern African coastline, where it has been determined that a favourable 10 kW/m of waterfront is available up to 1 km offshore and about 50 kW/m of waterfront up to 30 km offshore (UNEP 1983).

Non-energy mineral resources are exploited in the coastal zone of Sub-Saharan Africa. These are mostly placer minerals (e.g. in Sierra

Leone and Tanzania) and vast deposits of construction materials, including sand, gravel, and limestone. Phosphate mining and salt extraction are ongoing activities in some sectors of the African coastline, as is open-pit mining. Lead–silver ores were previously quarried in Kinangoni, Kenya. In addition, the coastal zone of Africa is known to have the potential to produce the vast array of minerals that would be expected from Africa's present-day geology and evolutionary history (Ibe 1982; Ibe et al. 1983).

The coastal zone and oceans, with their ecosystems of coral reefs, seagrass beds, mangroves, etc., are repositories of biological diversity in addition to serving as food "regenerating" factories.

Owing to the pattern of early contacts with the outside world, which were mainly coast based, most African cities of note are coastal cities. For example, in western Africa, the capitals of all but three of the countries from Mauritania to Namibia are situated on the coast and it is on the coast that the major industrial developments are taking place. In Ghana, 35 per cent of the population live in towns and 60 per cent of industry is concentrated in the coastal Accra/Tema metropolis. In Nigeria, about 10% of the total population of over 80 million live in Lagos, which is also the centre for 85% of the country's formal industry. The picture of coastal development in eastern Africa follows a similar pattern (Portmann et al. 1989). To promote international and national communication (transport) and trade, harbours and ports have often been constructed that are "out of tune" with the natural environment. Tourism is a booming industry in eastern Africa and a promising one in western Africa. Agriculture, including fishing and aquaculture, is practised on a largely artisanal, sometimes industrial, scale.

The coastal zone and oceans serve a number of indirect functions that nevertheless add to their usefulness as an integral component of a country's socio-economic fabric. Such functions include the removal of wastes, protection from storms, absorption of atmospheric carbon dioxide (CO_2), mediation of climate, purification of air, and recreation.

The main problems and their causes

It is perhaps ironic that the problems of the coastal zone and ocean in Sub-Saharan Africa derive from their usefulness and in particular from the settlement of humans on or near the coast.

The open ocean, however, seems as yet to be largely unaffected by either the environmental degradation wrought by humans or the overexploitation of its natural resources. For living resources in the open ocean, the only danger signal comes not from the activities of coastal states but from foreign fleets (from Japan, South Korea, Taiwan, and the former USSR, among others), which "poach" fish from these waters. For example, tuna in the western Indian Ocean (eastern Africa) is heavily exploited by these foreign fleets and recent indications are that yellow and southern blue fin tuna and bill fish are overexploited and that bigeye tuna and albacore are fully exploited (Ardill 1984). Bryceson et al. (1990) stated that this fishing pressure with highly sophisticated gear has an adverse impact on smaller-scale operations conducted by the fishing fleets of the region, and that artisanal fishermen have noticed marked decreases in catches of large pelagic migratory species.

On the Atlantic coast of Africa, similar pressures exerted by foreign fishing fleets have produced similar consequences (e.g. depletion of deep water prawn/shrimp resources) for the local fishing industry (Ajayi, personal communication).

Besides the operations of foreign fishing fleets, which are sometimes illegal, many of the fisheries of the region are artisanal and based mainly in the coastal zone. Here population pressures have increased consumption and demands and led to the use of destructive fishing methods.

In the coastal zone of eastern Africa, the most environmentally destructive method of fishing is dynamite blasting, mostly associated with coral reef habitats. Bryceson (1978a) reported that repeated blasting over a long period of time has meant the destruction of extensive areas of coral reef and the decline of their fisheries' productivity. The livelihood of artisanal fishermen who employ more traditional methods is threatened. Bryceson (1978a) also reported that spear-fishing had been banned in most countries of the region owing to its damaging effects on reefs and on populations of particularly vulnerable species. For the same region, Kayambo (1988) points out that depletion of the mollusc population as a result of its intensive collection for export and sale to tourists has been a cause for concern.

In the coastal zone of western Africa, in response to increasing demands for fish and fish products, trawling now prevails in areas formerly dominated by traditional fishermen. However, these operations are largely unregulated (or do not conform to regulations where they exist), with incorrect mesh sizes resulting in destructive fishing, including the catching of undersized fish (Ajayi, personal communication).

It is, perhaps, pertinent to mention that on the eastern and western coasts of Sub-Saharan Africa, the potential for aquaculture development is great and people are being urged to take it up as a way of increasing overall fish production. However, experience from its limited practice shows that the potential for environmental degradation (e.g. associated with clearing mangroves) is also great.

Mining of sand (siliceous and calcareous), gravel, and other construction materials (e.g. limestone) from estuaries, beaches, or the nearshore continental shelf is common (Ibe 1982, 1987a,b; Ibe and Quélennec 1989) in the coastal states and islands of Sub-Saharan Africa. The mining of sand and gravel from coastal rivers and particularly from estuaries tends to diminish the amount of fluvial sediment input to the coastline, thereby accelerating shoreline retreat. Sand extraction directly from beaches seriously depletes the sediment pool available, and beach retreat is either induced or accelerated. Dredging of sand from the inner continental shelf is an obvious cause of beach erosion in Africa. This is because the beaches along these coasts exist in dynamic equilibrium with the nearshore continental shelf. Therefore, dredging of sand/gravel for replenishment, land reclamation, or other civil engineering construction from the shore area or, for that matter, anywhere else within the dynamic system inevitably disrupts this equilibrium and enhances shoreline retreat. Countries where this problem has been documented include Liberia, Sierra Leone, Côte d'Ivoire, Nigeria, Mauritius, Tanzania, Kenya, the Seychelles, and Mozambique (Ibe et al. 1983; Ibe 1986c; Ibe and Quélennec 1989; Bryceson et al. 1990).

Besides the increased threat of erosion, the mining of construction materials from the coastal zone has a tendency to disrupt fragile ecosystems such as coral reefs and mangroves and affect their productivity (Ibe 1982; Ibe et al. 1985).

Lead–silver ores were quarried in Kinangoni, Kenya, and were a cause for concern as regards metal pollution, so that the quarries had to be closed (Muslim 1984).

The exploration, exploitation, refining, and transportation of oil and gas in Sub-Saharan Africa, although contributing to economic development, bring worrying problems because these activities routinely contribute a variety of pollutants to the coastal zone and oceans. These include hydrocarbons from occasional spills but, perhaps more importantly, from chronic low-level releases associated with leaking valves, corroded pipelines, ballast water discharges, and production water effluents. Drilling fluids contain diesel and some toxic chemicals that cause pollution. Heavy metals, particularly vanadium and nickel, are introduced through oil-field operations and are known to affect life forms.

Another impact of oil production is the initiation or exacerbation of subsidence in the fragile coastal zone. The main effect of fluid extraction is the reduction of fluid pressure in the reservoir, thus leading directly to an increase in the "effective stress" (or grain to grain stress) in the system. Compaction results and the sedimentary basin subsides (Cooke and Doornkamp 1974). The subsequent progressive inundation of the coastline results in accentuated erosion. Ibe et al. have documented this phenomenon in Nigeria's oil-producing Niger delta (Ibe et al. 1985; Ibe 1988b).

In oil-producing coastal states, a network of canals for hydrocarbon exploitation and transportation, on or near the coast, constitutes a visible structural modification of the coastal zone that has adverse effects on coastline migration.

As stated elsewhere, perhaps the greatest problem in the coastal zone arises from development activities linked with coastal settlements. Coastal towns are by far the most developed in Sub-Saharan Africa and, by implication, the location of residential, industrial, commercial (including harbour and port construction), agricultural, educational, and military facilities in the coastal zone is high (Ibe 1988a, 1989). The increasing awareness of the revenue-generating potential of tourism has also led to increased construction of tourist facilities on beaches along the coast. Construction activities in the coastal zone loosen the sediment binding by removing the surface revetments and increasing rainwater runoff. Thus soil erosion is enhanced. On the other hand, structures constructed on the coast, by strengthening the soil, may lead to decreased sediment supply to the shoreline. The opposite problems of increased siltation and sediment starvation along the coast result, depending on the local physiographic conditions.

The pollution caused by these settlements and the accompanying development activities threatens to make nonsense of the concept of sustainable development. The pollution results primarily from raw or insufficiently treated domestic sewage and from untreated toxic and deleterious wastes from industries, which generally discharge directly into rivers, estuaries, and the nearshore ocean. Preliminary results from pollution-monitoring projects instituted by United Nations agencies, including the Intergovernmental Oceanographic Commission of UNESCO in Eastern and Western Africa, show that pollution by pathogenic organisms, pesticides, chemical fertilizers, and petroleum hydrocarbons is widespread, while metal pollution occurs as hot spots close to industrial sites.

Solid matter (litter) from industries, households, shipping, and the tourist trade poses a problem of an unsightly and irritating nature, but it also has serious public health implications.

The construction of ports, harbours, and piers for national and international trade has a direct negative impact on the environment. This is because, for the most part, these structures lie perpendicular, or nearly so, to the littoral zone, thereby causing acute down-drift erosion. This problem has been documented in Benin, Togo, Nigeria, Liberia, Ghana, Côte d'Ivoire, South Africa, Tanzania, and Somalia, among others. In most of these cases, attempts at solving the harbour-induced erosion have further exacerbated the problem (Ibe 1986a,b).

Increased clearing of coastal vegetation at construction and mining locations or for the establishment of agricultural farms or the expansion of settlements leads to increased surface runoff and makes the exposed area extremely vulnerable to mass movement and to erosion by winds, currents, and water. Large areas of mangroves have been cleared in Kenya, Tanzania, Ghana, and Mozambique for the production of salt by evaporation (Ibe 1987a; Semesi 1988). In Mauritania, Guinea, Sierra Leone, Liberia, Togo, and Angola, open peat mining in littoral zones also contributes to the destruction of vegetation and the acceleration of coastal erosion. The clearance of mangroves is particularly serious because mangroves, in addition to serving as windbreaks, provide excellent spawning and nursery grounds for a variety of coastal organisms, including fish, crustaceans, and molluscs. The loss of mangroves therefore has serious implications for the productivity of coastal ecosystems.

An additional possible problem in coastal areas relates to the expected effects of global warming on shallow ocean and coastal zones, in particular the impact of the associated rise in sealevel. The negative implications of global warming, if they occur, will be considerable for natural and man-made ecosystems, human and animal health, and the spatial and temporal characteristics of natural and human resources (Ibe 1989; Ibe and Ojo 1993; Ojo 1992; Tobor and Ibe 1992).

207

Remedies

Owing to the abundant natural resources with which they are endowed, the coastal zone and oceans of Sub-Saharan Africa hold the key to the social and economic well-being of the coastal states. This is on condition that these resources are exploited in a rational and prudent manner that ensures economic gains while preserving the integrity of the environment. This is the central thrust of the concept of sustainable development.

Today, the exploitation of the natural resources of the coastal zone and near-shore ocean is almost haphazard and has very little respect for the quality of the environment. A degraded environment cannot sustain the renewable resources needed to support the teeming populations that have thronged to coastal areas on account of the presence, in the first place, of these resources; the quality of life of the people deteriorates, and the ensuing struggle for human survival puts additional pressures on the environment and the increasingly limited natural resources. A sort of vicious cycle comes into play. The need is therefore urgent to break this cycle. As has been emphasized elsewhere, the problems of Sub-Saharan Africa as far as the open ocean is concerned are few but they are multifarious for the coastal zone. It would appear reasonable, therefore, to focus suggested remedies on this critical zone.

Attempts at piecemeal solutions of coastal zone problems seem to have failed woefully on account of their intricately interwoven nature. The resulting conflicts are sometimes difficult to solve unless institutionalized frameworks exist. National coastal zone management policy, with adequate legal provisions and providing linkages between the exploitation of natural resources, the conservation of these resources, the preservation of environmental quality, and the promotion of human well-being, seems to be a pressing need. Such a policy, which should have as a core objective the relief of population pressures on the coastal environment, must state clearly not only the concern of a given country for rational coastal zone development but also the procedures to be applied in the coastal zone. In this regard, inspiration and lessons should be drawn from the prevalent practice in most countries in the industrialized world where, despite a variety of existing controls to reduce pressures on the coastal zone, specific laws have been passed to give greater precision to the legal status of coastal zone management and control. The Coastal Zone Management Act of 1972 in the United States of America and Decree no. 79-716 of 17 August 1979 in France are particularly instructive (Ibe 1987c, 1988a).

There will be a need to create (where they are lacking) or to strengthen (where they exist) appropriate national infrastructures to ensure effective compliance with such policies. However, although action at the national level is desirable, it must be borne in mind that, spatially, the oceans and the coastal waters (lagoons, estuaries, bays, creeks) that are in communication with them have no physical boundaries conforming to national jurisdiction. The transportation of pollutants originating from land-based sources in one country to neighbouring countries cannot be prevented physically; the down-drift erosion generated by structures perpendicular to the shore in one country will easily affect another country. The same goes for atmospheric inputs. Oil or toxic chemical accidents at sea transcend national boundaries in their impacts. The meaningful approach therefore should favour integrated and coordinated global resource development and global environmental protection strategies.

Even before but particularly since the 1972 Stockholm Conference on the Human Environment through the United Nations Law of the Sea Conference in 1982 to the 1992 United Nations Conference on Environment and Development in Rio de Janeiro, existing international agreements have implied this global view and contain, for the most part, explicit provisions for capacity building and the transfer of technologies and experience as well as financial assistance, and these issues are of legitimate concern to developing countries. It would appear prudent for coastal states in Sub-Saharan Africa to be parties to existing conventions aimed at the protection of the global ocean and coastal zone and to seek to negotiate from "within" in order to change any provisions that are not in their best interests. In the same vein, these states are encouraged to join the negotiations for future conventions to ensure that their specific concerns are catered for within the global view. Increased global solidarity is imperative in the quest for a healthier ocean and coastal zone and the rational exploitation of their resources towards sustainable development.

As a manifestation of this solidarity, the rich industrialized countries, despite their own troubles (real or perceived), should be willing (even enthusiastic) to assist developing countries, and in particular countries in Sub-Saharan Africa, in their attempts to alleviate poverty. As a developing country leader put it very lucidly many years ago, "poverty is the greatest pollution" in developing countries. Poverty is indeed the key element in the vicious cycle responsible for persistent environmental degradation in developing countries, and it would seem logical that any credible policy aimed at restoring and preserving the environment in Sub-Saharan Africa should have as a principal target the elimination of poverty. This could be done through a combination of the many schemes already proposed – for example, debt forgiveness, debt for nature swaps, interest-free loans for the installation of improved pollution-free technologies in Sub-Saharan Africa. In making the commitments called for, the rich industrialized countries must recognize that there are few or no other options open to them, because, if the developing countries "sink in a polluted ocean," the bonds and interrelationships that have made the world a global village mean that the developed world would be dragged down as well.

The time for concerted action is now. Fortunately, the Agenda 21 (Chapter 17) programme approved at the 1992 United Nations Conference on Environment and Development (UNCED 1992) affords an effective framework of global action towards the sustainable and equitable development of the entire ocean and coastal areas. It is hoped that the implementation of the provisions of Agenda 21 (Chapter 17) will bring significant improvement and protection to the ocean and coastal environment of Sub-Saharan Africa and will ensure, as was hoped for in the 1985 Brundtland Commission Report, that, in exploiting the resources of this environment, "the needs of the present generation should be satisfied without compromising those of future generations" (WCED 1987).

References

Ardill, J. D. 1984. Tuna fisheries in the south west Indian Ocean. In: S. A. Iversen and S. MyKlevoll (eds.), *Proceedings of the Seminar to Review the Marine Fish Stocks and Fisheries, Tanzania.* Bergen, Norway: Tanzania Fisheries Research Institute, Norwegian Agency for International Development, and Institute of Marine Research, pp. 97–119.

Bryceson, I. 1978a. Tanzanian coral reefs at risk. *New Scientist* 80: 115.

——— 1978b. A review of some problems of tropical marine conservation with particular reference to the Tanzanian coast. *Biological Conservation* 20: 163–171.

Bryceson, I., T. F. De Souza, I. Jehangeer, M. A. K. Ngoile, and P. Wynter. 1990. *State of the Marine Environment in the Eastern African Region.* UNEP Regional Seas Reports and Studies no. 113.

Cooke, R. U. and J. C. Doornkamp. 1974. *Geomorphology in Environmental Management: An Introduction.* Oxford: Clarendon Press.

Howell, K. M. 1988a. The conservation of marine mammals and turtles in Tanzania. Workshop on the Ecology and Bio-productivity of the Marine Coastal Waters of East Africa, University of Dar-es-Salaam, Tanzania, January.

——— 1988b. The conservation of coastal water-birds of Tanzania. Workshop on the Ecology and Bio-productivity of the Marine Coastal Waters of East Africa, University of Dar-es-Salaam, Tanzania, January.

Ibe, A. C. 1982. *A Review of Potential Economic Mineral Resources in Offshore Nigeria.* NIOMR Tech. Paper no. 8.

——— 1986a. Harbour development related erosion at Victoria Island, Lagos. In: Proceedings of the First International Conference on Geomorphology. Manchester, U.K.: 15–21 September 1985, *International Geomorphology*, Part 1, pp. 457–465.

——— 1986b. Impact of artificial structures on the Nigerian shoreline. In: J. H. Walker (ed.), *Artificial Structures and Shorelines.* Antwerp: Reidel, pp. 287–294.

——— 1986c. Experience from marine pollution monitoring in West and Central Africa. Symposium on Global Marine Pollution, Sixth Session of the IOC Scientific Committee on the Global Investigation of Pollution in the Marine Environment, Paris, 22–24 September.

——— 1987a. Marine erosion on a transgressive mud beach in western Niger delta. *Geomorphology and Environmental Management*, pp. 337–350.

——— 1987b. Port development related erosion at Excravos, Bendel State, Nigeria. In: Proceedings of the Symposium on Man and the Coastal Environment, Spain, *Thalassas Revista de Ciencias del Mar* 4(1): 91–96.

——— 1987c. Collective response to erosion hazards along the Nigerian coastline. In: Proceedings of the 5th Symposium on Coastal and Ocean Management, 1, pp. 741–754.

——— 1988a. *Coastline Erosion in Nigeria.* Ibadan, Nigeria: Ibadan University Press.

——— 1988b. The Niger delta and the global rise in sea level. In: J. Milliman (ed.), *Proceedings of the SCORE Workshop on Sea Level Rise and Subsidiary Coastal Areas, Bangkok, 7–14 November 1988.* Oxford: Pergamon Press.

——— 1989. Adjustments to the impact of sea level rise along the West and Central African coasts. In: *Proceedings of the International Workshop on Adaptive Options and Policy Implications of Sea Level Rise and other Impacts of Global Climate Change, Miami, 27 November – 1 December 1989.* Washington D.C.: US Environmental Protection Agency, vol. 1, pp. 1–14.

Ibe, A. C. and T. O. Ajayi. 1985. Possible upwelling phenomenon in offshore Nigeria. NIOMR Tech. Paper no. 25.

Ibe, A. C. and S. O. Ojo. 1993. *An Overview of Implications of Expected Climatic Changes on the Coastal and Marine Environment of West and Central Africa.* UNEP Regional Seas Reports and Studies no. 148.

Ibe, A. C. and R. E. Quélennec. 1989. *Methodology for Assessment and Control of Coastal Erosion in West and Central Africa.* UNEP Regional Seas Reports and Studies no. 127.

Ibe, A. C., E. E. Antia, and D. O. Lambert-Akhionbare. 1983. Offshore Nigeria as a source of raw materials for the steel industry. In: Proceedings of the First National Conference on Steel, Ovwian-Aladja, Bendel State, Nigeria, 18–20 April, pp. 165–176.

Ibe, A. C., L. F. Awosika, A. E. Ihenyen, C. E. Ibe, and A. I. Tiamiyu. 1985. *Coastal Erosion in Awoye and Molume Villages, Ondo State, Nigeria*. A report for Gulf Oil Co. Nigeria Ltd.

Kayambo, N. 1988. Ecology and fishery of gastropods and other molluscan species along the Dar-es-Salaam coast. Workshop on the Ecology and Bio-productivity of the Marine Coastal Waters of East Africa, University of Dar-es-Salaam, Tanzania, January.

Longhurst, A. R. 1962. Review of the oceanography of the Gulf of Guinea. *Bulletin de l'Institut Français d'Afrique Noire* (B) 24(3): 633–663.

Muslim, F. 1984. *Kenya National Report*. UNEP Regional Seas Reports and Studies no. 49, pp. 31–57.

Newell, B. S. 1957. A preliminary survey of the hydrography of British East African waters. Colonial Office Fisheries Publication 9. London: HMSO, pp. 1–21.

———— 1959. The hydrography of British East African Waters. Colonial Office Fisheries Publication 12. London: HMSO, pp. 1–18.

Ojo, S. O. 1992. Global climate change: Future perspectives. In: J. G. Tobor and A. C. Ibe (eds.), *Global Climate Change and Coastal Resources and Installations in Nigeria: Impacts and Response Measures. Proceedings of the National Seminar, Lagos, 20–21 Nov. 1990*. Lagos, Nigeria: Francis Graphics Publishers, pp. 135–145.

Portmann, J. E., C. Biney, A. C. Ibe, and S. Zabi. 1989. *State of the Marine Environment in the West and Central African Region*. UNEP Regional Seas Reports and Studies no. 108.

Semesi, A. K. 1988. Status and utilization of mangroves along Tonga coast, Tanzania. Workshop on the Ecology and Bio-productivity of the Marine Coastal Waters of East Africa, University of Dar-es-Salaam, Tanzania, January.

Tobor, J. G. and A. C. Ibe (eds.) 1992. *Global Climate Change and Coastal Resources and Installations in Nigeria: Impacts and Response Measures. Proceedings of the National Seminar, Lagos, 20–21 Nov. 1990*. Lagos, Nigeria: Francis Graphics Publishers.

UNCED (United Nations Conference on Environment and Development). 1992. *Nations of the Earth Report*, vols. 1–3. Geneva: UNCED.

UNEP (United Nations Environment Programme). 1983. *Ocean Energy Potential of the West African Region*. UNEP Regional Seas Reports and Studies no. 30.

WCED (World Commission on Environment and Development). 1987. *Our Common Future*. Oxford: Oxford University Press.

Winters, I. 1976. The oceanography of the east African coast. Paper presented at Co-operative Investigation of the North and Central Western Indian Ocean Conference, Nairobi, April.

Part 3
Environment and resource management

11

Agricultural development in the age of sustainability: Crop production

Humphrey C. Ezumah and Nkoli N. Ezumah

Introduction

It is estimated that by the year 2025 the population of Sub-Saharan Africa will double. A major concern is how to feed the population of over 480 million (without South Africa) whose 3 per cent rate of annual population increase is about the highest in the world. Climatic, ecological, and socio-economic problems plague Africa. Poor infrastructure for crop production, handling, and marketing, compounded by climatic extremes, causes fluctuations in food availability and subsequently hunger. About 100 million inhabitants of Sub-Saharan Africa (or 25 per cent) consume less than 80 per cent of the requirements recommended by the Food and Agriculture Organization of the United Nations (FAO), including the proportion filled by food imports (World Bank 1989). Because the food security of the majority of the Sub-Saharan African population that is dependent upon farming is directly influenced by agriculture, emphasis on agricultural productivity and related activities will most likely alleviate the food deficits of the most vulnerable sector. Production not only must increase but should be sustained in the long term.

The concern for sustainable development is reflected in the growing literature and policy initiatives on the issue. Definitions range from those that base sustainability on ecological balance to those that combine ecological with socio-economic concepts. Dover and Talbot (1987) view a sustainable production system as one whose productivity continues indefinitely with no noticeable degradation of the ecosystem. Earlier, Conway (1985) emphasized sustainability as the ability of a system to maintain its level of productivity in spite of a major disturbance such as is caused by an "intense or large perturbation." These definitions do not give the degree or level of production to be maintained and at what pressure on the environment. Thus the boundaries have not, according to Lynam and Herdt (1988), been ascertained in these definitions. In this paper, the explanation of sustainability that incorporates biophysical, socio-economic, and cultural concepts given by Okigbo (1989) is preferred. He defines a sustainable agricultural production system as "one which maintains an acceptable and increasing level of productivity that satisfies prevailing needs and is continuously adapted to meet the future needs for increasing the carrying capacity of the resource base and other worthwhile human needs" (1989: 3). Thus a production system leads to the development of people if it results in advancement from the current position. Development attains a sustainable level when its processes are controlled and perpetuated by resources within the reach of, and/or controlled by, the system such that any external influences do not upset the equilibrium attained. Highly developed people (or societies) attain a high quality of life using resources that they control or that are accessible to them to "own, maintain or hire" (Okigbo 1989).

The objective of this paper is to examine how agricultural development can be oriented to be highly productive and sustainable. Therefore the main discussion areas in this paper are:
- The ecological zones of Sub-Saharan Africa: their major crops and production constraints.
- General crop production constraints and the potential for overcoming them.
- Technologies with potential for sustained resource management.
- Women's underexploited potential.
- Approaches to sustainable crop production in Sub-Saharan Africa.

The ecological zones of Sub-Saharan Africa

Sub-Saharan Africa has over 23 million km² of land with a potential arable area estimated at 643 million hectares and forest at 700 million hectares, which is being cleared at the rate of 3.7 million hectares per year (World Bank 1989). Only 174 million hectares of the land are currently under cultivation. Sub-Saharan Africa is demarcated into five major ecological zones, which are determined mainly by rainfall and relief (table 11.1).

The humid forests of West and Central Africa

In the humid forests of West and Central Africa, tree crops such as oil-palm (*Elaeis guineensis*), cocoa (*Theobroma cacao*), rubber (*Hevea braziliensis*), and protected economic woody plants are grown in plantations or in multistorey associations with root and tuber crops. Rice is a major crop in both swamps and upland areas in the humid forest zone. Compound land (land immediately adjacent to the compound or homestead, often in permanent cultivation) is particularly important in these areas. Household refuse, including ash and plant and animal wastes, is used to maintain a stable multistorey plant production system. Protected trees, perennial herbaceous plants, including plantains and bananas, together with raffia are mixed with vegetables, spices, yams, and some maize in farms around the homesteads. The trees gradually decrease in number or completely disappear from farms as the distance from homesteads increases.

Soil fertility and structural instability are the most important plant production constraints of this zone. Luxurious forest growth soon gives way to eroded land when clearing is followed by intensive cropping (Kang and Juo 1981; Lal 1989). Soil acidity is common, and weeds, which flourish in the heavy rains, compete with tree and other food crops. Another important effect of forest clearing is loss of plant genetic diversity, exposure of soil to wind and water erosion, and the extinction of useful plant resources (Okigbo 1989). This resource waste is further accentuated by high average human (63 persons/km^2 in West Africa and 10/km^2 in Central Africa) and animal population pressure, intensive farming, overgrazing, construction development, hunting, and burning. A reduction in maize yield in this zone owing to cloudy skies and reduced insolation has been observed (IITA 1983).

The Southern Guinea Savanna and Derived Savanna

The humid forest of the Southern Guinea Savanna, sometimes called the sub-humid zone of West Africa, has been mostly cleared and

Table 11.1 **Major eco-zones and characteristics in Sub-Saharan Africa**

Zone	Number of humid months	Mean annual rainfall	Growing period (days)	Main soils
1. Forest: coastal West Africa and Central Africa	7–9+	1400–4000+ (mostly unimodal)	270–365	Mostly acidic (ultisols and oxisols); some non-acid (inceptisols, entisols, vertisols, alfisols, etc.)
2a. Derived Savanna	6–7	1300–1500 (bimodal, some areas)	240–270	Moderately leached soils (alfisols, some ultisols, etc.)
2b. Southern Guinea Savanna	5–6	1200–1500 (partially bimodal)	190–240	Mainly alfisols and related soils; acidic ultisols and oxisols in some wetter areas; also entisols and vertisols in some areas
3. Northern Guinea Savanna	4–5	880–1300 (unimodal)	140–200	As above, with greater proportion of non-acid alfisols
4. Sudan Savanna	2–4	500–880 (unimodal)	90–140	Alfisols and some drier aridisols, etc.
5a. Eastern and southern African highlands	7–12	750–1000 (unimodal)	270–365	Ultisols, oxisols, vertisols
5b. Eastern and southern African highlands	5–6	750–1000 (bimodal)	190–240	Alfisols, ultisols, oxisols

Source: Adapted from Papadakis (1966); FAO (1978); Kowal and Kassam (1978); Lawson (1979).

218

cropped for a long period and has been overtaken mainly by grasses and shrubs. At an early stage of succession from forest to savanna is the Derived Savanna, which is better known as Guinea Savanna (Ter Kuile 1987). Rainfall in the Derived Savanna may be slightly higher than that in the Southern Guinea Savanna (table 11.1). Sorghum and maize are important cereals, and root crops (cassava and yams) grow and yield highly.

The high infestation of tse-tse fly debars the use of oxen as sources of power; therefore labour at peak growing seasons is a major constraint. This zone is poorly served by roads and marketing systems. Weeds, particularly the parasitic *Striga*, attack the dominant cereal crops. The soils are relatively rich and are structurally more stable than humid forest soils but are frequently deficient in some major nutrients, whose efficiency may be reduced by negative interaction with minor elements, e.g. phosphorus (P) and zinc (Zn).

The Northern Guinea Savanna

The Northern Guinea Savanna of West Africa, also called the sorghum–millet belt of West Africa, receives lower rainfall than the southern part. It is excellent for maize growth and some of the highest yields in West Africa are obtained from this zone (IITA 1984). Sorghum is also important. However, drought at critical stages of maize development frequently reduces grain yields. High soil temperatures and high evaporation rates are also important constraints (Hullugale 1989). The parasitic weed *Striga* attacks cereals and grain legumes (cowpea), the two important food-crop groups grown in the Northern Guinea Savanna. The soil is more favourable for cropping and responds to N, P, and S applications. Soil erosion caused by wind and soil crusting and capping has also been reported (Charreau 1970).

The Sudan Savanna

The Sudan Savanna is located to the north of the Northern Guinea Savanna. Rainfall is unimodal, its duration is uncertain, and crop failures are common. Millet and cowpeas are the major food crops in this area. Cereals are grown on about 70 per cent of the total cultivated area of the Sudan Savanna (Matlon 1987). Cotton and groundnuts are the major commercial crops and are sometimes grown for export.

The eastern and southern African highlands

The generalizations about the preceding zones are modified by high elevation in Rwanda, eastern Zaire, Burundi, and the mountainous plains of eastern Africa. The monsoon tropical climate and the high incidence of radiation result in extremely high productivity.

In the area of the eastern and southern highlands where rainfall is unimodal, high maize yields are recorded. However, rainfall may limit production. Banana is an important staple and groundnuts are also grown commercially. Coffee and tea, particularly the former, are export crops.

In the area where rainfall is bimodal (March/April to May and November to January), the short duration of the rainfall requires very intensive labour in land preparation and planting, the consequences of which are frequent crop losses. The crops grown are maize, coffee, and bananas. High population pressure on the soils of both highlands, with only 5–7 months of rainfall, causes low productivity. Soil loss is high, particularly in the communal lands of Zimbabwe, where it is reported at 50 tons/ha/yr (Whitlow 1987) and results in reduced yields of crops (Collinson 1987).

There are, therefore, three broad zones: (a) the humid forest zones of West and Central Africa, (b) the savanna zone, demarcated by the level of available rainfall, and (c) the highlands, including plateaux.

General crop production constraints and potentials for overcoming them

Constraints

Paulino (1987) reports that cereals (wheat, maize, sorghum, millet, rice) constitute 54 per cent by calories of the food crops grown in Sub-Saharan Africa, while root and tuber crops (cassava, yams, potatoes, and taros) make up 27 per cent of calories. All other crops (plantains and bananas, grain legumes, fruits and vegetables, etc.) make up the balance of 19 per cent. Many traditional varieties of these crops are low yielding and the improved varieties released do not seem to have made an impact in the Sub-Saharan Africa region. De Bruijn and Fresco (1989) report relatively small increases in cassava yield (23 per cent) compared with maize (55 per cent) in developing countries during 1984–1986 compared with 1961–1965. The

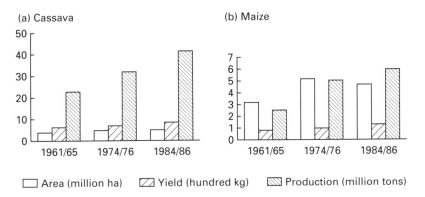

(a) Cassava (b) Maize

□ Area (million ha)   ▨ Yield (hundred kg)   ▧ Production (million tons)

Fig. 11.1 **Area, yield, and production of cassava and maize in Africa, 1961–1965, 1974–1976, and 1984–1986 (Source: adapted from de Bruijn and Fresco 1989)**

yield increases shown in figure 11.1 are small compared with the population increase, which stood at 71 per cent in Africa during the same period. The small increases in production and yield of cassava and maize during the two decades illustrate the small average effect of introducing improved crop varieties into Africa. Increases in other major crops such as yams, rice, wheat, sorghum, and millet were similarly low in comparison with human population increases. Sweet potato, which produces more dry matter per unit area and time than any other crop in Sub-Saharan Africa, is not a preferred crop, but, fed to pigs and poultry, it can be converted to protein and fats.

Insufficient and excess rains, as well as management and socio-economic factors, also result in reduced productivity. Across the ecological regions of Sub-Saharan Africa constraints are related to the amount and distribution of rains and to poor soil conditions for plant growth. Rainfall in Sub-Saharan Africa is highly variable, ranging from excessive in places such as Debunscha, Cameroon, with 10,000 mm average annual rainfall to about 200–300 mm in some areas of West Africa. Drought-induced crop losses in the drier areas of Sub-Saharan Africa occur frequently (Matlon 1987). In the tropical zone, drought-induced crop losses may occur during years in which the rains are poorly distributed (Ter Kuile 1987; Lawson 1985). The incidence of diseases and pests is enhanced by rainfall and soil condition. An example is the noxious weed spear grass (*Imperata cylindrica*), which thrives in areas where forest vegetation is replaced by grass. Many diseases such as *Pythium* and *Rhizoctonium* rots occur mainly in high-rainfall areas, as does cassava bacterial blight, *Xan-*

221

thomonas manihoti, which requires high humidity to survive (Lawson and Terry 1984), while the cassava mealybug (*Phenacoccus manihoti* MF) is very serious during dry seasons (Nwanze et al. 1977; Herren 1989). Multiple soil nutrient deficiencies, especially in areas with a high cropping intensity, low inherent soil fertility characterized by low cation exchange capacity (CEC), high acidity, rapid organic matter decomposition, high P fixation, high erodibility, and leaching – all compounded by a dominance of low activity clay (Kang and Juo 1981) – render most of the soils in Sub-Saharan Africa unsuitable for intensive crop production using available technologies.

Farmers with few resources, a large proportion of whom are women, dominate in Sub-Saharan Africa. They may manage efficiently at their resource level, which, unfortunately, is low in productivity. High resource inputs require more efficient and demanding managerial skills, which should be demonstrated by profit margins in competitive markets and not by ability to survive. Women who dominate in farming have very limited access to production resources.

Institutional and policy constraints have been discussed by Vallaeys et al. (1987), Olayide and Idachaba (1987), and other authors in Mellor et al. (1987). They emphasize the underdeveloped marketing and input/output infrastructure of the agricultural sector, low investment in research, amounting to about 0.5 per cent of gross agricultural product (Vallaeys et al. 1987), poor research-extension–farmer linkages, which reduce the effectiveness of technology transfer (Collinson 1987), and the high dependence of agricultural inputs on imports, which are becoming increasingly costly as foreign exchange becomes scarce. Yet the prices of farm outputs decline.

Potentials for overcoming constraints

In spite of the constraints enumerated above, crop production in Sub-Saharan Africa could increase tremendously if adequate human and institutional resources were available to manage the biophysical resources. To buttress this statement, Ruttan (1988) noted that the achievement of the level of development attained by developed countries will depend upon Africa's commitment to the investment in the institutional and physical infrastructure required to exploit the production potential of the resources with which Africa is endowed. De Wit et al. (1979) report a calculation by de Hoogh et al. (1976) that shows that, whereas the potential arable land in tropical Africa is 643 million ha, the area in use is only 174 million ha, or 27 per cent.

The same data indicate that yield expressed in 1965 grain equivalent for Africa was only 74,000 million out of a potential 9,474,000 million kilocalories, i.e. only 0.8 per cent. Thus the biophysical resources available in Sub-Saharan Africa and elsewhere in the world are grossly underutilized. Because these calculations were based upon biophysical potentials (fertilizer and water are not limiting, diseases and pests are controlled, optimal available solar radiation is captured), it was concluded that the main obstacles to increased crop production are socio-economic (capital, institutions, policy, culture). Sub-Saharan Africa could resolve its food deficit problem if even 25 per cent of this estimation were attained. How do we manage the resources of crop production (including human, with an emphasis on women farmers) so that resources are sustained? This question calls for a re-examination of the technologies available and their usefulness in sustained resource management.

Technologies with potential for sustainable resource management

Good technologies with missing links

In Sub-Saharan Africa, considerable efforts have been expended on the development of improved cereals, root and tuber crops, and food and fodder legumes by plant breeders, and also on the characterization and identification of the limitations of the soils. Pest control measures have also received attention, particularly from international (IITA, IRRI, ICRISAT, WARDA, ILCA, ICP),[1] national, and other research centres and universities in Africa. Agronomists and soil scientists have conducted a lot of research on responses to fertilizer application of various crops in different ecological settings, and breeders and disease and pest control specialists have documented results based on chemical, host plant resistance, biological, and chemical control measures.

Each of these results, introduced into a farmer's system, provides some relief to problems. The ephemeral nature of some of the relief is realized when the breeders' variety yields less than expected in the intensive multistorey crop association system of small-scale farmers (Juo and Ezumah 1992), and when the expected response to fertilizer is not realized, either because the increased crop pressure requires higher applications (Wahua 1983; Olasantan 1992), or because the soil physical conditions have deteriorated so much that the effectiveness of fertilizer is reduced in intensive systems (Lal and Greenland 1978). Similarly, the undesirable long-term effects of pest and disease control by a non-integrated approach have been documented (Maxwell 1990). A holistic approach to research and extension, which also incorporates the concepts of integrated pest management (IPM), could reduce the dangers of unsustainable crop production in Sub-Saharan Africa.

Technical innovation in agriculture is generally not designed so as to exploit the complementary and synergistic effects of the important results for sustained crop production enumerated earlier. Such complementarities are achievable when technologies are developed from current farmers' knowledge base, using multidisciplinary experiences (Norman 1982; Hildebrand 1990). The central thesis is that resource-poor farmers do not adopt technologies that require costly inputs of labour, cash, and materials or technologies for which inputs are not readily available. These technologies therefore do not fit in the farmers' production environment and frequently break the linkages that enhance resource conservation.

The International Institute of Tropical Agriculture, for example, developed an early maturing erect cowpea that, together with other improved varieties, required frequent applications of insecticide. Among the early varieties were TVX3236 and IT82E-60. As long as chemicals were subsidized when the Nigerian currency, the naira, was relatively strong, some farmers, particularly those on larger farms, grew these cowpea varieties. The majority of the small-scale farmers did not adopt the early, erect types because (a) they required insecticides that were not available or that they could not afford and (b) the vegetation required as animal feed was too scanty. Thus the improved variety that matured early enough in the low-rainfall zones did not satisfy the conditions for its adoption (Carr 1989). With respect to fertilizers, recommendations are available in virtually every country in Sub-Saharan Africa. The limited use of fertilizers, even when prices are subsidized, is attributed to poor distribution systems (Harrison 1987). Although many farmers in south-eastern Nigeria (Unamma et al. 1985) and in Zaire (Osiname et al. 1987) are aware of the importance of fertilizers and herbicides, most are not making use of them because (i) they may not be available either at all or when required, (ii) they are too costly, or (iii) they require equipment that the farmers do not own, e.g. knapsack sprayers. A common feature of the technologies cited – which also include tractorized tillage, liming, short-stalked, high-yielding sorghum for farmers who may require stalks for fencing or for fuelwood, and zero tillage unaccompanied by a weed control package for reduced tillage systems – is that they do not fit into farmers' production environments because some components that would facilitate their usefulness in existing systems are missing. Adoption of the early cowpea and of dwarf sorghum might, because of high yields, lead to a destruction of vegetation from other environments for animal feed and for fuelwood. It is also noted that the modern practices of conventional agriculture, which comprise land clearing and preparation (tillage systems), fertilization, weed control, and harvesting, have elements of environmental degradation.

Mimicking natural ecosystems

Almost all the sustainable systems currently available in Sub-Saharan Africa mimic natural ecosystems. These systems comprise traditional shifting cultivation, which is sustainable at low population pressures, well-managed multiple-cropping systems (which include compound land systems), the alley cropping system, and the fadama or inland valley systems. These systems may have some or all of the following attributes: extending the duration of growth of the plant community, increasing light-capturing potential through multi-layer interception over a longer period, and recycling nutrients from deep layers. The systems also integrate many groups of plant species – ephemerals, annuals, and perennials – in the same land area. By mimicking nature, microclimates suitable for the growth of many species of plants, and that therefore enhance diversity, are created (Okigbo and Greenland 1976; Juo and Ezumah 1992). Multiple-cropping (i.e. intercropping and rotation) leads to more efficient resource use and this is reflected in yield advantages (Osiru and Willey 1972; Okigbo and Greenland 1976; Willey 1979; Ezumah and Lawson 1984, 1990). Associations that exhibit yield advantage may be long-duration plants inter-cropped with short-duration plants (Okigbo and Greenland 1976; H. Ezumah 1990) or combinations of short-duration crops belonging to the same family, e.g. sorghum and millet (Willey 1979), or of different species, e.g. sorghum and pigeon pea (Rao and Willey 1983) or maize and cowpea (Ezumah and Ikeorgu 1993). Other advantages of multiple-cropping include improved physical and chemical soil conditions for growth (Lal 1976), reduced soil temperature (Lal 1976; Ikeorgu and Ezumah 1991), reduced soil surface evaporation, and increased water content (Lal 1976). Increased biological activity in

225

the soil (e.g. earthworm activity) in intercropping compared with monocrop rotations (Hullugale and Ezumah 1991) and a reduction in surface runoff and soil loss and therefore a reduction of soil degradation have also been reported for intercropped situations (Aina et al. 1977). In Ouagadougou, Hullugale (1989) showed that undersowing *Stylosanthes* with maize reduced soil temperature and increased soil moisture, which was significantly improved by conserving moisture through the erection of cross ridges or tying of ridges. Ikeorgu and Ezumah's (1991) results also showed reduced soil temperature in cassava intercropped in four complex mixtures with maize, okra, and egusi melon compared with sole cassava or cassava + maize intercrops. These results highlight the need to focus research on farmers' current systems and to improve on them. They also show the importance of conserving plants and animals in the wild, because their usefulness to humans, apart from the broad concept of ecological balance, is unknown.

Surface mulching

Some of the advantages of multiple cropping are also obtained by surface mulching of the soil with dead material (Lal 1976). Okigbo (1977) studied a wide range of mulching materials including gravel, sawdust from wood, translucent white and black plastics, as well as foliage and twigs from different plant sources including leguminous and non-leguminous plants. The short-term advantages of mulching on an alfisol in Nigeria appear to relate more to improvement of the soil microclimate for plant growth than to chemical properties, because higher crop yields were obtained from the plastic mulches than from the foliages and the twigs. These effects do not, however, negate the long-term benefits of mulching (Lal 1989). A major difficulty of mulching is the procurement of materials. Lawson and Lal (1980) estimated a threshold of 4–6 tons/ha for effective mulching on an alfisol in Nigeria. This quantity of mulch is too much for a low-resource farmer to carry. Akobundu (1980) reported higher maize yield without N fertilization over a five-year period of continuous cropping in association with living legume plants (*Psophocarpus palustris* and *Centrosema pubescens*). Little response to N fertilizer was observed in the legume-associated plots compared with the control, which responded to over 60 kg N fertilization per hectare. For greater benefits, a well-established legume plot is required (Mulongoy and Akobundu 1985). Cassava intercropped with maize generates enough mulch to sustain yields. The IITA (1985) reported stable yields of cassava and maize over four years on an alfisol in southern Nigeria. Longer-duration maize (over 120 days to maturity) with high dry matter gave higher yields than shorter-duration maize (less than 100 days to maturity). The short-duration maize allowed in more light to the associated cassava in their intercrop system.

Alley cropping

The most recent innovation in mimicking the natural ecosystem is the alley cropping system (Kang and Wilson 1987). In alley cropping, the multistorey association of the compound land setting is rearranged so that trees occupy adjacent hedges (hedgerows), about 4m apart. Crops are then grown in the alleys between the hedges. Trees are chosen for certain characteristics such as deep rooting (to recycle nutrients), ability to coppice and to produce high biomass (which is pruned for mulching and nutrient release), and, sometimes, rhizobia N-fixing ability. Legume trees in the hedges contribute N in excess of 40 kg/ha to associated crops (Kang 1988). Even non-legumes recycle deeply located nutrients at about 13–19 kg/ha. Although the alley system contributes to moisture conservation, organic residue, and structural and chemical improvements to the soil, a reduction in the yields of associated crops owing to reduced light because of the tree canopy has been observed (Lawson and Kang 1990). Considering its soil improvement features and the stability of alley cropping over a period of years (Kang and Wilson 1987; IITA 1989: fig. 2), alley cropping is a sustainable system that needs refining. Unlike compound farming, it is amenable to large-scale methods. The labour requirements for pruning, which often coincides with other important farm activities (e.g. weeding and harvesting of maize and melon), are a serious setback (Ngambeki 1985). Alley species suitable for acid soils are still being sought. Figure 11.2a shows a rapid decline of maize yields in a continuous cropping system, even if fertilizer is applied. Alley cropping can stabilize maize yields at levels that vary with inputs, e.g. fertilizer (fig. 11.2b). In the latter case, fertilizer augments biologically generated nutrients to sustain maize yields.

Inland valleys

Inland valleys or fadamas, though small individually, total tens of millions of hectares in West and Central Africa. International Insti-

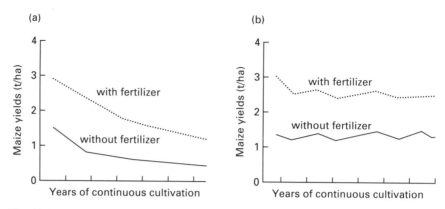

Fig. 11.2 **Maize production at IITA, Ibadan. (a) Relationship between length of continuous cultivation and maize yields. (b) Sustainability of maize production in alley cropping systems (Source: Kang and Wilson 1987)**

tute of Tropical Agriculture estimates for West Africa alone gave about 14 million ha (IITA 1980). Inland valleys are well watered and have enormous potential for producing food, especially rice. In China, inland valleys have been cropped continuously for centuries (Juo and Lowe 1986). The neglect of Sub-Saharan Africa's inland valleys, according to the International Institute of Tropical Agriculture (IITA 1990), is attributed to lack of knowledge about their management, which leads to their infection by vectors of many harmful diseases, such as *Schistosomiasis*, river blindness, malaria, and guinea worms. In addition to water availability, the inland valleys are sustainable and give higher rice yields because they are relatively high in fertility as a result of inflows of nutrients from the uplands. Increased fertility of the inland valleys of Sub-Saharan Africa can be attained by rotating rice with legumes tolerant of water logging, some of which are *Crotolaria* spp., soybean (*Glycine max*), and *Sesbania* spp. Thus, exploitation of the potential for sustainable plant production in the inland valleys of Sub-Saharan Africa requires more research.

Disease and pest control

Some known crop management methods to control diseases and pests include chemical and mechanical measures. These may require high capital and labour inputs. Host plant resistance and biological control measures, though requiring high initial investment at institutional levels, are sustainable and indirectly affordable by the low-resource farmers of Sub-Saharan Africa. Recent examples include the control of cassava bacterial blight (*Xanthomonas manihotis*) by resistance breeding (Hahn et al. 1979) and the effective reduction of the cassava mealybug pest (*Phenacoccus manihoti* Mat-Fer) by biological control (Neuenschwander and Hammond 1987). A parasitoid, *Epidino-carsis lopezi*, introduced from Latin America and released at strategic sites has contributed to the reduction of the cassava mealybug epidemic in Africa.

Many examples of disease and pest resistance through breeding have been documented for various crops in Sub-Saharan Africa. Claims that diseases and pests (except for weeds, for which it has been demonstrated) are controlled by intercropping need further research because reports have been inconsistent (IITA 1978; Francis 1989).

Women's underexploited potential

One of the causes of the "weak agricultural growth" in Africa is the underutilization of human resource potential (World Bank 1989: 2). This is particularly manifested in the gender gap in access to production resources. The majority of African food crop producers who are smallholder farmers, and women in particular, experience great difficulties in increasing production. To achieve sustainable agricultural production it is imperative to eliminate those factors that hinder the productivity of the majority of food producers.

African women are responsible for about 70 per cent of the labour input in food production. Their activities include hoeing, planting, weeding, transportation of crops and planting materials, food processing, and storage. Men, on the other hand, have been largely responsible for bush clearing, land preparation, staking of crops, and hunting (FAO 1982). Recent trends characterizing gender roles in African agriculture have been identified (Guyer 1986: 396–398), namely, that male tasks in agriculture are declining owing to: (a) the decrease in forest cover and game resources; (b) the greater participation of men in out-migration; and (c) male predominance in export crop production. As a corollary, women's agricultural work has been intensified. Factors responsible for this development are that: (a) shorter fallows are now used, resulting in increased weeding; (b) as the distance of farms from homes increases, there is greater demand for the transport of crops and planting materials; (c) as the food trade increases, the demand for food processing increases; and (d) the predominance of men in migration leads to an increased workload for women in food production.

Despite the increased responsibility of African women for food production, their productive capacity is deteriorating because they continue to suffer from less access to production resources and inputs, agricultural innovations, and extension services. Some specific constraints that are important for women farmers in Sub-Saharan Africa concern limited or no access to resources such as land, capital/credit, labour, and agricultural innovations.

Access to land

In most African societies women traditionally had use rights to land (Pala 1976). The introduction of the Western concept of private land ownership has been to the detriment of women (Boserup 1970). Some development programmes in Africa have also exacerbated women's restricted access to land. Pankhurst and Jacobs (1988) report women's loss of land through land reforms in Zimbabwe. The marginalization of women in the allocation of irrigated rice fields to men in the Gambia adversely affected rice production and gender relations and also culminated in the failure of the project (Dey 1981; Carney 1988).

Access to credit

Smallholder farmers, particularly women, who lack access to credit experience great difficulties in purchasing inputs to increase their production. Access to credit is often based on ownership of collaterals such as land or membership of cooperatives and farmers' associations, which many African rural women lack (Loutfi 1980; Cloud 1985). Consequently, most agricultural bank loans in the past went to "absentee" or "progressive" farmers (professionals, top bureaucrats, and military personnel) (Bukh 1979; D'Silva and Raza 1983; Okuneye 1984).

Access to labour

The male predominance in rural–urban migration for wage employment has resulted in the intensification of women's work in agriculture and in labour shortages in food production, particularly in female-headed households (Rogers 1980). Women's lack of access to credit has a concomitant effect on their ability to purchase paid labour (Roberts 1988). A greater number of women consequently dissipate a lot of energy that could be channelled towards increased productivity on their farms in other enterprises such as working as paid labour on other people's farms or providing exchange labour in return for labour received (Guyer 1984; N. Ezumah 1990). Women's cultural obligation to provide labour on their husband's farm also results in limitations on the amount of time they can devote to their own farms (Babalola and Dennis 1988).

Access to improved technologies

The dissemination of information about innovations in agriculture as well as access to training, fertilizers and other inputs, and extension services have been geared mainly to male farmers with adverse effects on women's productivity. Most training in agriculture has been directed to men. The marginalization of women in terms of access to production inputs has often resulted in the deterioration of women's productive capacity (Muntemba 1982). "Progressive" farmers, usually men, have received preferential allocation of extension visits and services (D'Silva and Raza 1983; Okuneye 1984). Some of the adverse consequences of this neglect of women's role in the implementation of agricultural innovations include a loss in adaptive efficiency when women's operational knowledge is not taken into consideration and lower adaptation rates owing to women's lack of access to technology and training (Kumar 1988: 142).

Suggested approaches to sustainable production

Wisdom from farmers' production systems

Systems that have a high potential for sustainability mimic natural ecosystems and ensure continuity in supply of some important resources for plant growth, e.g. vegetation, nutrients, and water, and prevent their losses from soils by erosion. These systems are those practised by farmers whose habitats scientists are trying to understand. Biological control is one of the benefits of maintaining the ecological diversity of plants and animals. Therefore, approaches that incorporate farmers' relevant knowledge and experience into designs for improvement will most likely be sustainable, as has been shown in the examples of mimicking natural ecosystems. The Association of Farming Systems Research and Extension (Norman 1982; Okigbo 1989; Hildebrand 1990) emphasizes approaches requiring a thorough diagnosis of existing systems and conditions before designing any improvements and experimenting and testing them in farmers' fields. Improvements will definitely be necessary because the existing farmers' systems, developed in a given set of conditions (such as shifting cultivation at low population densities with bush path highways), break down when practised in situations for which they are not meant. Such improvements should gradually build up from existing systems (Hildebrand 1990) instead of replacing them completely. When replacement is the adopted approach, the system breaks down and frustration occurs, as was noted by Nye and Greenland (1960: v), who reviewed the effectiveness of technologies generated in Europe and applied in tropical Africa and observed that "after a quarter of a century of experiment in the African tropics, we have failed to introduce to the forest regions any method of staple food production superior to the system of natural fallowing used in shifting cultivation." The current research emphasis on multiple cropping, agro-forestry, including alley systems, and mulching of various kinds to produce plant cover for the soil represents a refinement of farmers' shifting cultivation to fit emerging situations.

Requirements of new technologies

To be sustainable, new technologies should address the whole farm and interactions in plant production systems (Hildebrand 1990). Donor interest in Farming Systems Research and Extension (FSR/E) may no longer be strong, as was shown by the funding problems of FSR/E and the complete absence of donors during a recent international meeting (AFSR/E annual meeting, East Lansing, Michigan, September 1992). Yet sustainability and FSR/E are compatible concepts because whole farm situations and interactions of their components need to be understood. An implication is that the days of neatly laid out field experiments with one or two factors and high environmental controls may be over (Federer, personal communication, 1991). High levels of variability are to be expected at farm level and more attention to interactions than to the main effects may pay off in understanding farmers' real situations and problems.

232

Sub-Saharan Africa and water problems

At optimum water supply and disease and pest control, Linnemann and his co-workers (1979) showed that the potential annual grain production in Sub-Saharan Africa was about 10 billion metric tons. Burningh et al. (1975) estimated that the potential agricultural area in Africa in 1965–1973 was 23 per cent of Africa's total land area. Out of this area, only 6 per cent is cultivated, with a yield of 1,000 kg/ha, i.e. about 10 per cent of the 10,000 kg/ha potential. Burningh et al. (1975) concluded that the problem is one more of social and economic than of biophysical potential. Nevertheless, biophysical factors are of great importance if this potential is not exploited in a sustainable manner. Many of the improved crop varieties currently in use in Sub-Saharan Africa do not yield as much as they would if adequate water were available. In the humid zones of West and Central Africa, water distribution is such that crops are oversupplied for certain months of the year and undersupplied in others. A lack of water is also noted in some areas in the humid zone because of poor distribution, which often reduces the duration of crop growth (de Wit et al. 1979). Eastin et al. (1969) have shown that moisture stress adversely affects inflorescence development and grain filling and leads to inefficient use of nutrients. With stress, either fertilization is inhibited or grains that are already fertilized abort. Irrespective of breeders' expected yields, crop yields decline because of the reduced duration of growth attributed to the moisture stress of cereal grains (de Wit et al. 1979) or of roots and tubers (Lawson 1985). An urgent technical input is to ensure timely water distribution for plant growth. Even for cassava, which is tolerant of moisture stress, storage root yield is decreased during the dry season months of the transitional zone of West Africa (Lawson 1985).

Implications for plant breeding

For most plant breeders, favourable yields are based on high economic yields and the high harvest indices of improved varieties per unit of space and time. Varieties are usually evaluated in monocropping systems using the recommended levels of fertilizer and pest control. Evidence now available suggests that these values need to be reassessed in plant production systems aimed at sustainable development. To conserve soil resources, there is a need to conserve biological life: living organisms can be adversely affected by pesticides

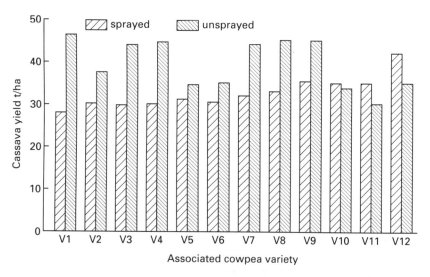

Fig. 11.3 **Effects on cassava root yields of insecticide protection applied to inter-cropped cowpeas in an IITA experiment in southern Nigeria, 1987/88 (Source: unpublished data from IITA Experimental Service)**

and other chemicals; ploughing accelerates soil and nutrient losses owing to erosion and leaching; good harvests at the expense of leaves, stems, and other plant parts may be detrimental because the additional vegetative materials needed for mulching the soil are lost. In highly vegetative plants, nutrients that could have been leached off or volatilized from soil may be held in plant parts and later released during decomposition.

The age of sustainability calls for a modification of breeding objectives. It may require new approaches in testing improved varieties and a re-examination of selection procedures. A trait lost may be hard to recover at later stages in a breeding cycle. An example is cassava, whose shoot and root yields may be reduced significantly by spraying cowpea intercropped with the cassava as compared with unsprayed cowpea and cassava (fig. 11.3). Without a systems approach, this interaction may be missed because cowpea protected from insect attack by spraying yielded higher than when unsprayed. Thus the limited objective of increasing cowpea yield is achieved but the broader objectives of ecological balance and of increasing total yield are not attained.

The lack of involvement of users in the development of technologies can lead to non-acceptance of the results. The success of intensive agricultural development in Taiwan is mainly the result of farmer pressure on researchers. In a study of 150 selected projects by US firms, Merrill-Sands (1992) reported a failure rate of about 67 per cent and a success rate of 15 per cent in cases where user influence on the products developed was characterized by hostility and distrust. The exact opposite, 67 per cent success and 14 per cent failure, was observed when client pressure or demand-pull led to product development. The high rate of cassava (TMS 30572) and sweet potato (TIB1) adoption in West Africa, particularly in Nigeria and Cameroon, respectively, appears to relate more to their development in unfertilized soil, which may have simulated the farmers' soil conditions, than to any other factor.

Virtually all the crops that generate export income, such as cocoa, coffee, and oil-palm, are declining in importance in the world market. For increased export earnings, Sub-Saharan Africa may need to produce specialized products in which it commands some advantages. The luxuriant vegetation, fruits, and nuts in African landscapes contain important oils, some protein, lubricants, and condiments (Okigbo 1980). Their potential benefits to Sub-Saharan Africa and in the world market remain unknown. For example, the cash income derived from some protected isolated stands of trees (*Elaeis guineensis*, *Irvingia gabonensis*, *Raphia* spp., and *Bytyrospermum paradoxum*) in southern Nigeria in 1980 was at least 2.3 naira per tree per day or over 10 naira (US$0.5) at 1980 rates (Okafor 1980). Multiplication and improvement of important plants can be effected by biotechnology, which also has considerable potential in health care (medicine, nutrition) and in the chemical and cosmetic industries. New, improved crops with desirable characteristics, as well as cheap pest and disease control measures, are other potential benefits of biotechnology that Sub-Saharan Africa may miss out on if action is not taken to utilize existing facilities and create new ones if necessary.

Enhancing women's productivity

To attain sustainable development arising from the increased agricultural productivity of Sub-Saharan Africa, the human resource potentials of both men and women should be developed. Concrete efforts should be geared towards enhancing the productivity of all those involved in food crop production. As women are now responsible for the bulk of the food crops produced on small farm holdings, the emphasis should be on providing them with access to the resources and inputs necessary to increase their productive capacity (specific resources have already been discussed).

Summary

This paper has discussed the potential for developing sustainable plant production systems for Sub-Saharan Africa. Only a small fraction of the biophysical potential for crop production in Sub-Saharan Africa is exploited. Although the constraints on plant production are many, they can be reduced to three main focus areas: rainfall, soil-related issues, and human resource management.

There is a need to develop methods of conserving the available water and to invest in water storage, particularly for those semi-arid areas of Sub-Saharan Africa where there is a serious lack of moisture. This requires investment, but approaches currently used by farmers (stone and plant barriers, surface catchments, tied ridges) need to be improved and inland valleys should be exploited. All these require more research. Agro-forestry species tolerant of acid soils and adapted to the semi-arid zone should be identified and evaluated for their usefulness in alley or related systems.

In the humid forests, the Guinea and moist savannas, and the highlands of eastern Africa, agro-forestry systems, multiple-cropping systems, and surface mulching using appropriate live mulch species need to be studied further. These have elements of sustainability that require additional research prior to their wide application. Of particular importance is the interaction of live mulches with soil moisture, especially in dry areas. With the increasing cost of imported chemicals, fertilizer research should be redirected to determining the minimum levels required for sustained yields and to augment nutrients generated through biological activity.

Holistic approaches to technological developments pay off in terms of their ease of adoption. Step-wise approaches to technology development, using farmers' current systems as the base, appear to have merits for the small-scale farmers of Sub-Saharan Africa. Research into whole farm systems requires a revision of the operational approach. Farm-level research is very complex and involves many interactions; it therefore requires multidisciplinary team efforts. Less rigorous but useful analytic approaches should be devised for interpreting data. Most of the farmers in Sub-Saharan Africa are women. Their neglect in resource allocation should be redressed by gearing efforts towards enhancing their productivity.

Finally, biotechnology may be the cheapest hope if it is applied to resolving some of the constraints, for example through multiplication of improved varieties, particularly clonal materials (Zok and Nyochembeng 1992), conservation of wild and exotic species, and breeding for disease and pest resistance and much other gene-related research. Regional laboratories to handle this specialized work need to be created, staffed, and funded for the mutual benefit of the countries of Sub-Saharan Africa, and special management procedures devised for the laboratories. Some existing laboratories – for example, the Jay P. Johnson Biotechnology Laboratory, Ekona, Cameroon, and the International Institute of Tropical Agriculture Biotechnology Laboratory at Ibadan, Nigeria – could be expanded to serve parts of the region, and the possibility of establishing others needs to be evaluated. Courses in biotechnology to acquaint researchers and policy makers with its potential (similar to the one designed by Ferguson et al. 1992) could be modified to fit Sub-Saharan African conditions and videotaped for popular use. Such a course could remind researchers and policy makers of the usefulness of cell biology in agriculture and of the basic training requirements.

Conclusions

1. Sub-Saharan Africa has more than enough biophysical resources to produce more food and other plants at sustained levels.
2. Research should be directed to exploiting existing biological complementarities in a holistic manner. Inorganic inputs should be used to complement, not to replace, biological inputs.
3. Post-harvest losses constitute a major source of productivity loss in Sub-Saharan Africa.
4. Since most crops in Sub-Saharan Africa are produced by women, gender issues are very important and should be addressed in developing plant production and utilization technologies.
5. Small-scale farming is not necessarily bad, and increased production does not necessarily call for increased farm size.
6. Given the adverse effects of mechanization in terms of the degradation of soil resources in the tropics, one must be cautious about introducing mechanization, especially because it is not a panacea for increased production and yield (see 5).
7. With serious effort and resource commitment, the perennial problem as regards water for crop production and for human needs could be resolved. This is an area in which investment probably

could be made to pay, bearing in mind that some parts of California, Nevada, and Israel, for example, which produce surplus food, are in deserts.

8. Continued conservation of species diversity, especially some wild species, is advocated. What is wild today may find a use tomorrow.
9. The potential of biotechnology needs to be exploited through organized groupings of Sub-Saharan African regions to invest in gene-related research.

Acknowledgements

We are grateful to Mr. George Gamze for help in reproducing this paper. To Mrs. C. N. F. Poubom, Mr. A. E. Efite, and Dr. Charles Yamoah we give thanks for proofreading the manuscript and making useful suggestions. In spite of these contributions, all responsibility for the contents of this paper is that of the authors.

Note

1. IITA: International Institute of Tropical Agriculture; IRRI: International Rice Research Institute; ICRISAT: International Centre for Research in Semi Arid Tropics; WARDA: West African Rice Development Association; ILCA: International Livestock Research Centre; ICP: International Centre for Insect Physiology.

References

Aina, P. O., R. Lal, and G. S. Taylor. 1977. Soil crop management in relation to soil erosion in the rainforest of Western Nigeria. In: *Soil Erosion Prediction and Control*. Soil Conservation Society of America, Special Publication 21: 75–84.

Akobundu, I. O. 1980. Live mulch: A new approach to weed control and crop production in the tropics. In: *British Crop Protection Conference: Proceedings of the 1980 British Weed Control Conference, 17–20 November, Brighton, England*. Oxford: ARC Weed Research Organization, pp. 377–382.

Babalola, S. O. and C. Dennis 1988. Returns to women's labour in cash crop production: Tobacco in the Igboho, Oyo State, Nigeria. In: J. Davidson (ed.), *Agriculture, Women and Land: The African Experience*. Boulder and London: Westview Press, pp. 79–89.

Boserup, E. 1970. *Woman's Role in Economic Development*. New York: St. Martin's Press.

Bruijn, G. H. de and L. O. Fresco. 1989. The importance of cassava in world food production. *Netherlands Journal of Agricultural Science* 37: 21–34.

Bukh, J. 1979. *The Village Woman in Ghana*. Uppsala, Sweden: Scandinavian Institute of African Studies.

Burningh, P., H. D. J. Van Heemst, and G. J. Staring. 1975. Computation of the absolute maximum food production of the world. Department of Tropical Soil Science, Agricultural University, Wageningen, The Netherlands.

238

Carney, J. A. 1988. Struggles over land and crops in an irrigated rice scheme: The Gambia. In: J. Davison (ed.), *Agriculture, Women and Land: The African Experience*. Boulder and London: Westview Press, pp. 59–78.

Carr, J. S. 1989. *Technology for Small-scale Farmers in Sub-Saharan Africa. Experience with Food Crop Production in Five Major Ecological Zones*. Technical paper no. 109. Washington D.C.: World Bank.

Charreau, C. 1970. Traditional African agricultural systems and their improvement. FAO/IITA Conference on Shifting Cultivation, Ibadan, Nigeria, mimeo.

Cloud, K. 1985. Women's productivity in agricultural systems: Considerations for project design. In: C. Overholt, M. B. Anderson, K. Cloud, and J. E. Austin (eds.), *Gender Roles in Development Projects. A case book*. West Hartford, Conn.: Kumarian Press, pp. 17–56.

Collinson, M. 1987. Potential and practice in food production technology development: Eastern and southern Africa. In: J. W. Mellor, C. L. Delgado, and M. J. Blackie (eds.), *Accelerating Food Production in Sub-Saharan Africa*. Baltimore, Md.: Johns Hopkins University Press.

Conway, G. R. 1985. Agroecosystem analysis. *Agricultural Administration* 20: 1–25.

Dey, J. 1981. Gambian women: Unequal partners in rice development project? In: N. Nelson (ed.), *African Women in the Development Process*. London: Frank Cass, pp. 109–122.

Dover, M. and L. M. Talbot. 1987. *To Feed the Earth: Agro-ecology for Sustainable Development*. Washington D.C.: World Resources Institute.

D'Silva, C. and M. R. Raza. 1983. Equity considerations in planning and implementing rural development projects in Nigeria: An evaluation of the Funtua Project. In: B. L. Green Shield and M. A. Bellamy (eds.), *Rural Development Growth and Inequity*. IAAE Occasional Paper no. 3. Brookfield, Vt.: Ashgate Publishing, pp. 101–106.

Eastin. J. O., F. A. Haskins, C. Y. Sullivan, and C. H. M. Van Bavel. 1969. Physiological significance of internal water relations to crop yield. In: *Physiological Aspects of Crop Yield*. Madison, Wis.: American Society of Agronomy and Crop Science Society of America, pp. 53–85.

Ezumah, H. C. 1990. Maize genotypes for intercropping with cassava in Southern Nigeria. Yield responses. *Discovery and Innovation* (African Academy of Sciences) 2(2): 63–72.

Ezumah, H. C. and J. E. G. Ikeorgu. 1993. Population and planting pattern effects on intercropped maize and cowpea. *Journal of Agronomy and Crop Science* 170: 187–194.

Ezumah, H. C. and T. L. Lawson. 1984. Maize plant "architecture". Important factor in intercropping with cassava. *IITA Research Highlights*. Ibadan, Nigeria: IITA, pp. 96–99.

———— 1990. Cassava and maize intercropping systems. 1. The effects of varieties and plant population. *Journal of Agronomy and Crop Science* 164: 334–342.

Ezumah, N. N. 1990. Women in development: The role of Igbo rural women in agricultural production. Unpublished Ph.D. dissertation, University of Ibadan, Ibadan, Nigeria.

FAO (Food and Agriculture Organization of the United Nations). 1978. *Food Balance Sheets and Per Capita Food Supplies*. Rome: FAO.

———— 1982. *Follow-up to WCARRD: The Role of Women in Agricultural Production*. Rome: FAO.

Ferguson, N. H., P. E. Adams, and R. E. Franklin. 1992. A plant biotechnology course in distance delivery. *Journal of Natural Resources and Life Sciences Education* 21(2): 133–136.

Francis, C. A. 1989. Biological efficiencies in multiple cropping systems. In: *Advances in Agronomy*, vol. 42. New York: Academic Press.

Guyer, J. I. 1984. Naturalism in models of African production. *Man* 19: 371–388.

———— 1986. Women's role in development. In: R. J. Berg and J. S. Whitaker (eds.), *Strategies for African Development*. Berkeley: University of California Press, pp. 393–421.

Hahn, S. K., E. R. Terry, K. Leuschnor, I. O. Akobundu, C. Okali, and R. Lal. 1979. Cassava improvement in Africa. *Field Crop Research* 2: 193–226.

Harrison, P. 1987. *The Greening of Africa*. Harmondsworth, Middlesex: Penguin Books.

Herren, H. R. 1989. IITA/Africa-wide biological control programme: History, achievements and prospects for sustainable pest control in Africa. In: *Seminar Report: Integrated Pest Management, 5–6 Sept 1988*. Sem, Asker, Norway: NOR-AGRIC, pp. 15–32.

Hildebrand, P. E. 1990. Agronomy's role in sustainable agriculture: Integrated farming systems. *Journal of Production Agriculture* 3(3): 285–288.

Hoogh, J. de, M. A. Keyser, H. Linneman, and H. D. J. van Heemst. 1976. Food for a growing world population: Some of the main findings of a study on the long-term prospects of the world food situation. *European Review of Agricultural Economics* 3: 459–499.

Hullugale, N. R. 1989. Effect of tied ridges and undersown *Stylosanthes hamata* (L) on soil properties and growth of maize in Sudan Savanna of Burkina Faso. *Agriculture, Ecosystems and Environment* 25(1): 39–51.

Hullugale, N. R. and H. C. Ezumah. 1991. Effects of cassava-based cropping systems on physico-chemical properties of soil and earthworm casts in a tropical Alfisol. *Agriculture, Ecosystems and Environment* 35: 55–63.

IITA. 1978, 1980, 1983, 1984, 1985, 1989, 1990. *Annual Report*. Ibadan, Nigeria: International Institute of Tropical Agriculture.

Ikeorgu, J. E. G. and H. C. Ezumah. 1991. Some analytical aspects of cassava/maize/eguei/okra melon complex mixture: Soil temperature in relation to leaf area variation. *Field Crops Research* 27: 51–60.

Juo, A. S. R. and H. C. Ezumah. 1992. Mixed root crop ecosystems in the wetter regions of Sub-Saharan Africa. In: C. J. Pearson (ed.), *Field Crop Ecosystems of the World*. Amsterdam: Elsevier Scientific Publishers, pp. 243–258.

Juo, A. S. R. and J. A. Lowe (eds.) 1986. *Wetland and Rice in Tropical Sub-Saharan Africa*. Ibadan, Nigeria: IITA.

Kang, B. T. 1988. Nitrogen cycling in multiple cropping systems. In: J. R. Wilson (ed.), *Advances in Nitrogen Cycling in Agricultural Ecosystems*. Wallingford, UK: CAB International.

Kang, B. T. and A. S. R. Juo. 1981. Management of soil with low activity clays for food crop production in tropical Africa. In: *Proc. International Soil Classification Workshop, Kigali, Rwanda*. Technical Monograph, Soil Management Support Service, USDA, Washington D.C.

Kang, B. T. and G. F. Wilson. 1987. The development of alley cropping as a promising agroforestry technology. In: H. A. Stepler and P. K. R. Nair (eds.), *Agroforestry: A Decade of Development*. Nairobi: ICRAF, pp. 227–243.

Kowal, J. M. and A. H. Kassam. 1978. *Agricultural Ecology of Savanna: A Study of West Africa*. Oxford: Clarendon Press.

Kumar, S. K. 1988. Women's role and agricultural technology. In: J. W. Mellor, C. L. Delgado, and M. J. Blackie (eds.), *Accelerating Food Production in Sub-Saharan Africa*. Baltimore, Md.: Johns Hopkins University Press, pp. 135–147.

Lal, R. 1976. *Soil Erosion Problems and an Alfisol in Western Nigeria and Their Control*. IITA Monograph no. 1, Ibadan, Nigeria.

———— 1989. Conservation tillage for sustainable agriculture: Tropics vs temperate environments. In: *Advances in Agronomy*, vol. 42. New York: Academic Press, pp. 85–119.

Lal, R. and D. J. Greenland. 1978. Effect of conditioners and moisture content on temperature profile and infiltration rate of a vertisol. In: W. W. Emerson, R. D. Bound, and A. R. Dexter (eds.), *Modification of Soil Structure*. London: John Wiley, pp. 191–198.

Lawson, T. L. 1979. Agroclimatology section. IITA Annual Report.

———— 1985. Agro-climatic consideration for cassava cropping. *IITA Research Highlights, 1981–1984*. Ibadan, Nigeria: Farming Systems Program, IITA.

Lawson, T. L. and B. T. Kang. 1990. Yield of maize and cowpea in alley cropping systems in relation to available light. *Agricultural and Forest Meteorology* 528: 347–357.

Lawson, T. L. and R. Lal. 1980. Response of maize to surface and buried straw mulch on a tropical Alfisol. In: R. Lal (ed.), *Soil Tillage and Crop Production*. Ibadan, Nigeria: IITA, pp. 63–74.

Lawson, T. L. and E. R. Terry. 1984. Weather and plant disease in Africa. In: D. L. Hawksworth (ed.), *Advancing Agricultural Production in Africa. Proceedings of CAB's First Scientific Conference, Arusha, Tanzania, 12–18 February 1984*. Slough, UK: CABI, pp. 314–320.

Linnemann, H., J. de Hoogh, M. A. Keyser, and H. D. J. van Heemst. 1979. *MOIRA: Model of International Relations in Agriculture*. New York: North-Holland.

Loutfi, M. F. 1980. *Rural Women Unequal Partners in Development*. A Wep study. Geneva: ILO.

Lynam, J. K. and R. W. Herdt. 1988. Sense and sustainability: Sustainability as an objective in international agricultural research. Paper presented at a CIP–Rockefeller Conference on Farmers and Food Systems, Lima, Peru, September.

Matlon, P. J. 1987. The West African Semi-arid Tropics. In: J. W. Mellor, C. L. Delgado, and M. J. Blackie (eds.), *Accelerating Food Production in Sub-Saharan Africa*. Baltimore, Md.: Johns Hopkins University Press.

Maxwell, G. F. 1990. Integrated pest management: Considerations for success in developing countries. In: S. K. Hahn and F. E. Caveness (eds.), *Integrated Pest Management for Tropical Root and Tuber Crops. Proc. Workshop on the Global Status of, and Prospects for, IPM for Root and Tuber Crops in the Tropics*. Ibadan, Nigeria: IITA.

Mellor, J. W., C. L. Delgado, and M. J. Blackie (eds.) 1987. *Accelerating Food Production in Sub-Saharan Africa*. Baltimore, Md.: Johns Hopkins University Press.

Merrill-Sands, D. 1992. Strategic initiatives in roles for FSR/E: Institutional linkages – linkages and impact: Station Research. 12th Annual AFSRE (Association of Farming Systems Research and Extension) meeting, 13–18 September, Michigan State University, East Lansing.

Mulongoy, K. and I. O. Akobundu. 1985. Nitrogen uptake in live mulch systems. In: B. T. Kang and J. van der Heide (eds.), *Nitrogen Management in Farming Systems in Humid and Sub-humid Tropics*. Harren: Institute of Soil Fertility, pp. 285–290.

Muntemba, S. 1982. Women as food producers and suppliers in the twentieth century: The case of Zambia. *Development Dialogue* 1–2: 29–50.

Neuenschwander, P. and W. N. O. Hammond. 1987. Biological control of the cassava mealybug, Phenacoccus manihoti, in Africa: A review of field studies. In: S. K. Hahn and F. E. Caveness (eds.), *Integrated Pest Management for Tropical Root and Tuber Crops*. Ibadan, Nigeria: IITA, pp. 42–57.

Ngambeki, D. S. 1985. Economic evaluation of alley cropping Leucaena with maize–maize and maize–cowpea in southern Nigeria. *Agricultural Systems* 17(4): 243–258.

Norman, D. W. 1982. *The Farming Systems Approach to Research*. Farming Systems Research Paper no. 3, Kansas State University, Manhattan, Kansas.

Nwanze, K. F., K. Leuchner, and H. C. Ezumah. 1979. The cassava mealybug: Phenacoccus sp. in the Republic of Zaire. *PANS* 25(2): 125–130.

Nye, P. H. and D. J. Greenland. 1960. *The Soil under Shifting Cultivation*. Technical Communication no. 51, Commonwealth Agricultural Bureau, England.

Okafor, J. C. 1980. Edible indigenous woody plants in rural economy of Nigeria forest zone. *Forest Ecology and Management* 3: 45–55.

Okigbo, B. N. 1977. Effects of mulching with a range of materials on crop yield. In: *Mulching and soil management*. IITA, Annual Report, Farming Systems Program.

——— 1980. Ahajioku Lecture. Government Printer, Ministry of Information and Culture, Imo State, Nigeria.

——— 1989. *Development of Sustainable Agricultural Production Systems in Africa: Roles of the International Agricultural Research Centers and National Research Systems*. First Distinguished African Scientist Lecturer Series, IITA, Ibadan, Nigeria.

Okigbo, B. N. and D. J. Greenland. 1976. Intercropping systems in tropical Africa. In: R. I. Papendick, P. A. Sanchez, and G. B. Triplett (eds.), *Multiple Cropping*. Special Publication 27. Madison, Wis.: American Society of Agronomy, pp. 63–101.

Okuneye, B. 1984. Farmers' characteristics and the theory and strategy of agricultural under-development and development. Paper presented at the National Seminar on Innovative Approaches to Development Theory. 23–27 January, Nigerian Institute for Social and Economic Research (NISER), University of Ibadan, Ibadan, Nigeria.

Olasantan, F. O. 1992. Nutrient requirement of cassava (*Manihot esculenta* Grantz)/maize (*Zea Mays* L) intercrop. Ph.D. thesis, University of Ibadan, Nigeria.

Olayide, S. O. and F. S. Idachaba. 1987. Input and output marketing systems: A Nigerian case. In: J. W. Mellor, C. L. Delgado, and M. J. Blackie (eds.), *Accelerating Food Production in Sub-Saharan Africa*. Baltimore, Md.: Johns Hopkins University Press.

Osiname, O. A., C. Bartlett, N. Mbulu, L. Simba, and K. Land. 1987. Diagnostic survey of cassava-based cropping systems in two ecological zones of Bas-Zaire. In: H. C. Ezumah and D. S. O. Osiru (eds.), *Cassava Based Cropping Systems Research*. Ibadan, Nigeria: IITA.

Osiru, D. S. O. and R. W. Willey. 1972. Studies on mixtures of dwarf sorghum and beans (Phaseous vulgaris) with particular emphasis on plant population. *Journal of Agricultural Research, Cambridge* 79(3): 531–540.

Pala, A. O. 1976. *African Women in Rural Development: Research Priorities*. OLC (Overseas Liaison Committee, American Council on Education) Working Paper no. 12, Washington D.C., December.

Pankhurst, D. and S. Jacobs. 1988. Land tenure, gender relations and agricultural production: The case of Zimbabwe's peasantry. In: J. Davison (ed.), *Agriculture, Women and Land: The African Experience*. Boulder and London: Westview Press.

Papadakis, J. 1966. *Crop Ecologic Survey in West Africa*, vols. I and II. Rome: FAO.

Paulino, L. A. 1987. The evolving food situation. In: J. W. Mellor, C. L. Delgado, and M. J. Blackie (eds.), *Accelerating Food Production in Sub-Saharan Africa*. Baltimore, Md.: Johns Hopkins University Press, chap. 23.

Rao, M. R. and R. W. Willey. 1983. Effect of genotype in cereal/cowpea intercropping on the alfisols of semiarid tropics of India. *Experimental Agriculture* 19: 67–78.

Roberts, P. A. 1988. Rural women's access to labour in West Africa. In: S. B. Stichter and J. L. Parpart (eds.), *Patriarchy and Class: African Women in the Home and the Workforce*. Boulder, Colo.: Westview Press, pp. 97–144.

Rogers, B. 1980. *The Domestication of Women: Discrimination in Developing Societies*. London: Kegan Paul.

Ruttan, V. W. 1988. Sustainability is not enough. *American Journal of Alternative Agriculture* 3: 128–130.

Ter Kuile, C. H. H. 1987. The humid and sub-humid tropics. In: J. W. Mellor, C. L. Delgado, and M. J. Blackie (eds.), *Accelerating Food Production in Sub-Saharan Africa*. Baltimore, Md.: Johns Hopkins University Press.

Unamma, R. P. A., S. O. Odurukwe, H. E. Okereke, L. S. O. Ene, and O. O. Okoli. 1985. *Farming Systems in Nigeria*. Agricultural Extension & Research Liaison Services, National Root Crops Research Institute, Umudike, Umuahia, Nigeria.

Vallaeys, G., M. T. Silvestre, M. J. Blackie, and C. L. Delgado. 1987. Development and extension of agricultural production technology. In: J. W. Mellor, C. L. Delgado, and M. J. Blackie (eds.), *Accelerating Food Production in Sub-Saharan Africa*. Baltimore, Md.: Johns Hopkins University Press.

Wahua, T. A. T. 1983. Nutrient uptake by intercropped maize and cowpeas and a concept of nutrient supplementation index (NSI). *Experimental Agriculture* 19: 263–275.

Whitlow, R. 1987. A national soil survey for Zimbabwe. *Journal of Soil and Water Conservation*, July/August.

Willey, R. W. 1979. Intercropping – Its importance and research needs. Part I. Competition and yield advantages. *Field Crops Abstracts* 32(1): 1–10.

Wit, C. T. de, H. H. Van Laar, and H. van Keulen. 1979. Physiological potential of crop production. In: J. Sneep and A. J. T. Hendriksen (eds.), *Plant Breeding Perspectives*. Wageningen, The Netherlands: PUDOC, pp. 47–82.

World Bank. 1989. *Sub-Saharan Africa. From Crisis to Sustainable Growth. A Long Term Perspective Study*. Washington D.C.: World Bank.

Zok, S. and L. M. Nyochembeng. 1992. Micropropagation of a tropical tuber food crop, Xanthosoma Sagittifolium (L) Schott, in Cameroon. Jay P. Johnson Biotechnology Laboratory, Institute of Agronomic Research, PMB 25 Buea, Cameroon, mimeo.

12

Agricultural development in the age of sustainability: Livestock production

Saka Nuru

Introduction

The livestock industry is an economic enterprise and can also be considered as a "survival enterprise" for millions of herdspeople throughout tropical Africa, especially in the arid, semi-arid, and sub-humid areas. Among the multiple roles of the livestock industry, food production and gainful employment are the most important. Over 12 million people in West Africa, of whom over 3 million are in Nigeria, depend primarily on livestock for their survival, while over 70 million people in the same region depend on livestock and livestock-related enterprises for their livelihood (Nuru 1982, 1983; McDowell and DeHaan 1986). One-third of the African continent's livestock population is in West Africa.

How can the African continent, particularly the Sub-Saharan region, increase its livestock product production to meet the ever-increasing demands of its people now and in the future, using all available natural resources, with no or minimum environmental degradation? Above all, how may the environment be preserved or sustained for future economic development when major environmental constraints such as drought and erosion could retard future progress in development?

Land degradation (soil erosion), drought, desert encroachment, etc. pose a significant threat to the use of land for crops and livestock production, especially in the arid and semi-arid zones where agricultural activities are the main occupation of the people of Sub-Saharan Africa. To prevent further deterioration and to increase the productivity of food animals, it is necessary to act now.

Because of its economic and social significance, the livestock enterprise must be considered or viewed holistically: the animal, its environment, and productivity. It is the interaction between the physical environment and the animal's genetic make-up that determines productivity and even the survival of both animal and plant species within a given ecosystem. In this holistic approach, human factors such as culture and social and economic status as related to other production factors are also important because they influence productivity. Most African cattle are still in the hands of pastoral livestock owners – the Fulanis, Shuwas, and Fulas in West Africa and the Masais in East Africa. Their husbandry methods are indigenous and based on low-input systems. However, their survival strategy is influenced by seasonal migration to areas with optimum forage resources to feed their animals. This has an effect not only on animal productivity but also on the ecosystem.

Livestock production, productivity, and feed resources

When considering ecological stability and increased animal protein production from domestic animal species, the two main natural factors of production are:
• the animals – in this case the ruminants but, to a lesser extent, the monogastrics;
• the land and climatic conditions.
Other factors of production are credit facilities, marketing, and the socio-economic status of the herd owners. These factors do not have a direct effect on environmental degradation, whereas the cultural practices in the husbandry system do.

The animal species: Contribution and spatial distribution

Among domestic animals, the ruminants – for example, cattle, sheep, and goats – form the largest number and are of paramount social and economic importance in tropical Africa. There are several reasons why ruminants should be given special attention when considering ecological change in Sub-Saharan Africa.

First, they supply the bulk of livestock products. The ever-increasing demand for these products owing to increased human population and better health education justifies greater attention to animal production if the continent is to avoid a huge animal protein deficit.

Secondly, because of the large population of ruminants and their dependence mainly on global grazing, large areas, especially in West and East Africa, are in danger of irreversible soil degradation and desertification. Ruminants, though not the sole factor in these ecological disasters, contribute through overgrazing and subsequent soil compaction and wind erosion. Their survival is based on genotype adaptability to the fragile environment and the vagaries of climatic conditions.

Cattle and a few other large ruminants constitute 83 per cent of food animals and produce over 45 per cent of meat products and over 90 per cent of available domestic milk supply. Sheep and goats (medium-large stock), on the other hand, constitute 15 per cent of the total number of food animals and contribute about 35 per cent of meat, as well as fibre. As of 1990, 187.8 million cattle, 205.0 million sheep, 173.9 million goats, and 13.6 million pigs were estimated to be in Africa (FAO 1991: 191 and 194). Of these, approximately 178.6 million cattle, 162.4 million sheep, 157.8 million goats, and 13.5 million pigs were in Sub-Saharan Africa. Sub-Saharan livestock produced 6.7 million metric tons of meat (slaughter weight), 14 million metric tons of milk, and 0.9 million metric tons of hens' eggs (FAO 1991: 199–226). However, there is a higher elasticity of demand than of supply. In West Africa alone, a deficit of 2–4 million tons of meat and 6.5–9.0 million tons of dairy products is envisaged by the year

Table 12.1 **Livestock numbers in Sub-Saharan Africa, West Africa, and the world, 1990**

	Cattle	Sheep	Goats	Pigs
World (m. head)	1,279.3	1,190.5	557.0	856.7
Sub-Saharan Africa (m. head)	178.6	162.4	157.8	13.5
% of world	14.0	13.6	28.3	1.6
West Africa (m. head)	42.8	42.2	59.5	6.4
% of SS Africa	24.0	26.0	37.7	47.4

Source: FAO (1991).

Table 12.2　**Human and livestock distribution in western Africa, 1979**

	Zone				
	Arid	Semi-arid	Sub-humid	Humid	Total
Area (km² million)	4.0	1.5	1.6	1.9	9.0
Agricultural population (m.)	6.9	36.1	16.1	31.1	90.2
Cattle (m. head)	9.0	21.6	6.2	3.8	40.6
Sheep (m. head)	13.2	10.1	6.7	6.0	36.0
Goats (m. head)	14.8	19.2	11.8	8.7	54.5
Ruminant TLU	10.8	16.7	6.2	4.3	38.0

Source: Adapted from Jahnke (1982) by McDowell and DeHaan (1986).
TLU, Tropical Livestock Unit = 250 kg livestock body weight.

Table 12.3　**Livestock densities in various ecological zones of West Africa**

	Zone			
	Arid	Semi-arid	Sub-humid	Humid
TLU/km²	2.7	11.1	3.8	2.2
Agricultural population density (n/km²)	1.7	24.0	10.1	16.4
TLU per agricultural capita	2.5	0.5	0.4	0.1

Source: McDowell and DeHaan (1986).
TLU, Tropical Livestock Unit = 250 kg livestock body weight.

2000 (McDowell and DeHaan 1986). Table 12.1 shows the distribution of some animal species in Africa compared with world estimates. These animals are not evenly distributed across the African continent. As shown in table 12.2, for the West African region, the semi-arid zones contain the largest number of ruminant species (16.7 TLU[1]) compared with the arid (10.8 TLU), sub-humid (6.2 TLU), and humid zones (4.3 TLU) (Jahnke 1982; McDowell and DeHaan 1986). In terms of stocking density (table 12.3), the arid zone has a low livestock per unit area (2.7 TLU/km²) compared with the semi-arid zone (11.1 TLU/km²). Thus the semi-arid areas have more animals per km² but this is possible because of higher land productivity. The highest number of ruminants is found in this zone in West Africa. Although the sub-humid and humid zones have greater forage potential, the climate and prevalence of typanosomes limit the use of these two zones for raising ruminant livestock, hence the very low numbers per unit area (2.2 TLU/km^2) in the humid zone.

The role of monogastric food animals – poultry and swine in particular – in increased animal production potential in Sub-Saharan Africa cannot be underestimated. These animals compete with human beings for available grain, especially maize and sorghum, which are the staple food of the African peoples. However, these species can have greater meat and egg turnover in a relatively short time. Although they are intensively raised on restricted land areas, their contribution to environmental problems can be great. Air pollution owing to odour from pig and poultry houses can be a nuisance to nearby inhabitants. Sustainability of productive capacity of these animals is more easily accomplished, especially with modern trends in housing and feed technologies. Recycling of manure by spreading it on arable cropland ensures increased crop production at reasonable cost as well as environmental conservation.

The land resource, climate, and production systems

Large areas of African soils are said to be fragile and are classified as of low productive capacity in many countries within the continent. Most of the available land for agricultural production is located within fragile and ecologically sensitive regions, e.g. tropical rain forest, arid savannas, and the drought-prone Sahel, where a large proportion of the cultivated area is not compatible with sustainable agriculture. Land-use systems are usually based on incomplete knowledge of the status of the land resources of the various areas (Anande-Kur 1992). These factors must be borne in mind because knowledge and information about the land resources of a given ecosystem for a particular production – arable or livestock – are essential, as can be seen when related to the stocking density and effect on the environment.

For the purpose of this paper, I am more concerned with the ecological and agro-climatic zones in Sub-Saharan Africa as they relate to livestock enterprises and to the sustainability of all production systems.

The ecological zone classification is based on the number of growing days, i.e. days with rainfall. Thus the arid zone has 0–90 days of rainfall, the semi-arid zone has 90–180 days, the sub-humid zone has 180–270 days, and the humid zone has rainfall for over 270 days annually (McDowell and DeHaan 1986). It is the agro-ecological zones that determine both crop and livestock production in a given zone. The intensity, frequency, and distribution of rainfall influence biomass production in a given area, and hence are a determinant factor in the carrying capacity of the land for the purpose of raising livestock. In general, the majority of ruminants in Sub-Saharan Africa are raised on range-land where feed resources are mostly naturally growing grasses and legumes but with occasional supplementation with leaves of shrubs and trees. The husbandry systems are either nomadic, semi-nomadic, or settled. Stock owners with large herds often practise full pastoralism, while those who are agro-pastoralists often have small herds and are sedentary or settled. The global grazing habit of a large number of domestic ruminants has a detrimental effect on the environment, especially as the stocking density can be very high in marginal grazing areas (table 12.3). Because of the high stocking density and fewer watering points in these zones, erosion due to constant trampling around water points can be an added detrimental effect of overgrazing.

The effect of seasonality on ruminant livestock production is also very important. In the mid wet season, forage biomass is higher in quality and quantity, with crude protein up to 9 per cent in most of the native grasses. Natural grasses and legumes are rich and highly digestible at this period. As the dry season sets in, the protein level drops and the roughage quantity increases. There is an increase in lignin content and voluntary intake decreases. This is a poor feed resource, resulting in weight loss and decreased fertility and milk yield for up to 4–5 months of the year. The severity and duration of low-quality feed differ from one country to the other within the region. To worsen the ecology and its available food resources further, there is widespread annual burning of native grasslands, thereby drastically reducing the amount of forage on offer. Indeed, it has been observed that a combination of these factors – low-quality roughage and bush burning, which reduce the biomass available in quantity and quality – could lead to weight losses ranging from 300 to 400 g per head per day for cattle (Zemmelink 1974) and up to 15 per cent of body weight in sheep (Otchere et al. 1977).

In the arid zone, nomadism and transhumant systems of livestock production prevail. In these systems, high mobility for global grazing habit is the most efficient adaptation to the erratic rainfall. Migration from one area to another in search of good quality and quantity of feed and water is the rule. Transhumant or semi-nomadic systems have a home base, although they too are very mobile, with the majority of animals and the family away for several months and only

2–6 lactating cows left at the base to provide milk for sale and for the utilization of the aged parents left behind. Feed from crop residue provides the main energy source during and shortly after harvesting periods.

In all the zones, the main constraints on feed resources are the destruction of perennial tree cover for firewood, bush fires caused by hunters and livestock rearers, and overgrazing. These man-made constraints often lead to serious degradation of the range resources and in some cases to an irreversible process of desertification, especially in the Sahel zone. The sub-humid zone (SHZ) has a high potential for ruminant production because of the high rainfall and vast land area for forage production. In Nigeria, the SHZ contains only 19.59 per cent of the total national livestock units (Otchere and Nuru 1988). This low percentage of TLU in the Nigerian SHZ is attributed partly to tse-tse infestation and high humidity.

The effect of government policy on livestock production

In a number of countries, Nigeria in particular, there are governmental policies on livestock production as well as on the environment. On livestock, the government is concerned with the grazing rights of stock owners in forest areas. The Grazing Reserve Law of 1964 in Nigeria is a good example. Shelter belts have been created to prevent desert encroachment. Federal or national environmental protection agencies have been set up by some governments within the region. A lot more emphasis is, however, placed on environmental pollution from oil spillage and on drought prevention rather than on natural herbage resource conservation. In many countries, the land tenure system is a major constraint on range conservation or increased production. Policies on the land tenure system and land use are mostly to the advantage of city dwellers and a few enlightened farmers. In many countries, the laws are hardly obeyed and people (hunters, etc.) are rarely penalized. In order to achieve their objective, such laws and regulations must be not only technically sound but also socially acceptable.

Suggested solutions

It can be seen that the present livestock production, based on global grazing husbandry systems, ecological destruction through bush fires, and overgrazing due to high stocking density in areas where feed or water resources cannot support the number of animals, does not augur well for present and future productivity and sustainability.

What then are the solutions to ensure sustenance of the ecosystem and its herbage and tree shrubs cover and of the grazing livestock species for the future economic development of Sub-Saharan Africa?

Livestock production is still very much based on traditional systems in Sub-Saharan Africa, even in such agriculturally advanced countries as Nigeria, Zimbabwe, or Egypt. One would have thought that, with a large number of livestock research institutions and faculties of agriculture and veterinary medicine in the region, a newer and more modern approach to livestock enterprise would have provided the answer for future productivity and the sustainability of both animals and the environment. It is true that old habits die hard and, therefore, the traditional herding system will continue in many African countries.

It will not be possible drastically to change the cultural and socio-economic status of the livestock producers for at least another decade. It has, however, been shown that their production systems are more efficient in terms of livestock product yield per animal per unit area, probably because of their husbandry knowledge and complete devotion to their vocation. Large-scale farms with modern techniques of production are not the only way to sustain productivity. They are too capital and labour intensive to guarantee a profit compared with the low-input systems of traditional owners. A lot of large-scale livestock and arable farmers have failed in many countries, Nigeria being a good example. Indeed, it has been shown that in Zimbabwe, Botswana, Kenya, and Mali the contribution of communal livestock production to the national animal protein yield is greater than that from commercial ranching enterprises in terms of kg of protein production per hectare per year (Barrett 1992). For these and other reasons, our attention must be primarily focused on how to improve the traditional systems, to introduce simple and adaptable innovations and techniques to enhance productivity and yet protect the environment from being abused to the extent of irreversible degradation.

Suggested solutions for sustaining the productivity of both the livestock and plant species for future development are therefore centred on the following strategies:
1. improved animal genetic resources to meet future needs;
2. improved nutrition;
3. improved management;
4. government policies and commitments;
5. active participation by the private sector.

Improved animal genetic make-up

Modern ideas about animal production are mostly based on: the use of bio-engineering to improve on the genetics of various animal species for higher output, embryo transfer, and immuno-genetics; artificial insemination and cross-breeding for quick genetic gain in heterosis; improvement of reproductive efficiency through the use of hormones and drugs to improve fertility rates. Developments in breeding animals with increased resistance to diseases and pests as well as in animal health and disease control through vaccine production are major contributions. Recombinant DNA technology has of recent years offered remarkable opportunities for restructuring animal phenotypes and ability to withstand viral and bacterial diseases. Cross-breds, if so adopted, would yield more meat (through faster growth) and higher milk output in a relatively short time. The goal of all these techniques is to produce a biologically efficient animal species for each ecosystem. However useful these techniques are, they are too advanced to be used by the present-day resource-poor subsistence farmers in Sub-Saharan Africa, but could be of advantage in future to conserve the ecosystem and yet increase livestock production to meet the needs of the year 2000. For the next decade, emphasis should be on animal health through effective control of "economic diseases" such as gastroenteritis due to helminth parasites, streptothricosis, trypanosomiasis, and other chronic diseases that give rise to wastage owing to abortion, infertility, stillbirths, and unthriftiness, and even deaths.

Improved nutrition

Improved nutrition is the key factor. One way of achieving it is through increased crop yields, because grains and tubers are used to supplement natural grasses. Other methods are: effective management and utilization of natural pastures; feed resources conservation; and use of arable crop wastes.

At present, the global grazing orbit is declining owing to physical development (roads, new HQs, etc.) and the expansion of cultivated land as a result of large agricultural schemes. Therefore, better and more efficient management of range land is essential, e.g. controlled grazing, controlled stocking density, avoidance of bush fires, range reseeding, and water supply.

In order to conserve feed resources, silage and hay could be made from high-quality grass and legumes, and agricultural crop residues such as groundnut and cowpea tops could be conserved when the nutritive value of the plants used is high. Unfortunately, the inputs for such technology (tractors, bailers, etc.) are hard to come by for many peasant livestock farmers.

Within the past two decades, the mechanization of agriculture for crop production has contributed immensely to increases in cereal crop production and therefore in crop residues. However, it must be noted that mechanized farming has also physically contributed to soil degradation, resulting in deterioration of the soil structure and compaction of the subsoil (Anande-Kur 1992). These effects in themselves render the soils prone to erosion. The integration of livestock and crop production systems on a given land area can improve soil fertility through the output of organic manure by the animals and the more effective utilization of crop residues.

The utilization of crop residues for increased animal protein production has received greater research attention within the past decade because of the higher quantities of crop residue, especially from sorghum, maize, and millet, and partly because of the astronomical increase in the prices of agricultural by-products such as wheat and maize offal residue used for livestock feed, groundnut and cotton seed cake, and brewers dried grain. The importance of crop residue in the dry season feeding of ruminants in the Northern Guinea Savannah has long been recognized. Van Raay and de Leeuw (1971) estimated that crop residue grazing accounts for 85 per cent of total grazing time from the harvest period in December, declining to 40 per cent in February in the Sudan Sahel zone of Nigeria. Alhassan (1985) estimated that for every kg of grain harvested, there are 4 kg dry matter of straw from sorghum, 8 kg from millet, and 4 kg from maize straw. From table 12.4 it can be seen that approximately 16.4 million metric tonnes of sorghum straw and 23.2 million metric tonnes of millet straw were available in Nigeria in 1980/81 from 6.1 million hectares of sorghum and 4.5 million hectares of millet, respectively. This may apply to other countries in Sub-Saharan Africa where these crops are grown on a large scale. By treating this straw with non-protein nitrogen sources or chemicals (e.g. urea, ammonia, and sodium hydroxide) the lignin content will be degraded and the feed value and palatability enhanced. If animal feed is supplied in this way, further destruction of the ecosystem by way of bush fires for early grass growth and overgrazing when feed resource is scanty can be prevented or minimized. Here again, education of the stock

254

Table 12.4 **Estimated area sown to sorghum and millet and their grain and straw production for various cropping years**

Year	Sorghum			Millet		
	Area (ha m.)	Grain production (m.t)	Estimated straw (m.t)	Area (ha m.)	Grain production (m.t.)	Estimated straw (m.t.)
1964/65	5.6	4.2	16.8	4.4	2.7	21.6
1969/70	5.8	4.3	17.2	4.2	3.2	25.6
1974/75	4.8	3.9	15.6	4.0	2.6	20.8
1980/81	6.1	4.1	16.4	4.5	2.9	23.2

Source: Nuru (1986).

rearers about the need to settle and adopt such simple technologies is essential. Other agricultural by-products with great potential for animal feed include sugarcane tops, molasses, bagasse, discarded cocoa beans, pineapple tops, and other rejects.

It can be seen that, for optimum resource usage, there is an urgent need for an integrated approach to livestock development for increased product availability at reasonable or affordable prices and enhanced natural resource management and conservation.

Similarly, the use of microbes has greatly enhanced our knowledge about the production and utilization of better nutrients to feed various species of animals for a higher output of meat, milk, and milk products. In addition, modern trends in production make use of anabolic steroids – a combination of progesterones, oestrogen, testosterone, and zeasolone (plant origin) – as feed additives to promote faster growth and therefore higher output; growth hormones to increase milk production in lactating cows; and ionospheres (antibiotics) and coccidiostats in poultry. These drugs are mentioned only in passing here, because the level of education, socio-economic status, and acceptance of these new techniques by the majority of livestock producers cannot at present be guaranteed. Only a few enlightened farmers in southern Africa are able to use these technologies. More appropriate and simple technological innovations therefore need greater emphasis.

Improved management techniques

Sedentarization
Change from a free-range production system to an acceptable market-oriented and sedentary system could be considered. Most of the de-

struction of ecosystems is due to bush burning, overgrazing, and lack of adequate water points. A more sedentary husbandry system with higher input and higher output could be desirable in some agro-ecological areas. This would not be easy in the arid zone, but it would be possible in the semi-arid and sub-humid zones. In the arid zones, a reduction of livestock numbers in keeping with the carrying capacity of the land is desirable. Agro-pastoralism is a solution in some areas where there is adequate rainfall. This is the emerging trend in the sub-humid zone of Nigeria, where more and more pastoralists are settling (ILCA 1979; Otchere et al. 1985). In this way, the concept of integrated farming systems can develop to great advantage. In the Congo, and other densely forested countries, the use of typano-tolerant breeds of animals is now more emphasized. These animal species are not only adapted to the environment but also more pro-ductive in such areas. It must be noted, however, that sedentarization and its acknowledged benefits can be achieved only through a dynamic and workable land tenure system that is the responsibility of the government.

Agro-forestry
According to Harrison (1987), forestry has been considered sepa-rately from agriculture and livestock. Foresters view farmers and herders as vandals and destroyers of forests, while peasants see for-esters as policemen who exclude them from land that was tradition-ally theirs to control and use. Farmers view tree planting as an alien activity carried out by unpopular professionals. Forestry nevertheless has a crucial role in farming and pastoralism in Africa. There is a need to integrate forestry fully into crop and livestock production in order to sustain agriculture in a stable ecosystem in the future. The Grazing Reserve Law in Nigeria is worthy of emulation by other countries. Suitable trees will provide fodder for animals at the end of the dry season and the beginning of the rains when feed is scarce. The most crucial role of appropriate forest trees would be the recycling of soil nutrients in an environment in which heavy rains leach nutrients below the reach of crop roots and the maintenance of soil organic matter in an environment in which high temperatures break down organic matter very quickly. A promising approach to agro-forestry to sustain crop and livestock production is alley farming. Suitable multi-purpose trees that provide abundant fodder or mulch from their leaves, fuelwood and stakes from their stems, as well as the ability to fix nitrogen are greatly recommended. At the moment, trees

such as *Leucaena leucocephala*, *Gliricidia sepium*, and *Sesbania seban*, among others, have been found suitable. There is, however, the need to increase the number of species that meet the requirements.

Pasture establishment

With the current increase in crop production through massive land-clearing in many countries in Sub-Saharan African, coupled with the growth of population and hence the physical development of more and larger towns and cities (urbanization), the land-use pattern is constantly changing and less land is available for crop and livestock production.

Intensive production systems and the use of crop residues and agricultural by-products are thus further emphasized. Because of the limiting factors on global grazing, which are even more likely to be a problem in the year 2000 if livestock and human population growth are not restrained, the need arises for sedentarization and pasture establishment if there is to be enough animal protein and at the same time the natural ecosystem is to be conserved. Technically, scientists have developed suitable pasture plants to meet the variations of the agro-ecological zones in Sub-Saharan Africa. The grasses and legumes required include *Digitaria* spp., Buffel grass, Guinea and Rhodes grasses, together with Stylosanthes, Centrosema, and other varieties of legumes. It will require social and cultural changes amongst the nomadic and livestock owners if they are to adopt the technologies that have been developed and to treat livestock ventures as viable commercial enterprises not just a way of life. In this respect, several African governments have a lot to do as regards land tenure systems and the provision of assistance in the acquisition of infra-structure and credit facilities for a profitable future livestock industry.

As part of the new technology in animal husbandry, improved pastures produce more dry matter of high nutritive value and lead to greater animal productivity than do native pastures. To date, the tra-ditional African livestock farmer has yet to adopt these new tech-niques. Throughout Sub-Saharan Africa, grazing land is communal; only a few private ownerships exist. Improvement of the range by individual stockowners by oversowing with legumes and by fertiliza-tion is not advantageous because grazing areas are for communal usage.

There must be more emphasis on the training of range and pasture specialists in order to achieve success in range improvement and con-servation and in pasture establishment and effective utilization, and also to prevent further range degradation and to ensure increased livestock productivity.

Government policies and commitments

Government policies and programmes to assist herdspeople and the millions of people engaged in livestock enterprise need to take cognizance of the following:

(a) The land tenure system must be revised in some countries to make it easier for those who really need land to obtain it. The need to instill pride of ownership and willingness to invest in development is crucial because communal grazing is free and therefore unattractive for commercial livestock enterprise.
(b) Nomadic education as presently carried out in Nigeria is encouraging and worth emulating by other countries.
(c) The supply of sufficient manpower/experts, e.g. animal scientists, range managers, and technical staff, is essential. Most African universities are non-starters in the production of such specialists.
(d) Regulatory control of herd size and distribution to achieve ecological balance and avoid overgrazing needs policy attention. The encouragement of herd owners to move to the sub-humid zone in Nigeria, which is rich in feed resources, is a very slowly developing programme.
(e) Greater incentives to producers – marketing, credit facilities, technical supervision, subsidized inputs, etc. – are essential.

Active participation by the private sector

Private sector participation in the primary production of livestock is highly desirable if the necessary output of livestock products is to be achieved in the future. Through this sector, environmental degradation can be minimized and increased productivity of livestock products ensured. So far, only in Zimbabwe, Botswana, Kenya, and South Africa are people engaged in modern commercial livestock production. The need to invest in the industry as a high-potential economic enterprise cannot be overemphasized if the future is to be safeguarded.

Summary and conclusions

The demand for food of animal origin is growing much faster than production because of better health education, higher income per capita, and ever-increasing population growth. Yet, owing to the application of Structural Adjustment Programmes, many African countries are poorer than before and livestock products are beyond the reach of the ordinary person. Many governments in Sub-Saharan Africa will face serious problems in terms of food self-sufficiency and food security if immediate and adequate measures for sustainability are not taken.

The two most important resource bases in livestock production are the animals and the range land on which they depend for survival. The genetics of the various species of animals and plants and their interaction within a given ecological zone form the basis of their productiveness or otherwise. The ability to maintain the pace of economic development from these resource bases (since they are governed by external factors, e.g. climate, social, cultural, and economic status of herdspeople) is the focus of the concept of sustainability. However, for any given system one may wish to sustain more than one aspect of the system. For example, in livestock systems, genetic considerations may be just as important in the tropical environment as the feed resource base, in which case conflict can arise. Again, the concept of sustainability without consideration of social objectives or goals is meaningless in terms of future economic development. The herd owners' social objectives may not tally with the government policy objective in that the herd owners may be more interested in maximizing the numbers of their stock whereas the government objective may be sedentarization of the herd owners in order to be able to increase the productivity of the animal per unit area using available technologies in animal husbandry, including nutrition and herd health management. Sustaining a given subset of a system therefore needs to be taken more seriously while thinking of overall future economic development gains.

Ruminants have a greater effect on ecosystems than other animal species. They are numerous and provide substantial quantities of animal protein. However, their production is based on age-old husbandry systems, which need to be gradually modified in order to meet the needs of consumers. A reduction of animal numbers in accordance with the resource capability of the land is essential. The various governments in Sub-Saharan Africa must try to achieve this through legislation and inducement packages. In addition, the sedentarization of nomads and the acquisition of land (i.e. a change in land tenure systems) can greatly increase the adaptation and use of new techniques in animal production systems.

The present poor system of livestock production of the majority of herd/flock owners should not be a deterrent to exploring future possibilities. In this context, therefore, one could stress the need to "domesticate" the environment so that it can cope with the production effort, especially for monogastrics. The alleviation of environmental stress through genetic improvement, hormonal regulation, feed intake, and control will be an important consideration for future needs.

Research into optimum environments for livestock will need to be addressed; for example, poultry houses with relative humidity, temperature, etc. controlled to make them conducive to rearing have led to higher output in Europe, the USA, and other countries. Comfort, productivity, and the economics of poultry and swine production will be the rule rather than the exception even in tropical environments. These are to be achieved through environmental control and animal welfare considerations.

Owing to space constraints, I have not considered the role of wild life in the preservation of ecosystems in this paper. They form part of Africa's cherished biodiversity and their significant role in the supply of bush meat, especially to rural people, needs no emphasis. However, with intensive hunting for game, they are declining in number, and the present number of herbivorous species is not a threat to the ecosystem. Destruction by bush fire and the cutting down of young and old trees for firewood or the clearing of dense natural forests for agriculture pose more threat to the system and should be regulated for future animal protein production.

Government assistance through research and the development of specialist skills, e.g. range management, pasture expertise, and animal science, is of paramount importance to ensure future economic growth and development in the livestock sector if Sub-Saharan Africa is to meet the challenges of the future.

Note

1. TLU (Tropical Livestock Unit) = 250 kg livestock body weight.

References

Alhassan, W. S. 1985. The advances in ruminant nutrition and their application to the utilization of poor quality forage. Paper presented at the 10th annual meeting of the Nigeria Society of Animal Production, University of Ife, Nigeria.

Anande-Kur, S. 1992. Land management and problems in large-scale farming in Nigeria. Paper presented at a conference on Large Scale Agriculture, Abeokuta.

Barrett, J. C. 1992. *The Economic Role of Cattle in Communal Farming Systems in Zimbabwe*. Pastoral Development Network Paper 32b, March.

FAO (Food and Agriculture Organization of the United Nations). 1991. *Production Yearbook 1990*, vol. 44.

Harrison, P. 1987. *The Greening of Africa. Breaking Through in the Battle for Land and Food*. London: Paladin Griffon.

ILCA. 1979. *Livestock Production in the Subhumid Zone of West Africa: A Regional Review*. ILCA Systems Study no. 2. Addis Ababa, Ethiopia: International Livestock Centre for Africa.

Jahnke, H. E. 1982. *Livestock Production Systems and Livestock Development in Tropical Africa*. Kiel: Kiefer Wissenschafts Verlag and Vauk.

McDowell, R. E. and C. DeHaan. 1986. *West African Agricultural Research Review: Livestock Research*.

Nuru, S. 1982. Problems and prospects of the Nigerian beef industry. In: O. A. Osinowo (ed.), *Proceedings of the National Conference on Beef Production*. Kaduna, Nigeria, pp. 12–43.

——— 1983. Effective harnessing of Nigeria's agricultural resources: The case for livestock production sub-sector. Annual Conference of the Agric. Society of Nigeria, Ilorin.

——— 1986. The role of research in increasing food production in Africa. In: B. Webster, C. Valverde, and A. Fletcher (eds.), *The Impact of Research on National Agricultural Development. A Report on the 1st International Meeting of National Agricultural Research Systems*. Brasilia, Brazil, pp. 53–63.

Otchere, E. O. and S. Nuru. 1988. Ruminant livestock production and feed resources in the subhumid zone in Nigeria: Constraints and perspectives. *Journal of Animal Research* 8(2): 147–168.

Otchere, E. O., C. B. M. Dadgie, D. A. Ayebo, and K. E. Erbynn. 1977. Response of grazing sheep to rice straw or cassava pellets fortified with urea and molasses as supplemented feed. *Ghana Journal of Agricultural Science* 10: 61–66.

Otchere, E. O., H. U. Ahmed, Y. M. Adesipe, M. S. Kallah, N. Mzamane, T. K. Adenowo, E. K. Bawa, S. A. A. Olorunju, A. A. Voh Jr., E. A. Lufadeju, and S. T. Balogun. 1985. Livestock production among pastoralists in Giwa District. Preliminary report of the Livestock System Research Project, NAPRI, Nigeria (unpublished).

Van Raay, H. G. T. and P. N. de Leeuw. 1971. The importance of crop residue as fodder: A resource analysis in Katsina province, Nigeria. *Samaru Research Bulletin* no. 139, Institute for Agricultural Research Samaru, Zaria.

——— 1974. *Fodder Resources and Grazing Management in a Savanna Environment: An Ecosystem Approach*. Occasional Paper no. 45. The Hague: Institute of Social Studies.

Zemmelink, G. 1974. Utilization of poor quality roughages in the Northern Guinea Savanna zone. In: J. K. Loosli, V. A. Oyenuga, and G. M. Babatunde (eds.), *Animal Production in the Tropics*. Ibadan, Nigeria: Heinemann.

13

The fuelwood/energy crisis in Sub-Saharan Africa

Elizabeth Ardayfio-Schandorf

Introduction

At the core of the question of the sustainable development of Sub-Saharan Africa (SSA) lies the problem of development itself. Without development there is the possibility that SSA's problems will multiply. Since the 1960s its gross domestic product (GDP) has declined steadily. Higher oil prices, fluctuating agricultural commodity prices, and a lack of adequate response strategies have contributed to aggravate this situation. Excessive borrowing from international financial institutions provided funds to support infrastructural development, but the inability of SSA to service these loans has resulted in the region's present debt crisis. Other factors such as the drought of the 1980s severely affected the food and energy supplies of most countries. Further decline in these countries may tend to undermine growth in the economy. Should population growth occur without development, SSA will be compelled to exploit its resources on a non-renewable basis, thus accelerating environmental deterioration. For effective development, SSA should aim at a type of development that is sustainable.

In this connection, an important element in the developmental system is the complex issue of energy.

The countries in SSA are rich in modern energy resources. A few have large oil and natural gas reserves, some have coal, and several have hydroelectric power. Albeit, the rate of consumption of these resources is limited, per capita consumption being the lowest in the world. The main commercial energy resources consumed in SSA are petroleum (41 per cent), natural gas (14 per cent), hydroelectricity (10 per cent), and coal (35 per cent). In the total resources, including traditional fuels, wood fuel is dominant (Ardayfio 1986). All these energy forms have their environmental effect. Contemporary biomass fuel use results in deforestation and land degradation, which is associated with non-sustainable use of land resources and environment. Air pollution is also linked with the use of coal, oil, gas, and water, and with solid waste problems. Policies relating to institutions and investments are needed to improve the energy situation and reduce the environmental impact.

Hence this paper seeks to appraise the extent of the energy problem in Sub-Saharan Africa with special reference to the fuelwood crisis. The problems of the energy sector in the rural and urban areas are considered, while subsequent sections are devoted to the socio-economic implications of the fuelwood crisis and the strategies that have so far been adopted to combat the crisis. Finally, the development of new and renewable energy is discussed before the conclusion.

Population and environmental concerns

The population of Sub-Saharan Africa is growing by leaps and bounds (3 per cent per annum), reaching over 459 million in 1990 (World Bank 1992) in spite of family planning measures to bring it under control. With a fast population growth rate, people are unable to feed themselves. Meanwhile energy demand is increasing with the rise in population. With increased urbanization and industrialization the situation is worsening as more energy is needed. At the same time, an increase in the demand for petroleum for food production and modernization is leading to an economic crisis. The cost of imports has risen and the value of exports has fallen. More cash crops have to be produced to provide foreign exchange. Meanwhile, farmers and nation-states in general are impoverished and indebted because they have to produce more for less cash. With the shortening of the fallow period marginal lands have to be exploited, leading to environmental crisis with rising economic and environmental costs of production (fig. 13.1). High fertility rates and a high percentage of child-bearing women are contributing to the high population growth rates. The issue at stake here is the distribution of the population and its influence on the existing resources of the region. Urbanization rates are even higher (5.6 per cent), though in many countries economic growth has been slow over the past few decades.

The upsurge of population growth has short- and long-term consequences for the existing forest resource base, land use, and fuelwood production. The economic crisis, with its concomitant high rates of unemployment and very low incomes, has encouraged the use of fuelwood in most African cities (fig. 13.1). These urban centres have become, as it were, a lucrative market for fuelwood[1] because it seems to be relatively available and cheaper than modern fuels, which hitherto have not proved a viable alternative in either rural or urban areas.

With growing population pressure on land use, a fuelwood gap is created, putting more pressure on the producing rural areas. Ultimately it is not only the sustainability of the environment that is at stake but the very survival of the urban poor and rural people, with women being the worst victims.

Though the countries of SSA may have divergent political systems and cultures, in broad terms they seem to have a common feature in so far as energy is concerned. They are literally being squeezed in a common energy problem. On the one hand, there is a heavy reliance on imported petroleum for the commercial sector, making petroleum shortages a chronic problem. On the other hand, there is a growing shortage of fuelwood in the predominant traditional sector and acute scarcity in some subregions.

The fuelwood crisis, as the "other energy crisis" is called, began to emerge during the oil crisis of the 1970s and has been aggravated by agricultural policies that aim at making African countries self-sufficient in food production (Eckholm et al. 1984). This has been achieved at the expense of existing forest lands, which are the main sources for fuelwood. National programmes tend to overlook this relationship between food and forest, so that the focus has been either wood or forest. This implies that wood energy is not being exploited in a manner that is sustainable in African countries. It appears that a more acceptable means for safe and sustainable energy production is yet to be found. Before this can be achieved, a good

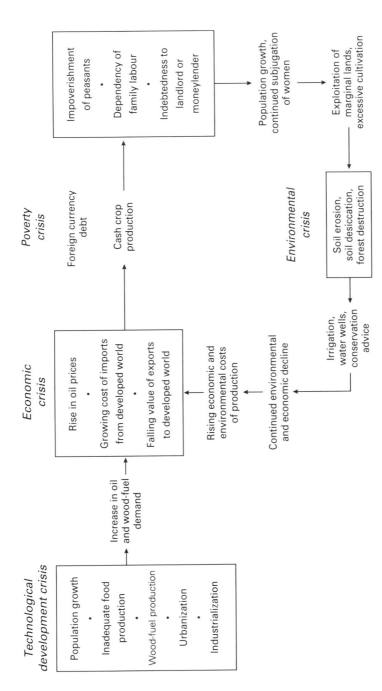

Fig. 13.1 **The crises of sustainability in Sub-Saharan Africa**

understanding of the African energy situation needs to be established as a basis for formulating a sustainable energy agenda.

According to Gamser (1980), little is known about the dependence of poor people in Africa on the use of forest resources for meeting their energy and subsistence needs. The measures needed to develop energy resources to ensure that rural interests can be served are also not well known. Gamser claims that there is not sufficient empirical understanding of the ecologically diverse lands involved in the tropical forest energy crisis. Neither have forest surveys provided adequate data on the dynamics of forest energy. He therefore calls for a concerted effort on the part of the international community to react positively to the shortfall in the existing data on forest energy production and consumption. At the moment most wood energy statistics, including those of the Food and Agriculture Organization (FAO), are based on estimates or unofficial sources, and this has been rather a weakness as regards knowledge about traditional energy. However, studies undertaken since the 1970s reveal the vulnerability of African countries so far as energy resources are concerned.

Although Africa accounts for 12 per cent of the global population, it consumes only 4 per cent of global energy. Besides, 40 per cent of its energy consumption is mainly in the form of biomass and it consumes no less than 40 per cent of this resource. On the global scale, the proportion of biomass in its total energy consumption is 6 per cent (see tables 13.1 and 13.2).

The rate of consumption varies within Africa when compared with other continents. In the Republic of South Africa, for example, out of the annual per capita consumption of 95GJ, only 5 per cent is biomass; in North Africa it is 11 per cent out of 34GJ. In Sub-Saharan Africa by contrast, out of the minimal per capita consumption of only 15GJ, 73 per cent is biomass (FAO 1987).

In the subregions of Africa the fuelwood situation may be determined by the political economy, the ecology, the geography, the demography, and the culture. Thus the fuelwood situation varies from the Sahel across humid West Africa, through Sudan, Kenya, and the SADCC countries.[2] However, within each of these countries, two energy crises, of petroleum and of fuelwood, are experienced.

The primary energy sector in Sub-Saharan Africa

Although SSA is rich in modern energy resources, some of these are underexplored. The energy potential is expressed in the abundance

Table 13.1   **Estimated energy consumption in Africa, 1990**

Fuel[a]	World		Africa		Africa as % of world
	Million TOE	EJ	Million TOE	EJ	
Gas	1,610	68.8	25	1.1	–
Oil	2,740	117.1	85	3.6	–
Coal	3,180	135.9	86	3.7	–
Hydro[b]	630	26.9	14	0.6	–
Subtotal	8,160	348.7	210	9.0	2.6
Biomass	600	25.6	140	6.0	23.4
Total	8,760	374.3	350	15.0	4.0
Population (million)	5,300		650		12.3

Source: United Nations (1990).
a. TOE = tons of oil equivalent.
  EJ = exajoules = 10^{18} J.
b. Primary energy equivalent.

Table 13.2   **Estimated energy consumption in Africa by region, 1990**

Fuel	North Africa		Sub-Sahara excl. R.S.A.		Republic of South Africa	
	Million TOE	EJ	Million TOE	EJ	Million TOE	EJ
Non-biomass fuels	80	3.4	47	2.0	83	3.6
Biomass fuels	10	0.4	126	5.4	4	0.2
Total	90	3.8	173	7.4	87	3.8
Percentage	26%		49%		25%	
Population (million)	114	(17%)	497	(77%)	39	(6%)

Source: United Nations (1990).

of oil reserves, which were estimated at about 21 billion barrels in 1990 and over 200 GW of hydropower (United Nations 1990). Figures 13.2 and 13.3 demonstrate the contrast between petroleum and hydroelectricity production and consumption of SSA. Clearly, when compared with other regions in both the developed and developing world, Africa consumes far less petroleum and electricity. SSA yearly consumption seems to be the lowest in per capita terms throughout the world. The energy resource distribution is

267

skewed and there are no appropriate institutions and mechanisms to ensure its integration, although there is some interregional trade in hydropower, coal, and petroleum.

Within Sub-Sabaran Africa only five countries account for almost all the oil produced – Nigeria, Angola, Gabon, Congo, and the Central African Republic (in descending order of output in 1991). The greater proportion is exported outside the region, even though petroleum is needed internally. Nigeria alone accounts for about three-quarters of the OPEC oil regulated quotas. On the whole, the total petroleum consumed is below 25 per cent of the total production (figs. 13.2 and 13.3).

Natural gas reserves on the continent are enormous and it is observed that the current reserves outweigh petroleum reserves if the current rate of production is taken into consideration. Coal reserves, which are more concentrated in the south, are expected to last for about 300 years. The growth rate of coal production has been slow, partly owing to greater reliance on petroleum for energy and to infrastructural and environmental problems.

Unlike coal, hydropower production is more widespread and has been increasing. It grew nearly four-fold between 1950 and 1988. Even at this growth rate, only 4 per cent of this power potential is exploited. Initial investment in production, environmental concerns, as well as old equipment and recurrent drought, have contributed to slowing down the growth of this power sector. Geothermal energy is utilized mainly in East Africa, and the possibility of its development needs to be explored for use elsewhere in SSA. The same goes for the production and supply of renewable energy sources. In these circumstances, wood fuels have become the predominant source of energy in the region.

Problems of the energy sector in Sub-Saharan Africa

Before the oil crisis in the 1970s, consumption of petroleum and its related products increased because oil was cheap and considered an infinite resource. The advanced industrialized countries developed a consumption infrastructure in the industrial and transport sectors. This meant that demand for petroleum was relatively inelastic. Sub-Saharan Africa unfortunately developed along these same lines, making it more vulnerable in the oil crisis.

The establishment of the Organization of Petroleum Exporting Countries (OPEC), which includes African countries such as Gabon,

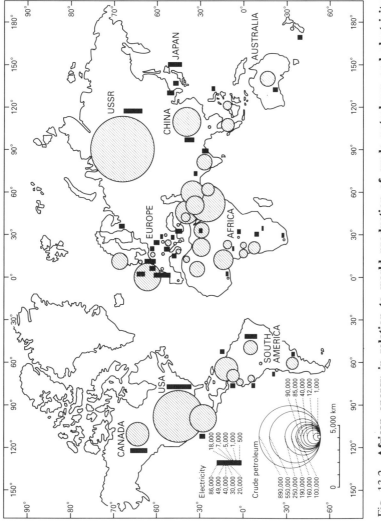

Fig. 13.2 **African energy in relation to world production of crude petroleum and electricity (quantities in '000 metric tons of coal equivalent) (Source: based on United Nations 1990)**

269

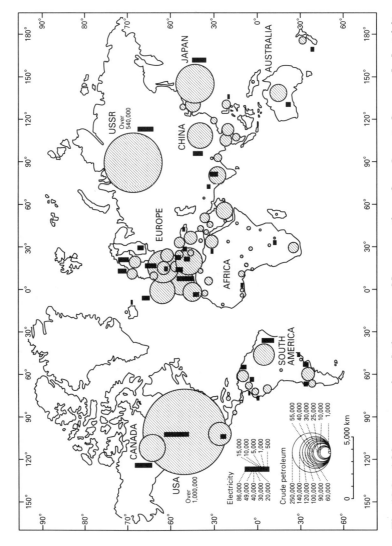

Fig. 13.3 **African energy in relation to world consumption of crude petroleum and electricity (quantities in '000 metric tons of coal equivalent) (Source: based on United Nations 1990)**

270

Nigeria, and Angola, was in response to the inelastic consumption pattern set up by the West in an effort to restrict oil output and to raise prices. Considering the high industrial development and the financial resources available, the West made attempts to move away from petroleum to alternative fuels. Such a move has not been possible in the non-oil-producing countries of Africa, where oil consumption in the energy balance is small and imports very high. For instance, Ghana spends 13 per cent of its foreign exchange on petroleum imports, but this rises to over 20 per cent in Tanzania and Kenya, and more than 40 per cent in Mozambique.

In spite of these huge financial burdens, the direct benefits that accrue from these exorbitant petroleum imports scarcely benefit the rural people. As O'Keefe (1990) remarks, even the recent fall in oil prices may be unlikely to ease the various rationing systems that operate in most non-oil-producing countries in Sub-Saharan Africa.

Because the rural and urban poor cannot afford high-priced petroleum products they have to depend on fuelwood in the various socioeconomic sectors. We therefore find in Sub-Saharan Africa a "paradox" of the wood-fuel situation: a situation of abundant wood-fuel resources in some countries and an acute shortage in certain areas as found in countries such as Ghana and Angola.

In 1981, the FAO undertook a global survey in order to determine fuelwood supplies and demand for them in developing countries such as Africa in 1980 and the year 2000. This was supposed to be one of its contributions to the United Nations Conference on New and Renewable Sources of Energy. Because there was a paucity of source material, the data were based on projections from the early 1980s, but the results present a reasonable picture of the status of fuelwood in Africa. Four major categories of the fuelwood situation were identified:

1. Areas where there has been overexploitation of biomass to the extent that there is fuelwood shortage.
2. Areas where fuelwood demand is in excess of sustainable supply – referred to as "crisis regions."
3. Areas where population growth is likely to give rise to crisis in the foreseeable future – categorized as satisfactory. In this regard the situation in the Sudano-Sahelian region is critical because acute shortages are expected, especially in the rapidly growing peri-urban areas. This is occurring because of increasing encroachment of agricultural land, and industrial, residential, and commercial developments. Bushfires and fuelwood production compounded

by population expansion have also resulted in gradual depletion of wood-fuel resources on an annual basis.

4. Areas estimated to be generally free of fuelwood supply problems – the humid and semi-humid areas. Nevertheless, large urban centres such as Yaoundé, Brazzaville, and Kinshasa located within the forest ecosystems are already experiencing local shortages. This is also occurring in the semi-humid areas of East Africa wherever very high population densities threaten wood-fuel resources. Communal land reserves are particularly in danger of fuelwood depletion.

As an example of the fuelwood situation in East Africa, the Kakamega District of the Western Province of Kenya can be cited. Having an area of 3,500 km², which constitutes only 0.5 per cent of Kenya's land area, the province harbours over 6.5 per cent of the population. As one of the most populous regions of the country, its population densities are over 800 persons per km² in localized areas. This has generated a mosaic of small fragmented farms of about 0.5 ha feeding large families of about 10. Consequently, considerable pressure has been put on the limited land to the extent that agriculture and fuel needs are severely threatened. Farmers have no viable alternatives other than to depend on their own tiny land-holding for fuelwood supplies.

Similarly, a fuelwood deficit is to be found in the small mountainous SADCC countries, where population pressure has created acute wood-fuel shortages in countries such as Malawi and Swaziland. The situation in island countries such as Madagascar is also critical, particularly in the central and western sections.

The dynamics of the fuelwood situation represent a growing crisis. Whereas, in 1980, 55 million people in Sub-Saharan Africa lived in areas where there was acute fuelwood scarcity and another 146 million lived in areas with an increasing deficit, it is estimated that by the year 2000 about 535 million people will experience a critical fuelwood deficit if exploitation continues at the current rate (United Nations 1990).

Wood-fuel exploitation is not solely responsible for environmental degradation. In the forest areas of SSA, deforestation is caused to a large extent by logging and forest clearance for cultivation. Many trees are also lost as fallow periods are shortened. Generally, areas with a high rate of tree regrowth can meet the needs of a larger population than those with low growth potential. Areas with wood-fuel deficits are those with low to moderate rainfall and high population densities. In areas such as the Sahel where there is very low population density and low rainfall, the demand for wood fuels has outstripped the slow growth potential of the woody plants, creating acute fuelwood problems in urban and rural areas.

Energy in rural Africa

Rural energy use in Africa is generally low, reflecting the low industrial and urban base of the African economy. The more rural and the lower the incomes of the community, the more use they make of traditional fuels. Cooking, heating, and local industrial establishments are major consumers of household energy, which is dominated by wood fuels (FRIDA 1980). On present trends it is unlikely that fuel switching will occur in the near future on a large scale. As the population expands one would expect a direct increase in fuelwood utilization.

This being the case, a "wood-fuel paradox" can be observed in operation at both local and national levels. In many African countries there is adequate forest stock for wood-fuel production. Within this apparent situation of plenty, however, specific localized wood-fuel shortages exist in western Kenya, northern Ghana, Angola, Zambia, and the Sudan. Arid and semi-arid areas have their share of scarcity just like the large deforested areas in Botswana, Lesotho, and Swaziland. The low carrying capacity of these countries means that growth is not sustainable for either agriculture or wood fuels. For example, in Zimbabwe, Chad, and Mali, advanced deforestation and soil erosion in infertile areas with poor rainfall have forced many people to migrate.

Deforestation is affecting many rural people, who have been accused of being the cause of deforestation. More often these people produce fuelwood from their own food farms, secondary forests, or fallow lands. Where trees are cleared from agricultural land, they are readily used as fuelwood. Deforestation is caused primarily by the need for fuelwood for the curing of tobacco and tea, by excessive felling of timber for domestic and export markets, by agricultural production, by urbanization, by bushfires, and, more significantly, by demand for wood fuel by urban households.

Urban fuel demand

Patterns of household energy use in urban areas are far more complex than in rural areas. As rural–urban migration opens up more avenues for the poor, it also brings about various problems with limited opportunities. Catering for the fuel needs of the poor is just one of the essential services that poor migrants have to provide in the urban area. These are services that would have been free if they were in the rural areas. As most towns in SSA are growing rapidly, urban growth is paralleled by increasing demand for energy to meet consumption needs. This is met by wood fuels. Hence it is estimated that, if the current rates of population growth continue, urban wood-fuel consumption will surpass that of rural areas in the next 20 years or so (O'Keefe 1990).

The significance of fuelwood in the urban energy balance is the limited access to alternative fuels. Fuelwood competes with other household fuels such as kerosene, liquefied petroleum gas (LPG), and electricity. The choice of fuelwood depends among other things on its cost relative to commercial alternatives, their availability and security, and supply bottlenecks. These encourage a lucrative black market in which prices are much higher than the official stated prices. The prohibitive costs tend to increase the reliance of poor women on fuelwood even if it is scarce and expensive. Besides, there is also the cost of modern cooking stoves, which is not affordable to many households that may want to switch fuels.

The available evidence indicates that urban fuelwood prices have been rapidly increasing, causing a household dilemma for poor women. In urban centres in poorer environments fuelwood prices are almost comparable to those of modern fuels. According to Leach and Mearns (1989), African cities such as Addis Ababa, Harare, Nairobi, and Abidjan are experiencing fuelwood price rises in excess of general inflation rates. Thus fuelwood prices in many large cities are increasing in real terms.

Urban demand for fuelwood is accelerating the degradation of woody vegetation. For example, in the Sudan an area of 31,000 km^2 of woodland is cleared each year for fuelwood production, especially for charcoal. In certain areas the resulting scarcity has created a disastrous effect on supplies. For example, in Burkina Faso the land surrounding the city of Ouagadougou has been completely cleared of woody vegetation for 45 km in all directions (French 1978: 1–3). As a result, bulky and low-value wood fuels are transported over hundreds of kilometres to urban markets where the fuels are badly needed. Similarly in East Africa, charcoal has to be transported for about 600 km to Nairobi and its environs. In Nigeria, the long-distance haulage of fuelwood to urban centres has been an official concern since early colonial times (Cline-Cole 1985).

As more land around the towns and cities is further depleted of its remaining vegetation, a vicious cycle of soil erosion is set in motion. In extreme cases, wood fuels gradually vanish from the urban market, as in the Cape Verde islands. Judicious urban energy planning may minimize the degradation and improve the access of women and the urban poor to other energy alternatives.

The socio-economic implications of the fuelwood crisis

Generally, the economic and social consequences of fuelwood exploitation and consumption are overlooked. In Ghana, for example, cooking in the home depends on fuelwood, which is responsible for more than 75 per cent of all energy consumed in the country annually. Most small-scale industries and food-processing enterprises that women undertake depend in large part on wood fuel. This dependence on wood fuels has contributed to the growing exploitation of the country's forest. In all, about 650,000 ha of forest are destroyed every year through the carbonization of charcoal. Alarmingly, between 1974 and 1990 wood-fuel consumption increased by 50 per cent in the country (Ardayfio-Schandorf 1993). This increase mainly reflects the urban demand previously discussed.

Urban demand has, as it were, created fuelwood markets, providing job opportunities for both men and women. Men are involved in the long-distance trade in fuelwood and charcoal, and women are in small-scale fuelwood businesses focused on villages and local markets. Charcoal production is undertaken by women in towns and villages, where they run family businesses more actively during the off farming season.

Though inefficient, wood-fuel production and distribution contribute to some extent to the national balance of payments at the macro level, as foreign exchange that might have been used for the purchase of imported fuels is saved through the use of traditional fuels. This notwithstanding, poor urban women have to pay higher prices for fuelwood and charcoal owing to commercialization. In the rural areas, women and children walk long distances to produce, harvest, and transport fuelwood to their households. However, in areas where forest resources are abundant the production of fuelwood is less problematic. In areas of high population density, women spend longer hours producing fuelwood. In such areas, women collect fuelwood on their return from the farm while they do other things as well (Ardayfio-Schandorf 1981). Similarly, in the semi-arid, arid, or savanna areas with low population density where wood-fuel resources are scarce, women have to walk for longer distances to produce fuelwood.

Where these problems exist, a bigger burden is put on women, who have to make some trade-offs. Women curtail cooking time and even cut down on economic enterprises to make time for fuelwood production. The production time varies from one region to another, with walking distances ranging from about 1 to about 10 km and even more in places such as Ethiopia. The distance covered is reflected in the cost of fuelwood.

In the Sahelian countries where deforestation is severe, fuelwood costs as much as food. Even in Ghana it has been found that women in the savanna (semi-arid) regions have cut down on their cooking time and are cooking less nutritious food because of the fuelwood crisis (Ardayfio, 1986). In view of these problems, some scholars argue that the real energy crisis is women's time. However, the energy crisis goes beyond women's time. In areas where fuelwood is the only energy input for commercial activities for women, they have been forced owing to cost and non-availability of fuelwood to discontinue many economic activities. Because of this pressure, women who are involved in household fuelwood production have developed an intimate knowledge of wood species critical for fuelwood and charcoal production. This knowledge could be exploited in planning to meet improved wood-fuel supplies.

Strategies to combat the fuelwood crisis

The oil crisis in the 1970s, which raised awareness of the wood-fuel problem, set in motion various strategies for combating it (Eckholm et al. 1984). One of the initial steps that have been taken to solve this problem has been the gathering of adequate data to enhance the understanding of the crisis.

One of the earliest institutions to contribute to the debate was the United Nations University in Tokyo, which recognized the wood-fuel issue as a pressing global problem within its programme of environmental resource utilization and management. Extensive studies were carried out in south-western and northern Nigeria. Among the other institutions that developed a similar focus was the International Labour Organization, whose studies embraced Africa as well as other countries in the developing world. Further information has also been provided by the Beijer Institute of Stockholm about the SADCC countries of southern Africa.

These studies, including the more current ones that are now being undertaken by national institutions, have shed some light on the fuelwood crisis, but more information is still needed to construct a much clearer picture to replace the existing one based on projections from the 1980s. For example, the question of measurement of fuelwood is yet to be solved through further studies throughout SSA.

In the supply and demand area, strategies included a focus on village woodlots, reafforestation, and afforestation programmes based on forest management technology. In Kenya, a study indicated that afforestation programmes projected to the middle of 1985 would contribute only 5 per cent to total fuelwood demand. If such forest plantations were embarked upon in order to solve the wood-fuel problem, the effect will be marginal because the viability of some of the programmes themselves has been questionable.

In spite of this, afforestation programmes have the potential of ensuring some degree of regeneration to conserve soil and water resources around urban centres. They could also provide industrial raw materials and possibly generate export income by exporting timber. In Kenya, for instance, woodlot programmes have been successful in areas that do not have problems with land ownership. They have helped to ease pressure on the natural forest, to protect the environment, and to satisfy the fuelwood needs of the local communities concerned.

Moving to West Africa, the concept of natural forest management, which had been practised since World War II to provide fuelwood, was revived in the Sudan savanna town of Ouagadougou. This move was made to supply wood from classified forests to meet the growing fuelwood needs. Agro-forestry is also being promoted throughout the semi-arid countries in the region, and is now practised in most countries, including Sierra Leone. This approach could be further promoted by giving incentives to local people to grow more of their own fuel on their own farmlands and on community land. The short rotation of non-indigenous and indigenous trees for fuels, food, fodder, and other industrial products would be beneficial to most villagers.

The policy implications of these programmes could be far-reaching. Owing to the environmental costs and benefits associated with forestry/energy projects, many countries in Africa are adopting policies that will also modify current energy consumption patterns. Energy policies are being enforced by the appropriate ministries, such as the Ministry of Energy in Ghana, the National Electric Power Authority of Nigeria, and the National Energy Administration of the Sudan. Some of these policies try to improve efficiency by narrowing the fuel energy production ratio. Energy-saving devices, including improved charcoal stoves, have been introduced to replace the traditional stove gradually. Some of these stoves could save up to 50 per cent of fuelwood demand and reduce the energy bill of women in urban centres (FAO 1987).

Other policies have focused on reducing national demand through appropriate pricing policies, improving the current supply of fuelwood through a more efficient charcoal-manufacturing process, and reducing fuelwood consumption patterns by increasing the use of conventional fuels such as petroleum and its by-products. Attempts have also been made to increase the supply and use of new and renewable energy sources.

New and renewable energy development

Many Sub-Saharan African countries have great potential for the development of hydropower, which is the major source of electricity production (70 per cent). The rest comes from thermal plants, which are fuelled by oil or in some countries by coal. Despite this potential, electricity represents only 10 per cent of total energy consumption in Sub-Saharan Africa (FAO 1987). Even though it was modest, the region experienced a rapid growth of its electric power sector until the economic crisis of the 1980s.

The downturn that occurred had a negative impact on the economy and the electric power sector. The electricity production of Sub-Saharan Africa is far below that of other major developing regions. Of the amount generated, mining and processing industries absorb up to 80 per cent, with a limited amount being consumed by households. As the consumption rate of electric power increases, the level should be maintained so that many more urban and suburban populations may be supplied with electricity. But the question is, how can this be achieved?

Economic and financial constraints on African countries have been major causes of the inadequate development and slackening growth of the power sector. Being the poorest of the developing countries, the deterioration of their terms of trade has affected their economic growth, which is further worsened by population explosion. The necessary investments for the energy sector are enormous. At the same time it appears that electrification in rural areas could help slow down rural–urban migration, which is on the increase, and pave the way for the conditions for sustained economic development. However, given that rural electrification programmes are capital intensive and usually unprofitable, the possibility of providing electric power to most of the rural population is a forlorn hope. For it is doubtful whether Sub-Saharan Africa has the potential to mobilize adequate resources to develop this sector.

None the less, technologies now exist for generating electricity based on renewable energy sources apart from hydropower generation. Solar photovoltaic systems, wind generators, and gasifiers are a few of the examples. In 1981, a national conference was organized on New and Renewable Sources of Energy (NARSE) by the United Nations in Rome. A lot of enthusiasm about these resources was generated but one has to be cautious about the technological developments suggested at such energy meetings. The conference painted a rosy and conflict-free picture of solar and wind energy projects. To this end, between 1981 and 1986 there was dissemination of solar and other renewable energy technologies. However, because oil was cheap at the time and the fuelwood crisis had not yet reared its ugly head, not much attention was devoted to research and development of these appropriate technologies.

With the oil crisis, industrial countries made efforts to expand their development endeavours in appropriate technology. In Africa, solar technology was seen as a potential alternative. It was even assumed that African countries could bypass an era of fossil fuel and switch straight to solar energy, which is abundant, ubiquitous, and free (Goodman 1985). But this was not to be realized on a large scale because economic constraints hindered the diffusion of the NARSE technologies. Those NARSE technologies, such as solar cookers, that were initially acceptable appear to have lost their original attraction. Other applications, including solar crop driers, solar water heaters for institutional applications, passive solar heating, wind pumps, and mini-hydro and bio-energy in the form of biogas, have, however, achieved some measure of success.

Considering the existing status of NARSE, it seems the energy sector in SSA will continue to be largely based on wood fuels. But this does not mean that alternative sources must not be pursued. Wood energy must be seriously considered as an integral part of a global and multisectoral energy strategy.

In this connection, increasing numbers of action programme initiatives are being developed at both regional and national levels to harmonize and improve rational forest management and wood-fuel availability. Among the national programmes are the Desertification Control Programme, the Environmental Action Plan, and the Tropical Forest Action Plan, which have wood fuel as one of their priority areas. The regional programmes include the Inter-States Committee on Drought Control, the Intergovernmental Authority on Drought and Development, the Southern Africa Development Coordinating Conference, and the Agroforestry Network for Africa Programme.

Donor agencies have been particularly supportive in assisting developing countries to formulate and execute environmentally sound energy policies. One such example is the Energy Sector Management Assistance Programme funded by the United Nations Development Programme and the World Bank. This project, which operates in many African countries, has an elaborate research agenda that emphasizes the promotion of energy-efficient technologies and environmentally benign fuels.

Conclusion

By all indications the fuelwood paradox is a critical issue in the sustainable development of Sub-Saharan Africa. As the terms of trade of the countries of Africa deteriorate, it becomes even more difficult to allocate foreign exchange to petroleum imports and the development of new and renewable sources of energy, which are more efficient. As such, we could not agree better with Brooks that:

We cannot conceive of development without changes in the extent or nature of energy flows of Africa. And because energy is so fundamental, every one of those change flows has environmental implications. The implications of this are profound. It means that there is no such thing as a simple energy choice. They are all complex. And they will all involve trade-offs. However, some of the choices and some of the trade-offs appear to be unequivocally better than others, in the sense that they offer more development and less environmental damage. (Brooks 1986; cited in WCED 1987: 173)

Wood fuels offer least potential in economic and industrial development even though they are the predominant household fuel. In the short term, energy policies should include strategies for the production and supply of wood energy to ensure its consumption in a more sustainable manner.

To formulate an effective basis for doing this, due attention should be given to analysis of the special needs and priorities of rural populations with reference to women and community participation in identifying actions as well as decentralized energy planning. In the process of fuelwood supply, modified patterns should be determined through studies at the national level. Remunerative producer prices should also be established to satisfy urban fuelwood needs. Coupled with this, national and local programmes, including dissemination of cheap and efficient charcoal and wood-burning stoves, should be launched to reduce wood-fuel consumption.

The development of modern fuels such as coal, petroleum, and natural gas should be more fully explored and developed. National and international institutions should be encouraged to invest in the sector. Regional cooperation could also be explored as a useful instrument for furthering this goal and for enhancing energy development and independence in SSA. This cooperation has already been demonstrated with the formation of the African Petroleum Producers' Association (APPA) in 1987. Other regional groupings, as well as multilateral institutions, could help to accelerate sustainable energy development in the region.

Notes

1. Fuelwood refers to firewood, whilst wood fuel refers to fuelwood, charcoal, and agricultural waste.
2. SADCC refers to Southern Africa Development Coordinating Conference. The nine countries concerned are Angola, Botswana, Lesotho, Malawi, Mozambique, Swaziland, Tanzania, Zambia, and Zimbabwe.

References

Ardayfio, E. 1986. *The Rural Energy Crisis in Ghana: Its Implications for Women's Work and Household Survival.* Geneva: International Labour Organization.

Ardayfio-Schandorf, E. 1981. *Rural Energy Production and Consumption in Southwestern Nigeria: The Role of Women.* Obafemi Awolowo University, Ile-Ife, Nigeria.

———— 1983. Rural energy consumption in south-western Nigeria. *Bulletin of Ghana Geographical Association* 1(1).

———— 1993. Commercialization of fuelwood in Ghana. Paper presented at a Conference on Women and Forestry in Ghana, Accra.

Brooks, D. 1986. Friends of the Earth, cited in WCED, *Our Common Future.* Oxford: Oxford University Press, 1987.

Cline-Cole, R. 1985. Energy, environment and man in tropical Africa: The case of the Freetown woodfuel market. Paper presented to the Bamako International Symposium on Urban–Rural Relationships, Bamako.

Eckholm, E. et al. 1984. *Fuelwood: The Energy Crisis That Won't Go Away*. London: Earthscan.

FAO (Food and Agriculture Organization of the United Nations). 1987. *Ghana Forestry Project Preparation Report*. Rome.

French D. 1978. *Renewable Energy for Africa: Needs, Opportunities, Issues*. Washington D.C.: United States Agency for International Development.

FRIDA (Fund for Research and Investment for the Development of Africa). 1980. *Domestic Energy in Sub-Saharan Africa: The Impending Crisis. Its Measurement and Framework for Practical Solutions*. London.

Gamser, M. S. 1980. The forest resource and rural energy development. *World Development* 8: 769–780.

Goodman, G. T. 1985. Energy and development. Where do we go? *Ambio* 14(4–5).

Leach, G. and R. Mearns. 1989. *Beyond the Woodfuel Crisis: People, Trees and Land in Africa*. London: Earthscan.

O'Keefe, M. 1990. A new energy agenda for Africa. Paper presented at the International Seminar on Energy in Africa, 27–30 November, Abidjan, Côte d'Ivoire.

United Nations. 1990. *United Nations Statistical Year Book*.

WCED (World Commission on Environment and Development). 1987. *Our Common Future*. Oxford: Oxford University Press.

World Bank. 1992. *World Development Report*. Washington D.C.

14

The case for mineral resources management and development in Sub-Saharan Africa

Lloyd A. K. Quashie

"Sustainable development" implies that economic activity should be designed to create wealth for the use of present and future generations. If natural resources cannot be developed and exploited to create wealth for the nation, the result may be poverty and deprivation. Crisis management soon takes over from sustainable economic development. So far, experience in Sub-Saharan Africa for the past 20 years would indicate that almost all the countries in this region have suffered negative growth; that is, the economies of Sub-Saharan Africa are in a state of decline and the development of the rich natural resources has come to a virtual standstill. The Sub-Saharan region has turned into a region of "beggar nations" in the midst of plentiful natural resources. In this regard, the least harnessed resources of this beautiful continent include minerals and energy.

The economic crisis has become endemic and is now becoming pandemic in the region. A solution to the problems must be found in order to reverse the condition of exponential decay and bring the countries back on the track of viable and sustainable economic growth.

The thesis of this paper is that the road to sustainable development and growth of the Sub-Saharan economies will be mainly via rational

283

development and exploitation of the mineral and energy resources rather than by agricultural development. The track record of the Sub-Saharan economies since independence, and certainly for the past 20 years, would support the argument that agriculture has so far failed as the engine for economic development in most countries of mainland Sub-Saharan Africa. For example, countries such as Côte d'Ivoire, Senegal, and Kenya have succeeded for only a limited period in using agriculture and agro-based industries as an "engine" for the sustainable growth of their economies.

On the other hand, countries such as Botswana, Zimbabwe, and, more recently, Ghana have proved that a country with a strong minerals industry and a cheap energy resource can aspire to positive economic growth that can be sustained, depending on the life of the resource and changes in demand, and can also provide the necessary catalyst for the development of other sectors of the economy. This growth pattern has also been the backbone of the sustainable development of certain industrialized countries such as the United States, Canada, some West European countries, and Australia. Other highly developed countries lacking or with only limited mineral and energy resources, such as Germany (i.e. former West Germany) and Japan, have had to import the necessary mineral raw materials and fuel energy to feed and sustain their huge industrial base for economic growth.

The industrialized countries would rather hoard or subsidize agricultural production, much to the detriment or the disadvantage of the developing countries, in particular Sub-Saharan Africa, which provide most of the mineral raw materials and part of the fuel energy for the industrialized countries. Production of selected minerals by the leading producing countries in Sub-Saharan Africa in 1989 is shown in table 14.1 and the value of minerals exported in 1989 in table 14.2.

In order for Sub-Saharan Africa to recover from its development stagnation, it is imperative that a new development agenda be forged, with more emphasis on the exploration, development, exploitation, and rational management of its mineral and energy resources for sustainable economic growth. Curbing population growth or demobilizing the public sector of the economy cannot open the gates to sustainable development in the medium to long term. Preserving the pristine countryside in the interests of good environmental practice and health would also cause the otherwise necessary industrial development of the subregion to stagnate. A happy medium has to be found between unguarded development and sustainable development

Table 14.1 **Sub-Saharan Africa: Major mineral producers and share of world mine supply, 1989 (volume of selected minerals)**

Country	Mineral						
	Copper '000 m.t.	Bauxite '000 m.t.	Rutile m.t.	Diamonds '000 carats	Manganese ore '000 m.t.	Cobalt m.t.	Uranium '000 m.t.
Angola	–	–	–	1,272	–	–	–
Botswana	22	–	–	15,251	–	–	–
CAR	–	–	–	447	–	–	–
Gabon	–	–	–	–	2,600	–	900
Ghana	–	382	–	290	280	–	–
Guinea	–	17,547	–	230	–	–	–
Namibia	38	–	–	932	–	–	3,629
Niger	–	–	–	–	–	–	2,962
Sierra Leone	–	1,562	128	600	–	–	–
Swaziland	–	–	–	55	–	–	–
Zaire	430	–	–	17,652	–	8,314	–
Zambia	445	–	–	–	–	4,490	–
Zimbabwe	16	–	–	–	–	–	–
Total SSA	951	19,491	128	36,729	2,880	12,804	7,491
World supply	9,082	107,963	450	98,500	22,100	19,867	35,586
SSA share	11%	18%	28%	37%	13%	64%	21%

Source: World Bank (1992: 1).

285

Table 14.2 **Sub-Saharan Africa: Value of mineral exports, 1989 (US$ m.)**

Country	Mineral[a]													
	Copper	Bauxite	Ore	Gold	Diamonds and gems	Lead/ zinc	Manganese ore	Nickel	Tin	Cobalt	Uranium	Phosphate rock	Misc.	Total
Angola	—	—	—	—	230	—	—	—	—	—	—	—	—	230
Botswana	60	—	—	—	1,300	—	—	140	—	—	—	—	—	1,500
Burkina Faso	—	—	—	30	—	—	—	—	—	—	—	—	—	30
CAR	—	—	—	—	40	—	—	—	—	—	—	—	—	40
Gabon	—	—	—	—	—	—	175	—	—	—	50	—	—	225
Ghana	—	5	—	150	15	—	15	—	—	—	—	—	—	185
Guinea	—	400	—	45	55	—	—	—	—	—	—	130	—	630
Liberia	—	—	200	—	—	—	—	—	—	—	—	—	—	200
Mali	—	—	—	25	—	—	—	—	—	—	—	—	—	25
Mauritania	—	—	180	—	—	—	—	—	—	—	—	—	—	180
Namibia	125	—	—	10	320	60	—	—	10	—	250	25	—	800

Senegal	–	–	–	–	–	–	–	–	–	80	–	80
Sierra Leone	–	25	–	–	–	–	–	–	–	–	55	90
Swaziland	–	–	–	20	–	–	–	–	–	–	10	30
Togo	–	–	–	–	–	–	–	–	–	115	–	115
Zaire	1,245	–	30	250	90	–	15	170	–	–	–	1,800
Zambia	1,230	–	–	–	40	–	–	70	–	–	–	1,340
Zimbabwe	30	10	175	–	–	110	–	–	–	–	85	410
Others	–	–	15	10	–	–	15	–	–	–	20	60
Total formal	2,690	430	480	2,250	190	250	40	240	530	195	325	8,200
Artisanal/informal			300	500								800
Total SSA[b]	2,690	430	780	2,750	190	250	40	240	530	195	325	9,000

Source: World Bank (1992: 2).

a. Excludes aluminium exports of about US$300 million from Ghana and Cameroon.

b. Over 95 per cent of SSA's mineral production is estimated to be exported and available statistics do not readily permit a separation of the value of production and the value of exports.

that takes into account the health of the population and the preservation of a sound environment for future generations.

Africa is almost certainly endowed with enormous mineral resources yet to be discovered. Exploration for these mineral resources has not been conducted in a systematic manner since independence in the Sub-Saharan countries. As such, the full impact of the minerals industry sector on the economies of these countries has been minimal or non-existent. The countries that could boast of a significant minerals industry sector are: Botswana, Ghana, Guinea, Zaire, Zambia, Zimbabwe, and the Republic of South Africa; including oil, one would add Nigeria, Gabon, and Angola (see table 14.3). These countries, however, had a mining tradition during colonial times and in several

Table 14.3 **Sub-Saharan Africa: The economic contribution of mining, selected countries, 1989**

Country	Formal mining exports (US$ m.)	Mining exports as % of total exports	Mining value-added as % of GDP	Mineral taxes as % of total taxes
Zaire	1,798	83	16	35
Botswana	1,506	83	51	58
Zambia	1,337	95	13	16
Namibia	799	76	29	36
Guinea	627	82	25	72
Zimbabwe	411	26	6	n.a.
Niger	232	75	6	16
Angola	230	8	2	n.a.
Gabon	225	16	5	n.a.
Liberia	200	58	n.a.	n.a.
Ghana	186	23	2	n.a.
Mauritania	181	41	10	n.a.
Togo	115	22	8	n.a.
Sierra Leone	89	80	6	5
Senegal	76	10	1	n.a.
CAR	40	25	3	n.a.
Burkina Faso	33	15	1	n.a.
Swaziland	30	10	1	n.a.
Mali	25	9	1	1
Total	8,140	47	10	30[a]

Source: World Bank (1992: 3).
a. Estimate.

cases even before. Some governments built strong geological surveys, mining, and metallurgical departments, which conducted geological mapping and exploration of known mineral deposits (usually ancient artisanal mining sites) for allocation to mining companies for development and exploitation. The mining leases granted by the colonial governments virtually gave the companies perpetual mineral rights and tenure on very disadvantageous terms to the colonies. Upon the attainment of independence, these countries enacted new mining laws, which vested the minerals resources in the state. The countries therefore achieved sovereign rights over the mineral deposits (including petroleum and natural gas) with a view to exploiting these resources, this time more to the benefit of these sovereign nations. However, with the exception of the Republic of South Africa, and recently Botswana, none of the Sub-Saharan countries can boast of a strong and viable minerals industry sector in their economies that could contribute to sustainable development in the coming decades. So far, attempts to develop the mineral resources of these countries have been limited to half-hearted policy reforms and the enactment of mining legislation and investment codes, which have failed to attract the necessary investment in the minerals industry sector. Many factors have contributed to the poor performance of the minerals industry sector of the Sub-Saharan countries. However, before proceeding to discuss these factors, I should like to examine the new slogan "sustainable development" as it may be applied to mineral management and development in the Africa region.

Minerals occur naturally in the subsoil and they have to be discovered by systematic exploration. Their distribution in the subsoil is governed by certain physical and chemical principles, host-rock characteristics, and the structural history of the mineral location. Unlike crops, minerals cannot be planted, watered, fertilized, or made to grow to produce "food" to feed the nation. The mineral endowment of a country can be made available for utilization only through sustained investment in systematic exploration, development, mining, and processing. The minerals that can be developed, mined, and processed economically should occur in such proven quantities and grades that they may contribute to the wealth and growth of the economy when exploited. A viable mineral enterprise should also be able to generate sufficient funds from operations to finance further exploration and development of the mineral resource base for future exploitation, otherwise the enterprise will perish.

Without exploration for ore reserves there can be no sustainable development of a mining enterprise and the sector cannot contribute to economic growth for the future wealth of the nation.

In the minerals industry, "sustainable development" would therefore imply sustained investment in exploration and development to access economic ore deposits for extraction and for use at a profit. There are, however, certain imperatives for the development of a strong and viable minerals industry sector. It needs a realistic management and administrative policy that takes account of the needs of society and, at the same time, guarantees equitable distribution of the wealth generated by the mineral asset to the investor and the host country. This mineral development policy should be stable in the long term in order to attract the much-needed investment in the sector, which, by its very nature, is "high risk" and requires long lead-times for development, start-up, and operations. Above all, society is now demanding that mining operations should, in addition to contributing to wealth, be environmentally friendly and sustainable for the use of future generations. This is what a rational and realistic mineral development policy has always been about. This policy has been described as a "mineral conservation policy" by economic geologists, and progressive mining laws and regulations include provision for such a policy. Sustainable environmental practice should be compatible with good mining industrial practice. Good mining practice should also take into account the health and safety of the workers and the people living near the mining operations.

Furthermore, mineral conservation requires that the depletion rate of the mineral deposit should be in balance with the rate of discovery of mineable reserves and in accordance again with good environmental practice. Environmentalists have tended to confuse conservation of the natural resource and environment with preservation, an attitude that may preclude the utilization and development of natural resources.

If all these factors and policy issues are brought into harmony under mineral development legislation and fiscal regimes that are realistic and dynamic, sustainable development of the minerals industry could be carried out for economic growth to meet the basic needs of the population, while conserving the natural resource base for the socio-economic needs of future generations in a sound environment. However, Botswana should be singled out for special mention as the only country that has been able to develop its mineral sector as an "engine" for economic growth during the past 10 years.

The country is blessed with minerals of very high intrinsic value, a realistic mineral legislation policy, and a relatively stable investment climate. After many decades of massive investment in agriculture and agro-based industries, Botswana has shown that agriculture alone cannot suffice to sustain economic development.

Many constraining factors have contributed to the near-stagnation of the development of the minerals industry in the Sub-Saharan economies. These factors occur in varying degrees from country to country, but those that are fundamental and common to all the countries are identified briefly below:

- a lack of investment in systematic geological mapping and exploration, and inadequate technical data on the mineral endowment;
- a weak institutional and policy framework for mineral development and exploitation;
- inadequate fiscal and financial regimes for mining development;
- poorly developed infrastructural bases, including transportation, communications, and engineering services;
- a lack of cheap, reliable energy resources for industrial projects;
- the deterioration of the economic performance of the Sub-Saharan countries, exacerbated by deteriorating terms of trade and inadequate pricing of primary mineral commodities produced by these countries;
- the unusually high cost of capital for mining projects in the region compared with the capital cost of similar mining projects in South-East Asia, Australia, and South America;
- the perception by the international mining community of an unstable "investment climate," political instability, and corruption in Sub-Saharan Africa;
- the scarcity of indigenous professional and technical manpower capable of formulating viable policy reforms, estimating the feasibility of mineral development projects, or negotiating equitable joint-venture mining agreements with transnational corporations.

Despite these difficulties, the Sub-Saharan countries should be able to develop their mineral resources as an "engine" for sustainable growth and in an environmentally friendly manner. The continent is endowed with enormous mineral potential, including: diamonds, gold, silver, the platinum group metals, emeralds, rubies, and other semi-precious minerals, bauxite, manganese, nickel, cobalt, copper, cadmium, chrome, lead, zinc, and other non-ferrous metals, iron ores (hematite and magnetite), cassiterite, rutile, ilmenite, zirchon, monazite, mica, vermiculite, limestone, gypsum, barytes, potash, phosphate, kaolin, "granites" for dimensional stones, and other industrial minerals. Africa is also known for proven reserves of high-quality petroleum, natural gas, peat, lignite, and coal with low sulphur content (i.e. Gondwana coal). African countries are yet to develop these rich mineral resources and exploit them for industrialization and sustained growth. The World Bank (1989: 122) describes the "relative mineral abundance" as a "mixed blessing" to many African countries. It could also be described as a situation of *poverty in the midst of plenty!*

However, the failure to develop the full potential of the minerals industry in the Sub-Saharan economies is not entirely the fault of the governments concerned. Certain important exogenous factors have also contributed to the near-stagnation of the development agenda of the African countries. For the past 20 years, Africa has missed the investment boom of international finance in mineral exploration and development. Most of the mining investments have been directed away from Africa to South America, Canada, Australia, Papua New Guinea, and the fast-growing countries of South-East Asia (see fig. 14.1). Some of these apparently more attractive countries have little comparative advantage in terms of political stability. In fact, there is evidence that many of the transnational corporations that were operating profitably in Africa during colonial times pulled out of Africa just before or immediately after independence to invest in mining ventures elsewhere. Fortunately for Sub-Saharan Africa, many of the ventures have failed in those countries and the Africa region has another opportunity to attract the transnational corporations back to the very high-grade near-surface ore deposits of the continent that they virtually abandoned more than 20 years ago. The country most likely to offer stiff competition for scarce mining venture capital over the next few years is Australia. However, the mining companies of Australia have already committed most of their sales contracts for the supply of mineral products to Japan and the ASEAN countries, which until recently have been experiencing an economic boom.

In today's Sub-Saharan Africa investors will find the host countries more realistic in asserting their sovereign rights over natural resources. The private sector will be encouraged to participate in the development of mineral resources without undue intervention from the state. Governments are more prepared to confine themselves to the roles of good landlord and regulator of the industry. Investment codes have been enacted that have entrenched in them special bene-

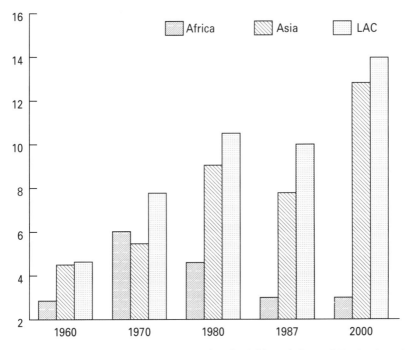

Fig. 14.1 **Comparison of mineral production in Africa, Asia, and Latin America–Caribbean for eight selected minerals and metals, 1960–2000 (1985 US$ billion) (Note: actual and projected gross value of production of aluminium, copper, iron ore, zinc, nickel, lead, tin, and gold. Source: World Bank 1992: 5)**

fits and incentives for investing in the mining sector. More competitive and stable fiscal and financial regimes have been passed into law with guarantees for the repatriation of capital and profits. However, the host countries also expect a fair and equitable share of the revenues generated from the mining operations for financing sustainable development and the growth of their economies. Having undertaken painful macroeconomic reforms in order to attract foreign investment, these countries will expect that joint-venture mining projects would not be operated as offshore or enclave enterprises and that they would be more integrated into the domestic economies and become net foreign exchange earners. Import substitution projects would be encouraged only if it could be demonstrated that they would conserve foreign exchange, that the products would be of high quality, and that they would be sold at competitive prices. Host countries would also expect that the plant employed for added-value processing of minerals and mineral products would utilize proven

293

technology that reduces unit costs and does little or no damage to the environment.

As discussed above, in my view agriculture has failed to provide a satisfactory engine for growth in the past two decades in several Sub-Saharan countries. The monocultural export economies of developing countries, and of Africa in particular, have suffered heavily from worsening terms of trade. Apart from poor agricultural commodity prices, war and drought have exacerbated the situation in the region. The devastation of the human ecology and the environment by war and plunder is often overlooked or taken for granted by the so-called animal lovers and Greenpeace activists. There is also evidence that large-scale farm mechanization and the application of chemical fertilizers have damaged the soils in some areas of intensive agricultural development, although Sub-Saharan Africa uses less chemical fertilizer than any other major global region. However, it must be recognized that countries whose economies are "mono-mineralic" arc also vulnerable to the vagaries of the international mineral market, with the exception to some extent of the countries that produce precious minerals such as gold and gemstones. Countries that are endowed with both large areas of fertile/arable land and mineral resources stand the best chance of stable economic development. The majority of African countries fall into this category. The Republic of South Africa (RSA) is the only country with a strong and long-lasting mining tradition in the Sub-Sahara that has successfully developed its minerals industry as the backbone of its economy, including the agricultural sector. It should also be noted that the mining industry of the RSA is fully integrated into the domestic economy with minimal foreign exchange content in the cost of operations. The country possesses efficient and competitive import-substitution industries, and the minerals and metals exporting companies are net foreign exchange earners. There are no "enclave" or "offshore" transnational enterprises in the RSA. The government regulates and intervenes to rescue the industry during bad times and participates in the revenue via royalties, not by equity holdings. The fundamental difference here is that the currency of the RSA is freely convertible into prime currencies and has purchasing power. This makes the investment climate very attractive, in spite of political instability.

The objectives set more than 30 years ago by many Sub-Saharan countries to exploit their mineral and energy resources for import substitution and value-added production of manufactures have not been achieved. Although there are indications of mineral deposits of economic value, the exploration effort in many countries has been inadequate or non-existent. Informal artisanal mining, particularly for gold, diamonds, emeralds, rubies, and amethyst, and small-scale quarrying for industrial minerals and aggregate are the main activities in the mining sector. Large-scale mining of iron ore, non-ferrous metals (e.g. copper, bauxite, manganese, nickel), petroleum products, and coal is undertaken by transnational corporations in economic enclaves, and the products are exported as concentrates with very little or no added value. For the foreseeable future, many of the Sub-Saharan countries will be unable to establish downstream processing/ extraction plants to refine and produce finished products of metals and mineral substances. The continent will for a long period remain a primary producer of metal and mineral raw materials for the industrialized countries of the North. As such, environmental degradation and pollution are more likely to occur at the mining and ore-dressing stage. Those countries that would like to establish downstream plant for the production of finished products should beware of the dumping of obsolete technology by companies that may be forced to sell old plant owing to the environmental regulations of their home countries.

For the present and immediate future the areas of environmental concern include the following mining-related activities:

- large-scale open-pit operations (e.g. porphyry copper deposits, bauxite, lateritic nickel, manganese, phosphate rock, oxidized gold ores, and placer deposits);
- large-scale dredging operations in rivers with extensive drainage systems and in beach sands;
- roasting of refractory ores containing arsenic, sulphides, and radioactive substances;
- open-pit coal mining and processing of coal and briquetting;
- small-scale mining, especially alluvial mining of gold and diamonds, and the use of toxic chemicals and unsafe mining methods by artisanal operators;
- metallurgical processing, extraction, refining, and manufacture of metals and chemicals for local use and for export to earn foreign exchange.

Environmental impact assessment of the above mining activities and control measures should be instituted with the objective of conserving the environment for the well-being of the present generation and for future use. There is an urgent need to develop an implementable environmental policy that will promote the efficient extraction and utilization of the mineral and energy resources of Africa in order to achieve sustainable growth. Failure to explore, access, and develop the natural resources for fear of damaging the countryside will bring only economic stagnation, poverty, disease, and degradation of life in the Sub-Saharan countries. Environmental preservation is not the same as environmental conservation. Furthermore, preservation of the natural resources should not be confused with conservation of the ecological equilibrium of an area. The former attitude is fraught with hypocrisy and the latter takes account of the realities and imperatives of sustainable development and sustainable economic growth. It is the great industrial countries that are the greatest polluters of the earth's environment. The African countries should learn some useful lessons from the industrialized countries if they are ever going to break the spiral of decay and poverty in the midst of plenty. The natural resources must be harnessed for economic development and growth. There is no other alternative for Africa's survival and sustainability in the global environment.

Minerals have to be mined where they are found. Fortunately, they are usually found in remote locations where industrial activity is non-existent, and the environment itself is sensitive to sudden change. As such, an environmental impact assessment must be carried out by the investing company in cooperation with decision makers of the government. Both sides must be environmentally aware so that environmental protection needs may be determined realistically before the implementation of the mining project. Preliminary information gathered in a "green-field" area should provide the baseline or reference point for future assessment and monitoring of the impacts of the mining operations on the environment. Many industrialized countries of the North, particularly in Eastern Europe, with long histories of mining minerals, processing, and the use of low-grade fuels, are now paying the price for not tackling the problems of damage to the health of the population and complete destruction of the environment.

However, legislation that sets standards for environmental protection should not be onerous or non-implementable. It should be dynamic and, as much as possible, should be project specific because every mining project is different and specific to a particular area.

Finally, it is very important that management and the entire workforce on a mining project are made aware of their responsibilities to the environment in which they are working and making a living. Many of the workers may not originate from the area and management must endeavour to maintain this awareness from top to bottom throughout the life of the project cycle. Environmental impact studies and assessment methods are relatively new in the curriculum of minerals industry schools. The Sub-Saharan countries should strengthen their institutional capacity to monitor environmental impacts through sustained training. Training of indigenous personnel in environmental work should be provided for in all agreements with developers. Training in environmental assessment methods is an area where the bilateral and multilateral organizations could make a valuable contribution to human resource development for capacity-building in Africa.

I hope that I have been able to put the case for the need to institute a rational, pragmatic, and, above all, realistic policy reform in Sub-Saharan Africa for the sustained exploration and development of its minerals and energy resources for the creation of wealth on an exponential basis to sustain the improved well-being of its long-suffering population and for the survival of future generations. What Sub-Saharan Africa has experienced so far is the decay of economies supervised by incompetent governments, the majority of which have no democratic mandate to rule their people. I refuse to believe that Africa cannot succeed. Given the right political atmosphere, free from utopian and unworkable foreign ideologies, the intelligent and enterprising people of Africa, at all levels of society, can and should be allowed to develop the economy for sustainable growth. Africa is not short of intelligent, capable, and experienced people. They have been prevented from participating in the development process for the past 30 odd years, during which private initiative, entrepreneurship, and the private sector of the economies were destroyed. I pray that it will not take that long to rebuild the mining sector and bring African countries back to the path of sustainable development and social equity.

References

World Bank. 1989. *Sub-Saharan Africa: From Crisis to Sustainable Growth*. Washington D.C.: World Bank.
———— 1992. *Strategy for African Mining*. Technical Paper no. 181. Washington D.C.: World Bank.

Part 4
Institutional issues

15

Modes of international and regional research cooperation

Juha I. Uitto and Walther Manshard

Introduction

The global environmental agenda appears more complex than ever before. There has been a distinct shift in environmental problems from localized disruptions to long-term potentially catastrophic changes at regional and global scales. There is also a growing awareness of the complex interlinkages between the various parts of the physical environment and human actions.

The United Nations Conference on the Human Environment held in Stockholm, Sweden, in 1972 showed just the beginnings of a more marked awareness of the emerging environmental problems and led to, for example, the creation of ministries for the environment in many countries. The United Nations Conference on Environment and Development (UNCED) in Rio de Janeiro, Brazil, in 1992 brought to the forefront the challenges of sustainable development and the urgent need for active international cooperation. The responses, as outlined in the *Agenda 21* emanating from UNCED and its scientific counterpart, *Ascend 21*, prepared by the International Council of Scientific Unions (ICSU), require concerted efforts at national, regional, and global scales. It is no longer enough to "think globally and act locally"; it is also increasingly necessary, while continuing to work at a local level, to begin to "act globally."

The aim of this paper is to outline the responses of the international scientific community to the challenges posed by global environmental change, with particular emphasis on Africa, and to discuss the role and future outlook of such scientific cooperation. The paper focuses on the main global change programmes – the International Geosphere–Biosphere Programme (IGBP) and the Human Dimensions of Global Environmental Change Programme (HDP) – as well as the environmental programme area of the United Nations University (UNU).

The global change programmes

One of the most important points on the international agenda (although at first by no means universally accepted) is the sharing and exchange of scientific data and knowledge about environmental matters. With the assistance of organizations such as the United Nations Environment Programme (UNEP) and the UNESCO Man and the Biosphere Programme, as well as non-governmental organizations such as the ICSU and the IUCN (the World Conservation Union), this goal has now been reached in most countries. Depending on their respective scientific infrastructure, many countries are now in a position to assess the importance of their national environmental data and research findings for their own development agenda.

However, for the evaluation of global and regional scientific implications there still remain many problems. Even when the data are available, it is in many cases not known how the earth's ecosystems will respond to significant environmental changes, and what the results will be in various parts of the world. To shed further light on some of these questions is the basic goal of the two global change programmes under discussion here.

The International Geosphere–Biosphere Programme

Established in 1986 by the ICSU, the IGBP has now reached its implementation phase. The aim of IGBP is stated as:

To describe and understand the interactive physical, chemical and biological processes that regulate the total Earth system, the unique environment that it provides for life, the changes that are occurring in this system, and the manner in which they are influenced by human activities. (IGBP 1992: 5)

The present programme is organized to tackle a number of key questions. Core projects have been established or proposed to answer each question, and potential projects are being considered.

Question 1: How is the chemistry of the global atmosphere regulated, and what is the role of biological processes in producing and consuming trace gases?
   Core project: International Global Atmospheric Chemistry (IGAC).

Question 2: How will global changes affect terrestrial ecosystems?
   Core projects: Global Change and Terrestrial Ecosystems (GCTE); Land Use/Land Cover project.

Question 3: How does vegetation interact with the physical processes of the hydrological cycle?
   Core project: Biospheric Aspects of the Hydrological Cycle (BAHC).

Question 4: How will changes in land use, sealevel, and climate alter coastal ecosystems, and what are the wider consequences?
   Core project: Land–Ocean Interactions in the Coastal Zone (LOICZ).

Question 5: How do ocean biogeochemical processes influence and respond to climate change?
   Core projects: Joint Global Ocean Flux Study (JCOFS); Global Ocean Euphotic Zone Study (GOEZS).

Question 6: What significant climatic and environmental changes occurred in the past, and what were their causes?
   Core project: Past Global Changes (PAGES).

Within the core projects there is a distinction between core research, regional/national research, and other relevant research. Much of the work is based on a network of national committees. There are currently 66 national IGBP committees all around the world. In Sub-Saharan Africa, national committees have been established in Benin (1992), Botswana (1993), Côte d'Ivoire (1992), Ghana (1993), Kenya (1990), Niger (1991), Nigeria (1992), Sierra Leone (1993), South Africa (1987), Togo (1992), Uganda (1990), Zambia (1990), and Zimbabwe (1989).
   In addition to the core projects, there are three other IGBP activities with overarching and integrative goals: the Task Force on Global

Analysis, Interpretation, and Modelling (GAIM); the Data and Information System (IGBP-DIS); and the System for Analysis, Research, and Training (START).

The START programme (the somewhat halting abbreviation stands for SysTem for Analysis, Research and Training) is a new initiative responding to the need to ensure global coverage of the global change research programmes in both developed and developing countries and regions (Eddy et al. 1991). START is organized under the joint auspices of the IGBP, the World Climate Programme, and HDP, with the aim of providing the necessary structure of networks, centres, and sites to address the regional origins and impacts of global change. Its major objective is to strengthen the participation of developing countries in IGBP research through the research networks as well as training.

For the purposes of START, the world has been divided into 14 ecological regions, each with networking functions. Africa is divided into two regions: North Africa (NAF), with headquarters in Ghana, and South and East Africa (SAF), with headquarters in Malawi.

The Human Dimensions of Global Environmental Change

It is recognized that understanding global environmental change will not be possible without acknowledging the intricate ways in which human activities affect the physical environment. Themes such as land degradation and society, population pressure and carrying capacity, land use and resource management, marginality and criticality, resilience and sustainability of social groups have increasingly come to the attention of research in various disciplines.

The Human Dimensions of Global Environmental Change Programme (HDP) was set up as a complement to the IGBP to bring together social and natural scientists, as well as those involved in the management of human activities, to carry out research and related activities in key areas of human interactions with the earth (Jacobson and Price 1990). It was initiated at a symposium in 1988 jointly by the UNU, the International Social Science Council (ISSC), the International Federation of Institutes for Advanced Studies (IFIAS), and UNESCO. The broad objectives of the programme were defined as (HDP 1989):

1. to foster a global network of scientists and other concerned parties, and to encourage this network – in collaboration with other relevant research initiatives – to engage in research directed towards the dynamics of human interactions with the global ecosystem;

2. to understand selected core projects central to the purposes of the programme;
3. to develop appropriate information systems and methodologies that will enable the execution of a research programme of this scope;
4. to explore the ethical, cultural, and legal traditions and frameworks that underlie and shape the human aspects of global change;
5. to propose procedures and techniques for assisting in the translation of research findings into policy-relevant terms; and
6. to promote educational efforts devoted to human activities having significant effects on the global environment.

One of the important projects is the one on global risk assessment. Risk assessment has emerged as a tool for exploring the potential impacts of proposed technological innovations and large-scale industrial activities. This working group is exploring various aspects of risk assessment theory and practice at the level of global risks. Other themes covered in the context of global risks are uncertainty, critical regions, technology, and corporations. Special attention is given to high-risk regions and potential sealevel rise.

The project on Critical Zones in Global Environmental Change is carried out as a collaboration between the UNU and the International Geographical Union (IGU). Nine regions around the world are explored, where large-scale environmental degradation threatens current or future human occupance and well-being (Kasperson et al. 1995). One of these case-studies is concerned with the dry hill region of Kenya, the Ukambani Mountains.

A closely related activity co-sponsored by the IGU and the UNU is an initiative on Famine Vulnerability and Most Critical Zones and Regions (Bohle et al. 1993).

Since the UNU's 1988 Tokyo symposium, HDP has been continuously evolving, changing, and attracting new partners and scholars. It is to be hoped that it will continue to adapt itself to the actual needs perceived worldwide and will be designed to address global environmental issues with a long-term perspective.

The UNU environmental programmes

UNU environmental research programmes, other than those directly related to HDP, emphasize the importance of local and regional ecological sustainability through appropriate environmental and resource management (Manshard and Uitto 1993).

Major initiatives include the long-term collaborative research project on People, Land Management, and Environmental Change (PLEC) launched in 1992. PLEC emphasizes the consequences for land management, and hence for the environment, of population and production pressure in the smallholder agricultural areas of developing countries. On the basis of field research clusters in various parts of the world, PLEC seeks to obtain data-based, policy-related propositions concerning the adaptation of farming systems to population growth and demographic change, to changing socio-economic conditions, and to environmental deterioration. Strong emphasis is placed on: (i) the study of adaptive agro-diversity and its relations to biodiversity; (ii) identification of what is sustainable and what is unsustainable; (iii) the provision of researched options for the better management of land, its waters and biota, under societal, demographic, and environmental change in different bio-geophysical settings, and evaluation of capacity to adopt these options; and (iv) the creation or enhancement of baseline data that could form the basis of long-period ecological monitoring research, incorporating human use and socio-economic elements (Brookfield 1993).

Five clusters have been established. Two of them are in Africa – one based in Ghana with extension into Guinea, the other covering East Africa (Kenya, Tanzania, Uganda).

A major effort has been made by the University to develop the Institute for Natural Resources in Africa (INRA) headquartered in Ghana. UNU/INRA's objectives emphasize human resource development and institutional capacity-building related to the strategies and priorities of *Agenda 21* through collaboration with African universities and networking within a "college of research associates." The programme focuses on three key areas: (i) soil and water conservation and management; (ii) indigenous African food and other useful plants – conservation of biodiversity, improvement, production, and utilization; and (iii) mineral resources management, development, and the environment. The activities focus on research and capacity-building in the field of environmentally sustainable development, including surveys, research meetings/workshops, and training courses related to soil and water management, indigenous African food and other useful plants, and home gardens, as well as environmental monitoring.

Following UNCED and the ratification of the Convention on Biological Diversity, questions relating to sustainable production and to genetic and ecological biodiversity are receiving significant attention

306

in the international community in terms of improved regional economic cooperation. All of the above topics have a direct bearing on the preservation and management of biological diversity in Africa.

Networking

One thing in common between all the above and other similar efforts is that they are based on a networking principle. International networks of research and training institutions as well as individual scholars are set up in order to agree on a joint research agenda, to focus efforts, and to benefit from economies of scale. The networks also have the central function of capacity-building in developing countries.

To demonstrate this point, consider international cooperation in agricultural research. One of the questions is whether our present concepts of international and national resources research as related to African farmers are still capable of meeting the challenges of the more systemic approach that is now required.

Much of the research is based on cooperation between the centres within the Consultative Group on International Agricultural Research (CGIAR), national research bodies, and actors at the "grass-roots" level. The main function of international centres such as the International Institute for Tropical Agriculture (IITA) or the International Livestock Centre for Africa (ILCA) and their related networks seems to be to provide technologies that in a second step could be adapted to national and local conditions. This strategy has been largely successful, and some national administrations have been able to adopt the right research topics at the user level.

In many national research systems, however, this does not work because of the lack of trained professional staff, limited funding, and other administrative and fiscal obstacles. It has also been difficult to introduce priority problems from the farmers' and resource users' level into the research agendas of the international bodies. Investigations have shown time and again that, particularly as regards the small traditional peasant farmer, there still exist great problems of acceptance (Hatch 1976; Chambers 1983; Jazairy et al. 1992). The technological application gap seems to be as wide as ever, and much of the extension work of past decades has not been very successful (Merrill-Sands 1986).

From the farmers' point of view, the world looks very different compared with an international expert's view. Innovations may be refused because too much risk is involved or because they do not fit within the socio-economic reality of the farmers' environment. Risk minimization is of central importance to smallholders, who by processes of trial and error have generally acquired long experience in resource management, which they will not easily give up for something unknown, however promising.

What is needed is an even stronger reorientation of at least some of the international research towards the level of smallholders' problems, including a better appraisal of their traditional knowledge. Several of the new initiatives, including UNU/INRA and PLEC, are designed with this in mind.

This approach, which has been accepted for some time, also calls for increased interdisciplinary cooperation, including social scientists. A number of new concepts have been tried out during the past 10–20 years. The work on farming systems research (Shaner et al. 1982), on on-farm research (Byerlee and Collinson 1980), on the "farmer-first-and-last" model (Chambers and Ghildyal 1985), and on on-farm client-oriented research (Merrill-Sands and McAllister 1989) may serve as examples.

A participatory approach will improve the probability that internationally advocated technological innovations will eventually be adopted at the local and national levels. It is to be hoped that UNU/INRA can also make a substantial contribution here.

Another example of successful research networking for capacity-building in developing countries is the UNU–International Mountain Society programme on Mountain Ecology and Sustainable Development. The programme has been operational since 1978 and, in recognition of its contribution in the field, it was selected to prepare the UNCED mountain agenda (Stone 1992). One of the central objectives since its initiation has been institutional support to mountain and highlands research in developing countries. For example, the programme was instrumental in establishing the African Mountain Association, which is now a fairly self-sufficient network of mountain researchers from Africa. The mother programme continues to support the global as well as regional networking activities through the journal *Mountain Research and Development* and newsletters.

Environmental governance

Effective environmental governance at national, regional, and global levels is vital to the achievement of sustainable development. A better understanding of the interactions between government, governance, and environmental policy is necessary. International agreements and conventions perform functions of governance in the absence of central governments.

On the other hand, the establishment of international regimes and conventions cannot replace effective national decision-making. Some international conventions have been successfully accepted and implemented, while others have been disappointing. More often, the institutional forms of international environmental governance are not yet efficient enough to achieve their objectives. In order to improve our knowledge in this field, further work is necessary.

Besides the more specialized environmental research that goes on in universities and research institutions, further international work is needed in two main fields:
1. well-focused research programmes on governance, policy implementation, and institutional change; and
2. improvements in the field of training and dissemination.

A significant part of the work under the Human Dimensions Programme has been directed towards research into environmental governance and policies and the multilateral action needed to understand and deal with environmental change that may affect the earth as a whole. Recent work under the HDP has focused on, for example, environmental law and institutions, and governance (Young et al. 1991; Brown Weiss 1992).

Another UNU project under the umbrella of the HDP was concerned with the scientific, economic, and political issues pertaining to determining the responsibility for greenhouse gases, calculating the obligations of countries to pay, and measuring the costs of different policies for creating a global regime for coping with greenhouse gas emissions that is just and fair to both the North and South (Hayes and Smith 1993). One of the project's case-studies focused on carbon abatement potential in West Africa (Davidson 1993).

Outlook

Only a marked acceleration of international cooperation will lead to a better understanding of the global environment as a common and shared resource. All countries must be partners in the solution of the world's problems. In this respect we have come to recognize that in Africa, too, environment and development are closely linked, a fact that has profound implications for the well-being of its inhabitants.

Poverty, which contributes so much to the environmental degradation of Africa, can in the long run be overcome only by improving economic development, for which in turn a strengthening of environmental institutions and of environmental education in Africa will be necessary.

The key concept of "sustainable development" may in the long run also clarify the so far rather vague concept of "carrying capacity" (Davis and Bernstam 1990; UNFPA 1991). Parameters related to demographic characteristics, consumption patterns, and productive technologies must increasingly be based on a more concrete understanding of the ecological, social, and economic trade-offs (Rockwell and Moss 1992).

To sum up, if we have to decide on some basic international modes of action, one could also quote US Vice-President Al Gore in his book *Earth in the Balance: Ecology and the Human Spirit* (1992). Following the experiences of the Marshall Plan in Europe, he focuses on five strategic goals:
1. stabilization of the world population;
2. the development of ecologically appropriate technologies;
3. changing some of the economic "rules of the game," which would allow the measurement of the consequences of environmental decision-making;
4. negotiating a new generation of international agreements; and
5. the establishment of a cooperative educational plan for the enlightenment of the world population on global environmental matters.

References

Bohle, H.-G., T. E. Downing, J. O. Field, and F. N. Ibrahim (eds.) 1993. *Coping with Vulnerability and Criticality: Case Studies on Food-Insecure People and Places.* Freiburg Studies in Development Geography 1. Saarbrücken and Fort Lauderdale: Verlag Breitenbach.

Brookfield, H. 1993. What is PLEC about? *PLEC News and Views*, no. 1: 2–8.

Brown Weiss, E. (ed.) 1992. *Environmental Change and International Law: New Challenges and Dimensions.* Tokyo: United Nations University Press.

Byerlee, D. and M. P. Collinson. 1980. *Planning Technologies Appropriate to Farmers – Concepts and Procedures.* Mexico: CIMMYT.

Chambers, R. 1983. *Rural Development: Putting the Last First.* London: Longman.

Chambers, R. and B. P. Ghildyal. 1985. *Agricultural Research for Resource-Poor Farmers: The Farmer-First-and-Last Model.* IDS Discussion Paper 302. Sussex: Institute of Development Studies.

Davidson, O. R. 1993. Carbon abatement potential in West Africa. In: P. Hayes and

K. Smith (eds.), *The Global Greenhouse Regime: Who Pays?* London: Earthscan, and Tokyo: United Nations University Press, pp. 210–232.

Davis, K. and M. S. Bernstam (eds.) 1990. *Resources, Environment and Population: Present Knowledge, Future Options*. New York and Oxford: Oxford University Press.

Eddy, J. A., T. F. Malone, J. J. McCarthy, and T. Rosswall (eds.) 1991. *Global Change System for Analysis, Research and Training (START)*. Report of a Meeting in Bellagio. Global Change Report no. 15, Boulder, Colo.

Gore, A. 1992. *Earth in the Balance: Ecology and the Human Spirit*. Boston: Houghton Mifflin.

Hatch, J. K. 1976. *The Corn Farmers of Motupe: A Study of Traditional Farming Practices in Northern Coastal Peru*. Land Tenure Center Monographs no. 1, University of Wisconsin, Madison.

Hayes, P. and K. Smith (eds.) 1993. *The Global Greenhouse Regime: Who Pays?* London: Earthscan, and Tokyo: United Nations University Press.

HDP (Human Dimensions of Global Environmental Change Programme). 1989. *Human Dimensions of Global Change: An International Programme on Human Interaction with the Earth*. Report of the Tokyo International Symposium on the Human Response to Global Change, 1988. Toronto: IFIAS/ISSC/UNU.

IGBP (International Geosphere–Biosphere Programme). 1992. *Global Change: Reducing Uncertainties*. Stockholm: IGBP.

Jacobson, H. K. and M. F. Price. 1990. *A Framework for Research for the Human Dimensions of Global Environmental Change*. Paris: ISSC/UNESCO.

Jazairy, I., M. Alamgir, and T. Panuccio. 1992. *The State of World Rural Poverty: An Inquiry into Its Causes and Consequences*. International Fund for Agricultural Development. London: IT Publications.

Kasperson, J. X., R. E. Kasperson, and B. L. Turner, II (eds.) 1995. *Regions at Risk*. Tokyo: United Nations University Press.

Manshard, W. and J. I. Uitto. 1993. Environmental studies in the humid tropics: UNU programmes and future perspectives. In: J. I. Uitto and M. Clüsener-Godt (eds.), *Environmentally Sound Socio-economic Development in the Humid Tropics: Perspectives from Asia and Africa*. Tokyo: United Nations University, pp. 7–29.

Merrill-Sands, D. 1986. *The Technology Applications Gap Overcoming Constraints to Small Farmer Development*. FAO Research and Technology Paper no. 1. Rome: FAO.

Merrill-Sands, D. and J. McAllister. 1989. *Strengthening the Integration of On-Farm Client-Oriented Research and Experiment Station Research in National Agricultural Research Systems. Management Lessons from Nine Country Case Studies*. OFCOR Comparative Study no. 1. The Hague: International Service for National Agricultural Research.

Rockwell, R. C. and R. H. Moss. 1992. The view from 1996. *Environment* 34(1): 12–38.

Shaner, W. W., P. F. Philipp, and W. R. Schmehl. 1982. *Farming Systems Research and Development Guidelines for Developing Countries*. Boulder, Colo.: Westview Press.

Stone, P. B. (ed.) 1992. *The State of the World's Mountains: A Global Report*. London: Zed Books.

311

UNFPA. 1991. *Population, Resources and the Environment: The Critical Challenges.* New York: United Nations Population Fund.

Young, O. R., G. J. Demko, and K. Ramakrishna. 1991. *Global Environmental Change and International Governance.* Summary and Recommendations of a Conference held at Dartmouth College. United Nations University, Dartmouth College, World Resources Institute, and Woods Hole Research Center, Hanover, New Hampshire.

16

National, regional, and international cooperation for sustainable environmental and resource management: The place and roles of NGOs

Shimwaayi Muntemba

Introduction

Sustainable development must have as its aim the management of natural resources and the regenerative capacity of nature in such a manner as to maintain their productivity and resilience over time. Over decades, non-governmental organizations (NGOs) and the environment movement have been struggling for sound environmental management and prudent use of natural resources. In recent years, they have been sustained in these struggles by the knowledge and evidence that the grass-roots communities among whom they work, and in some cases from whom they are derived, have understood and practised sound management over time, although there have been some disruptions to their knowledge base. Moreover, Southern NGOs in particular consider that there are socio-economic aspects in terms of which sustainable development implies prevention of the friction and disequilibrium that may arise if economic development is, on the one hand, out of step with the existing natural resource endowments and, on the other, remains insensitive to social and cultural realities; it implies economic constraints but also opportunities in a given country. Although these concerns are shared by all sectors of humanity, this last one is particularly pertinent to NGO philosophy and work.

We must recognize from the outset, however, that NGOs are diverse in scope, interest, and size. Some NGOs are *of* the people, that is, formed by them. These operate at the village/community level, but they may also express themselves in wider movements. Others are *for* the people. Such organizations are external to the communities but they constitute important development partners. They comprise individuals who are committed to the cause of the poor, change agents, and front-line workers. Often, these organizations are considered partners because they work with the "beneficiaries" at all stages of the activity – from conception to evaluation – interacting and providing feedback. Some organizations are welfare oriented; others are research based. In Africa, very few organizations belong only to the last category. The majority of the few that carry out research include this task among their many other activities, as demanded of front-line activists.

The list of the nature and scope of NGOs can be long, and the diversity within the NGO community cautions us against conceptualizing NGOs in a monolithic manner. Despite this diversity, however, NGOs share certain fundamental elements:

- uneasiness about today's economic order, an order in which the majority remain materially deprived;
- uneasiness about the state of the resource base, which in the majority of cases is responsible for the deprivation;
- uneasiness and anger over social injustice:
- a commitment to fight, in many ways, against those forces responsible for the injustice;
- a commitment to change at all levels;
- in varying degrees, weaker capacities compared with governmental institutions and, especially, compared with the private sector, mainly because NGOs are "of" the poor, who remain distanced from power-controlling structures.

The diversity, yet commonalities, and levels of capacity of NGOs are correspondingly reflected in the multitude and magnitude of liaisons, networking, collaboration, and cooperation within the NGO community itself and with other institutions.

In order to strengthen their own efforts in their daily work and to tackle the challenges from a broader base, some NGOs are forging links among themselves, with the people on the ground, with research

institutions, and, now, even with governmental organs. They believe that, through sound management, a more sustainable resource base and a more just world may be attained by these strategies. They are doing this in many ways, including:
- information sharing, for which transformable data are needed;
- partnerships with various institutions and groups;
- dialogues with governmental and industry organs for effective advocacy work;
- linking with policy institutions;
- working with monitoring institutions to ensure effective implementation and accountability.

Information sharing

As with many other actors in the process of sustainable development, efforts that NGOs undertake can be strengthened by the information supplied, on the one hand, by independent policy and research institutions and, on the other, by local village surveys, which offer feedback from users. Village surveys can reflect the resources available to people at the household and community levels – land, trees, grass, water, etc. They can also reflect the services provided by the government and other agencies, including NGOs, time use, household job distribution and resource allocation, control and access.

The past 20 years or so have witnessed fundamental shifts in the role and place of research in the development process, including planning and resource management. The most conceptually powerful shifts have occurred in the area of the practical usability of research findings in strengthening the efforts of poor people to manage their destinies and cope with their poverty. Gradually, therefore, research is being seen by many development agencies, and some researchers, as a tool for empowering the disadvantaged and marginalized: the poor, women, and the young. Research is seen as a tool for this because:
(a) it could provide data and information to influence policy in favour of the poor and other marginalized groups;
(b) it could provide information that NGOs as front-line workers could use in their daily work with and for the people, and in their advocacy work on behalf of the poor communities; and, most important,
(c) it could provide the poor communities with information that they

315

themselves could use to strengthen their own efforts, and also enable them to carry out advocacy work on their own behalf. Thus the research process and results would empower the poor.

Yet, despite research's noble intention, most research remains peripheral to developmental efforts. NGOs experience even greater difficulties with much of the existing research-generated information, couched as it is in unusable language and form. In addition, they see problems with the nature of that information. The prevailing scientific information order, especially the international one, is generally skewed in favour of vested interests (basically Northern and Northern outposts in the South). Thus, for example, research and information produced by/for industry sources are much more readily available than is information resulting from data gathered from the South.

Today, knowledge is a major source of power and control. Producers of knowledge, particularly researchers, claim objectivity. Yet much of this knowledge contributes to continued inequality and deprivation. Producers of the dominant forms of knowledge have also taken it upon themselves to define the nature of knowledge. Consequently, the people and others outside or on the fringes of the power structures have become dependent on experts who tell them what is good for them. In the process, their capacity to produce some of their own knowledge has become eroded, and in some cases, completely destroyed. A case in point is the knowledge of indigenous peoples in rainforest areas; this knowledge is being destroyed at a frightening pace, in some instances faster than the destruction of the forest itself. (Environment Liaison Centre International 1988: 20)

Part of the reason for NGO frustration lies in the assumptions of research as reflected in much of its present approaches, i.e. that the researcher, and not the people, will provide answers and ultimately solutions to the plight of the disadvantaged. Many front-line workers acknowledge the store of indigenous knowledge and the ingenuity of grass-roots communities in developing coping strategies, which should provide a solid base for any strategies for the alleviation of poverty and ultimately its elimination. Moreover, the concepts of the dominant culture of the ruling classes are carried over by most researchers through the dominant methodologies, which are mainly extractive, distancing the researcher from the "researched." Because the research methodologies, the language, and the images end up distancing the communities, NGOs find much of the information unusable.

The nature and quality of much available information, therefore, present particular dilemmas and challenges to NGOs as front-line

316

workers, working with the people for sustainability of the environment and societies. NGOs are close to and, in some cases, of the people. They have the capacity to crystallize the needs as felt by the people and to distill researchable questions and problems for them. Because they are close to the people, they would and can ensure that the research done is directly relevant to what goes on at the grass roots and is oriented towards the actual research needs of the people.

NGOs have been grappling to gain access to useful and usable information derived from solid scientific data. Yet they acknowledge the inherent shortfalls and biases in traditional research, particularly for situations in the South. This is why there have been debates within and with the NGO community about how to deal with this dilemma. Below are some of the possibilities and options NGOs have considered and are experimenting with in information generation and creation.

Linking with scientific research institutions

Some NGOs are establishing loose links with individuals from universities and independent research institutes, in some cases inviting members from these institutions to become permanent associates. Others are linking up with governmental research organs and yet others with intergovernmental organizations. The idea is to gain access to any relevant, up-to-date data and information on threats to the resource base, which information they can use in their advocacy work and in their work with the communities, and also in awareness-raising. They can use it to articulate and strengthen their struggles in local-level resource management and at the same time feed into national/regional environmental data collection, interpretation, and use. Thus strengthened, NGOs could play lead roles, as some already do, in the use of research results to achieve sustainable livelihoods and development.

Seeking assistance from international NGOs

Often, academic research is not directly usable by NGOs and village-level groups. Where they are not already doing so, NGOs wish to link with the stronger members within the NGO community to transform the data into usable information through more easily comprehensible media. To date, however, many NGOs do not have the capacity to do this. Thus, even as they are using their networks, they need to have

317

their own capacities independently strengthened. For this, some NGOs are turning to the international community of NGOs for assistance.

Building internal research capabilities

NGOs remain uneasy with the nature of traditional research, which does not seem directly to support popular and NGO attempts to identify the main causes of adverse environmental processes in the communities concerned. As currently focused and carried out, this research cannot provide the knowledge needed to build strong movements in Africa, whose aim is to try to influence regional and global environmental change with African perspectives and for a more sustainable society generally. This points to the need to build the NGO research capacity, and especially research that is action and grass-roots oriented. Many, therefore, are trying to build internal research capabilities. To meet these research needs, international cooperation through internship schemes offered by fellow NGOs, through university schemes, and with the official donor community is becoming important.

Participatory Action Research

NGOs also want research that will generate information that is owned, controlled, and, therefore, more easily used by the people who provide it in the first place. Thus some NGOs are spearheading links with universities, individual researchers, and other NGOs who are pushing for Participatory Action Research (PAR), a derivative of Rapid Rural Appraisal (RRA) and a close ally of Participatory Rural Appraisal (PRA) methodologies. Some of the advantages of PAR are that:
- it is people based;
- its goal is to empower local communities, and it empowers them because they form part of the investigative team into their own problems and they join in the search for solutions;
- it acknowledges the importance of secondary sources, but also believes that the targeted community may be able to lead the way to some of these sources – local leaders (churches, individuals) often hold information sources that provide a more living portrait of the neighbourhood;
- the traditionally "researched" are full members of the research

318

team, so that within a short time the multidisciplinary outside researchers become facilitators only;
- research findings are more likely to be true reflections of the people's
concerns, fears, and aspirations;
- in enhances the liberation, knowledge, and capabilities of the local
people, strengthening their ability to champion their demand for
services and self-dignity;
- it enables the creation of an ongoing rapport with the outside researchers through whom the local communities might identify other
partners in their struggles.

The output of PAR is: (a) directly used by the communities for any
follow-up action that they themselves may agree upon – development
action plans, land use, resource allocation, and management, etc.; (b)
more easily usable by front-line workers, and the research process
itself will have inculcated a team spirit among NGOs, local community leaders, local government officials, policy makers, and a cross-
section of the community.

Partnerships with other institutions

NGOs are also developing, or are being called upon to enter into,
partnerships with many other actors to empower both themselves and
also other weaker groups from among themselves. Other groups may
be considered weaker because, in addition to information gaps, they
may need technical support, or mobilization skills, or supporters and
advocators as they struggle for control over the resources they use
and manage as part of their daily work, or machinery to link them to
national power systems in order to strengthen their work, or the
strength of numbers as an empowering strategy for coping with forces
that appear too bewildering to be tackled singly.

The ways in which they are doing this include the following.

Networking among the like-minded

Umbrella or membership organizations engaged in networking can
identify strengths and weaknesses within their community of NGOs.
Then, they either provide the information so that members can
contact each other directly, or link members to each other through
various schemes. NGOs in Zaire and Tanzania, for example, have
strengthened their forestry-related activities and management by
learning on the ground and enhancing their skills through networking

with NGOs in Kenya: the GreenBelt Movement and Kenya Energy and Environment NGOs (KENGO). NGOs in Kenya and Zimbabwe enriched their organic farming skills by spending time at each other's locations and learning as they worked. In the process they were also experimenting and improving the methods. Similarly, NGOs from Kenya and Uganda have enhanced each other's skills through exchange visits. Many others, including some from other third world regions, have strengthened their networking and management skills through visits to the Environment Liaison Centre International, a membership organization based in Nairobi, Kenya. It is clear that NGOs will enhance their resource-management skills through exchange visits among themselves within Africa and on a South–South basis.

Partnerships with groups at the village/community level

In some cases, NGOs are linking up with local-level groups as a strategy for forging lasting and more result-oriented relationships. But they are also being called upon by the groups themselves to enter into partnerships with them in order to enhance their own efforts. Examples are women's groups, and I don't mean middle-class women, but the groups that depend directly on the resource base for their livelihoods and those of their households. Increasing degradation of the resource base is inflicting a harsher "onslaught" on women resource-users. These are the women who, to a greater extent, have retained what indigenous knowledge of resource management is extant. They are the managers of the resources they use on a daily basis. Therefore they hold a key to the sustainability of the resources. Yet their knowledge and roles remain unrecognized, though talked about. Women continue to represent the majority who are struggling for control over and easier access to the resources.

The idea of partnerships is not new to African women. Recognizing the need for partners, women have developed mutual-aid societies. The Kenyan word *"harambee"* is the most appropriate one I have come across to describe this. Whether they are known as clubs, groups, or cooperatives, the spirit behind them is the same.

As the environmental issues move from the local to the national and on to the wider world, as ownership of the resources shifts from women to men and from local to national power structures, and as support systems move out of the locality to the national capitals, women's partners must in turn reflect this wider horizon and especially be able to link them to the distant power brokers. NGOs, being of and for the people, fulfil this role. NGOs are already providing invaluable partners, strengthening women's groups in many ways: enhancing their capacities by improving the women's knowledge base, making it more efficient and reflective of the changing environment; empowering women through the acquisition of managerial and other technical skills; carrying out advocacy work on behalf of women to local and national power holders and brokers and to policy makers. Those NGOs that are able to carry out research can facilitate people-centred research, in order to strengthen local-level resource management, by bringing women into the research process. Thus women would be enabled to play lead roles in the use of research results for sustainable development.

Coalitions with other groupings

NGOs are working with an array of other institutions for sustainable management of the resources. Peasant societies and unions, farmers' unions, which in some cases mean large-scale farmers (to be distinguished from peasant unions), legal aid associations, fishermen's cartels, and in a few cases trade unions are some such groupings. NGOs work with them in their struggles against powerful forces whose practices are dangerous to the environment. In other third world regions these types of coalition have grown into movements. This has rarely been the case in Africa. Nevertheless, these unions are emerging and need to be encouraged and supported as a means of sustaining efforts at resource management. They will play major roles in the years ahead.

Dialogues with governmental and industry organs

Traditionally, much advocacy work by NGOs *vis-à-vis* governments (and industry) has been confrontational. This yielded results in other parts of the world, but now everyone, including government and industry, claims to have been converted and to be, therefore, environmentally conscious. Moreover, the targets of protests of 10–20 years ago seem not to be affected by such methods any more. For Africa, in addition, confrontational methods have often led to harassment of the individuals singled out as ring-leaders, without evident results. Often, too, globalization of the environment agenda has thrown African NGOs and governments on to one side of the arena, as both belonging to the globally deprived. Because of these developments, a number of African NGOs have sought more effective ways of carrying out their advocacy work on behalf of nature and people. These have included penetrating key organs within government as entry points into policy and governmental sanctuaries.

The ways in which this is happening include the following.

Individual links to the power structures

Many African countries attained their political independence in the past 30 years or so. Thus, many front-line workers and activists have links with the power structures through some friend, uncle, cousin, etc. These, in turn, introduce them to more of their kind. Some activists have found that they can use these contacts to press their case. The higher the contact is in the power hierarchy, the greater the chances of influencing the views of many. With the opening up of political systems and structures, parliamentarians are also being approached by their constituency members.

It must be admitted that these are not easy methods and it is doubtful whether such alliances can be sustained or depended upon. But there have been a few situations where they have worked and some NGOs would like to explore these methods of bringing about desirable change.

Dialogue with the relevant governmental organs

NGOs recognize that many governments and nascent industry in Africa are under tremendous pressure to meet short-term needs out of the limited natural resources available to the countries. More recently, they have also had to meet the demands of debt clearing. African countries therefore set aside long-term or even medium-term perspectives in favour of incessant political demands to meet day-to-day requirements. Market demands and economic and financial interest in reaping short-term gains blur the link with damaging costs to society. Therefore, a better appreciation of the costs and benefits of resource conservation through sound management is necessary before leaders in government and industry will accept the rigours of sustainable development.

NGOs involved in advocacy work see a role in influencing leaders in these areas, but they need solid, well-researched data to support their case. Confrontational approaches that might work in other instances are not likely to impress the targets in these cases. A number of NGOs have adopted this subtle yet effective way of going about their advocacy work, and it seems to be a method that should be pushed.

Until recently, the dialoguing method has been tried on a case-by-case basis. However, many NGOs whose mandates include advocacy have felt that this method, although it has proved effective in many instances, is reactive. They want to be proactive, particularly if the goal is to change policy so that national development strategies become more ecologically sound, economically viable, and socially and culturally acceptable to the people.

NGOs see an effective way of making any impact to be through: (i) identifying from among themselves those NGOs that share the same concerns, and (ii) initiating a series of dialogues with policy makers at national and subregional levels. The United Nations Conference on Environment and Development (UNCED) in Rio de Janeiro in 1992 provided an opportunity for some NGOs to initiate dialogues with their national governments, researchers, and others for effective participation. Since Rio, some NGOs have been attempting to engage in dialogue with governmental organs and researchers so that, together, they may initiate some follow-up action (UNDP 1992). This strategy has the advantage of, in the process, educating concerned policy makers about the state of the resources and about the important roles that grass-roots people, and especially women, play in the sustainable management of the resources. Many NGOs concerned with the sustainability of resources and societies have plans to explore this mechanism further.

The use of external links to penetrate local power structures

Many indigenous NGOs would not resort to the use of external links, but there have been cases, and there are indications that this is likely to occur again, where NGO interventions on behalf of equity of access have fallen on deaf ears in their countries, whereas external forces have been seen to influence change. With careful assessment of the likely implications, and if it is deemed not to be injurious to African dignity, some NGOs will turn to this form of pressure.

Linking with policy institutions

Many NGOs recognize the importance of policy in their daily work. They find that, unless policy is in line with sustainability on the one hand and people friendly on the other, much of their work will be short lived. Yet, although they acknowledge the need to understand the policy implications of their work and, where possible, influence it, they admit their shortcomings. They see these shortcomings in the following ways:

(a) Very few NGOs are intellectually equipped to analyse the long-term implications of national and international environmental and development policies for them, their work, and the societies they work with/for. Moreover, there are very few organizations addressing policy in Africa. These gaps handicap NGO work further.

(b) Most policies are evolved by governments behind closed doors. Societies and NGOs that work with them rarely make inputs into or shape the outcome of policies.

(c) As a result, most policies do not create the physical or moral environment for effective implementation of NGO work.

(d) In many countries, environmental concerns remain theoretical. They are not linked to issues of sustainability and sustainable livelihoods and development. As a result, the resource base continues to be degraded, thus undermining the very basis of the work of those NGOs that are either concerned with creating or raising awareness or working with poor people in their struggles to increase productivity.

For these and many other reasons, some (albeit few) NGOs have started to address the need to include policy in their work. They do so in many ways.

Direct participation in policy-formulation processes

Some NGOs see an effective way of accomplishing direct participation through dialogue: seminars, roundtables, discussion groups. Those involved either seek ways through which they can be invited by the governmental organs concerned, or organize seminars to which key governmental functionaries and politicians are invited. It is acknowledged that very few governments in Africa have opened themselves to NGO intervention. Therefore, it is rare for governments to have invited NGOs to interact with them. However, there are indications that, after the UNCED, the trend of dialogue that the summit process initiated in some countries will be built upon.

Advice to governments

Some NGOs advise governments through submissions, while others get themselves invited to comment on documents. None the less, it must be mentioned that the trend has been for the involvement of larger NGOs, some of them Northern. True, these are better equipped to handle policy issues, but many of them are removed from the daily concerns and struggles of the direct users and managers of the natural resources. Those working at the grass roots question the knowledge and objectivity of such NGOs, especially Northern ones. They wonder to what extent they can truly represent people's perspectives. Therefore, there are tendencies for grass-roots NGOs to seek other ways of directly influencing policies.

Seeking organizations specifically devoted to policy

Some NGOs see a need for organizations that will devote their attention specifically to policy development, formulation, and analysis. These would assist in mobilizing NGO participation, particularly by the smaller NGOs and community groups, and would also support governments in developing environmentally friendly policies rooted in Africa's social and cultural reality. In addition, NGOs see such organizations as playing a role in facilitating NGO appreciation of the implications of international policies for their work and the communities they work with. There are indications that NGOs are searching for such organizations and that, where possible, they are initiating them. The trends is for such nascent organizations to link up with similar institutions in the North, in an effort to inform governments worldwide, and as humanity searches for sustainable livelihoods and development.

Working with monitoring institutions for effective implementation and accountability

NGOs are often of and for the people. In recent years, there have been concerns about accountability by governments and NGOs themselves to the people and to the sustainability of natural resources and of societies. More immediate shifts towards democratization worldwide have strengthened NGO calls for participation and accountability. They see this happening in many ways.

Holding governments to their pledges

Governments have gone through two decades of agreements, resolutions, and conventions. Many of these have very good points that, if implemented, would have positive impacts on the resource base and societies. NGOs are concerned that governments honour what they have pledged to undertake. Through many channels, including the media and dialogues, NGOs want to hold governments to their pledges.

Reminding governments of their responsibilities

Governments are now accepted as being in place for the people and that their utmost priority is to uphold the well-being and welfare of their populations. NGOs are joining hands at either national or international levels to watch over governments, acting as their consciences and in some cases as their executioners. More NGOs are defining such roles for themselves and it is clear that, as society moves into new forms of democratization, a unity among NGOs will emerge to press for greater change and participation.

Calling for participatory democracy

NGOs now distinguish between representative and participatory democracy, seeing the latter as central to sustainability:

Participatory democracy is central to sustainability: how are all poor rural women struggling for livelihoods to be heard? How will development paradigms ensure the sustainability of their assets? What about indigenous people in the Amazonia and North America; the Maoris in New Zealand; the urban poor in our cities, the young, men and women, outside main-stream structures? Many of us in the NGO world believe that these are central to the sustainability of life-support systems, of cultures and ultimately of entire societies. Participatory democracy is a cornerstone of respect for human rights and of ensuring civil liberties. Governments everywhere must address the question of civil liberties. (Environment Liaison Centre International 1992: 12)

It is clear that, in the post-Rio era, participatory democracy is becoming an organizing theme for NGOs nationally and regionally,

linking African NGOs to those outside the continent on a South–
South, South–North basis.

Holding themselves accountable

There are two main ways in which NGOs hold themselves accountable. First, some have started to include organizational and programme audits in their structures. In this way, and on their own, they
attempt to ensure accountability to their constituencies. Are the
structures they have in place conducive to participation and delivery?
Are the programmes reflective of the concerns of the people for
whom they were initiated? Are the programmes delivering the goods
such that the identification, planning, and implementation process
actually empowers the intended "beneficiaries"?

Secondly, NGOs are coming up with alternative treaties, a phenomenon that gathered momentum during the UNCED process and
especially in Rio. NGOs are developing and evolving mechanisms for
monitoring themselves, ensuring that the same rules they apply to
governments are applied to themselves. As we enter a period of more
conventions and treaties, we shall see NGOs develop more articulate
mechanisms for self-monitoring.

Conclusion

Non-governmental organizations have been concerned about the
sustainability of resources and have spearheaded strategies for and
work in wise resource management. They have done this in many
ways. They have been building their own capacities for information
generation and packaging in order to reinforce grass-roots efforts.
They have been establishing and building partnerships for resource
management. They have been bridging gaps between themselves
and governmental and industry leaders in order to raise the latter's
awareness. NGOs believe that governments and leaders in industry
will accept the rigours of sustainable development only after a better
appreciation of the costs and benefits of environmental conservation
and sound resource management. Awareness might both lead to policies conducive to sustainability and reduce inefficiency in resource
use, which is a cause of resource loss. NGOs, therefore, have initiated
many ways of working together to strengthen their pioneer work in
resource management for sustainability. The coming years will see
more links being forged across NGO borders, as NGOs reach out to

partners from universities, research and training institutes, governmental organs, and perhaps even industry. Africa's own plight and the globalization of the environment are pushing NGOs in these more accommodating directions.

References

Environment Liaison Centre International. 1988. *Earth 1992, ELCI's Strategies for Sustainable Development, 1989–1992*. Nairobi: Environment Liaison Centre International.
———— 1992. Speech by Shimwaayi Muntemba. *Ecoforum, Focus on the Agenda ya Wananchi* 15(5/6).
UNDP (United Nations Development Programme). 1992. *Africa 2000 Network News* 1(2).

Part 5
Environment and development in Ghana

17

Institutional issues on the environment and resource management with reference to Ghana

George Benneh

Introduction

Environment and resources are two sides of the same coin that is required for development. It is impossible, over the long term, to manage one without the other. The term "environmental resources" is appropriate in discussions on the problems of managing development on a sustainable basis. The wide spectrum of environmental resources and the complex relationships that link them in structure and functioning over time and in space make their management difficult, particularly with respect to organization for conservation.

The successful management of environmental resources in any country depends to a large extent on the effectiveness of the institutional arrangements put in place by government for their management. These institutional arrangements refer to the types of organizational units involved, such as ministries, agencies, and committees, and to the responsibilities and authorities of these units, and the relationships between them. Because the management of environmental resources cuts across all sectors of government, it also requires the active coordination and participation of virtually all segments of government.

There is no common institutional framework or formula for managing environmental resources in African countries because situations differ. Indeed, the institutional framework for addressing environmental concerns in a particular country may also change with time, depending on the perception of the government of the scope and seriousness of these concerns. This is exemplified by the case of Ghana.

Early developments

In Ghana, concern about the land and environmental degradation has been expressed since the early decades of the twentieth century, notably since the 1930s (Agyepong 1987; Benneh et al. 1990). Legislation to protect specific aspects and components of the land were put in place in the early years of the century. For instance, in 1901, the Wild Animals Preservation Ordinance was passed, followed by the Rivers Ordinance in 1903. Forest reservation was initiated in 1907, followed a year later by the establishment of the Forestry Department. The Mining Rights Regulations Ordinance was introduced in 1925. Severe degradational problems in the northern savannas led to the institution of land planning and soil erosion measures in those areas. These introduced conservational practices in the agricultural use of land, water, and grazing resources. Planning and execution involved the Departments of Agriculture and Forestry and the local people. The Land Planning and Soil Erosion Ordinance was passed in 1953, and amended in 1957, to create permanent committees of the areas designated for planning (Benneh 1985).

The institutional arrangements that have developed over the years charge government departments or committees with responsibility for specific resources. This was the case with the Forestry Department and the Geological Survey Department. The Land Survey Department was established in 1919, the Soil Survey Division, now the Soil Research Institute, came into existence in 1947, and the Game and Wildlife Department was established in 1961. Between the early 1950s and the beginning of the 1970s, several enactments empowered various official agencies to exercise executive responsibilities as far as the care and protection of the environment and resources were concerned. In addition, a number of research institutes were established. The responsibilities for environmental resources were therefore widely distributed, with no one agency having an oversight of the wider environment or significant portions of it. This sectoral arrangement of institutional responsibilities has been characteristic of the management of the environment and resources in the country. Twenty-two departments, commissions, corporations, and institutes have been identified in Ghana as having responsibility for land and other resources management (Benneh et al. 1990). Responsibilities range from policy formulation, survey and evaluation, planning, production, conservation, research, and training to monitoring.

The problems of achieving an ecologically and environmentally comprehensive perspective on resources and the resource processes in these circumstances are many and have impeded optimal management.

The Stockholm Conference and after

The United Nations Conference on the Environment in Stockholm in 1972 created a situation where the environment emerged as a global issue, and the social and economic implications of resource use, environment, and development became a major concern for many governments.

National and global strategies have been widely discussed and formulated since 1972, as evidenced in the two landmark reports *The World Conservation Strategy* (IUCN 1980) and *Our Common Future* (WCED 1987). The United Nations Environment Programme was set up after the conference as the global environmental conscience.

These emerging concerns found clear expression in the establishment of departments and other institutions of the environment and natural resources in a number of countries. These institutions were vested with legislation to provide wide overviews and functions involving environmental impact procedures, standard setting, monitoring, and training programmes. Ghana was one of the first of the developing countries to set up an environmental institution. The Environmental Protection Council (EPC) was established in 1974 by National Redemption Council Decree 23 under the supervision of the Ministry of Finance and Economic Planning.

The functions of the EPC contained in its mandate were:
- to advise the government generally on all environmental matters relating to the social and economic life of Ghana;
- to coordinate the activities of all bodies concerned with environmental matters and to serve as a channel of communication between these bodies and the government;
- to conduct and promote investigations, studies, surveys, research, analyses, including the training of personnel, relating to the im-

provement of Ghana's environment and the maintenance of sound ecological systems;

• to serve as the official national body for cooperating and liaising with national and international organizations on environmental matters;

• to undertake such studies and submit such reports and recommendations with respect to environmental matters as the government may request;

• to embark upon general environmental educational programmes for the purpose of creating enlightened public opinion regarding the environment;

• without prejudice to the economic and social advancement of Ghana, to ensure the observance of proper safeguards in the planning and execution of all development projects, including those already in existence, that are likely to interfere with the quality of the environment; and

• to perform functions as the government may assign to the Council of all or any of the foregoing functions.

The membership of the EPC was drawn from ministries, universities, research institutions, public boards, and the general public. The EPC was to operate through specialized committees in the exercise of its functions. It was also to seek advice and to consult any public body in the discharge of its functions. Through the supervising ministry, legislative instruments and regulations may be made for the purpose of giving effect to the provisions of the decree establishing the EPC. In 1976, an amendment was made to the decree empowering the EPC to request information and enter premises to undertake inspection for the purposes of giving effect to the decree, backed by fines and imprisonment terms.

The ministerial location of the EPC varied with its perceived role. Its original location in the Ministry of Finance and Economic Planning was changed to that of Health in 1981, and a year later it was reassigned to the Ministry of Local Government. The roles shifted from an emphasis on planning, to health (sanitation), and to local issues. Problems still existed in developing the relevant concepts and the institutional framework to take in the functions of a single agency charged with overseeing the varied facets of the environment. Environmental management continued to be ad hoc and sectoral through the specialized committees of the EPC, e.g. natural ecosystems, human settlements, industrial pollution, water, and hazardous chemicals. The environmental problems persisted and increased in occurrence and intensity. Notable were deforestation, soil erosion, water and air pollution, and urban waste disposal. Decisions reached by the committees could not be effectively implemented, and the EPC had to rely on the goodwill and understanding of the ministries and agencies concerned.

The EPC sometimes found itself in a situation where it had to take over the responsibilities of other institutions owing to the inability of these agencies to perform their assigned roles effectively. The EPC was then accused of taking on too much. This situation arose because, as environmental problems increased, the general public tended to look to the Council to resolve these problems.

With the EPC shying away from accusations of taking over the role of others, a situation was created where some problems that did not fall within the sphere of responsibility of any one body were left unattended to. In addition, and with time, the mandate of sectoral agencies proved inadequate to cope with the increasing problems resulting from increasing development and also from inadequate personnel, equipment, and enforcement powers.

The Environmental Action Plan (EAP)

Beginning in the early 1980s, especially following a severe drought in 1983 that affected the whole country and resulted in widespread bush fires, the protectionist and sector-oriented approach to environmental management with limited scope began to change as the state of the natural resource base deteriorated rapidly and began to pose a problem for the future prospects of development. The EPC initiated and led the way in the preparation of a number of plans and programmes, including the National Oil Spill Contingency Plan (1985), the National Plan of Action to Combat Desertification (1986), the Draft National Conservation Strategy (1987), and the National Environmental Protection Programme (1987). The new approach was aided by the launching of the World Conservation Strategy in 1980 by the International Union for the Conservation of Nature and Natural Resources (IUCN) in which the term "sustainable development" was used.

One major principle of sustainable development was to provide a framework for integrating development and conservation, in terms of laws, institutions, and policies. Following on these developments, one of the specialized committees of the EPC, the Natural Ecosystems Committee, initiated moves in 1986 to prepare a National Conservation Strategy for Ghana. To do this a national conference on the theme "Resource Conservation for Ghana's Sustainable Development" was organized in 1987. The conference brought together scientists, planners, economists, and decision makers to discuss how Ghana's development could be made sustainable. After the conference, the ideas gathered were to be used for the preparation of the National Conservation Strategy.

During this period the country had embarked on its Economic Recovery Programme (ERP), beginning in 1983, to reverse the economic decline of the country. The key factors accounting for the initial achievements of the ERP included the exploitation of the natural resource systems of the country. The environmental degradation that accompanied the economic growth and exploitation of the natural resources imposed costs on the economy of the country. This led the government to direct the EPC in March 1988 to set up a "think tank" "to develop environmental issues for incorporation into the second phase of the ERP." The work of the "think tank" was followed by the setting up of sectoral working groups on land, forestry and wildlife, water management, marine and coastal ecosystems, mining, manufacturing industries, and hazardous chemicals, and human settlements to address in detail the issues identified in the think tank's report and the proceedings of the 1987 national conference. These, together with the issues identified during a series of regional and district forums on the environment in 1987, led to the preparation of an Environmental Action Plan (EAP) for Ghana (EPC 1991), which was to address the nation's environmental problems in a comprehensive and integrated manner. It was to provide a technical, institutional, and legal framework for dealing with the problems of land and water degradation, diminishing forest and wildlife resources, and problems associated with mineral extraction and other industrial activities (fig. 17.1).

The concept of sustainable development runs through the Plan, which integrates the previous ad hoc programmes, which were sectoral in nature, into a comprehensive strategy addressing all issues of concern not only to Ghanaians but also to the international environmental movement at large. The Plan seeks to redirect national development into more environmentally sustainable programmes and practices through the following:
• the protection and preservation of the resource base;
• prior assessment of the potential environmental impacts of development projects;
• alternative or multi-purpose uses of land and water resources;

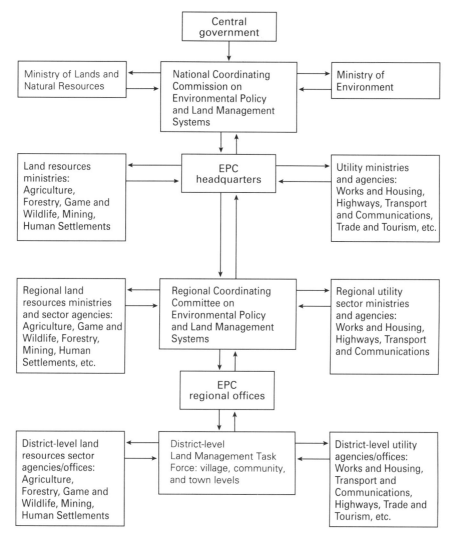

Fig. 17.1 An integrative institutional framework for environmental management and policy (Source: EPC 1991)

- the promotion of popular participation in planning, evaluating, and implementing environmental and development strategies.

The Plan sets out an environmental policy for Ghana and makes the attainment of a high-quality environment a key element in the country's economic and social development. It also provides guidance and sets out an action-oriented strategy that specifies the role of sectoral ministries, agencies, non-governmental organizations (NGOs), and indeed of every Ghanaian in its implementation. It is recognized that the realization of the objectives in the EAP and the national environmental policy can be attained only through collaboration and cooperation among institutions with responsibility for various aspects of resource management and environmental protection.

Institutional problems and issues

During the EAP preparation process, a number of institutional issues were identified in six areas: land management, water resource management, marine and coastal ecosystems, mining industry and hazardous chemicals, human settlements, and forest and wildlife.

In the area of land management, the institutional issues were that:
– there were a multiplicity of land management agencies, in fact as many as 22 with varying responsibilities;
– the coordinating management functions among agencies were not clear because they saw themselves as autonomous units, each with a specific mandate under different ministries; and
– each agency saw the problems or potentialities of the environment from its professional technical point of view and in terms of its mandate.

In the water resource management sector the major problems were:
– the improper definition of areas of responsibility, resulting in overlapping of efforts and different standards of measurement and analysis;
– the lack of an organization responsible for the overall management of water resources – functions were diffused among a number of agencies with respect to the abstraction of water and the discharge of effluents, and many of the water agencies dealt with individual aspects of water use to serve individual sectors of the economy.

In the marine and coastal ecosystems area, the issues were mainly a lack of the necessary manpower, equipment, and training in existing agencies.

In the mining industry and hazardous chemicals, problems were:
– an absence of an appropriate legislative framework for hazardous chemicals – there was a need for clear-cut arrangements for the enactment and enforcement of laws of the environment and a need for a dispute settlement procedure;
– weak institutional strength in terms of staffing, training, equipment, and logistical and financial support.

In the human settlement sector the issues were that the overall direction and integration of human settlement policy were inadequate to ensure consistency in the training of personnel and execution of policy with regard to population distribution and the provision of infrastructure and services.

In the forest and wildlife sector, training in modern techniques was recognized as an important requirement.

The implementation of the Environmental Action Plan

The above institutional problems and issues were to be addressed by the Environmental Protection Council (EPC), which is responsible for coordination of action by various individuals and organizations, monitoring action, and reporting to government. Generally, this role of the EPC is undisputed and there is broad public acceptance of the authority of the EPC, even though it has been argued that it needs to be given enforcement powers in order to prosecute.

The role of the EPC in the implementation of the EAP has remained unchanged. However, the focus of its operations, based on the provisions of the national environmental policy and related policy orientations, has shifted from an emphasis on environmental protection to environmental resource management. The need for effective management of the environment is a recurrent theme of the EAP. In the light of this, the EPC has been given increased functions, which include the following:

- to issue environmental permits and pollution abatement notices for controlling the volume, types, constituents, and effects of waste discharges, emissions, deposits, or other sources of pollutants and of substances that are hazardous or potentially dangerous to the quality of the environment or any segment of the environment;
- to issue notices in the form of directives, procedures, or warnings to such bodies as it may determine for the purpose of controlling the volume, intensity, and quality of noise in the environment;
- to ensure compliance with any laid down environmental impact assessment procedures in the planning and execution of development projects, including compliance in respect of existing projects;
- to impose and collect environmental protection levies in accordance with the Act or regulations made under the Act setting up the EPC.

To reflect these changes and to invest the EPC with more powers, the Council has been redesignated as the Environmental Protection Agency (EPA) within the new Ministry of Environment, Science and Technology.

In order to resolve the institutional issues, the Ghana Environmental Resource Management System (GERMS) has been made part of the implementation programme of the Environmental Action Plan. The proposed system would ensure that there is no duplication of roles. The system envisages the development of an Environmental Information System (EIS) incorporating topographic, land capability, and current land-use information, the processing of meteorological information, and the determination of land ownership on the scale of 1 : 250,000. GERMS will involve communities and government institutions in the planning, implementation, and monitoring of the sustainable use of environmental resources.

GERMS will provide a framework for policy formulation, planning, monitoring, problem solving, and implementation. Because most environmental concerns are intersectoral in nature and decisions involve choices between alternatives and possibly conflicting courses of action that carry costs and benefits, the management system should ensure that all possible options are considered, as well as the technical, economic, financial, social, or political implications of issues, by the various sectoral agencies involved to reflect national, district, or community development priorities.

GERMS is to create intersectoral linkages to bring together sectoral agencies and communities whose activities impinge on the environment. There are four intersectoral networks: built environment, natural resources, mining, and education. These networks will be supported by specialists in the areas of environmental economics, environmental impact assessment, environmental quality, and data management. The EPA therefore provides a forum for detailed discussions of environmental issues prior to making recommendations to government decision makers.

At the local level, district assemblies, which are the district planning authorities, together with district environmental management committees will provide a firm basis for local management of the environment. This is in line with the government's decentralization programme, which allows district, municipal, and metropolitan assemblies to have a central role in ensuring the protection and management of the environment.

Conclusion

Ghana's current institutional arrangements for the management of resources and the environment emphasize participatory planning

340

involving local communities and institutions, non-governmental organizations, and decentralized sectoral organizations. Technical implementation will be undertaken by the technical departments. The Environmental Protection Agency provides coordinating and monitoring functions, which is a desirable departure from the sectorally segmented approaches in the past. Already a lot of education to increase awareness of the nature of the resource and environmental problems has been undertaken with favourable indications that the new philosophy and approach will succeed in minimizing the problems.

References

Agyepong, G. T. 1987. *Perspectives on Land Resource Planning for Conservation in Ghana*. Report of National Conference on Resource Conservation for Ghana's Sustainable Development, EPC, Accra, 28–30 April.

Benneh G. 1985. Population, disease and rural development programme in the Upper East Region of Ghana. In: J. I. Clark et al. (eds.), *Population and Development Projects in Africa*. Cambridge: Cambridge University Press, pp. 206–218.

Benneh, G. et al. 1990. *Land Degradation in Ghana*. Commonwealth Secretariat/University of Ghana.

EPC (Environmental Protection Council). 1991. *Environmental Action Plan*, vol. 1. Accra: EPC.

IUCN (International Union for the Conservation of Nature and Natural Resources). 1980. *The World Conservation Strategy*. IUCN.

WCED (World Commission on Environment and Development). 1987. *Our Common Future*. Oxford: Oxford University Press.

18

The environmental impact and sustainability of plantations in Sub-Saharan Africa: Ghana's experiences with oil-palm plantations

Edwin A. Gyasi

Introduction

This paper discusses the environmental impact and sustainability of plantations in Sub-Saharan Africa, mainly on the basis of Ghana's experiences with oil-palm plantations. Sub-Saharan Africa refers to the approximately 22 million km² region of some 451 million inhabitants in 1987, located generally south of the Sahara desert, excluding South Africa and Namibia (Goliber 1989; World Bank 1989; Population Reference Bureau 1990).

Agriculture has, traditionally, formed the principal economic activity in Sub-Saharan Africa. It generates the bulk of employment and incomes, and is the major land-use factor. In Ghana, for example, agriculture contributes 50 per cent of the gross domestic product (GDP) and 60 per cent of export earnings, and occupies 57 per cent of the total land area (Ministry of Agriculture 1991). As the major land-use factor, agriculture exerts a powerful modifying influence on the natural environment, especially through vegetation removal, with profound implications for the living conditions of the Sub-Saharan inhabitants.

Agricultural practices may be categorized as three major systems:

the more or less pure livestock and cropping systems, and the mixed system, which integrates both livestock and crops in significant proportions (Benneh 1972; La-Anyane 1985; FAO 1991). The cropping system includes small-scale indigenous methods such as the classical shifting cultivation and its offshoot, land rotation or bush fallow, and exotic methods, notably the large-scale plantation system, whose environmental impact and sustainability in Sub-Saharan Africa form the central subject of discussion in this paper.

Plantations are distinguished not only by their large size but also by their monocultural character, systematic layout, and advanced infrastructure. Their other typical characteristics include: corporate and factory-like organization; high capital outlay; mechanization; extensive use of hired labour; and high reliance on artificial external inputs, notably agro-chemicals, for biological regeneration. These characteristics stand in sharp contrast to the small peasant farms that usually surround the plantations; these employ intercropping and a mosaic layout, are less capitalized, have low artificial external inputs, and are more nature based, labour intensive, and family operated.

Economies of scale are the major advantage of the plantation system. The sheer level of farming enhances efficiency by permitting greater specialization or division of labour, systematic research, utilization of by-products, access to capital and markets, and mechanization, especially of processing. As a result, plantations often yield a higher return per hectare and per worker, generate steadier and more regular high-quality produce, and provide greater and more readily taxable income than do smallholdings. Other major advantages include: carbon and oxygen cycling and minimization of soil erosion by the densely distributed plants; and rural development in the plantation areas through provision of modern infrastructure, introduction of advanced agricultural and other technical skills, and reduction of rural out-migration by the employment generated by the plantation. These advantages underlie the perception of plantations as a better alternative for agricultural development in the tropics, their long-standing central economic role in several countries, and growing popularity in others (Courtenay 1965; Hasselman 1981; La-Anyane 1961; Ruthenberg 1971; Symons 1966; Udo 1982).

However, the advantages must be balanced against various social, economic, and environmental problems associated with the plantation system. The problems include exploitation of the indigenes in the plantation areas and of the massive numbers of African slaves and indentured Asiatic labour imported to work under cruel conditions on the plantations in the eighteenth and nineteenth centuries in tropical areas of the Americas, the Far East, and eastern and southern Africa. Other problems include the racial, political, and land rights conflicts associated with the abrupt juxtaposition of large numbers of culturally different foreign and native plantation workers. Additionally, the plantation system tends to involve higher labour costs, is often plagued by labour disputes between workers and management, and appears less adaptable to short-term changes than the small-scale diversified systems. Plantations may also dislocate local people; create land shortage and land tenure problems among them; weaken local food security by export crop specialization; reduce biodiversity; and cause pollution and general destabilization or disturbance of the socio-economic system, including the land or natural environment that supports the plantations and the other economic activities (Jones and Darkenwald 1954; La-Anyane 1961; Courtenay 1965; Gourou 1966; Symons 1966; Ruthenberg 1971; Hasselman 1981; Udo 1982; Dickenson et al. 1983; Thomas 1984).

Overview of the plantation system in the Sub-Sahara

Plantations were introduced into the tropics during the sixteenth century by European colonists as a system of cheaply exploiting the hot humid environment and the native labour as well as slave and indentured or contract labour, for the purpose of producing tropical crops such as sugar cane for export to temperate countries, especially Europe. Initially the plantations were concentrated in South America and the West and East Indies. Subsequently, they spread to Sub-Saharan Africa and other areas of the tropics, with their mode of ownership evolving from paternalist resident planters, through absentee landlords and limited liability companies, to transnational or multinational corporations and national or state enterprises.

The plantation system grew in importance in Sub-Saharan Africa following the partitioning of Africa among the European colonial powers in 1885. This was particularly so in the Belgian Congo (now Zaire) where, in 1911, Lever Brothers, the giant transnational conglomerate, acquired vast freeholds and concessions of land, portions of which were developed into oil-palm plantations. The spread of plantations slowed during the depression years between 1920 and 1940. However, following the return of peace and favourable conditions for international trade and investments after the end of World War II in 1945, the plantation system started expanding once again, especially in Zaire, Nigeria, Cameroon, Côte d'Ivoire, Liberia, and Angola, with Lever Brothers playing a leading role. The expansion continued through the following two decades. It accelerated during the immediate post-independence era, about 1960–1965, which saw direct involvement of the national governments of the newly independent states in the establishment and running of plantations. Thereafter, the expansion slackened, mainly because of a decline in external investments following the growing political instability and state control of the national economies and the attendant erosion of foreign investors' confidence in them (Courtenay 1965; Gourou 1966; Udo 1982; Dickenson et al. 1983; Dinham and Hines, 1983; Halfani and Barker 1984; Thomas 1984).

Of late, most especially since about 1975, the plantation system has witnessed rejuvenation as a strategy for stimulating agricultural production, which has, since the mid-1960s, fallen below the average population growth of 3 per cent per annum (Dinham and Hines 1983; Halfani and Barker 1984; World Bank 1989; Gyasi 1987, 1992a; Goliber 1989; Population Reference Bureau 1990).

The rejuvenation of the plantation system, notably in Cameroon, Côte d'Ivoire, Nigeria, Kenya, and Ghana, poses several important issues, including its impact on production, employment, and incomes. Others include its environmental impact and sustainability, which this paper examines mainly on the basis of the experience with oil-palm (*Elaeis guineensis*) plantations in Ghana. More specifically, the paper addresses the following questions:

(a) what have been the impacts of the plantation system, especially on the environment;

(b) what do the impacts imply for the sustainability of the system; and,

(c) assuming that the impacts are generally negative, how might the system be rendered sustainable, or what other farming system might be recommended as a better alternative?

As used here, the term "impact" means effect, which implies change; "environment" describes the biotic and abiotic world within which human society lives and derives sustenance; while the term "sustainability" refers to the capacity to ensure survival or continuity of an activity, event, phenomenon, or situation such as the environment and the resources therein.

The paper is justified, firstly, by the need to gain better understanding, for planning purposes, of the significant impact that the growth of the extensive and monocultural plantation system is likely to have on the environment and its living conditions, particularly in the wake of increasing population pressure and the attendant diminishing supplies of land, the basic source of livelihood in Sub-Saharan Africa. Secondly, growing reliance on the plantation system as a strategy of agricultural development calls for critical analysis of its sustainability as part and parcel of the general search for an optimum way of increasing agricultural production at minimal environmental cost.

The evolution of plantations in Ghana

Ghana is 238,000 km^2, a predominantly agricultural country of some 15 million inhabitants located on the Gulf of Guinea in western Sub-Saharan Africa. There are four principal agro-ecological zones in Ghana, namely: the dry interior Guinea–Sudan savanna; derived savanna or forest savanna; humid forest; and the dry coastal savanna where the plantations reportedly started before spreading to the more favourable humid forest zone in the interior.

The Dutch were the first to introduce the plantation system in Ghana about the beginning of the eighteenth century. Dickson (1969) reports the establishment or attempted establishment of several Dutch plantations near the coast during the eighteenth and nineteenth centuries. Other plantations included those established by German, British, and other European interests about the end of the nineteenth century and in the early decades of the twentieth century, particularly after the passing of the Oil Palm Ordinance of 1913, when "Numerous oil-palm plantations [including those at Butre, Sese, and Winneba] were made" (Dickson 1969: 148). The Ordinance empowered the government to grant a mill operator the exclusive right to extract oil, by mechanical means, from the pericarp of palm fruits produced within 16 km of the mill. But the plantation system failed to gain a significant hold, partly because of the internal political insecurity engendered by inter-tribal warfare and by rivalry among the European powers seeking territorial hegemony, and also because of the negative attitude towards the system by the British Crown, which, from about 1850 onwards, gained the upper hand in the European struggle to colonize Ghana (Dickson 1969; Howard 1978).

It appears that, despite pressure by external private commercial interests, plantations were not very much favoured by the dominant British colonial administration. This was partly because of the fear that, by dispossessing the owners of their land, the extensive land acquisitions necessary for the plantations would alienate the peasants, seriously disrupt their export production system, and precipitate local opposition of the kind provoked by the abortive Crown Lands Bill of 1894 and the Land Bill of 1897, which sought to vest in the British Crown all "waste" or unoccupied lands, forest lands, and minerals. Another reason was the conviction among British government advisers that the indigenous small-scale peasant farming system was more resilient economically than the exotic large plantations. Furthermore, the peasant system was considered to be a tried and inexpensive method of producing tropical export crops. The official ambivalence towards the plantation system had been reinforced by a decision much later against the system at a conference on the West African oil-palm industry in 1926 in Nigeria (Shephard 1936; La-Anyane 1961, 1963; Johnson 1964; Usoro 1974; Udo 1982; Kotey 1990). Consequently, plantations did not make much impact on the environment and agricultural production during the colonial era in Ghana.

The inability of peasant production to keep pace with the growing demand for palm oil and other agricultural products arose from the rapidly expanding population, the government's import-substitution policy, and its desire for accelerated socio-economic improvements. After 1957, during the post-independence period, there was a policy change involving greater emphasis on the plantation system centred on the oil-palm and rubber, *Hevea brasiliensis* (Ghana Office of the Planning Commission 1964; Ghana, Republic of, 1987; ILO 1989; Ministry of Agriculture 1990). The policy change, up to the time of the 1966 military coup d'état, favoured state-owned and state-operated plantations. However, mainly because of capital constraints, political interference, poor planning, mismanagement, and the rigidity of the centralized state control system, these state-owned farms did not prove economically viable (Miracle and Seidman 1968). They succeeded only in worsening rural living conditions by dispossessing the peasants of their most fundamental natural resource, the land, with little or no compensation (Gyasi forthcoming), and by the deforestation and other forms of ecological and economic disturbance associated with the removal of natural vegetation to make room for monocultural plantations (Gyasi 1990). Subsequently, some of the state plantations were sold. Others were abandoned, sometimes after felling of the palms, a practice that invariably left behind derived savanna or even grass in place of the original forest cover, as in the case of Kwamoso, 60 km north-east of Accra. Attempts were made to reorganize the remaining plantations into viable economic units under decentralized state control.

On the whole, however, the new policy, especially after the 1981 coup d'état and the subsequent liberalization of the economic system, has sought to promote plantations through private enterprise, foreign-aided government ventures, and joint government–private projects. The resultant plantations include the three major ones established by the government-owned but foreign-assisted Ghana Oil Palm Development Co. (GOPDC) located around Kwae; the government/privately owned Twifo Oil Palm Plantations Ltd. (TOPP) located around Twifo Praso/Ntafrewaso; and the government/privately ownd Benso Oil Palm Plantations Ltd. (BOPP) located around Benso/Adum Banso (fig. 18.1). They were to grow oil-palms for the purpose of producing oil from the fruit of the palm, "probably the heaviest producer of vegetable fats" (Van Royen 1954: 166). This agro-industrial crop, which has a wide variety of uses, was a leading foreign exchange earncr for Ghana, mainly on the basis of small-scale peasant production in an oil-palm belt near the littoral, from about the mid-nineteenth century to the beginnings of the twentieth century (Gyasi 1992a).

The three major new palm plantations (GOPDC, TOPP, and BOPP), which have engaged my research attention since 1988, form the primary basis of the following discussion of the impact and sustainability of the plantation system in Sub-Saharan Africa.

Managed on modern corporate agro-business lines, the plantations have been developed on land compulsorily acquired from peasants by the government in the humid tropical environment of the interior, which favours the oil-palm. In addition to developing the acquired areas into palm plantations, the companies involved were to encourage palm fruit production among the peasants in the plantation hinterland through the nuclear or nucleus estate system to help sustain their huge palm-oil-processing mills located inside the plantations.

The positive impacts of the plantations

Since about 1977, when they started, the three plantations, GOPDC, TOPP, and BOPP, have developed rapidly and contributed significantly towards the expansion of Ghana's oil-palm hectares from 18,000 to 103,000 between 1970 and 1990 (Gyasi 1992a). This growth of 24 per cent per annum has resulted in the re-emergence of the palm as a major commercial crop rivalling cocoa; has served as a basis for the fast-developing palm oil and other agro-industrial processing

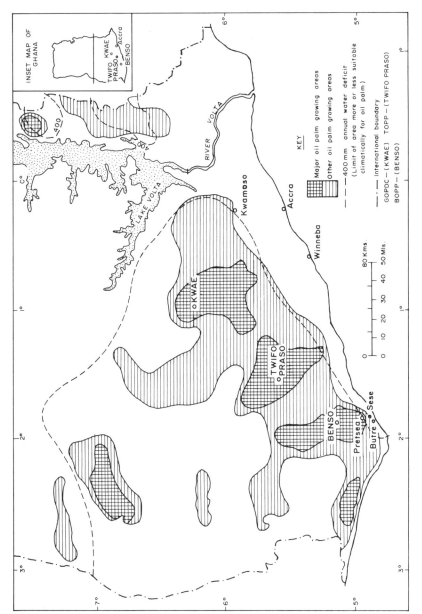

Fig. 18.1   **The location of the GOPDC, TOPP, and BOPP plantations (Source: Gyasi 1992a)**

349

industries; and rendered the country more than self-sufficient in palm-oil production.

During 1989, GOPDC, TOPP, and BOPP contributed about 20 per cent of the national palm hectares and 40 per cent of the palm-oil output, which traditionally had been dominated by small home-based producers. The three companies, which directly engaged over 4,500 people in their farming, milling, and other operations, were the largest single employers in their localities.

By 1989, the companies had organized over 2,700 farmers into out-growers operating more than 6,700 oil-palm hectares with the companies' support. Additionally, GOPDC and TOPP were assisting 409 smallholders, peasants dislocated by the plantations, to grow 2,250 ha of palms on leased portions of the plantation concessions.

It appeared from my field study, including interviewing the companies' management, that the new job opportunities were registering a positive rural developmental impact in the plantation areas through:

(a) income, expenditure, and investment enhancement;
(b) reduction in migration out of the rural areas; and
(c) improvement in agricultural and other technical skills through experience acquired on the job and training programmes mounted by the companies on the plantations.

Employment and income improvements were consistently ranked by both the company management and the small farmers as the most important benefits accruing from the plantations.

Other benefits included improved medical services, transportation, and education provided by the companies. Rural development had been further enhanced by backward linkages with the areas adjoining the plantations, particularly through palm fruit purchases from the small farmers to feed the plantation mills, which, together with the large number of smaller village-based semi-mechanical mills and manual establishments, generate substantial amounts of income from the value gained by processing the palm fruit into oil. Other benefits had accrued by forward linkages through palm kernels, a by-product used by rural women for making kernel oil. Other beneficial forward linkages had been through the selling of palm oil to sustain the big import-substituting and increasingly export-oriented soap, margarine, deodorized cooking oil, vaseline, and related products manufactures located mostly in the urban centres.

Thus, to the extent that the three plantations had achieved their principal objective of boosting oil-palm and palm-oil production, and had generated highly significant ancillary socio-economic benefits, particularly within their rural setting, the plantation system could be said to be an appropriate strategy for development in Sub-Saharan Africa.

A major factor underlying the significant positive socio-economic impact registered within the short time-span by the three Ghanaian plantations, as well as others in Kenya, Cameroon, and Nigeria, is their nuclear or nucleus estate method. This involves a core estate with an agro-processing mill together with other modern infrastructure. From the nucleus estate, advanced farming methods and other forms of assistance are extended to enable the peasants dislocated by the plantations to grow palms on leased portions of the estate, and to enable the "outgrowers" to grow the same crop on their own land within a specified radius. These smallholders and outgrowers are jointly called "contract farmers" because they are under a contractual obligation to sell the harvested palm fruit to the nuclear estate companies in exchange for their assistance.

Other factors underlying the plantations' positive impact include:
- the large-scale production methods facilitated by mechanization, foreign-assisted capitalization, and modern corporate management;
- the plantations' higher oil extraction rate of 95–100 per cent, compared with 75–80 per cent for the medium-scale mechanical mills, and 50–60 per cent for the small-scale manual or semi-mechanical processors;
- easier access to land, credit, and other inputs facilitated by Ghana government support;
- worker incentives such as bonuses, free medical care, and subsidized housing on the estate;
- minimization of harvesting, transportation, and management costs by the provision of road networks inside the estates, and the location of outgrower farms near motorable roads;
- the systematic phasing of development (Halfani and Barker 1984; Gyasi 1987, 1990, 1991, 1992a).

These factors had allowed the GOPDC, TOPP, and BOPP to operate profitably, unlike the strictly state-controlled plantations, notably NOPL (National Oil Palms Ltd.) at Pretsea (fig. 18.1).

Adverse environmental impacts and sustainability

However, the question is whether the gains can be sustained. An answer was sought by examining the plantations' adverse impacts, particularly on the natural environment.

Traditionally, the natural environment, including the land, has constituted the basis of the farming, hunting, and gathering economies in the plantation areas. Consequently, the expropriation of over 16,000 ha of peasant lands for the plantations, with little or no compensation for the cottages, camps, and farms lost, together with various land-use or proprietary rights, could be expected to precipitate social resistance. This, indeed, had been the case, as illustrated by the dramatic refusal of the migrant Ningo farmers of Atobriso and Okaikrom to grant government and GOPDC officials entry into their acquired land. As in the case of land expropriated for the RISON-PALM nucleus estate in Nigeria (Gyasi 1987, 1990), other manifestations of the peasants' resistance had included: a group petition to the government and to the management of the plantations; threatened court action; pilfering of palm fruit from the plantations; and acts of sabotage, which had necessitated a tightening of security at considerable cost to the plantation companics. The insecurity engendered by the compensation factor partly accounts for the companies' inability to establish effective control over portions of their concessions used illegally by land-short local people, including squatter farmers.

But perhaps the most serious adverse effect has been the rapid transformation of the forest ecosystem and its resilient diversified ecologically based traditional economy into a vulnerable artificial monocultural system. Instability, risks, or uncertainties are inherent features of the natural environment, which the peasant farmers recognize. Traditionally, the peasants try to minimize these environmental risks, combat soil erosion, optimize utilization of the different soil nutrients, and enhance food security by intermixing crops of varying degrees of environmental sensitivity and different nutritional value, and by other forms of agricultural diversification and risk minimization. The resilient, diversified indigenous agriculture, modelled on the forest ecosystem and based on eco-farming principles borne out of the peasants' intimate knowledge of the natural environment, is being replaced by the risk-prone monocultural system, with devastating consequences for the forest ecosystem.

Of a sample of farmers, 47 per cent perceived a trend towards palm monoculture as a result of the activities of the plantation companies in their locality; 62 per cent of the farmers considered the monocultural trend desirable, because they saw the palm as lucrative, dependable, and a steadier income-generator owing to the high value placed on it, its robust character, and its bi-monthly fruiting habit. However, a significant 38 per cent of the farmers did not consider the trend towards palm monoculture desirable, primarily because it was leading to shortages of local staple foods, a problem also reported by the management of the plantations. A second reason was the vulnerability of the monocultural palm farms to insect pests and diseases (table 18.1), an agro-ecological problem most vividly demonstrated by the unusually massive and destructive insect invasion of the monocultural palm farms in 1986–1987. A third reason was the difficulty of marketing palm fruit and oil associated with poor marketing facilities for the increased output, and the higher production cost in Ghana, related to the less favourable moisture conditions and less effective radiation utilization by the palm (BOPP 1990), which has led to the growing premature felling of the palm trees for production of the local gin, *akpeteshie*. Other reported or observed adverse effects were:

- deforestation, and the associated growing cost and scarcity of forest products such as "bush meat" (game), medicinal plants, and wood, an important constructional material and the basic fuel source;
- the high cost, erratic supplies, and polluting effect of the agro-chemicals used to boost palm yields and to control pests and weeds, especially in the large plantations;
- environmental pollution by the palm fruit and palm oil effluents, a potentially rich source of organic fertilizer.

Although these reports or observations require further investigation, they nevertheless point to the environmental shortcomings of the system.

On the one hand, the plantation system, especially the nuclear estate version, appears attractive as a development strategy in the Sub-Sahara because of its ability to accelerate agricultural production and generate other important socio-economic benefits, including employment, income, agro-industrial growth, and modern infrastructure, especially in the rural areas. On the other hand, the system does not appear attractive because its vulnerable character and adverse effects on traditional landholding and land-use rights, on food and fuel security, and, above all, on the natural environment throw its sustainability into serious doubt.

Perhaps the plantation system might be rendered sustainable by encouraging its modification into smaller diversified farms on the basis of organic and other eco-farming and the principles of low external inputs that underpin proven sustainable systems such as modern agro-forestry and traditional African systems, notably:

- the bush fallow system, which intermixes diverse crops amidst

353

Table 18.1 **Insect pests and diseases of the oil-palm**

INSECT

Scientific name	Common name	Category
Coelaenomonadera minuta (Coleoptera: Hispidae)	Oil palm leaf miner	Primary pest
Pimelophila ghasquieri (Lepidoptera: Pyralidae)	African spear borer	Primary pest
Temoschoita quadripustulata (Coleoptera: Curculionidae)	Oil palm weevil	Primary pest
Rhynchophorusphoenicis (Coleoptera: Curculionidae)	Red striped weevil	Primary pest
Oryctes spp. (Coleoptera: Dynastidae)	Rhinoceros beetle	Primary pest
Latoia viridissima (Lepidoptera: Limacodidae)	West African slug caterpillar	Secondary pest
Zonoceros variegatus (Orthoptera: Acrididae)	Grasshopper	Secondary pest
Augosoma contaurius (Orthoptera: Dynastidae)	N.A.	Secondary pest
Adoretus umbrosus (Coleoptera: Dynastidae Rutelidae)	N.A.	Secondary pest
Schizonycha africana (Coleoptera: Nololunthidae)	N.A.	Secondary pest
Parasa viridissima (Lepidoptera: Limacodidae)	West African slug caterpillar	Secondary pest
Spodoptera litura (Lepidoptera: Noctuidae)	N.A.	Secondary pest
Phenacoccus spp. (Hemiptera: Coccoidea)	Mealy bug	Secondary pest
Pinnaspis marchali (Hemiptera: Coccoidea)	Scale insect	Secondary pest
Sufetula nigrescens (Lepidoptera: Pyralidae)	Oil palm aerial root caterpillar	Potential pest
Metisa plana (Lepidoptera: Psychedae)	Oil palm bag worm	Potential pest
Leptonatada siostedti (Lepidoptera: Notodontidae)	N.A.	Potential pest
Monolepta apicicornis (Coleoptera: Chrysomelidae)	N.A.	Potential pest

DISEASE

Anthracnose
Cercospora leaf spot
Blast

Source: Gyasi (1991).
N.A. = not available.

354

selected uncleared trees and bushes in the form of proto-agro-forestry;
- the more or less permanent farming system on compound land, which often integrates both livestock and assorted crops around the household or living compound (Benneh 1972; Benneh and Gyasi 1991; Gyasi 1992b; Kopke and Schulz 1992).

The principles underlying the native African systems have much to recommend them because they derive from intimate knowledge of the local environment, form an integral part of the traditional culture, and, as such, offer a strong basis for agricultural development. Other possibilities for improving the environmental impact and sustainability of plantations include the "*i*'th" or "*n*'th" row method whereby every second, third, etc. row in the plantation is reserved for crops other than the primary plantation crop. Another is the arrangement whereby the outgrowers and the smallholders devote a portion of their land to the industrial crop required by the nuclear estate mill and the rest to food or other crops. Others include the intermixing of the principal plantation crop with other crops.

Conclusion

To sum up, what one may envision on the basis of this preliminary enquiry is a network of smaller diversified plantations of the nucleus estate type at appropriate locations, whereby modern ecologically based farming methods are extended to surrounding contract farmers to sustain agriculture and the environment in Sub-Saharan Africa.

References

Benneh, G. 1972. Systems of agriculture in tropical Africa. *Economic Geography* 48(3): 244–257.

Benneh, G. and E. A. Gyasi. 1991. Home gardens in West Africa: Progress in research role in agricultural production, nutrition, income generation and constraints to realizing their full potential as a sustainable agroforestry system. Paper presented at UNU/INRA Programme Consultative Meeting, University of Ghana, Legon, 22–26 April.

BOPP (Benso Oil Palm Plantation). 1990. An analysis of the palm sector's problems, mimeo, Adum Banso.

Courtenay, P. P. 1965. *Plantation Agriculture*. London: Bell.

Dickenson, J. P. et al. 1983. *A Geography of the Third World*. Cambridge: Cambridge University Press.

Dickson, K. B. 1969. *A Historical Geography of Ghana*. Cambridge: Cambridge University Press.

Dinham, B. and C. Hines. 1983. *Agribusiness in Africa*. London: Earth Resources.

FAO (Food and Agriculture Organization of the United Nations). 1991. *Sustainable Agriculture and Rural Development*. Regional Document no. 1 (FAO/Netherlands Conference on Agriculture and the Environment: Strategies and Tools for Sustainable Agriculture and Rural Development, S-Hertogenbosch, the Netherlands, 15–19 April, 1991). Rome: FAO.

Ghana Office of the Planning Commission. 1964. *Seven-Year Plan for National Reconstruction and Development: 1963/64 – 1969/70*. Accra.

Ghana, Republic of. 1987. *National Programme for Economic Development*. Accra.

Goliber, T. J. 1989. Africa's expanding population: Old problems, new policies. *Population Bulletin* 44(3): 1–50.

Gourou, P. 1966. *The Tropical World*. London: Longman.

Gyasi, E. A. 1987. The Risonpalm nucleus estate of Nigeria: An agricultural plantation and its effects on the surrounding area. *Malaysian Journal of Tropical Geography* 15: 26–38.

——— 1990. Nucleus agricultural estates and food security. *Rural Systems* 7(2): 61–68.

——— 1991. The oil palm industry and its implications for the rural economy in Ghana. Unpublished study funded by the University of Ghana, Department of Geography and Resource Development, University of Ghana, Legon.

——— 1992a. Emergence of a new oil palm belt in Ghana. *Journal of Economic and Social Geography* 83(1): 39–49.

——— 1992b. Sustaining oil palm farming by organic methods in Ghana. In U. Kopke and D. C. Schulz (eds.), *Proceedings 9th IFOAM International Scientific Conference on Organic Agriculture. A Key to a Sound Development and Sustainable Environment*, 16–21 November, Sao Paulo. Tholey-Theley, Germany: International Federation of Organic Farming Movements, pp. 233–238.

——— forthcoming. State expropriation of land for a plantation and its impact on peasants in Ghana. *Proceedings of Commonwealth Geographical Bureau Indigenous Land Rights Workshop*. Wellington: Department of Geography, University of Canterbury, and Christchurch: Ngai Tahu Maori Trust Board for the Commonwealth Geographical Bureau.

Halfani, M. S. and Barker, J. 1984. Agribusiness and agrarian change. In J. Barker (ed.), *The Politics of Agriculture in Tropical Africa*. Beverly Hills, Calif.: Sage Publications, pp. 35–63.

Hasselman, K.-H. 1981. Liberia. In H. De Blij and E. Martin (eds.), *African Perspectives: The Economic Geography of Nine African States*. New York: Methuen, pp. 137–171.

Howard, R. 1978. *Colonialism and Underdevelopment in Ghana*. London: Croom Helm.

ILO (International Labour Organization). 1989. *From Redeployment to Sustained Employment Generation: Challenges for Ghana's Programme of Economic Recovery and Development*. Addis Ababa: Jobs and Skills Programme for Africa.

Johnson, M. 1964. Migrants' progress. *Bulletin of the Ghana Geographical Association* 9(2): 4–27.

Jones, C. F and G. G. Darkenwald. 1954. *Economic Geography*. New York: Macmillan.

Kopke, U. and D. C. Schulz (eds.) 1992. *Proceedings 9th IFOAM International Sci-*

entific Conference on Organic Agriculture. A Key to a Sound Development and a Sustainable Environment, 16–21 November, Sao Paulo. Tholey-Theley, Germany: International Federation of Organic Farming Movements.

Kotey, E. N.-A. 1990. Indigenous land tenure and registration of title to land in Ghana: Legal and political problems. Paper presented at World Bank-sponsored Seminar on Land Tenure and Agricultural Productivity in Ghana, Accra.

La-Anyane, S. 1961. The oil palm belt in Ghana. *Ghana Bulletin of Agricultural Economics* 1(1): 7–43.

———— 1963. *Ghana Agriculture: Its Economic Development from Early Times to the Middle of the Twentieth Century*. London: Oxford University Press.

———— 1985. *Economics of Agricultural Development in Tropical Africa*. Chichester: John Wiley.

Ministry of Agriculture. 1990. *Ghana Medium Term Agricultural Development Programme (MTADP): An Agenda for Sustained Agricultural Growth and Development (1991–2000)*, vol. I. Accra.

———— 1991. *Agriculture in Ghana: Facts and Figures*. Accra: Policy Planning, Monitoring and Evaluation Department.

Miracle, M. P. and A. Seidman. 1968. *State Farms in Ghana*. LTC Paper 43, Madison, Land Tenure Center, University of Wisconsin.

Population Reference Bureau. 1990. *1990 World Population Data Sheet*. Washington D.C.

Ruthenberg, H. 1971. *Farming Systems in the Tropics*. London: Oxford University Press.

Shephard, C. Y. 1936. *Report on the Economics of Peasant Agriculture in the Gold Coast*. Accra: Government Printer.

Symons, L. 1966. *Agricultural Geography*. London: G. Bell.

Thomas, C. Y. 1984. *Plantations, Peasants and State: A Study of the Mode of Sugar Production in Guyana*. Los Angeles: Center for Afro-American Studies, University of California; Mona, Jamaica: Institute of Social and Economic Research, University of West Indies.

Udo, R. K. 1982. *The Human Geography of Tropical Africa*. Ibadan, London and Nairobi: Heinemann.

Usoro, E. J. 1974. *The Nigerian Oil Palm Industry (Government Policy and Export Production, 1906–1965)*. Ibadan Social Science Series. Ibadan: Ibadan University Press.

Van Royen, W. 1954. *The Agricultural Resources of the World*. New York: Prentice-Hall.

World Bank. 1989. *Sub-Saharan Africa: From Crisis to Sustainable Growth: A Long Term Perspective Study*. Washington D.C.: World Bank.

Contributors

Tade Akin Aina Council for the Development of Social Science Research in Africa (CODESRIA), Dakar, Senegal

Christine Amoako-Nuama Hon. Minister of Environment, Science and Technology of Ghana

Elizabeth Ardayfio-Schandorf Professor, Department of Geography and Resource Development, University of Ghana, Legon, Ghana

George Benneh Vice-Chancellor, University of Ghana, Legon, Ghana

Edouard G. Bonkoungou Regional Coordinator, International Centre for Research in Agroforestry (ICRAF), Ouagadougou, Burkina Faso

Humphrey C. Ezumah Consultant in Agronomy, Enugu, Nigeria; formerly Principal Agronomist, International Institute of Tropical Agriculture, Ibadan, Nigeria

Nkoli N. Ezumah Sociologist, Department of Sociology/Anthropology, University of Nigeria, Nsukka, Nigeria

Edwin A. Gyasi Professor, Department of Geography and Resource Development, University of Ghana, Legon, Ghana

A. Chidi Ibe Project Co-ordinator and Director, Regional Co-ordination Centre, United Nations Industrial Development Organization (UNIDO), Abidjan, Côte d'Ivoire

Rattan Lal Professor of Soil Science, School of Natural Resources, Ohio State University, Ohio, USA

Walther Manshard Professor, Department of Human Geography, University of Freiburg, Freiburg i. Br., Germany

William B. Morgan Professor Emeritus, Department of Geography, King's College, University of London, London, UK

Shimwaayi Muntemba Environmental Policy Specialist, Environmentally Sustainable Development Division, Africa Region Technical Department, World Bank, Washington D.C., USA

Saka Nuru Former director, National Animal Production Research Institute, Zaria, Nigeria

Bede N. Okigbo Director, The United Nations University Institute for Natural Resources in Africa (UNU/INRA), Accra, Ghana

John O. Oucho Professor and Director, Population Studies and Research Institute (PSRI), University of Nairobi, Nairobi, Kenya

Lloyd A. K. Quashie Resources Development Consultant, St. Jerome, Quebec, Canada

Robson M. K. Silitshena Professor and Head, Department of Environmental Science, University of Botswana, Gaborone, Botswana

David Simon Director, Centre for Developing Areas Research (CEDAR), Department of Geography, Royal Holloway, University of London, Surrey, UK

Juha I. Uitto Academic Officer, The United Nations University, Tokyo, Japan

359

Index